The Pergamon Oxford Dictionary of Perfect Spelling

CHRISTINE MAXWELL

A DIVISION OF PERGAMON PRESS

A. Wheaton & Company Limited
A Division of Pergamon Press
Hennock Road, Exeter EX2 8RP

Pergamon Press Ltd,
Headington Hill Hall, Oxford OX3 0BW, England

Pergamon Press, Inc.,
Maxwell House, Fairview Park, Elmsford, New York 10523, U.S.A.

Pergamon of Canada Ltd,
75 The East Mall, Toronto, Ontario M8Z 2L9, Canada

Pergamon Press (Australia) Pty Ltd,
19a Boundary Street, Rushcutters Bay, N.S.W. 2011, Australia

Pergamon Press GmbH,
6242 Kronberg/Taunus, Pferdstrasse 1, West Germany

First edition 1977

Library of Congress Cataloging in Publication Data

Maxwell, Christine.
The Pergamon Oxford dictionary of perfect spelling.

  1. Spellers. I. Title.
PE1146.M345 1977   428′.1   77-23541
ISBN 0-08-021425-8
ISBN 0-08-021902-0 pbk.
ISBN 0-08-021426-6 non net
ISBN 0-08-021427-4 pbk. non net

Printed in Great Britain by A. Wheaton & Co. Ltd, Exeter

Contents

Preface

This dictionary, the first of its kind in Great Britain (as far as the compiler knows), and its accompanying booklet, *Practise Your Spelling*, aim at being of service to children and adults of all ages who are weak at spelling and who therefore fail to locate quickly and easily the words they seek in standard dictionaries.

Compilers and publishers of English-language dictionaries overseas have long recognised this problem, and have successfully provided phonetically-arranged dictionaries to help pupils overcome these serious difficulties which so impede their progress.

Recent experience gained as a teacher in an Oxford middle school (age-group 9–13) and with students learning English as a foreign language has brought the compiler face to face with the problem. This has made her aware of the inordinate amount of time that has to be spent by teachers helping students with spelling difficulties which they could so easily have overcome for themselves had they had access to a phonetically-arranged dictionary.

The compiler gratefully acknowledges the co-operation of teachers and students in Oxfordshire schools for their help in testing the dictionary and its accompanying booklet, *Practise Your Spelling*, in a classroom environment. These successful tests, which were also carried out in several establishments that teach English as a foreign language, have revealed the following:

I. Students who assisted with the tests quickly understood that words printed in RED were incorrectly spelt and that only words printed in BLACK were correctly spelt. In tests which involved several hundred students, not one copied down incorrect spellings. Some teachers' initial concern over the possible negative effect of showing students incorrect spellings has proved unfounded.

II. Teachers (besides saving themselves time) found that regular use of the dictionary and the exercise booklet improved their pupils' ability to locate words easily and quickly and spell them correctly.

The mis-spellings (mainly phonetic) are printed in RED (RED is wrong), with the correct spellings given alongside in BLACK (BLACK is right). Even when users are unsure of the first two letters in a word, they may still find its correct spelling with the help of this dictionary. For instance, the word 'pheasant' will be found under the phonetic groups <u>fes</u> and <u>fez</u> as well as in its correct alphabetical place under <u>phe</u>:

fesant	pheasant
fezant	pheasant

pheasant

Some of the commonest spelling errors are made in adding suffixes and in forming derivatives from root words which in themselves may be quite easy to spell. In a conventional dictionary a student may be able to find the spellings of infinitives like 'picnic', 'abandon' and 'span', but may encounter difficulties spelling their present and past participles. How is one to know that the words 'spanning' and 'spanned' are not spelt 'spaning' and 'spaned'? There may be no indication that one must insert 'k' after 'picnic' in order to spell 'picnicking' and 'picnicked' correctly. This dictionary leaves no room for error in this respect, as difficult and irregular word derivatives are included.

It is hoped that this dictionary (and its accompanying booklet) will prove to be of practical, daily help, solving spelling problems and helping to increase the spelling skills of both children and adults—in the classroom, at home and at work.

Oxford, July 1977   CHRISTINE MAXWELL

On Choice of Words, Spelling and Arrangement of Entries

The words in this dictionary have been chosen because they are difficult to spell. Accordingly, many common words are omitted. Obsolete and highly technical words have also been left out, though special attention has been given to the selection of scientific and technical words. Very few proper names are given and foreign words are included only if they have passed into common use.

Where alternative spellings exist these have mostly been omitted. In the case of words ending in -ise, -isation, the -ize and -ization versions have not been given (nor have they been given as mis-spelt versions since they cannot be counted as such). In a very few instances two spellings have been given; where only one spelling is given the reader can assume that it is widely accepted as being correct. To help the user decide upon the correct spelling, brief word definitions are given in the case of words that are (1) pronounced alike but differ in meaning and spelling, (2) often mispronounced to give the same or almost the same sound but are entirely different in meaning and spelling, e.g.:

(1) sail (of boat) (2) poplar (tree)
    sale (of goods)   popular (well known)

The spellings and mis-spellings in the dictionary are arranged in alphabetical order.

Endings of words: It has not been possible to put in every derivation and many comparative endings have been excluded. In many cases there has been insufficient space for all the derivatives to be placed in one entry. They have therefore been split up in what the author considers to be the most obvious and practical way, e.g.:

abnormal /ly
abnormalit y /ies

Abbreviations Used in the Dictionary

adj(s).   adjective(s)
fem.   feminine
n.   noun
pl(s).   plural(s)
v.   verb

How to Use the Dictionary

1. Think hard about the word you wish to spell and try to decide with which two letters it starts.

2. Find the two letters in the dictionary and look down the <u>left-hand column</u> under these two letters until you find the word you want. If you find the word printed in BLACK, then you have found the correct spelling. However, if the word is printed in RED, then you are not spelling the word correctly, but if you look across the same line you will find the correct spelling printed in BLACK, e.g.:

palis   palace

3. (a) It may be necessary to add the word endings which are individually separated by oblique strokes (/) in order to build up the complete word you want. In the example below you can see how this works:

neat /er/est/ly/ness

> By adding <u>er</u> to <u>neat</u> you spell <u>neater</u>.
> By adding <u>est</u> to <u>neat</u> you spell <u>neatest</u>.
> By adding <u>ly</u> to <u>neat</u> you spell <u>neatly</u>.
> By adding <u>ness</u> to <u>neat</u> you spell <u>neatness</u>.

(b) Where the last letter or letters of a word are in *italics* these <u>must</u> be left off before adding the endings, e.g.:

nast*y* /ier/iest/ily/iness

Here, the *y* must be left off before making:

nastier, nastiest, nastily, nastiness

(c) The plurals of most nouns may be formed by simply adding the letter **s**. Only where this does not apply, or where the spelling of a plural often gives trouble, is the plural spelling noted, e.g.:

dais*y* /ies	(daisies)	cello /s	(cellos)
cargo /es	(cargoes)	minutia /e	(minutiae)
circus /es	(circuses)		

4. NOTE

If the correct spelling given alongside a mis-spelling has a $^+$ sign after it, then this means that all other given derivations of the word may only be found by looking up the correct spelling again, but in its PROPER ALPHABETICAL PLACE, e.g.:

hapen	happen [1]
hapier	happier $^+$
hapless	
happen [1]	
happi*er* /est/ly/ness	

Where the word <u>happier</u> occurs in its correct alphabetical place other forms of the word are given:

happiest, happily, happiness

If you thought that the word <u>elastic</u> began with an **i** you would find that you are spelling the word wrongly <u>and</u>, as the following example shows, the correct spelling of <u>elastic</u> has a $^+$ sign after it:

ilastic   elastic $^+$

Now if you look up <u>elastic</u> under **e** instead of **i** you will find that other forms of the word are given:

elastic /ally/ity

5. All the words with the number ¹ or ² or ³ or ⁴ after them are verbs (doing words) or may be used as verbs. If you require the word to end in either <u>ed</u> or <u>ing</u>, then you must remember the following:

(a) If you see ¹ after a word you may add <u>ed</u> or <u>ing</u> to the word without changing it, thus:

add ¹   add <u>ed</u>   add <u>ing</u>

(b) If you see ² after a word ending in **e**, the **e** must be dropped before adding <u>ed</u> or <u>ing</u>, thus:

name ²   nam <u>ed</u>   nam <u>ing</u>

(c) If you see ³ after a word you must double the final consonant (the last letter) before adding <u>ed</u> or <u>ing</u>, thus:

pat ³   patt <u>ed</u>   patt <u>ing</u>

(d) If you see ⁴ after a word (all words with a ⁴ after them end in **y**) you MUST change the **y** to an **i** before adding <u>ed</u>, but you may add <u>ing</u> to the word without changing it, thus:

carry ⁴   carri <u>ed</u>   carry <u>ing</u>
cry ⁴   cri <u>ed</u>   cry <u>ing</u>

BEWARE

A word having an asterisk (*) after it has the same sound, or almost the same sound, as another word, but it has a different meaning and spelling.

Explanations in brackets (not exact definitions) are only included where the words occur in their correct alphabetical place in the book, e.g.:

berr y * (fruit) /ies
berry   bury ⁴*
bury ⁴* (cover)

If you want to check the meaning of the word <u>bury ⁴*</u>, you must look it up in its correct alphabetical place under <u>bu</u> and not under <u>be</u>.

NOTES. (1) Where a dagger (†) appears after the *, the word definition is given on the next line, e.g.:

farth er *† /est
†(distant)

(2) The **hyphen** (-) is a sign used to join words and must not be left out, e.g.:

far /-fetched/-flung (far-fetched, far-flung)
fire-engine

KEY TO DICTIONARY SYMBOLS

A list of meanings of the various symbols used appears on the inside back cover of the dictionary.

Dictionary Exercises

Although the instructions on the use of the dictionary are set out clearly enough for a pupil to follow and understand, it would be helpful for the teacher to read through the rules with the pupils and make them do the exercises set out below. There is an exercise to help reinforce each rule, and the final exercise (V) gives the pupil practice in the use of all the rules.

Most pupils will quickly learn how to use the dictionary and the teacher can check whether they are using it accurately simply by giving a verbal test requiring written answers. For those who may need further practice, the teacher may use the exercises set out in *Practise Your Spelling* (O. B. Gregory/C. Maxwell, Wheaton, 1977), which exploit further the special features of the dictionary—and are designed to aid spelling, word study and development of vocabulary.

EXERCISE I

Look up the following words and write out in full all the other words that you can make up from the information you find. (The first question has been done for you.)

1. bite *(biting, bitten)*
2. abundant
3. bleak
4. bush
5. door
6. feeble
7. wealth
8. luck
9. sharp
10. tooth

EXERCISE II

Remember: When the last letter or letters of a word are in *italics*, these must be LEFT OFF before adding the other endings, e.g.:

nast*y* /ier/iest/ily/iness

The *y* in nast*y* must be left off before making the words

nastier, nastiest, nastily, nastiness

Look up the following words and write out in full all the other words that you can make up from the information you find. (The first question has been done for you.)

1. difficulty *(difficulties)*
2. rowdy
3. geography
4. giddy
5. mightier
6. lady
7. someone
8. greedier
9. busier
10. army

EXERCISE III **Using the numbers 1, 2, 3, and 4**

Use the following example as a guide,

Verb	Past participle	Present participle
peck	pecked	pecking

and write out the corresponding parts of the verbs listed in the following sections A–D. (The first items of sections A–D, respectively, have been done for you.)

A. Using the number **1**

1. tick *(ticked, ticking)*
2. bang
3. dismay
4. help
5. thump
6. link
7. lisp
8. hurl
9. shatter
10. drill

10

B. Using the number **2**

1. cripple *(crippled, crippling)*
2. mime
3. rinse
4. blaze
5. slope
6. tremble
7. wrestle
8. fuse
9. chuckle
10. ache

C. Using the number **3**

1. dab *(dabbed, dabbing)*
2. skid
3. beg
4. whiz
5. jar
6. chip
7. hum
8. zigzag
9. prod
10. expel

D. Using the number **4**

1. dignify *(dignified, dignifying)*
2. satisfy
3. disqualify
4. pity
5. busy
6. marry
7. terrify
8. try
9. fry
10. crucify

EXERCISE IV

Combination of numbers and other word endings: e.g. dance² /r
In the above entry the ² tells us that we can write <u>dancing</u> and <u>danced</u>.
If we add the **r** to the main word <u>dance</u>, we get <u>dancer</u>.

See if you can do this exercise. Write out in full as many forms of the words as you can from the information given. (The first question has been done for you.)

1. attract *(attracting, attracted, attraction)*
2. coach
3. narrow
4. dissatisfy
5. guide
6. hedge
7. learn
8. thin
9. mouth
10. travel

EXERCISE V

You are now ready to tackle an exercise containing a mixture of all the rules.

Look up the following words and write out as many words as you can from the information given. (The first question has been done for you.)

1. close *(closed, closing, closure)*
2. further
3. playful
4. run
5. young
6. clever
7. police
8. wide
9. knife
10. water

Your teacher will now ask you to spell a number of words, and if you use the dictionary correctly, you will get every word right.

You may also work with another member of your group or class, taking turns to ask each other how to spell words that you are presently using, until you are quite confident that you can use the dictionary successfully.

Remember, on the inside back cover there is a key to the symbols used in this dictionary.

A

<table>
<tr><td>à la carte</td><td></td></tr>
<tr><td>aback</td><td></td></tr>
<tr><td>abac us /i (pl.)</td><td></td></tr>
<tr><td>abait</td><td>abate $^{2+}$</td></tr>
<tr><td>abanden</td><td>abandon $^{1+}$</td></tr>
<tr><td>abandon ^{1} /ment</td><td></td></tr>
<tr><td>abash /ed</td><td></td></tr>
<tr><td>abate ^{2} /ment</td><td></td></tr>
<tr><td>abawd</td><td>aboard</td></tr>
<tr><td>abawshun</td><td>abortion $^+$</td></tr>
<tr><td>abawt</td><td>abort $^{1+}$</td></tr>
<tr><td>abawtion</td><td>abortion $^+$</td></tr>
<tr><td>abayans</td><td>abeyance $^+$</td></tr>
<tr><td>abbey /s</td><td></td></tr>
<tr><td>abb ot /ess (fem.)</td><td></td></tr>
<tr><td>abbreviat e ^{2} /ion</td><td></td></tr>
<tr><td>abdicat e ^{2} /ion</td><td></td></tr>
<tr><td>abdomen</td><td></td></tr>
<tr><td>abdomin al /ally/ous</td><td></td></tr>
<tr><td>abduct ^{1} /ion/or</td><td></td></tr>
<tr><td>abet ^{3} /tor</td><td></td></tr>
<tr><td>abetor</td><td>abettor</td></tr>
<tr><td>abeyan ce /t</td><td></td></tr>
<tr><td>abeyans</td><td>abeyance $^+$</td></tr>
<tr><td>abhaw</td><td>abhor $^{3+}$</td></tr>
<tr><td>abhor ^{3} /rence</td><td></td></tr>
<tr><td>abhorence</td><td>abhorrence</td></tr>
<tr><td>abhorens</td><td>abhorrence</td></tr>
<tr><td>abhorent</td><td>abhorrent $^+$</td></tr>
<tr><td>abhorrent /ly</td><td></td></tr>
<tr><td>abidans</td><td>abidance</td></tr>
<tr><td>abid e ^{2} /ance</td><td></td></tr>
<tr><td>abilit y /ies</td><td></td></tr>
<tr><td>abismal</td><td>abysmal $^+$</td></tr>
<tr><td>abiss</td><td>abyss</td></tr>
<tr><td>abject /ion/ly/ness</td><td></td></tr>
<tr><td>ablative</td><td></td></tr>
<tr><td>ablbodid</td><td>able-bodied</td></tr>
</table>

<table>
<tr><td>able /-bodied/r/st</td><td></td></tr>
<tr><td>ablie</td><td>ably</td></tr>
<tr><td>ably</td><td></td></tr>
<tr><td>abnawmal</td><td>abnormal $^+$</td></tr>
<tr><td>abnawmalitey</td><td>abnormality $^+$</td></tr>
<tr><td>abnormal /ly</td><td></td></tr>
<tr><td>abnormalit y /ies</td><td></td></tr>
<tr><td>aboard</td><td></td></tr>
<tr><td>abode</td><td></td></tr>
<tr><td>aboli sh ^{1} /tion</td><td></td></tr>
<tr><td>abolishun</td><td>abolition</td></tr>
<tr><td>A-bomb</td><td></td></tr>
<tr><td>abominabl e /y</td><td></td></tr>
<tr><td>abominabul</td><td>abominable $^+$</td></tr>
<tr><td>abominashun</td><td>abomination</td></tr>
<tr><td>abominat e ^{2} /ion</td><td></td></tr>
<tr><td>abord</td><td>aboard</td></tr>
<tr><td>aborigin al /es</td><td></td></tr>
<tr><td>aborshun</td><td>abortion $^+$</td></tr>
<tr><td>abort ^{1} /ive</td><td></td></tr>
<tr><td>abortion /ist</td><td></td></tr>
<tr><td>abound ^{1}</td><td></td></tr>
<tr><td>about</td><td></td></tr>
<tr><td>above /-board</td><td></td></tr>
<tr><td>abownd</td><td>abound ^{1}</td></tr>
<tr><td>abowt</td><td>about</td></tr>
<tr><td>abracadabra</td><td></td></tr>
<tr><td>abrashun</td><td>abrasion $^+$</td></tr>
<tr><td>abras ion /ive</td><td></td></tr>
<tr><td>abrawd</td><td>abroad</td></tr>
<tr><td>abreast</td><td></td></tr>
<tr><td>abrecadabra</td><td>abracadabra</td></tr>
<tr><td>abrest</td><td>abreast</td></tr>
<tr><td>abreviashun</td><td>abbreviation</td></tr>
<tr><td>abreviate</td><td>abbreviate $^{2+}$</td></tr>
<tr><td>abreviation</td><td>abbreviation</td></tr>
<tr><td>abridge ^{2} /ment</td><td></td></tr>
<tr><td>abrige</td><td>abridge $^{2+}$</td></tr>
</table>

abroad		abyewse	abuse [2]+
abrord	abroad	abysmal /ly	
abrupt /ly/ness		abyss	
absaloot	absolute +	abyusiv	abusive
absawb	absorb [1]+	abzawb	absorb [1]+
absawbency	absorbency +	abzawbent	absorbent
absawbensey	absorbency +	abzolv	absolve [2]+
absawbent	absorbent	acacia	
absawpshun	absorption +	academic /al/ally	
abscess /es		academician	
abscond [1] /er		academishun	academician
absent /ee/eeism		academ y /ies	
abserd	absurd +	acapuncture	acupuncture
abserditey	absurdity	accede [2] /nce	
absess	abscess +	accelerat e [2] /ion/or	
absolushun	absolution	accent [1] /ual	
absolut e /ely/ism		accentuat e [2] /ion	
absolution		accept [1] /ability	
absolv e [2] /able		acceptabl e /y	
absorb [1] /able		acceptabul	acceptable +
absorben cy /t		acceshun	accession +
absorbensey	absorbency +	access /ibility/ible	
absorpshun	absorption +	accessar y * (legal) /ies	
absorpt ion /ive		accession /al	
abstain [1] /er		accessor y *† /ies	
abstayn	abstain [1]+	† (accompaniment)	
abstemious /ness		accident /al/ally	
abstemius	abstemious +	acclaim [1] /er	
abstenshun	abstention	acclamashun	acclamation +
abstention		acclamat ion /ory	
abstinen ce /t		acclaym	acclaim [1]+
abstinens	abstinence +	acclimatis e [2] /ation	
abstract [1] /ion/or		accolade	
abstroos	abstruse +	accommodat e [2] /ion	
abstruse /ness		accompani st /ment	
absurd /ity/ities		accompany [4]	
abul	able +	accomplice	
abundanc e /y		accomplish [1] /ment	
abundans	abundance +	accompliss	accomplice
abundant /ly		accord [1] /ance/ingly	
abundent	abundant +	accordion /ist	
abunduns	abundance +	accordyun	accordion+
abus e [2] /ive/iveness		accost [1]	
abut [3] /ment		account [1] /ancy/ant	
abuv	above +	accountab le /ility	

14

accountabul	accountable +	acootrements	accoutrements
accoutrements		acord	accord [1]+
accredit [1] /ation		acorn	
accru *e* [2] /al		acost	accost [1]
accumpany	accompany [4]	acount	account [1]+
accumulat *e* [2] /ion/or		acoustic /s	
accumulative		acownt	account [1]+
accuracy		acquaint [1] /ance	
accurasey	accuracy	acquiesce [2] /nce/nt	
accurate /ly/ness		acquire [2] /ment	
accursed /ly/ness		acquisit *ion* /ive	
accusative		acquit [3] /tal	
accus *e* [2] /ation/er		acre /age	
accustom [1]		acrid /ity/ness	
ace		acrimonious /ly	
acer	acre +	acrimonius	acrimonious +
acerige	acreage	acrimony	
acetate		acrobat /ic/ically	
acetic		acromatic	achromatic
acetone		acronim	acronym
acetylen *e* /ic		acronym	
ache [2]		acropolis	
achevabul	achievable	across	
acheve	achieve [2]+	acseed	accede [2]+
achievable		acselerate	accelerate [2]+
achieve [2] /ment/r		acselerater	accelerator
achromatic		acsent	accent [1]+
acid /ic/ity		acsentuate	accentuate [2]+
acidul *ate* [2] /ous		acsept	accept [1]+
acknoledge	acknowledge [2]+	acseptable	acceptable +
acknolidge	acknowledge [2]+	acsesary	accessary *+
acknowledge [2] /ment		acsesary	accessory *+
aclaim	acclaim [1]+	acseshun	accession +
aclamashun	acclamation +	acsess	access +
aclamation	acclamation +	acsessorey	accessory *+
aclaym	acclaim [1]+	acshun	action +
acme		acsident	accident +
acne		act [1] /able	
acolight	acolyte	actini *c* /um	
acolyte		action /able	
acommodate	accommodate [2]+	activat *e* [2] /ion/or	
acomodate	accommodate [2]+	active /ly/ness	
acompaniment	accompaniment	activis *m* /t	
acompany	accompany [4]	activit *y* /ies	
acompliss	accomplice	act *or* /ress (fem.)	

actual /ly	
actualit *y* /ies	
actuar *y* /ies	
actuat *e* ² /ion/or	
acumen	
acumpany	accompany ⁴
acumpliss	accomplice
acumulate	accumulate ²⁺
acupuncture	
acupunkcher	acupuncture
acuracy	accuracy
acustic	acoustic ⁺
acurate	accurate ⁺
acustum	accustom ¹
acute /ly/ness	
ad	add ¹
ad hoc	
ad infinitum	
ad lib.³	
adage	
adagio /s	
adamant /ine	
adament	adamant ⁺
adapt ¹ /ation/ive	
adaptab *le* /ility	
adaptabul	adaptable ⁺
adapter ★ (person)	
adaptor ★ (electric)	
add ¹	
addend *um* /a (pl.)	
addenoids	adenoids
adder	
addict ¹ /ion/ive	
addition /al/ally	
addle ²	
address ¹ /ee/er	
ade	aid ¹⁺
adement	adamant ⁺
adendum	addendum ⁺
adenoids	
adept /ly/ness	
adequacy	
adequasey	adequacy
adequate /ly/ness	
adhear	adhere ²⁺

adhearence	adherence
adhere ² /nce/nt	
adheshun	adhesion ⁺
adhes *ion* /ive	
adicshun	addiction
adiction	addiction
adidge	adage
adieu	
adige	adage
adikwacy	adequacy
adikwat	adequate ⁺
adiquacy	adequacy
adiquate	adequate ⁺
adishun	addition ⁺
adition	addition ⁺
adjacent /ly	
adjectiv *e* /al	
adjoin ¹	
adjourn ¹ /ment	
adjudge ²	
adjudicat *e* ² /ion/or	
adjunct /ion/ive	
adjust ¹ /able/ment	
adjutan *cy* /t	
adle	addle ²
administ *er* ¹ /rable	
administrat *e* ² /ion/or	
administrater	administrator
administrative	
admirabl *e* /y	
admirabul	admirable ⁺
admiral /ty	
admirashun	admiration
admir *e* ² /ation/er	
admirul	admiral ⁺
admishun	admission ⁺
admisibul	admissible ⁺
admissib *le* /ility	
admiss *ion* /ive	
admit ³ /tedly	
admitance	admittance
admitans	admittance
admittance	
admonish ¹ /er/ment	
ado	

adobe		advis *edly* /er/ory	
adobi	adobe	advocacy	
adolescen *ce* /t		advocasey	advocacy·
adolesence	adolescence +	advocat *e* ² /or	
adolesens	adolescence +	advurse	adverse +
adolesent	adolescent	advurtisment	advertisement
adoor	adore ²⁺	aegis	
adopshun	adoption	aerat *e* ² /ion/or	
adopt ¹ /er/ion/ive		aerial /ly	
adorabl *e* /y		aerobatics	
adorabul	adorable +	aerodrome	
ador *e* ² /ation		aerodynamics	
adorn ¹ /ment		aerofoil	
adrenal /in		aeronaut /ical/ics	
adrift		aeroplane	
adroit /ly/ness		aerosol	
adsorpshun	adsorption +	aesthet *e* /ic/icism	
adsorpt *ion* /ive		afable	affable +
adue	adieu	afabul	affable +
adul	addle ²	afair	affair
adulashun	adulation	afare	affair
adulat *e* ² /ion/or		afecshun	affection
adult /hood		afecshunate	affectionate +
adulterat *e* ² /ion/or		afect	affect ¹⁺
adulterus	adulterous	afectation	affectation
adulter *y* /er/ous		afection	affection
advance ² /ment		afectionate	affectionate +
advans	advance ²⁺	afective	affective
advencher	adventure ²⁺	afeild	afield
advencherous	adventurous +	afeld	afield
advencherus	adventurous +	aferm	affirm ¹⁺
advent ⸜		afermativ	affirmative +
adventishus	adventitious +	affab *le* /ility/ly	
adventitious /ly/ness		affair	
adventure ² /some		affect ¹ /ion/ive	
adventurous /ly/ness		affectation	
adverb /ial		affectionate /ly/ness	
adversar *y* /ies		affidavit	
adverse /ly/ness		affiks	affix ¹⁺
adversit *y* /ies		affiliat *e* ² /ion	
advertise ² /ment		affinit *y* /ies	
advice ★ (a suggestion)		affirm ¹ /ation	
advisabl *e* /y		affirmative /ly	
advisabul	advisable +	affix ¹ /er	
advise ² ★ (suggest)		afflict ¹ /ion	

affluen *ce* /t		after	
affluens	affluence +	afterbirth	
afford [1] /able		afterburth	afterbirth
afforest [1] /ation		aftermath	
affray /s		afternoon	
affront [1]		afterthort	afterthought
afid	aphid +	afterthought	
afidavit	affidavit	afterwards	
afield		afterwerds	afterwards
afiks	affix [1]+	afurm	affirm [1]+
afiliashun	affiliation	afurmashun	affirmation
afiliate	affiliate [2]+	afurmation	affirmation
afiliation	affiliation	afurmativ	affirmative +
afinitey	affinity +	again	
afire		against	
afirm	affirm [1]+	agast	aghast
afirmativ	affirmative +	agate	
afix	affix [1]+	agayn	again
aflaim	aflame	age [2] /less	
aflame		agen	again
aflicshun	affliction	agenc *y* /ies	
aflict	afflict [1]+	agenda	
afliction	affliction	agensey	agency +
afloat		agenst	against
aflote	afloat	agent /ial	
afluence	affluence +	agglomerat *e* [2] /ion	
afluens	affluence +	aggrandise [2] /ment	
afluent	affluent	aggravat *e* [2] /ion	
aford	afford [1]+	aggregat *e* [2] /ely/ion	
aforesaid		aggreshun	aggression +
aforest	afforest [1]+	aggress *ion* /or	
aforestashun	afforestation	aggressive /ly/ness	
aforestation	afforestation	aggrieved	
aforism	aphorism +	aghast	
aforistic	aphoristic	agil *e* /ity	
aforsed	aforesaid	agitat *e* [2] /ion/or	
afrade	afraid	aglomerashun	agglomeration
afraid		aglomerate	agglomerate [2]+
afray	affray +	aglomeration	agglomeration
afrayd	afraid	aglow	
African		agnostic /ism	
Afrikaans		agonie	agony +
Afrikans	Afrikaans	agonis *e* [2] /ingly	
afrodisiac	aphrodisiac	agon *y* /ies	
afront	affront [1]	agorafobia	agoraphobia

agoraphobia		air hostess /es	
agrafobia	agoraphobia	airial	aerial [+]
agrandise	aggrandise [2+]	airily	
agrarian		airline /r	
agravate	aggravate [2+]	air-lock	
agree /d/ing/ment		airmail [1]	
agreeabl e /y		airmale	airmail [1]
agregate	aggregate [2+]	airobatics	aerobatics
agrement	agreement	airodinamics	aerodynamics
agreshun	aggression [+]	airodrome	aerodrome
agresion	aggression [+]	airofoil	aerofoil
agresiv	aggressive [+]	airofoyl	aerofoil
agression	aggression [+]	aironort	aeronaut [+]
agreved	aggrieved	aironortics	aeronautics
agriculcher	agriculture [+]	airoplane	aeroplane
agricultur e /al/ally		airosol	aerosol
agrieved	aggrieved	air-pocket	
aground		airport	
agrownd	aground	air raid	
agu e /ish		airworth y /iness	
ahead		airy /-fairy	
ahed	ahead	aisle ★ (passage)	
ahoi	ahoy	aisle	isle ★
ahoy		ajar	
aid [1] /er		ajasent	adjacent [+]
ail [1]★ (trouble)		ajectiv	adjective [+]
ail	ale ★	ajency	agency [+]
ailment		ajenda	agenda
aim [1] /less/lessly		ajensey	agency [+]
air [1]★ (gases)		ajent	agent [+]
air	ere ★	ajile	agile [+]
air	heir ★	ajilitey	agility
airate	aerate [2+]	ajitashun	agitation
airborne		ajitate	agitate [2+]
air-brake		ajoyn	adjoin [1]
aircondishner	air-conditioner	ajudicate	adjudicate [2+]
air-conditioner		ajunct	adjunct [+]
air-cooled		ajurn	adjourn [1+]
aircraft		ajusment	adjustment
aires	Aries	ajust	adjust [1+]
airey	airy [+]	ajustable	adjustable
airfeild	airfield	ajutancy	adjutancy [+]
airfield		akimbo	
air force		akin	
air-gun		aksiomatic	axiomatic [+]

19

aksis	axis [+]	alegation	allegation
aksium	axiom	alege	allege [2+]
akwaintance	acquaintance	alegiance	allegiance
akwalung	aqualung	alegians	allegiance
akwamarine	aquamarine	alegorey	allegory [+]
akwaplane	aquaplane	alegorical	allegorical [+]
akwarium	aquarium [+]	alelooya	alleluia
akwarius	Aquarius	aleluia	alleluia
akwatic	aquatic	alergey	allergy [+]
akwatint	aquatint	alergic	allergic
akwiduct	aqueduct	alert [1] /ly/ness	
akwiesence	acquiescence	aleviate	alleviate [2+]
akwiesent	acquiescent	alfa	alpha
akwiline	aquiline	alfabet	alphabet [+]
akwire	acquire [2+]	alfabetical	alphabetical
akwisition	acquisition [+]	alfresco	
akwisitiv	acquisitive	alga /e (pl.)	
akwit	acquit [3+]	algebra	
akwital	acquittal	algibra	algebra
alabaster		ali	ally [4+]
alack		aliance	alliance
alacrit*y* /ous		alians	alliance
alagro	allegro	alias /es	
alah	Allah	alibi /s	
alarm [1] /ist		aliby	alibi [+]
alas		alien /able	
alay	allay [1+]	alienat*e* [2] /ion/or	
albatross		aligater	alligator
albeit		alight [1]	
albeno	albino [+]	align [1] /ment	
albino /s		alike /ness	
album		alimenta *ry* /tion	
albumen *†		alimentrey	alimentary [+]
†(white of egg)		alimony	
albumin *†		aline	align [1+]
†(soluble protein)		alite	alight [1]
alchem*y* /ist		aliterashun	alliteration
alcohol /ic/ism		aliterate	alliterate [2+]
alcove		aliteration	alliteration
alder		alive	
alderman /cy		alkali /s	
ale ★ (drink)		alkalin*e* /ity	
ale	ail [1★]	alkemey	alchemy [+]
alegashun	allegation	alkemist	alchemist
alegater	alligator	all ★ (everyone)	

all	awl ★	almon *er* /ry	
Allah		almost	
allay [1] /er		alms ★ (charity)	
allegashun	allegation	alms	arms ★
allegation		alms-house	
allege [2] /dly		alocate	allocate [2+]
allegiance		alocation	allocation
allegorical /ly		aloft	
allegor *y* /ies		aloi	alloy [1]
allegro		alone	
alleluia		along /side	
allergic		alood	allude [2★]
allerg *y* /ies		aloof /ness	
alleviat *e* [2] /ion		alot	allot [3+]
alley /s/way		alotment	allotment
alli	ally [4]	aloud	
alliance		alow	allow [1+]
allians	alliance	alowable	allowable
alligator		alowabul	allowable
alliterat *e* [2] /ion/ive		alowance	allowance
allmost	almost	alowans	allowance
allocat *e* [2] /ion		alowd	aloud
allot [3] /ment		aloy	alloy [1]
allotropes		alp /ine	
allow [1] /able/ance		alpaca	
alloy [1]		alpaka	alpaca
all right		alpha	
allrite	all right	alphabet /ical/ically	
allso	also	alpine	
allude [2★] (refer to)		already	
allude	elude [2★]	alredy	already
allure [2] /ment		alright	all right
allushun	allusion ★	alrite	all right
allusion★ (reference to)		alsashun	Alsatian
allusion	illusion ★	Alsatian	
allusive ★† /ly/ness		also	
† (suggestive)		altar ★ (church)	
allusive	elusive ★+	altarpiece	
allusive	illusive ★	alter [1★] (change)	
alluvi *al* /um		altera *ble* /tion	
all *y* [4] /ies		alterabul	alterable +
ally	alley +	alterashun	alteration
almanac		altercat *e* [2] /ion	
almighty		alternashun	alternation
almond		alternat *e* [2] /ion/or	

21

alternative /ly	
alterpeace	altarpiece
alterpiece	altarpiece
altho	although
although	
altimeter	
altitude	
alto /s	
altogether	
altrooism	altruism
altrooist	altruist +
altrooistic	altruistic
altruism	
altruist /ic/ically	
alude	allude ²★
alum	
aluminium	
aluminum	aluminium
alure	allure ²+
alurt	alert ¹+
alushun	allusion ★
alusion	allusion ★
alusiv	allusive ★+
always	
amaise	amaze ²+
amalgam	
amalgamashun	amalgamation
amalgamat e² /ion	
amass¹ /able/ment	
amater	amateur +
amateur /ish/ism	
amaze² /ment	
Amazon /ian	
ambasader	ambassador +
ambassador /ial	
amber	
ambiant	ambient
ambidekstrus	ambidextrous
ambidextrous	
ambidextrus	ambidextrous
ambien ce /t	
ambiens	ambience +
ambiguit y /ies	
ambiguous /ly/ness	
ambiguus	ambiguous +

ambishun	ambition
ambishus	ambitious +
ambit	
ambition	
ambitious /ly/ness	
ambivalen ce /t	
amble² /r	
amboosh	ambush ¹+
ambrosia /l	
ambul	amble ²+
ambulance	
ambulans	ambulance
ambulat e² /ory	
ambush¹ /er	
ame	aim ¹+
ameba	amoeba
amelierashun	amelioration
amelierate	ameliorate ²+
ameliorat e² /ion	
amen	
amenabl e /y	
amenabul	amenable +
amend¹ /ment	
amenit y /ies	
American	
ameter	ammeter
amethyst /ine	
amfibian	amphibian
amfibious	amphibious +
amfibius	amphibious +
amfitheater	amphitheatre
amiab le /ility/ly	
amiabul	amiable +
amicab le /ility/ly	
amicabul	amicable +
amid /st	
amiss	
amiter	ammeter
amitey	amity
amithist	amethyst +
amity	
ammeter	
ammonia /c/cal	
ammonya	ammonia +
ammunishun	ammunition

ammunition	
amnest *y* /ies	
amoeba	
amoner	almoner +
among /st	
amonia	ammonia +
amonya	ammonia +
amoral /ity/ly	
amorfus	amorphous +
amorous /ly	
amorphous /ly/ness	
amortise ²	
amorus	amorous +
amount ¹	
amownt	amount ¹
ampar	ampere +
amper *e* /age	
amperige	amperage
amphibian	
amphibious /ly/ness	
amphitheatre	
ampl *e* /y	
amplie	amply
amplifi	amplify ⁴⁺
amplif *y* ⁴ /ier	
amplitude	
ampool	ampoule
ampoule	
ampul	ample +
amputashun	amputation
amputat *e* ² /ion	
amulet	
amung	among +
amunishun	ammunition
amunition	ammunition
amuse ² /ment/r	
anachronism	
anachronistic /ally	
anaconda	
anacronism	anachronism
anacronistic	anachronistic +
anaemi *a* /c	
anaesthe *sia* /tic/tist	
anaesthetis *e* ² /ation	
anagram /matic	

anakey	
anakronism	
anal	
analgesi *a* /c	
analise	analyse ²⁺
analisis	analysis +
analist	analyst
analitic	analytic +
analog	analogue
analogey	analogy +
analogous /ly	
analogue	
analogus	analogous +
analog *y* /ies	
anals -	annals
analyse ² /r	
analys *is* /es (pl.)	
analyst	
analytic /al/ally	
anarchi *c* /sm/st	
anarch *y* /ical	
anarkey	anarchy +
anarkick	anarchic +
anarkism	anarchism
anarkist	anarchist
anathema	
anatomic *al* /ally	
anatomise ²	
anatom *y* /ist	
ancest *or* /ress (fem.)	
ancestr *y* /al	
anchor ¹ /age	
anchov *y* /ies	
ancient /ly/ness	
ancillar *y* /ies	
andante	
androginus	androgynous +
androgyn *ous* /y	
anecdot *e* /al/ic	
aneks	annex ¹★
aneks	annexe ★
aneksashun	annexation
aneksation	annexation
anemia	anaemia +
anemic	anaemic

23

anemomet *er* /ry	
anemone	
anemya	anaemia [+]
aneroid	
anesthesia	anaesthesia [+]
anesthetic	anaesthetic
anesthetise	anaesthetise [2+]
anesthetist	anaesthetist
anew	
angel ★ (heavenly)	
angel	angle [2]★
angelic /al/ally	
angena	angina
anger	
angina	
angle [2]★ (geometry)	
angler	
Anglican /ism	
anglicise [2]	
anglisise	anglicise [2]
anglosaksen	Anglo-Saxon
Anglo-Saxon	
angora	
angrie	angry [+]
angr *y* /ier/iest/ily	
angsietey	anxiety [+]
anguish [1]	
angular /ity	
anguler	angular [+]
angwish	anguish [1]
anhidrus	anhydrous
anhydrous	
anihilate	annihilate [2+]
aniilate	annihilate [2+]
anilen	aniline
aniline	
animal /ism/istic	
animashun	animation
animat *e* [2] /ion	
animatedly	
animosit *y* /ies	
animul	animal [+]
aniseed	
aniversarey	anniversary [+]
anjelic	angelic [+]

anjelical	angelical
anker	anchor [1+]
ankerage	anchorage
ankerige	anchorage
ankle /bone/t	
ankshous	anxious [+]
ankshus	anxious [+]
ankul	ankle [+]
annals	
anneal [1]	
annex [1]★† /ation	
† (take possession of)	
annexe ★ (of house)	
annihilat *e* [2] /ion	
anniversar *y* /ies	
Anno Domini	
annon	anon
annotat *e* [2] /ion/or	
announce [2] /ment/r	
announs	announce [2+]
annoy [1] /ance/ingly	
annoyans	annoyance
annual /ly	
annuit *y* /ies	
annul [3] /ment	
annular ./ity	
annunciat *e* [2] /ion	
Ano domini	Anno Domini
anod *e* /al	
anodine	anodyne
anodyne	
anoi	annoy [1+]
anoiance	annoyance
anoians	annoyance
anoint [1] /er/ment	
anomaley	anomaly [+]
anomalous /ly	
anomalus	anomalous [+]
anomal *y* /ies	
anon	
anonimitey	anonymity
anonimous	anonymous [+]
anonimus	anonymous [+]
anonymity	
anonymous /ly/ness	

anorak	
anotashun	annotation
anotate	annotate $^{2+}$
anotation	annotation
another	
anounce	announce $^{2+}$
anouns	announce $^{2+}$
anounser	announcer
anownce	announce $^{2+}$
anowns	announce $^{2+}$
anoy	annoy $^{1+}$
anoyance	annoyance
anoyans	annoyance
anoynt	anoint $^{1+}$
anser	answer $^{1+}$
anserable	answerable
anserabul	answerable
ansester	ancestor $^+$
ansestrul	ancestral
ansestry	ancestry $^+$
anshent	ancient $^+$
ansilarey	ancillary $^+$
answer ^{1} /able/er	
ant /-eater/-hill	
ant	aunt $^+$
antacid	
antagonis e ^{2} /m	
antagonist /ic/ically	
Antarctic	
antasid	antacid
anteceden ce /t	
antecedens	antecedence $^+$
antechamber	
antedate ^{2}	
antediluvian	
anteek	antique $^+$
antelope	
antena	antenna $^+$
antenatal	
antenna /e (pl.)	
anterier	anterior
anterior	
anteroom	
anthem	
anther	

antholog y /ies/ist	
anthracit e /ic	
anthraks	anthrax
anthrasite	anthracite $^+$
anthrax	
anthropoid /al	
anthropologey	anthropology $^+$
anthropologist	
anthropolog y /ical	
anthropoyd	anthropoid $^+$
anti-aircraft	
antibiotic	
antibod y /ies	
antic	
antichamber	antechamber
antichrist	
anticiclone	anticyclone $^+$
anticipat e ^{2} /ion/ory	
anticlimaks	anticlimax $^+$
anticlima x /ctic	
anticyclon e /ic	
antidate	antedate ^{2}
antidiloovian	antediluvian
antidot e /al/ally	
anti-freeze	
antihistamine	
antikwarian	antiquarian
antikwate	antiquate ^{2}
antikwerey	antiquary $^+$
antikwitey	antiquity $^+$
antilope	antelope
antimon y /ial	
antinatul	antenatal
antipathey	antipathy $^+$
antipath y /etic	
antipodes	
antiquar y /ies/ian	
antiquate ^{2}	
antique /ness	
antiquit y /ies	
antiroom	anteroom
antisedens	antecedence $^+$
anti-semiti c /sm	
antiseptic /ally	
antisiclone	anticyclone $^+$

25

antisipashun	anticipation	aparishun	apparition
antisipate	anticipate ²⁺	aparition	apparition
antisipation	anticipation	apart	
antisocial /ly		apartat	apartheid
antisoshal	antisocial ⁺	apartheid	
antithes *is* /es (pl.)		apartied	apartheid
antithisis	antithesis ⁺	apartment	
antitoksic	antitoxic ⁺	apase	apace
antitoksin	antitoxin	apathetic /al/ally	
antitoxi *c* /n		apathy	
antler /ed		ape ²	
anu	anew	apeace	apiece
anual	annual ⁺	apeal	appeal ¹⁺
anuitey	annuity ⁺	apear	appear ¹⁺
anul	anal	apearance	appearance
anul	annul ³⁺	apearans	appearance
anular	annular ⁺	apease	apiece
anulment	annulment	apeel	appeal ¹⁺
anunciashun	annunciation	apeer	appear ¹⁺
anunciate	annunciate ²⁺	apeice	apiece
anunciation	annunciation	apeks	apex ⁺
anunsiashun	annunciation	apellant	appellant ⁺
anunsiate	annunciate ²⁺	apellashun	appellation
anunsiation	annunciation	apellation	appellation
anus		apend	append ¹⁺
anuther	another	apendage	appendage
anvil		apendicitis	appendicitis
anxiet *y* /ies		apendige	appendage
anxious /ly/ness		apendiks	appendix ⁺
any		apendisitis	appendicitis
anybody		apendix	appendix ⁺
anyhow		aperance	appearance
anyone		aperans	appearance
anything		apercher	aperture
anyual	annual ⁺	apergey	apogee ⁺
anyway		aperitif	
anywere	anywhere	apertain	appertain ¹
anywhere		aperture	
aorta		apetiser	appetiser
apace		apetising	appetising ⁺
Apache		apetite	appetite
apal	appal ³⁺	ap *ex* /exes/ices (pls.)	
aparatus	apparatus ⁺	aphid /ian	
aparel	apparel ⁺	aphoris *m* /tic	
aparent	apparent ⁺	aphrodisiac	

26

apiar *y* /ies	
apiece	
apissul	epistle +
apitite	appetite
aplaud	applaud [1]
aplause	applause
aplawd	applaud [1]
aplawse	applause
aple	apple +
apli	apply [4]
apliance	appliance
aplians	appliance
aplicable	applicable +
aplicabul	applicable +
aplicant	applicant
aplicashun	application
aplication	application
aplom	aplomb
aplomb	
apocalips	apocalypse +
apocalyp *se* /tic	
apocrifal	apocryphal
apocryphal	
apoge *e* /an	
apoint	appoint [1]+
apologetic /ally	
apologey	apology +
apologise [2]	
apolog *y* /ies/ist	
apoplectic /ally	
apopleksey	apoplexy
apoplexy	
aporshun	apportion [1]+
aportion	apportion [1]+
aposishun	apposition
aposit	apposite
aposition	apposition
aposle	apostle +
apost *le* /olate/olic	
apostrofey	apostrophe
apostrophe	
aposul	apostle +
apothecar *y* /ies	
apoynt	appoint [1]+
appal [3] /ingly	

apparatus /es	
apparel /led	
apparent /ly	
apparishun	apparition
apparition	
appeal [1] /ingly	
appear [1] /ance	
appease [2] /ment/r	
appella *nt* /tion	
append [1] /age	
appendices (pl.)	
appendicitis	
appendiks	appendix +
appendix /es (pl.)	
appertain [1]	
apperture	aperture
appetiser	
appetising /ly	
appetite	
applaud [1]	
applause	
applawd	applaud [1]
applaws	applause
apple /-cart/-pie	
appli	apply [4]
appliance	
applians	appliance
applicab *le* /ility	
applicant	
applicashun	application
application	
apply [4]	
appoint [1] /ment	
apporshun	apportion [1]+
apportion [1] /ment	
apposishun	apposition
apposite	
apposition	
appreciabl *e* /y	
appreciabul	appreciable +
appreciat *e* [2] /ion/ive	
apprehend [1]	
apprehenshun	apprehension
apprehension	
apprehensive /ly/ness	

27

apprentice² /ship		aproximation	approximation
apprentis	apprentice²⁺	apt /ly/ness	
apprise²		aptitude	
approach¹ /able		aptley	aptly
approbation		apul	apple⁺
approch	approach¹⁺	aqualung	
appropriate² /ly/ness		aquamarine	
appropriat*ion* /or		aquaplane	
approval		aquarelle	
approve²		aquari*um* /a/ums (pls.)	
approximashun	approximation	Aquarius	
approximate² /ly		aquatic	
approximation		aquatint	
aprehend	apprehend¹	aqueduct	
aprehenshun	apprehension	aqueous	
aprehensiv	apprehensive⁺	aquiline	
apren	apron¹	aquius	aqueous
aprentis	apprentice²⁺	ar	are⁺
apreshabul	appreciable⁺	arabel	arable
apreshiable	appreciable⁺	arabesk	arabesque
apreshiativ	appreciative	arabesque	
apresiashun	appreciation	Arabi*an* /c	
apricot		arable	
April		arabul	arable
aprise	apprise²	araign	arraign¹⁺
aprize	apprise²	arain	arraign¹⁺
aproach	approach¹⁺	Aramaic	
aprobashun	approbation	arange	arrange²⁺
aprobation	approbation	arant	arrant⁺
aproch	approach¹⁺	aray	array¹⁺
aprochabul	approachable	arayn	arraign¹⁺
aproksimashun	approximation	arber	arbour
aproksimat	approximate²⁺	arbiter	
aproksimation	approximation	arbitrar*y* /ily/iness	
apron¹		arbitrashun	arbitration
aproov	approve²	arbitrat*e*² /ion/or	
aprooval	approval	arbour	
apropo	apropos	arc★ (curved line)	
apropos		arc	ark★
apropriashun	appropriation⁺	arcade	
apropriate	appropriate²⁺	arch /es/ly/ness	
apropriation	appropriation⁺	archaeolog*y* /ical/ist	
aproval	approval	archai*c* /sm	
aprove	approve²	archangel	
aproximate	approximate²⁺	archaologey	archaeology⁺

archbishop		aright	
archdeacon		ariley	airily
archduke		arina	arena
archeologey	archaeology +	arise /n	
archer /y		aristocracy	
archetype		aristocrasey	aristocracy
archfeind	archfiend	aristocrat /ic	
archfiend		arite	aright
archipelago /s		arithmetic /ian	
architect /ure		arithmetical /ly	
architectural /ly		arival	arrival
archiv es /ist		arive	arrive 2+
archley	archly	arizen	arisen
archway		ark * (floating vessel)	
arcipeligo	archipelago +	ark	arc *
arcitect	architect +	arkade	arcade
arcitectural	architectural +	arkaic	archaic +
arcives	archives +	arkangel	archangel
arc -lamp /-light		arkiologey	archaeology +
Arctic		arkiologist	archaeologist
ardent /ly		arkipeligo	archipelago +
arder	ardour	arkitect	architect +
ardewus	arduous +	arkitectural	architectural +
ardour		arkives	archives +
arduous /ly/ness		arktic	Arctic
arduus	arduous +	arktipe	archetype
are /n't		arm 1 /ful/let	
area * (surface)		armada	
area	aria *	armadillo /es	
arears	arrears	armament	
arees	Aries	armchair	
arena		armer	armour +
arent	aren't	armey	army +
arest	arrest 1+	armistice	
argew	argue 2+	armistis	armistice
argu	argue 2+	armoner	almoner +
arguabul	arguable	armour /ed	
argu e 2 /able/ably		arms * (limbs)	
argument /ative		arms	alms *
ari	awry	arm y /ies	
aria * (song)		arnt	aren't
aria	area *	arogance	arrogance +
arial	aerial +	arogans	arrogance +
arid /ity		arogant	arrogant
Aries		arogate	arrogate 2+

29

aroma /s/tic	
arora	aurora
aroroot	arrowroot
arose	
around	
arouse²	
arow	arrow⁺
arownd	around
arowroot	arrowroot
arowse	arouse²
arpeggio /s	
arpejo	arpeggio⁺
arraign¹ /ment	
arrange² /ment	
arrant /ly	
array¹ /s	
arrears	
arrest¹ /er	
arrival	
arrive² /r	
arrogan *ce* /t/tly	
arrogans	arrogance⁺
arrogat *e*² /ion	
arrow /-head	
arrowroot	
arsenal	
arsenic /al	
arsnic	arsenic⁺
arson /ist	
artefact	
arter *y* /ies	
arteshun	artesian
artesian	
artful /ly/ness	
arthriti *c* /s	
arthropod	
artichoke	
article²	
articul	article²
articular	
articulat *e*² /ion	
artifice /r	
artificial /ity/ly	
artifis	artifice⁺
artifishal	artificial⁺

artiller *y* /ies	
artisan	
artist * (painter)	
artiste * (performer)	
artistic /ally	
artistry	
artizan	artisan
artless /ly/ness	
asail	assail¹⁺
asailant	assailant
asalant	assailant
asale	assail¹⁺
asalt	assault¹⁺
asassin	assassin
asassinashun	assassination
asassinate	assassinate²⁺
asassination	assassination
asault	assault¹⁺
asay	assay¹⁺
asayl	assail¹⁺
asbestos /is	
ascend¹ /ancy/ant	
ascenshun	ascension
ascension	
ascent * (rise)	
ascent	assent¹*
ascertain¹ /able	
ascetic /ally/ism	
ascrib *e*² /able	
ase	ace
asemblage	assemblage
asemble	assemble²⁺
asembley	assembly⁺
asemblige	assemblage
asembul	assemble²⁺
asend	ascend¹⁺
asendancy	ascendancy
asendansey	ascendancy
asendant	ascendant
asenshun	ascension
asension	ascension
asent	ascent *
asent	assent¹*
asep *sis* /tic	
asershun	assertion

asert	assert [1+]	asistance	assistance
asertain	ascertain [1+]	asistans	assistance
asertane	ascertain [1+]	asistant	assistant
asertayn	ascertain [1+]	asitic	acetic
asertion	assertion	ask [1]	
asertive	assertive	askance	
asess	assess [1+]	askans	askance
asesser	assessor	askew	
asessment	assessment	asku	askew
aset	asset	asleep	
asetic	ascetic [+]	asma	asthma [+]
aseticism	asceticism	asmatic	asthmatic
asfalt	asphalt	asociate	associate [2+]
asfixia	asphyxia	asociation	association
asfixiate	asphyxiate [2+]	asonance	assonance [+]
ash /es/en/-tray/y		asonans	assonance [+]
ashamed		asonant	assonant
ashfalt	asphalt	asort	assort [1+]
ashor	assure [2*]	asoshiashun	association
ashorance	assurance	asoshiate	associate [2+]
ashorans	assurance	aspadistra	aspidistra
ashore * (on beach)		asparagus	
ashore	assure [2*]	aspect	
aside		aspen	
asiditey	acidity	asperit y /ies	
asidulate	acidulate [2+]	aspershun	aspersion
asiduous	assiduous [+]	aspersion	
asiduus	assiduous [+]	asphalt	
asign	assign [1+]	asphyxia	
asignashun	assignation	asphyxiat e [2] /ion	
asignation	assignation	aspic	
asignment	assignment	aspidistra	
asilum	asylum	aspirashun	aspiration
asimetrical	asymmetrical	aspir e [2] /ation	
asimilashun	assimilation	aspirin	
asimilate	assimilate [2+]	asprin	aspirin
asimilater	assimilator	ass /es	
asimilation	assimilation	assail [1] /able/ant	
asimitrey	asymmetry [+]	assassin	
asinable	assignable	assassinat e [2] /ion	
asinabul	assignable	assault [1] /er	
asine	assign [1+]	assay [1] /er	
asinement	assignment	assembl e [2] /age	
asinin e /ity		assembl y /ies	
asist	assist [1+]	assembul	assemble [2+]

31

assend	ascend [1+]
assendancy	ascendancy
assendant	ascendant
assenshun	ascension
assension	ascension
assent [1]★ (agree)	
assent	ascent ★
assert [1] /ion/ive	
assess [1] /ment/or	
asset	
assiduous /ly	
assign [1] /able/ation/ment	
assignee	
assimilat e [2] /ion/or	
assine	assign [1+]
assist [1] /ance/ant	
associat e [2] /ion	
assonan ce /t	
assonans	assonance [+]
assort [1] /ment	
assoshiate	associate [2+]
assuage [2] /ment	
assum e [2] /able/ably	
assumption	
assumshun	assumption
assurance	
assurans	assurance
assure [2]★ (make certain)	
aster ★ (flower)	
aster	astir ★
asterisk	
astern	
asteroid	
asthma /tic	
astigmati c /sm	
astir ★ (motion)	
astonish [1] /ment	
astound [1] /ingly	
astownd	astound [1+]
astral /ly	
astray	
astrel	astral [+]
astride	
astringen cy /t	
astrolog y /er/ical	

astronaut /ic/ical	
astronomy	
astronort	astronaut [+]
astronortic	astronautic
astrul	astral [+]
astur	astir ★
asturn	astern
astute /ly/ness	
asume	assume [2+]
asumpshun	assumption
asumption	assumption
asunder	
aswage	assuage [2+]
asylum	
asymetrey	asymmetry [+]
asymmetr y /ical	
atach	attach [1+]
atachable	attachable
atachabul	attachable
atachay case	attaché case
atack	attack [1+]
atain	attain [1+]
atane	attain [1+]
ate ★ (did eat)	
ate	eight ★
ateen	eighteen [+]
atempt	attempt [1+]
atend	attend [1+]
atendance	attendance
atendans	attendance
atendant	attendant
atenshun	attention [+]
atention	attention [+]
atentiv	attentive
atenuashun	attenuation
atenuate	attenuate [2+]
atenuation	attenuation
aterney	attorney [+]
atest	attest [1+]
atestashun	attestation
atestation	attestation
atey	eighty [+]
atheis m /t/tic	
athiism	atheism [+]
athiist	atheist

athleet	athlete
athlete	
athletic /ism/s	
atic	attic
atipical	atypical +
atire	attire 2
atitude	attitude
Atlantic	
atlas /es	
atmosfere	atmosphere +
atmosferic	atmospheric
atmospher e /ic	
atom /ic/ically	
atomise 2 /r	
atone 2 /ment	
atract	attract 1+
atraction	attraction
atractiv	attractive +
atribushun	attribution
atributable	attributable
atributabul	attributable
atribute	attribute 2+
atribution	attribution
atrishun	attrition
atrition	attrition
atrium	
atrocious /ly/ness	
atrocit y /ies	
atrofey	atrophy 4+
atroph y 4 /ic	
atroshus	atrocious +
atrositey	atrocity +
attach 1 /able	
attachabul	attachable
attaché case	
attachment	
attack 1 /er	
attain 1 /able/ment	
attempt 1 /able	
attend 1 /ance	
attendant	
attenshun	attention +
attent ion /ive	
attenuat e 2 /ion	
atterney	attorney +

attest 1 /ation	
attic	
attire 2	
attitude	
attorney /s	
attract 1 /ion	
attractive /ly/ness	
attributable	
attribut e 2 /ion/ive	
attrishun	attrition
attrition	
attune 2	
atune	attune 2
aturney	attorney +
atypical /ly	
au pair	
aubergine	
auburn	
aucshun	auction 1+
auction 1 /eer	
audacious /ly	
audacity	
audashus	audacious +
audasitey	audacity
audib le /ility/ly	
audibul	audible +
audience	
audiens	audience
audiomet er /ric/ry	
audio-typist	
audio-visual	
audishun	audition 1
audit 1	
audition 1	
auditor	
auditorium	
auditory	
auditrey	auditory
auger * (tool)	
aught * (anything)	
aught	ought *
augment 1 /ation	
augur 1* (predict)	
augur y /ies	
August	

aunt /ie/y	
aura	
aural *(of the ear) /ly	
auric le /ular	
aurora	
auspic es /ious	
auspishus	auspicious
austere /ly/ness	
austerit y /ies	
Australian	
authentic /ally/ity	
authenticat e [2] /ion	
author /ess (fem.)	
authoris e [2] /ation	
authoritarian /ism	
authoritative /ly	
authorit y /ies	
autis m /tic	
autobiografey	autobiography [+]
autobiografical	autobiographi-cal [+]
autobiographical /ly	
autobiograph y /ies	
autocrac y /ies	
autocrasey	autocracy [+]
autocrat	
autocratic /ally	
autograf	autograph [1+]
autograph [1] /ic	
automat e [2] /ion	
automatic /ally	
automatism	
automaton	
automobile	
autonomous /ly	
autonomus	autonomous [+]
autonomy	
autopilot	
autops y /ies	
autum	autumn [+]
autumn /al	
auxiliar y /ies	
avaidable	available [+]
avaide	evade [2+]
avail [1]	

availab le /ility	
avalable	available [+]
avalabul	available [+]
avalanche	
avale	avail [1]
avarey	aviary [+]
avaric e /ious	
avenew	avenue
avenge [2] /r	
avenue	
aver [3] /ment	
average [2] /ly	
averige	average [2+]
averishus	avaricious
averiss	avarice [+]
averse /ly/ness	
avershun	aversion
aversion	
avert [1] /edly	
aviar y /ies	
aviashun	aviation [+]
aviater	aviator
aviat ion /or	
avid /ity/ly	
avlanch	avalanche
avocado	
avocashun	avocation
avocation	
avoid [1] /able/ably	
avow [1] /al/edly	
avoyd	avoid [1+]
avoydable	avoidable
avoydabul	avoidable
avrige	average [2+]
avur	aver [3+]
avurs	averse [+]
avurshun	aversion
avursion	aversion
avurt	avert [1+]
await [1]	
awake [2]	
awaken [1]	
award [1] /able/er	
aware /ness	
awate	await [1]

34

B

away	
awb	orb [1]
awe [2]*(fear)/some/struck	
awear	aware +
awful /ly/ness	
awgsiliarey	auxiliary +
Awgust	August
awgy	orgy +
awhile	
awile	awhile
awiyul	awhile
awkward /ly/ness	
awl * (tool)	
awning	
awoard	award [1]+
awoke	
awry	
axe [2]	
axial	
axident	accident +
axiom	
axiomatic /ally	
ax *is* /es (pl.)	
axle	
axseed	accede [2]+
axsel	axle
axselerate	accelerate [2]+
axsent	accent [1]+
axsentuate	accentuate [2]+
axsept	accept [1]+
axseptable	acceptable +
axseptabul	acceptable +
axsesorey	accessory +
axsess	access +
axsessible	accessible
axsessibul	accessible
ay * (yes) /es *	
ay	eye [2]*+
ay	I *+
aya	ayah
ayah	
aye * (always)	
azalea	
azalia	azalea
azure	

babble [2]	
babie	baby +
babmingten	badminton
babminten	badminton
baboon	
babul	babble [2]
bab *y* /ies	
baby-sitter	
baccarat	
bach	batch
bacheler	bachelor +
bachelor /hood	
bacill *us* /i (pl.)	
back [1] /ache/bone/er	
backara	baccarat
backbencher	
backbit *e* /er/ing	
backbone	
backcloth	
backfire [2]	
backgammon	
background	
backgrownd	background
backhand /ed/er	
backlash	
backlog	
backslid *e* /er/ing	
backspace [2]	
backstage	
backstitch [1]	
backstroke	
backward /ness/s	
backwater	
bacon	
bacteriological /ly	
bacteriolog *y* /ist	
bacteri *um* /a (pl.)	
bad * (no good) /ly	
bade * (asked)	
badge	
badger [1]	
badley	badly

35

badminton		balistic	ballistic +
baffle² /r		balk¹	
baful	baffle² +	balkoney	balcony +
bag³ /gy/gier/giest		ball * (dance) /room	
bagatelle		ball	bawl*
baggage		ballad /ry	
baggidge	baggage	ballast	
baggi ly /ness		ball-bearing	
bagier	baggier	ballerina	
bagiley	baggily +	ballet	
bagpipe /r		ballistic /s	
baige	beige	balloon¹ /er/ist	
bail * (security, sport)		ballot¹	
bail	bale²*	ball-point	
bailee * (person)		ballyhoo	
bailey * (castle wall)		balm /y * (mild)	
bailful	baleful +	balmoral	
bailiff		baloney	
bain	bane +	baloon	balloon¹+
bainful	baneful	balot	ballot¹
bairn		balsa	
baist	baste²	balsam	
bait¹* (fishing)		baluster	
bait	bate²*	balustrade	
baize		bamboo	
baje	beige	bamboozle² /r	
Balaclava		bamboozul	bamboozle²+
balad	ballad +	ban³	
balalaika		banal /ity/ities	
balalika	balalaika	banalitey	banality
balance² /r		banana	
balans	balance²+.	band *(stripe, group)/s*	
balast	ballast	band	banned *
balay	ballet	bandage²	
balcon y /ies		bandanna	
bald * (no hair)		bandey	bandy +
bald	bawled *	bandie	bandy +
balderdash		bandige	bandage²
bald-headed		bandit /ry	
bald ing /ness		bands	banns *
bale²* (bundle)		bandstand	
bale	bail *	bandwagon	
baleful /ly		bandy /-legged	
balerina	ballerina	bane /ful/fully	
balihoo	ballyhoo	baner	banner

bang ¹	
bangle	
bangul	bangle
banish ¹ /ment	
banister	
banjo /s	
bank ¹ /er/note	
bankrupt ¹ /cy	
bankwet	banquet ¹
banned * (barred)	
banner	
banns * (marriage)	
banquet ¹	
bans	banns *
bantam /-weight	
banter ¹ /ingly	
Bantu	
baonet	bayonet ³
baptis e ² /m	
bar /red * (stop) /ring *	
barack	barrack ¹
barb	
barbarian	
barbar ic /ism/ous	
barbarit y /ies	
barbarus	barbarous
barbecue	
barbed wire	
barber	
barbican	
barbique	barbecue
barbiturate	
bard * (poet)	
bard	barred *
bare ²* (naked) /foot	
bare	bear *
bareback	
barefaced	
bareheaded	
barel	barrel ³+
barelegged	
baren	baron *+
baren	barren *+
bareskin	bearskin
bargain ¹ /er	

barge ² /-pole	
bargen	bargain ¹+
baricade	barricade ²
barier	barrier
barige	barrage
baring * (exposing)	
baring	barring *
baring	bearing *
barister	barrister
baritone	
barium	
bark ¹ /er	
barley /-sugar	
barly	barley +
barm	balm +
barmade	barmaid
barmaid	
barmy * (crazy)	
barmy	balmy *
barn /yard	
barn	bairn
barnacle /d	
barnicul	barnacle +
barograf	barograph
barograph	
barok	baroque
baromet er /ric	
baron * (noble) /et/y	
baroness (fem.)	
baroque	
barow	barrow
barrack ¹	
barrage	
barrel ³ /ful	
barren * (empty) /ness	
barricade ²	
barrier	
barrister	
barrow	
barter ¹ /er	
barul	barrel ³+
basalt	
base * (station, foundation)	
base	bass *

baseball	
base *less* /ly/ness	
basement	
baset	basset
bashful /ly/ness	
basic /ally	
basillus	bacillus +
basin /ful	
basis * (groundwork)	
basit	basset
bask [1]	
basket /ball/ful/ry	
baskit	basket +
basoon	bassoon
bas-relief	
bass * (deep tone)	
bass clef	
bass drum	
basset	
bassoon	
bastard /ly	
bastardis *e* [2] /ation	
baste [2]	
basterd	bastard +
bastion	
bastyun	bastion
bat [3] /sman	
batalion	battalion
batalyun	battalion
batch	
bate [2]* (lessen)	
bate	bait [1]*
baten	baton *
baten	batten [1]*
bater	batter [1]
baterey	battery +
batering ram	battering-ram
bathe [2] /r	
bathroom	
batie	batty +
batik	
batle	battle [2]+
baton * (staff of office)	
battalion	
batten [1]* (wood, grow fat)	

batter [1]	
battering-ram	
batter *y* /ies	
battle [2] /dress/ship	
battle-axe	
batt *y* /ier/iest	
batul	battle [2]+
baty	batty +
bauble	
baubul	bauble
bauxite	
bawble	bauble
bawdie	bawdy
bawdi *ly* /ness	
bawd *y* /ier/iest	
bawk	balk [1]
bawksite	bauxite
bawl * (cry)/ed * /ing	
bawl	ball *
bawl-baring	ball-bearing
bawldedash	balderdash
bawldheded	bald-headed
bawldness	baldness
bawlpoint	ball-point
bawlroom	ballroom
baylif	bailiff
bayonet [3]	
bayth	bathe [2]+
bazaar	
bazar	bazaar
bazooka	
be * (is-[verb]) /ing	
be	bee *
beach [1]* (shore) /es	
beach	beech *+
beachcomber	
beachhead	
beacon	
bead /y	
beadle	
beadul	beadle
beaf	beef +
beafeter	beefeater
beafstake	beefsteak
beagl *e* /ing	

beagul	beagle [+]	bed [3] /ridden/rock	
beak /er		bedaub [1]	
beam [1]		bedawb	bedaub [1]
bean * (vegetable)		beday	bidet
bean	been *	bedevil [3]	
beanstalk		bedlam	
bear * (carry, animal)		bedouin	
bear	bare [2]*[+]	bedowin	bedouin
bearback	bareback	bedraggle [2]	
beard [1]		bedragul	bedraggle [2]
bearfased	barefaced	bedriden	bedridden
bearfoot	barefoot	bedroom	
bearheded	bareheaded	bed-sitter	
bearing * (carrying)		bedspread	
bearing	baring *	bedstead	
bearleggid	barelegged	bedtime	
bearskin		bee * (insect) /hive	
beast /ly		beech * (tree) /es	
beastli er /est/ness		beech	beach [1]*[+]
beat * (strike) /en		beechcomer	beachcomber
beat	beet *	beechhed	beachhead
beatif y [4] /ic/ication		beecon	beacon
beatitude		beed	bead [+]
beatle	beetle	beedle	beadle
beatroot	beetroot	beef /y	
beatul	beetle	beefeater	
beau * (dandy)		beefi er /est/ly/ness	
Beaufort scale		beefsteak	
beauteous		beegle	beagle [+]
beautician		beek	beak [+]
beautie	beauty [+]	beekun	beacon
beautiful /ly		beeline	
beautify [4]		Beelzebub	
beautishun	beautician	beem	beam [1]
beaut y /ies		been * (past of be)	
beaver		been	bean *
becalmed		beenstork	beanstalk
became		beer * (drink)	
becarmed	becalmed	beer	bier *
because		beerd	beard [1]
beck		beest	beast [+]
beckon [1] /ingly		beestlier	beastlier [+]
becom e /ing		beeswaks	beeswax
becon	beacon	beeswax	
becos	because	beet * (vegetable)	

beet	beat *+	bel	bell *
beetle		bel	belle *
beetroot		belaber	belabour [1]
beetul	beetle	belabour [1]	
beever	beaver	belated /ly	
befall /en		belay [1]	
befell		belch [1]	
befier	beefier +	beleaf	belief
befit [3]		beleager	beleaguer [1]
before /hand		beleaguer [1]	
befrend	befriend [1]	beleavabul	believable +
befriend [1]		beleave	believe [2]+
befuddle [2]		belfrey	belfry +
befudul	befuddle [2]	belfr y /ies	
beg [3]		Belgian	
began		beli	belie *+
beger	beggar [1]+	belicose	bellicose +
beggar [1] /liness/ly		belie * (untruth) /d	
begile	beguile [2]+	belief	
begin /ner/ning		believabl e /y	
begone		believe [2] /r	
begot /ten		beliful	bellyful
begrudge [2]		beligerence	belligerence +
beguile [2] /ment/r		beligerency	belligerency
begun		beligerent	belligerent
behalf		beline	beeline
beharf	behalf	belittle [2] /r	
behave [2]		belittul	belittle [2]+
behavier	behaviour +	beliying	belying
behaviour /ism		bell * (rings)	
behead [1]		belle * (beauty)	
behed	behead [1]	bellicos e /ity	
beheld		belligerenc e /y	
behest		belligerent	
behind		bellow [1] /er	
behive	beehive	bellows	
behold /en/er/ing		bell y * (stomach) /ies/ied	
behove		bellyful	
beige		belong [1] /ings	
being		belose	bellows
bekoz	because	beloved	
bekweath	bequeath [1]+	below * (beneath)	
bekwest	bequest	below	billow [1]*+
bel *†		below	bellow [1]+
†(unit = 10 decibels)		belows	bellows

40

bely	belly ★+	beril	beryl +
belying		berilium	beryllium
bemoan [1]		berkelium	
bemuse [2]		berlap	burlap
bench /er/es		berli	burly +
bend /ing		bern	burn [1]+
beneath		bernish	burnish [1]+
benefaction		berry ★ (fruit) /ies	
benefact or /ress (fem.)		berry	bury [4]★
beneficen ce /t		berserk	
beneficial		bersurk	berserk
beneficiar y /ies		berth [1]★ (moor, bunk)	
benefisens	beneficence +	berth	birth ★+
benefisent	beneficent	bery	berry ★+
benefisharey	beneficiary +	bery	bury [4]★
benefishul	beneficial	beryl /line	
benefit [3]		beryllium	
benevolen ce /t/tly		beseech [1] /er	
benevolens	benevolence +	beseige	besiege [2]+
benifacshun	benefaction	beset [3]	
benifacter	benefactor +	beside /s	
benifactress	benefactress	besiege [2] /ment	
benifit	benefit [3]	besort	besought
benign /ant/ly		besot [3]	
benine	benign +	besought	
bent		bespatter [1]	
benum	benumb [1]+	best /-seller	
benumb [1] /ment		bester	bestir [3]
benzene ★†		bestial /ism/ly	
†(from coal-tar)		bestialit y /ies	
benzine ★ (from		bestir [3]	
mineral oils)		bestow [1] /al/er	
bequeath [1] /ment		bestrew [1] /n	
bequest		bet [3]	
berate [2]		beta particles	
beray	beret	betle	beetle
bereave [2] /ment		betoken [1]	
bereft		betray [1] /al/er	
beret		betroth [1] /al	
bereve	bereave [2]+	better [1] /ment	
bergler	burglar	betul	beetle
berial	burial	between	
beriberi		betwixt	
berie	berry ★+	beverage	
berie	bury [4]★	beveridge	beverage

beverige	beverage
bevie	bevy +
bev y /ies	
bewail¹ /er	
beware	
bewayl	bewail¹+
bewich	bewitch¹+
bewilder¹ /ment	
bewitch¹ /er	
beyond	
bezurk	berserk
bi election	by-election
biannual *† /ly	
†(twice a year)	
biannual	biennial *+
bias¹ /es	
biatifi	beatify⁴+
biatitude	beatitude
Bibl e /ical	
bibliografey	bibliography +
bibliografic	bibliographic +
bibliographic /al	
bibliograph y /ies/er	
bibul	Bible +
bicalmed	becalmed
bicame	became
bicarbonate	
bicarmed	becalmed
bicentenar y /ies	
bicentennial	
bicentenyul	bicentennial
biceps	
bich	bitch +
bicicle	bicycle²+
biciclist	bicyclist
bicker¹ /er	
bicycl e² /ist	
bide²	
bidet	
bidevil	bedevil³
biennial *† /ly	
†(every two years)	
biennial	biannual *+
bier	beer *
bier	byre *

bifell	befell
bifocal	
bifurcat e² /ion	
big /ger/gest/gish	
bigam ist /ous	
bigamus	bigamous
bigam y /ies	
bigan	began
bighead	
bigile	beguile²+
bigin	begin +
biginer	beginner
bigining	beginning
bigon	begone
bigone	bygone +
bigot /ed/ry	
bigrudge	begrudge²
bigun	begun
biharf	behalf
bihave	behave²
bihavier	behaviour +
bihed	behead¹
bihest	behest
bihove	behove
bike	
bikweath	bequeath¹+
bikwest	bequest
bil	bill¹
bilaber	belabour¹
bilated	belated +
bilateral /ism/ly	
bilaw	by-law
bilay	belay¹
bilberie	bilberry +
bilberr y /ies	
bild	build +
bilding	building
bile	
bileager	beleaguer¹
bileavable	believable +
bileavabul	believable +
bileave	believe²+
bileger	beleaguer¹
bileif	belief
bilet	billet¹

bilge		biografical	biographical [+]
bilief	belief	biographical /ly	
bilingual /ism/ly		biography /ies/er	
bilingwal	bilingual [+]	biokemist	biochemist [+]
bilious		biologey	biology [+]
bilittle	belittle [2+]	biological /ly	
bilitul	belittle [2+]	biology /ist	
bilius	bilious	biopsey	biopsy [+]
bilk [1] /er		biopsy /ies	
bill [1]		biparti te /san	
billabong		bipartizan	bipartisan
billet [1]		bipass	by-pass [1]
billiards		biped	
billion /aire		biplane	
billit	billet [1]	biplay	byplay
billow [1★] (wave) /y		bipolar /ity	
bilong	belong [1+]	biproduct	by-product
bilow	below [★]	birate	berate [2]
bilow	billow [1★+]	birch /es	
biluvd	beloved	bird	
bilyards	billiards	birdie	
bilyon	billion [+]	bird's-eye	
bilyus	bilious	bireft	bereft
bimetalli c /sm		bireve	bereave [2+]
bimoan	bemoan [1]	birode	byroad
bimonthly		birth ★ (born) /day	
bimuse	bemuse [2]	birth	berth [1★]
bin ★ (box)		biscuit	
bin	been [★]	bisecshun	bisection
binacle	binnacle	bisect [1] /ion/or	
binacul	binnacle	biseech	beseech [1+]
binary		biseege	besiege [2+]
bind /er/ery/ing		biseksual	bisexual [+]
bineath	beneath	bisentenary	bicentenary [+]
bineeth	beneath	bisentenial	bicentennial
binge		bisentenyal	bicentennial
bingo		biseps	biceps
binine	benign [+]	biset	beset [3]
binnacle		bisexual /ly	
binocular /s		bishop /ric	
binomial		bisicle	bicycle [2+]
binum	benumb [1+]	bisiclist	bicyclist
biochemist /ry		biside	beside [+]
biografer	biographer	bisier	busier [+]
biografey	biography [+]	bisiley	busily

43

biskit	biscuit	blaber	blabber
bismuth		black [1] /out	
bisness	business [+]	black-beetle	
bison		blackberie	blackberry [+]
bisort	besought	blackberr *y* /ies	
bisot	besot [3]	blackbird	
bispatter	bespatter [1]	blackboard	
bistander	bystander	blacken [1]	
bistow	bestow [1+]	blackguard	
bistowal	bestowal	blackleg [3]	
bistru	bestrew [1+]	blacklist [1]	
bistur	bestir [3]	blackmail [1] /er	
bisun	bison	blacksmith	
bisy	busy [4]	bladder	
bitch /es		blade	
bit *e* /ing/ten		blader	bladder
biter	bitter [+]	blagard	blackguard
bitoken	betoken [1]	blaid	blade
bitray	betray [1+]	blaim	blame [2+]
bitrayal	betrayal	blaimless	blameless [+]
bitroth	betroth [1+]	blair	blare [2]
bitter /est/ly/ness		blaise	blaze [2]
bitum *en* /inous		blaizer	blazer
bitween	between	blam *e* [2] /able	
bitwixt	betwixt	blameless /ly	
bivalve		blameworthy	
bivouac /ked/king		blamonge	blancmange
bivuac	bivouac [+]	blanch [1]	
biwail	bewail [1+]	blancmange	
biware	beware	bland /ly/ness	
biwayul	bewail [1+]	blank /ly	
biwear	beware	blanket [1]	
biwhich	bewitch [1+]	blare [2]	
biwich	bewitch [1+]	blarney	
biwilder	bewilder [1+]	blasfeim	blaspheme [2+]
biword	byword	blasfemey	blasphemy [+]
biyond	beyond	blasfemus	blasphemous
bizar	bizarre [+]	blasphem *e* [2] /ous	
bizarre /ly/ness		blasphem *y* /ies	
bizier	busier [+]	blast [1] /-off	
biziley	busily	blast-furnace	
bizmuth	bismuth	blatancy	
bizness	business [+]	blatansey	blatancy
bizy	busy [4]	blatant /ly	
blab [3] /ber		blaze [2]	

44

blazer	
blazon [1] /er	
bleach [1] /er	
blead	bleed +
bleak /er/est/ly/ness	
blear [1] /y	
bleari er /est/ly	
bleat [1] /er	
bled	
bleech	bleach [1]+
bleed /er/ing	
bleek	bleak +
bleer	blear [1]+
bleerey	bleary
bleerier	blearier +
bleet	bleat [1]+
blemish [1] /er	
blench [1] /er	
blend [1] /er	
bless [1]	
blest	
blew * (wind)	
blew	blue *+
blewbell	bluebell
blewberie	blueberry +
blewbery	blueberry +
blew-chip	blue-chip
blewish	bluish
blewprint	blue-print
blight [1] /er	
blind [1] /est/ly/ness	
blinder /s	
blind-man's-buff	
blink [1]	
bliss /ful/fully	
blister [1]	
blite	blight [1]+
bliter	blighter
blith	blithe +
blithe /ly/ness	
blithering	
blits	blitz [1]
blitz [1]	
blizard	blizzard
blizzard	

blo	blow +
bloat [1] /edness	
bloater	
blob [3]	
bloc * (group)	
blochie	blotchy
block *† /age	
†(solid piece, stop)	
block	bloc *
blockade [2] /r	
blockhead /ed	
blond /ish/ness	
blone	blown
blood [1] /y	
blood pressure	
blood vessel	
bloodhound	
blood ied /ier/iest	
bloodi ly /ness	
blood shed /shot	
bloodthirst y /iness	
bloom [1] /ers	
blossom [1] /y	
blosum	blossom [1]+
blot [3] /ter	
blot	bloat [1]+
blotch [1] /y	
bloter	bloater
bloter	blotter
blouse	
blow /er/ing/n/y	
blowse	blouse
blowter	bloater
blowze	blouse
blowzey	blowzy +
blowz y /ier/iest	
blu	blue *+
blubber [1] /y	
blubell	bluebell
bluberie	blueberry +
blubery	blueberry +
blud	blood [1]+
blud presher	blood pressure
blud vesel	blood vessel
bludey	bloody

45

bludgen	bludgeon [1]	bob-sled	
bludgeon [1]		bob-sleigh	
bludhound	bloodhound	boby	bobby [+]
bludhownd	bloodhound	boch	botch [1+]
bludid	bloodied [+]	bode [2]	
bludie	bloody	bodice	
bludily	bloodily [+]	bodie	body [+]
bludshed	bloodshed [+]	bodi *ed* /ly	
bludshot	bloodshot	bodigard	bodyguard
bludthurstey	bloodthirsty [+]	bodiley	bodily
blue ★ (colour) /bell		bodiss	bodice
blue	blew ★	bodkin	
blueberr *y* /ies		bod *y* /ies	
bluebottle		bodyguard	
blue-chip		bogey ★ (golf)	
blue-print		bogey	bogy ★+
bluf	bluff [1+]	boggle [2]	
bluff [1] /er		bogul	boggle [2]
bluish		bogus	
blummers	bloomers	bog *y* ★ (devil) /ies	
blunder [1] /er		bohemian	
blunderbuss		boi	boy ★
blunt /er/est/ly/ness		boi	buoy [1★+]
blur [3] /riness/ry		boiansey	buoyancy [+]
blurb		boiant	buoyant
blurie	blurry	boicot	boycott [1+]
blurt [1]		boil [1] /er	
blush [1] /es/ingly		boisterous /ly	
bluster [1] /y		boisterus	boisterous [+]
boa-constrictor		boks	box [1+]
boar ★ (swine)		Boksing Day	Boxing Day
boar	boor ★	bolard	bollard
boar	bore [2★+]	bolaro	bolero
board [1] /er ★ (lodger)		bold	
boarding /-house/-school		bolder ★ (braver)	
boast [1] /er		bolder	boulder ★
boastful /ly/ness		bold *ly* /ness	
boat [1] /-house/-race		bole ★ (tree trunk)	
boater		bole	bowl [1★]
boatswain		bolero	
bobbin		bollard	
bobb *y* /ies		boloney	
bobie	bobby [+]	Bolshevi *k* /sm/st	
bobin	bobbin	bolster [1] /er	
bobslay	bob-sleigh	bolt [1]	

bom	bomb [1+]	boraks	borax
bomb [1] /er		borasic	boracic
bombard [1] /ment		borax	
bombardier		bord	board [1+]
bombast /ic/ically		border [1*] (edge) /line	
bomberdeer	bombardier	border	boarder *
bomer	bomber	bording	boarding +
bona fide		bordum	boredom
bonanza		bordy	bawdy +
bond [1] /age		bore [2*†] /dom	
bondige	bondage	† (drill, dull)	
bon e [2] /y		bore	boar *
bonet	bonnet	bore	boor *
bonfire		born * (birth)	
bonie	bonny	borne * (carried)	
bonier	bonnier +	boron	
bonit	bonnet	borough * (town)	
bonnet		borow	borrow [1+]
bonni er /est/ly/ness		borrow [1] /er	
bonny		borstal	
bonus /es		bort	bought
bony	bonny	bos	boss [1+]
boo [1] /er		bosie	bossy
boobie	booby +	bosier	bossier +
boob y /ies		bosily	bossily
boodwar	boudoir	bosn	bosun
book /able/ish/let		bosn	boatswain
bookay	bouquet	bosom	
bookie		boss [1] /es/y	
boolvar	boulevard	bossi er /est/ly/ness	
boomerang		bost	boast [1+]
boor * (bad-mannered)		bostful	boastful +
boor	boar *	bosun	
boorgwa	bourgeois	bosy	bossy
boost [1] /er		bot	boat [1+]
boot /ee * (shoe) /less		botaney	botany +
booteek	boutique	botanical /ly	
booth		botan y /ist	
bootie	booty *	botch [1] /y	
bootik	boutique	boter	boater
bootleg [3] /ger		both	
booty * (spoils)		bother [1] /ation/some	
booty	bootee *	botherashun	botheration
booze [2] /r		bothersum	bothersome
boracic		botom	bottom +

47

bottle²	
bottom /less/most	
botul	bottle²
boudoir	
bough * (tree)	
bough	bow¹*
bought	
boukay	bouquet
boulder * (big rock)	
boulder	bolder *
boulevard	
bounce² /y	
bound¹ /er	
boundary /ies	
boundless	
bounteous	
bountius	bounteous
bounty /ies/iful	
bouquet	
bourgeois	
bourgwa	bourgeois
bout	
bouteek	boutique
boutique	
bovine	
bow¹* (bend, arrow)	
bow	beau *
bow	bough *
bowel	
bower	
bowl¹* (cricket, basin)	
bowl	bole *
bownce	bounce²⁺
bownd	bound¹⁺
bowndarey	boundary⁺
bowndless	boundless
bowncy	bouncy
bowns	bounce²⁺
bowntey	bounty⁺
bowntiful	bountiful
bowntius	bounteous
bowt	bout
box¹ /er/es/-office	
Boxing Day	
boy * (lad)	

boy	buoy¹*
boyancy	buoyancy⁺
boyansey	buoyancy⁺
boyant	buoyant
boycott¹ /er	
boykot	boycott¹⁺
boyl	boil¹⁺
boysterus	boisterous⁺
brace²* (strap up)	
bracelet	
bracken	
bracket¹	
brackish	
brackit	bracket¹
brade	braid¹
brag³ /gart	
braget	braggart
Brahma /in	
brai	bray¹
braid¹	
brail	Braille
Braille	
brain /wave/y	
brain-drain	
brainier /est/ly	
brainwash¹	
braise²* (cook)	
braise	braze²*⁺
braisen	brazen⁺
brakable	breakable
brakabul	breakable
brake²* (stop)	
brake	break*⁺
brakedown	breakdown
braken	bracken
brakeneck	breakneck
brakethrew	breakthrough
brakethrough	breakthrough
brakewater	breakwater
brakige	breakage⁺
braking	breaking
brakish	brackish
brale	Braille
brama	Brahma⁺
bramble /y	

brambul	bramble +	breadth	
bramin	Brahmin	break * (destroy) /able	
branch¹ /es		break	brake²*
brand¹ /-new		break age /er/ing	
brandie	brandy +	breakdown	
brandnu	brand-new	breakfast	
brandy /-snap		breakneck	
brane	brain +	breakthrew	breakthrough
branedrain	brain-drain	breakthrough	
branewash	brainwash¹	breakwater	
branier	brainier +	bream	
bras	brass +	breast¹ /bone/plate	
brase	brace²*	breast stroke	
brase	braise²*	breath /less/lessly	
brase	braze²*+	breathalyse² /r	
brash /ly		breathe² /r	
brasier	brassiere *	breathtaking	
brasier	brazier *	bred * (reared)	
braslet	bracelet	bred	bread *
brass /ier/iest/ily/y		bredth	breadth
brassiere *†		breech * (part of gun)	
†(undergarment)		breech	breach¹*
brasy	brassy	breed /er/ing	
brasyer	brazier *	breef	brief¹+
brat		breef case	brief-case
bravado		breem	bream
brave² /ly/ry		breez e² /ily/iness	
bravo		breez y /ier/iest	
bravoora	bravura	breif	brief¹+
bravrey	bravery	breif case	brief-case
bravura		brekfast	breakfast
brawd	broad +	Bren-gun	
brawl¹ /er		brest	breast¹+
brawn /ier/iest/y		brestbone	breastbone
bray¹		brestplait	breastplate
brayd	braid¹	breststroke	breast stroke
braze²* (solder) /r		breth	breadth
braze	braise²*	breth	breath +
brazen /ly/ness		brethalise	breathalyse²+
brazier * (fire basket)		brethless	breathless
breach¹*†		brethren	
† (gap, violation)		brethtaking	breathtaking
breach	breech *	brevit y /ies	
bread * (food)		brew¹ /er	
bread	bred *	brewer y /ies	

breze	breeze 2+
brezy	breezy +
briar	
bribabul	bribable
brib e² /able/er	
briber y /ies	
bric-à-brac	
brick /bat/yard	
bricklay er /ing	
bridal * (of bride)	
bridal	bridle 2*+
bride /groom	
bridel	bridal *
bridel	bridle 2*+
bridelpath	bridle-path
bridesmaid	
bridge² /able	
bridle²*† /-path	
†(for a horse)	
bridle	bridal *
brief¹ /s/ly	
brief-case	
brigade	
brigadear	brigadier
brigadier	
brigand /age	
brige	bridge 2+
bright /ly/ness	
brighten¹	
brillianc e /y	
brilliant /ly	
brilliantine	
brilyance	brilliance +
brilyancy	brilliancy
brilyans	brilliance +
brilyansey	brilliancy
brilyant	brilliant +
brilyantine	brilliantine
brim³ /ful	
brimstone	
brindled	
brin e /y	
bring /ing	
brink	
brisk /ly/ness	

brisket	
brisle	bristle 2+
bristl e² /y	
brisul	bristle 2+
brite	bright +
briten	brighten 1
brittle /ness/r/st	
britul	brittle +
broach¹ *†	
† (tool, discuss)	
broach	brooch *+
broad /ly	
broadcast	
broadcloth	
broaden¹	
broadside	
broad ways /wise	
brocade²	
broccoli	
broch	broach ¹*
broch	brooch *+
brochure	
brock	
brocoli	broccoli
brog	brogue
brogue	
broil¹ /er	
broke /r	
broken /-hearted	
bromide	
bromine	
bronchial	
bronchitis	
bronco	
bronkitis	bronchitis
bronkiul	bronchial
bronkyul	bronchial
bronze²	
brooam	brougham
brooch * (clasp) /es	
brood¹ /iness/y	
brook¹ /let	
broom /stick	
broonet	brunette
broose	bruise 2+

broot	brute +	buccaneer /ing	
brootal	brutal +	buck¹	
brootalitey	brutality +	buckaneer	buccaneer +
brorn	brawn +	bucket /ful	
brornie	brawny	buckle² /r	
brorny	brawny	buckshot	
brort	brought	buckskin	
brosher	brochure	buckwheat	
broth		bucolic	
brothel		Buddhis*m* /t	
brother /hood		budge²	
brother(s)-in-law		budgerigar	
brotherl*y* /iness		budget¹ /ary	
brougham		budgigar	budgerigar
brought		Budism	Buddhism +
brow /s ★ (eyebrows)		budist	Buddhist
browbeat /en/ing		buf	buff
brown¹ /er/est		bufalo	buffalo +
browney	brownie	bufer	buffer¹
Brownian motion		bufet	buffet¹
brownie		buff	
browse²★ (read) /r		buffalo /es	
broyl	broil¹⁺	buffer¹	
brud	brood¹⁺	buffet¹	
brudy	broody	buffoon¹.	
bruer	brewer	buffooner*y* /ies	
bruerey	brewery +	bufit	buffet¹
bruise² /r		bufoonerey	buffoonery +
brunet	brunette	bufune	buffoon¹
brunette		bufunerey	buffoonery +
brunt		bug³ /bear	
bruse	bruise²⁺	bugbare	bugbear
brush¹ /wood		bugerigar	budgerigar
brusk	brusque +	buget	budget¹⁺
brusque /ly/ness		bugg*y* /ies	
Brussels sprouts		bugie	buggy +
brutal /ly		bugl*e* /er/ing	
brutalis*e*² /ation		bugul	bugle +
brutalit*y* /ies		bugy	buggy +
brut*e* /ish		build /er/ing	
bubbl*e*² /y		built	
bublie	bubbly	buksom	buxom +
bubly	bubbly	buksomness	buxomness
bubonic plague		bulb /ous	
bubul	bubble²⁺	bulbus	bulbous

51

buldoze	bulldoze²⁺	bungul	bungle²⁺
bulet	bullet⁺	bunie	bunny⁺
buletin	bulletin	bunion	
bulfinch	bullfinch⁺	bunk¹	
bulfite	bullfight	bunker¹	
bulg e² /y		bunkum	
bulie	bully⁴⁺	bunn y /ies	
bulit	bullet⁺	Bunsen burner	
bulit proof	bullet-proof	buny	bunny⁺
bulk /ier/iest/iness/y		bunyon	bunion
bulkey	bulky	buoy¹* (float)	
bulkhead		buoyan cy /t	
bull /fight		buoyansey	buoyancy⁺
bulldoze² /r		bur	
bullet /-proof		bura	borough*
bulletin		burble² /r	
bullfinch /es		burbul	burble²⁺
bullion		burch	birch⁺
bullock		burd	bird
bullring		burden¹ /some	
bull's-eye		burdey	birdie
bull y⁴ /ies		burdie	birdie
bulock	bullock	burds eye	bird's-eye
bulring	bullring	bureau /x (pl.)	
bulrush		bureaucrac y /ies	
bulseye	bull's-eye	bureaucrat /ic	
bulwark		burgandey	Burgundy
buly	bully⁴⁺	burger	burgher
bulyon	bullion	burgher	
bumbelbe	bumble-bee	burglar	
bumble-bee		burglar y /ies	
bump¹ /er/ily/iness		burgle²	
bumpey	bumpy⁺	burgler	burglar
bumpkin		burgul	burgle²
bumpshus	bumptious⁺	Burgundy	
bumptious /ly/ness		burial	
bump y /ier/iest		burlap	
bumshus	bumptious⁺	burlesk	burlesque²⁺
bunch¹ /es/y		burlesque² /r	
bundle²		burlie	burly⁺
bundul	bundle²	burl y /ier/iest/iness	
bung¹ /-hole		burn¹ /able/er/t	
bungalow		burnish¹ /er	
bungkum	bunkum	buro	bureau⁺
bungle² /r		burocracy	bureaucracy⁺

burocrasey	bureaucracy +	butress	buttress 1+
burocrat	bureaucrat +	butrey	buttery +
buro	bureau +	butt 1* (end)	
burow	burrow 1*+	butter 1 /-fingered	
burra	borough *	buttercup	
burrow 1* (hole, dig) /er		butterey	buttery +
burrow	borough *	butterfly	
bursar /y		buttermilk	
burser	bursar +	butterscotch	
burst /ing		butter y /ies	
burth	birth *+	buttock	
burthday	birthday	button 1 /hole	
bur y 4* (cover)		buttress 1 /es	
bus 3 /es		buxom /ness	
busbie	busby +	buy *† /ing/er * †(purchase)	
busb y /ies		buy	by *
bush /ily/iness		buy	bye *
bushel		buzz 1 /es	
bushie	bushy +	buzzard	
bush y /ier/iest		by * (near)	
busi er /est/ly		by	buy *+
business /-like		by	bye *
bust		by-and-by	
bustle 2 /r		bycicle	bicycle 2+
busul	bustle 2+	byciclist	bicyclist
busy 4		bye * (sport)	
but * (however)		by-election	
but	butt 1*	byer	buyer
butcher 1 /y		byfocal	bifocal
buten	button 1+	bygone /s	
buter	butter 1+	bying	buying
buter fingerd	butter-fingered	byke	bike
butercup	buttercup	by-law	
buterfly	butterfly	byle	bile
butermilk	buttermilk	bylore	by-law
buterscotch	butterscotch	bymetalic	bimetallic +
butey	beauty +	bymonthly	bimonthly
butician	beautician	bynomial	binomial
butify	beautify 4	byopsey	biopsy +
butique	boutique	bypartisan	bipartisan
butishun	beautician	bypartite	bipartite +
butler		by-pass 1	
butn	button 1+	byped	biped
butock	buttock	byplane	biplane
buton	button 1+		

53

byplay	
bypolar	bipolar [+]
by-product	
byre ★ (barn)	
byroad	
byrode	byroad
bysecshun	bisection
bysect	bisect [1+]
bysection	bisection
byseksual	bisexual [+]
bysexual	bisexual [+]
bystander	
byvalv	bivalve
byword	

C

cab /man	
cabal [3]	
cabaray	cabaret
cabaret	
cabbage	
cabbidge	cabbage
cabb y /ies	
cabie	cabby [+]
cabin /-boy	
cabinet	
cable [2] /gram/way	
cabul	cable [2+]
cacao	
cach	catch [+]
cachay	cachet
cache [2]★ (hidden store)	
cache	cash [1]★
cachet	
cachou	cashew
cachwerd	catchword
cackle [2]	
cacofony	cacophony [+]
cacophon y /ous	
cact us /i (pl.)	
cacul	cackle [2]
cad /dish	
cadaver /ous	

caddey	caddie ★
caddie ★ (golf)	
caddis /-worm	
cadd y [4]★ (for tea) /ies	
cadence	
cadens	cadence
cadentsa	cadenza
cadenza	
cadet corps	
cadge [2]	
cadis	caddis [+]
cadmium	
Caesar	
Caesarean	
caesium	
café /s	
cafene	caffeine
cafeteria	
caffeine	
cafiene	caffeine
cafiteria	cafeteria
cage [2] /y	
cagi er /est/ly/ness	
cain	cane [2+]
cairn	
cairngorm	
caison	caisson
caisson	
cajole [2] /ry	
cake [2]	
calabash	
calamine	
calamit y /ies/ous	
calcareous	
calcarius	calcareous
calcif y [4] /ication	
calcin e /ation	
calcium	
calculable	
calculabul	calculable
calculashun	calculation
calculat e [2] /ion/or	
calculus	
cale	kale
Caledonian	

calendar ★ (time)	
calender ¹★ (machine)	
calf /ves (pl.)	
caliber	calibre
calibrashun	calibration
calibrat e ² /ion/or	
calibre	
calicks	calyx
calico /es	
calif	caliph +
californium	
caligrafey	calligraphy +
caligraphy	calligraphy +
calipers	callipers
caliph /ate	
calipso	calypso
calix	calyx +
calk ¹★ (horseshoe)	
calk	caulk ¹★
call ¹★ (cry out)	
call	caul ★
calligraph y /er/ist	
callipers	
callisthenics	
callosity	
callous ★ (unfeeling)	
callous ly /ness	
callow	
callus ★ (hard skin)	
calm ¹ /ly/ness	
calomel	
calorie /s	
calorific	
calorif y ⁴ /ier	
calorimet er /ric/ry	
calory	calorie +
calositey	callosity
calow	callow
calsify	calcify ⁴+
calsine	calcine +
calsium	calcium
calumniat e ² /ion/or	
calumn y /ies/ious	
calus	callous ★
calus	callus ★

Calvary	
calve ²★ (produce a calf)	
calve	carve ²★
Calvinis m /t/tic	
calypso	
calyx /es	
cam /shaft	
camaflage	camouflage ²
camaraderie	
camber ¹	
Cambrian	
cambric	
came	
camellia	
camelya	camellia
Camembert	
cameo /s	
camera /man	
camerarderey	camaraderie
camfor	camphor +
camforated	camphorated
camio	cameo +
camisole	
camombare	Camembert
camomile	
camouflage ²	
camp ¹ /-follower	
campaign ¹	
campain	campaign ¹
campanile	
campanology	
camphor /ated	
campus /es	
can ³ /not/'t ★	
canabis	cannabis
Canadian	
canal	
canalis e ² /ation	
canar y /ies	
cancan	
cancel ³ /lation	
cancer /ous	
cancerus	cancerous
candela	
candelabrum	

cander	candour	cantankerous /ly/ness	
candey	candy +	cantata /s	
candid * (frank)		canteen	
candid	candied *	canter [1]	
candidac y /ies		cantilever /ed	
candidat e /ure		cantle	
candie	candy +	canton [1] /al/ment	
candied * (sugared)		cantul	cantle
candle /light/stick		canvas * (cloth) /es	
candour		canvass [1]* (solicit)	
candul	candle +	cany	canny
cand y /ies		canyon	
cane [2] /-sugar		caolin	kaolin
canery	cannery +	caos	chaos +
cangaroo	kangaroo	caotic	chaotic
canibal	cannibal +	cap [3]	
canibalise·	cannibalise [2]+	capabilit y /ies	
canie	canny	capabl e /y	
canine		capabul	capable +
canister		capacious /ly/ness	
canker [1]		capacit ance /ive/or	
cannabis		capacitans	capacitance +
canner y /ies		capacitate [2]	
cannibal /ism/istic		capacit y /ies	
cannibalis e [2] /ation		capashus	capacious
cannon [1]* (gun)		capasitey	capacity +
cannonade		capasitor	capacitor
canny		cape	
canoe [2] /s		caper [1]	
canoeist		capilarey	capillary +
canon * (law) /ical		capillar y /ies	
canon	cannon [1]*	capital /ism/ly	
canonaid	cannonade	capitalis e [2] /ation	
canonis e [2] /ation		capitalist /ic	
canonry		capitashun	capitation
canooist	canoeist	capitation	
canop y [4] /ies		capitulat e [2] /ion	
cansel	cancel [3]+	capon	
canselashun	cancellation	capric e /ious	
canselation	cancellation	Capricorn	
canser	cancer +	caprishus	capricious
canserus	cancerous	capshun	caption [1]
cant * (hypocrisy)		capshus	captious
cant	can't *	capsiz e [2] /able	
cantaloup		capstan	

capsul *e* ² /ar	
captain ¹ /cy	
capter	captor
captin	captain ¹⁺
caption ¹	
captious	
captivashun	captivation
captivat *e* ² /ion	
captiv *e* /ity	
captor	
capture ² /r	
car /park	
caracter	character
caracteristic	characteristic ⁺
carafe	
caramel	
carat ★ (unit of gems)	
carat	caret ★
carate	karate
caravan ³	
caraway	
carbine	
carbohydrate	
carbolic	
carbon /aceous/ate	
carbon dioxide	
carbon monoxide	
carbonis *e* ² /ation	
carbuncle	
carbuncul	carbuncle
carbureter	carburettor
carburettor	
carcass	
carcino *ma* /genic	
card /board	
cardiac	
cardigan	
cardinal	
cardiograf	cardiograph ⁺
cardiogram	
cardiograph /y	
care ² /worn	
careen ¹	
career ¹ /ism/ist	
carefree	

careful /ly	
careless /ly/ness	
caress ¹	
caret ★ (mark)	
caret	carat ★
caretak *er* /ing	
cargo /es	
cariage	carriage ⁺
caribou	
caricacher	caricature ²⁺
caricatur *e* ² /ist	
caricter	character
caricteristic	characteristic ⁺
caridge	carriage ⁺
carie	carry ⁴⁺
carier	carrier
carion	carrion
carisma	charisma
carkey	khaki
carki	khaki
carm	calm ¹⁺
carmine	
carnage	
carnal /ity/ly	
carnashun	carnation
carnation	
carngorm	cairngorm
carnidge	carnage
carnival	
carnivor *e* /ous	
carol ³ /ler	
carot	carrot ⁺
carous *e* ² /al	
carowsal	carousal
carowse	carouse ²⁺
carp ¹ /er	
carpent *er* ¹ /ry	
carpet ¹	
carpus	
carriage /way	
carrier	
carrion	
carrot /y	
carr *y* ⁴ /ier	
carryon	carrion

carsinoma	carcinoma +	casserole²	
cart¹ /-horse		casset	cassette
cartel		cassette	
cartilage		cassock	
cartilidge	cartilage	cast * (throw) /ing	
cartografer	cartographer	cast iron	
cartografey	cartography +	castanet	
cartograph y /er/ic		castaway	
carton		caste *† /less	
cartoon¹ /ist		† (social class)	
cartridge		castigat e² /ion/or	
cartrite	cart-wright	castle²	
cart-wheel		cast-off	
cart-wright		castor	
carve²* (cut)		castor-oil	
carve	calve²*	castrashun	castration
cary	carry⁴+	castrat e² /ion	
cascade²		casual /ly/ness	
cascara		casualt y /ies	
case²		casuist /ic/ry	
casein		cat /tish/ty/walk	
casement		catabolism	
caserole	casserole²	cataclysm /ic	
casette	cassette	catacomb	
cash¹* (money)		catacoom	catacomb
cash	cache²*	catalep sy /tic	
cashay	cachet	catalise	catalyse²+
casheer	cashier¹	catalisis	catalysis+
cashew		catalist	catalyst
cashier¹		catalitic	catalytic
cashmere		catalog	catalogue²+
cashoo	cashew	catalogue² /r	
cashual	casual+	catalys e² /ation	
cashuist	casuist+	cataly sis /tic	
cashultey	casualty+	catalyst	
casing		catamaran	
casino /s		catapiler	caterpillar
cask * (wine)		catapult¹	
cask	casque*	catar	catarrh+
caskaid	cascade²	cataract	
casket		catarrh /al	
caskit	casket	catastrofey	catastrophe
casock	cassock	catastrofic	catastrophic +
casque * (helmet)		catastrophe	
cassel	castle²	catastrophic /ally	

catcall [1]
catcawl — catcall [1]
catch /ing/ment
catchword
catechis e [2] /m
categoric /al/ally
categorise [2]
categor y /ies
cater [1] /er
caterpillar
caterwaul [1]
catgut
cathar sis /tic
cathedral
Catherine-wheel
cathod e /ic
catholic /ism
caticise — catechise [2]+
catigorey — category +
catigoric — categoric +
catigorise — categorise [2]
catikism — catechism
catish — cattish
catkin
catle — cattle
catnap [3]
cat-o'-nine-tails
cat's-eye
cattle
catul — cattle
caucashun — Caucasian
Caucasian
caucus /es
caught * (did catch)
caught — court [1]*
cauk — caulk [1]*
caul * (membrane)
caul — call [1]*
cauldron
cauliflower
caulk [1]* (seal)
caulk — calk [1]*
causal
causat ion /ive
cause [2] /less

causeway
caustic /ally
cauteris e [2] /ation
caution [1] /ary
cautious /ly/ness
cavalcade
cavalier
cavalr y /ies
cave [2] /man
cavern /ous
caveson
caviare
cavil [3]
cavisun — caveson
cavit y /ies
cavort [1]
caw [1]* (cry of a crow)
caw — core *
caw — corps *
cawcashun — Caucasian
cawcasian — Caucasian
cayenne
cazm — chasm
cease [2] /-fire/less
cedar
cede [2]* (give up)
cede — seed [1]*
ceder — cedar
cedilla
ceeling — ceiling *
ceese — cease [2]+
cefalic — cephalic +
ceiling * (top)
ceiling — sealing *
celandine
celebrant
celebrashun — celebration
celebrat e [2] /ion
celebrit y /ies
celerey — celery
celerity
celery
celestial /ly
celiba cy /te
celibasey — celibacy +

celibrant	celebrant	centileter	centilitre
celibrate	celebrate²⁺	centilitre	
cell * (prison, unit)		centime	
cell	sell *⁺	centimeter	centimetre
cellar * (cave)		centimetre	
celler	seller *	centipede	
cellist		centor	centaur
cello /s		central /ity/ly	
cellophane		centralis e² /ation	
cellular		centre² /board	
cellule		centre-forward	
celluler	cellular	centrifugal /ly	
celluloid		centrifuge	
cellulose		centripetal	
celofane	cellophane	centuple	
Celsius		centupul	centuple
Celt /ic		centurion	
cement¹ /ation		centur y /ies	
cemeter y /ies		cephali c /tis	
cemetrey	cemetery⁺	ceramic /s	
cemical	chemical⁺	cerculer	circular
cemist	chemist⁺	cercumcise	circumcise²⁺
cemistrey	chemistry	cercumference	circumference
cenotaf	cenotaph	cercumferens	circumference
cenotaph		cercumflex	circumflex
censer * (for incense)		cercumnavigate	circumnavi-gate²⁺
censer	censor¹*⁺		
censership	censorship	cercumscribe	circumscribe²
censher	censure²⁺	cercumscripshun	circumscription
censor¹*† /ious/ship †(moral overseer)		cercumscription	circumscription
censur e² /able		cercumsise	circumcise²⁺
census /es		cercumspect	circumspect⁺
cent * (money)		cercumstance	circumstance
cent	scent¹*	cercumstans	circumstance
cent	sent *	cercumstanshul	circumstantial⁺
centaur		cercumstantial	circumstantial⁺
centeem	centime	cercumvent	circumvent¹⁺
centenarian		cercus	circus⁺
centenar y /ies		cereal * (grain)	
centennial /ly		cereal	serial *⁺
center	centre²⁺	cerebellum	
center forwud	centre-forward	cerebra l /tion	
centigrade		cerebrum	
centigram		ceremonial /ly	
		ceremonious /ly	

ceremonius	ceremonious [+]
ceremony /ies	
cerial	cereal [*]
cerial	serial [*+]
ceribelum	cerebellum
ceribrum	cerebrum
cerise	
cerkit	circuit [1+]
cert	
certain /ly	
certainty /ies	
certen	certain [+]
certifiable /y	
certifiabul	certifiable [+]
certificate [2] /ion	
certify [4] /ier	
certinty	certainty [+]
certitude	
cervical	
cervicul	cervical
cerviks	cervix [+]
cervix /es	
cesashun	cessation
cesation	cessation
ceshun	cession [*]
ceshun	session [*]
cespit	cesspit
cespool	cesspool
cessation	
cession [*] (yielding)	
cession	session [*]
cesspit	
cesspool	
chacoal	charcoal
chafe [2*] (rub)	
chaff [*] (grain husks)	
chaffer [1]	
chaffinch /es	
chagrin /ed	
chain [1] /-gang	
chain-armour	
chain-mail	
chain-reaction	
chain-store	
chair [1] /man	

chalenge	challenge [2+]
chalet	
chalice	
chalinge	challenge [2+]
chalis	chalice
chalk [1] /y	
challenge [2] /r	
chamber /-music	
chamberlain	
chamberlin	chamberlain
chambermade	chambermaid
chambermaid	
chameleon	
chamie	chamois
chamois	
champ [1]	
champagne	
champain	champagne
champion [1] /ship	
champyun	champion [1+]
chamwa	chamois
chance [2] /y	
chancel	
chancellery /ies	
chancellor	
chancelor	chancellor
chancelrey	chancellery [+]
chancery /ies	
chandelier	
chandler	
chane	chain [1+]
chane reacshun	chain-reaction
chanel	channel [3]
change [2] /able/-over	
changeling	
channel [3]	
chans	chance [2+]
chansel	chancel
chanseler	chancellor
chanselrey	chancellery [+]
chanserey	chancery [+]
chansey	chancy
chansie	chancy
chant [1]	
chaos /tic	

61

chap³	
chapel	
chaperon¹ /age	
chaplain /cy	
chaplet	
chaplin	chaplain⁺
chapter /-house	
char³ /woman/women	
character	
characteris e² /ation	
characteristic /ally	
charade	
charcoal	
chare	chair¹⁺
charey	chary⁺
charge² /able	
chargé-d'affaires	
charger	
charie	chary⁺
chariot /eer	
charisma	
charitabl e /y	
charitabul	charitable⁺
charit y /ies	
charlatan	
charlot	charlotte
charlotte	
charm¹ /er	
charman	chairman
chart¹	
charter¹ /er	
chartis m /t	
char y /ily/iness	
chas ed* (pursued) /ing	
chased	chaste*
chasen	chasten¹
chasis	chassis
chasm	
chassie	chassis
chassis	
chaste* (pure)	
chaste	chased*
chasten¹	
chastise² /ment	
chastity	

chat³ /ty	
chateau /x (pl.)	
chater	chatter¹⁺
chaterbox	chatterbox
chattel	
chatter¹ /er	
chatterbox	
chaty	chatty
chauffeur	
chauvinis m /t/tic	
cheap* (inexpensive)	
cheap	cheep¹*
cheap ish /ly/ness	
chear	cheer¹⁺
chearful	cheerful⁺
chease	cheese⁺
cheat¹ /er	
check¹* (stop) /er	
check	cheque*⁺
Check	Czech*
checkmate²	
check-up	
Cheddar	
cheder	Cheddar
cheef	chief⁺
cheek y /ier/iest/ily/iness	
cheep¹* (bird sound)	
cheep	cheap*
cheer¹ /less	
cheerey	cheery⁺
cheerful /ly/ness	
cheerie	cheery⁺
cheerio	
cheer y /ier/iest/ily/iness	
chees e /y	
cheesecake	
cheese-cloth	
cheet	cheat¹⁺
cheeta	cheetah⁺
cheetah /s	
cheeter	cheetah⁺
chef	
chef-d'oeuvre	
cheif	chief⁺
cheiften	chieftain⁺

chelist	cellist
chelo	cello +
chemical /ly	
chemise	
chemist /ry	
chemistrey	chemistry
cheque *† /-book	
†(money)	
cherie	cherry +
cherio	cheerio
cherish [1]	
cheroot	
cherp	chirp [1]+
cherr y /ies	
cherub /ic	
chery	cherry +
ches	chess +·
chesbord	chessboard
chess /board	
chest	
Chesterfield	
chestnut	
chevalier	
chevron	
chew [1] /ing-gum	
chic * (stylish)	
chicanery	
chicory	
chick *† /weed	
†(baby bird)	
chide [2]	
chief /s	
chieftain /cy	
chiffon	
chil	chill [1]+
chilblain	
child /ren (pl.)	
childbaring	childbearing
childbearing	
child birth /hood	
child ish /less/like	
chili * (food) /es	
chilie	chilly *
chilier	chillier +
chill [1] /y * (cold)	

chilli er /est/ly/ness	
chime [2]	
chimeric /al	
chimney /-piece	
chimnie	chimney +
chimpanzee	
chin	
china /-clay	
Chinese	
chink [1]	
chintz /es	
chip [3]	
chipendale	Chippendale
chipmunk	
chipolata	
Chippendale	
chiropod y /ist	
chirp [1] /y	
chirrup [1]	
chisel [3] /ler	
chit /-chat	
chivalrus	chivalrous
chivalr y /ous	
chive	
chlorate	
chloride	
chlorinat e [2] /ion	
chlorine	
chlorofill	chlorophyll
chloroform [1]	
chlorophyll	
chloroplast	
chock /-a-block	
chock-full	
choclut	chocolate
chocolate	
choice /st	
choir * (singers)	
choir	quire *
chois	choice +
choke [2] /r	
choler * (rage) /ic	
choler	collar [1]*+
cholera	
cholester in /ol	

63

choo	chew ¹⁺
choos e /ing/y	
chop ³ /per	
chopp y /ier/iest	
chopsooey	chop-suey
chopstick	
chop-suey	
chopy	choppy ⁺
choral ★ (singing) /ly	
chorale ★ (metric hymn)	
chord ★ (music)	
chord	cord ★⁺
chore	
choreograph y /er	
chorister	
chork	chalk ¹⁺
chortle ²	
chortul	chortle ²
chorus ¹ /es	
chose /n	
chow	
chrisalis	chrysalis ⁺
chrisanthemum	chrysanthemum
Christ	
christen ¹	
Christendom	
Christian /ity	
Christmas /sy	
chromate	
chromatic /ally	
chromatin	
chromatograf	chromatograph ⁺
chromatogram	
chromatograph /y	
chrom e /ic/ium	
chromosome	
chronic /ally	
chronicle ² /r	
chronicul	chronicle ²⁺
chronograph /ic	
chronological /ly	
chronolog y /ies	
chronometer	
chrysalis /es	
chrysanthemum	

chub /by	
chubbi er /est/ly/ness	
chubier	chubbier ⁺
chuck ¹	
chuckle ²	
chucul	chuckle ²
chug ³	
chukker	
chum ³ /my	
chump	
chunk /y	
church /es/warden	
churl /ish	
churn ¹	
churp	chirp ¹⁺
chute ★ (drop)	
chute	shoot ★⁺
chutney	
chyle	
chyme	
cianide	cyanide
cibernetics	cybernetics
cicada	
cicatrice	
cicatricks	cicatrice
ciclamate	cyclamate
ciclamen	cyclamen
cicle	cycle ²
ciclic	cyclic ⁺
ciclist	cyclist ⁺
ciclometer	cyclometer
ciclone	cyclone ⁺
ciclops	Cyclops
ciclostile	cyclostyle
ciclotron	cyclotron
cicul	cycle ²
cider	
cifer	cipher ¹
cigar /ette	
cigaret	cigarette
cignet	cygnet ★
cignet	signet ★
cilestial	celestial ⁺
cilinder	cylinder
cilindrical	cylindrical ⁺

cilium	
cimbal	cymbal *+
cimbal	symbol *+
ciment	cement 1+
cinamon	cinnamon
cinch /es	
cinder	
Cinderella	
cine camera	
cinema /tic	
cinematograph /er/y	
cinerama	
cinic	cynic +
cinical	cynical +
cinicul	cynical +
cinima	cinema +
cinimatograf	cinematograph +
cinimatograph	cinematograph +
cinnamon	
cinosure	cynosure
cipher 1	
cipress	cypress
circa	
circit	circuit 1+
circle 2	
circuit 1 /ous/ry	
circul	circle 2
circular	
circularis e 2 /ation	
circulat e 2 /ion	
circulator /y	
circumcis e 2 /ion	
circumference	
circumferens	circumference
circumflex	
circumfrence	circumference
circumnavigat e 2 /or	
circumscribe 2	
circumscription	
circumspect /ion	
circumstance	
circumstans	circumstance
circumstanshul	circumstantial +
circumstantial /ly	
circumvent 1 /ion	

circus /es	
cirosis	cirrhosis
cirrhosis	
cirro-cumulus	
cirro-stratus	
cist	cyst +
cistern	
cistitis	cystitis
citadel	
cit e 2* (quote) /ation	
cite	sight 1*+
cite	site 2*
citie	city +
citizen /ship	
citologey	cytology
citric acid	
citr on /ate/ic	
citrus	
cit y /ies	
civet	
civic /ism/s	
civil /ian/ly	
civilis e 2 /ation	
civilit y /ies	
civit	civet
clad /ding	
claim 1 /able/ant	
clairvoyan ce /t	
clam	
clamant	
clamber 1	
clame	claim 1+
clamer	clamour +
clamerous	clamorous
clamerus	clamorous
clamm y /ily/iness	
clamo ur /rous	
clamp 1	
clamy	clammy +
clan /nish	
clandestine /ly	
clang 1 /our	
clank 1	
clansman	
clap 3 /per	

claptrap	
claret	
clarif*y*⁴ /ication/ier	
clarinet /tist	
clarion	
clarity	
clark	clerk +
claryun	clarion
clash¹	
clasify	classify⁴⁺
clasroom	classroom
class¹ /less/y	
classic /al/ally/s	
classicis*m* /t	
classif*y*⁴ /ication/ier	
classroom	
clatter¹	
clause	
claustrofobia	claustrophobia
claustrophobia	
clavichord	
clavic*le* /ular	
clavicord	clavichord
clavicul	clavicle +
claw¹	
clay /more	
claym	claim¹⁺
clean¹ /able/liness/ly	
cleanse²	
clear¹ /ance/ly/ness	
cleave² /age	
cleavidge	cleavage
cleek	clique +
clef	
cleft	
clematis	
clemen*cy* /t	
clemensey	clemency +
clench¹	
clenliness	cleanliness
clense	cleanse²
clergy /man	
cleric /al/alism	
clerk /ship	
clever /er/est/ly	

clew¹* (thread)	
clew	clue *⁺
clichay	cliché
cliché	
click¹	
client /ele	
cliff /s	
climactic /ally	
climaks	climax¹⁺
climat*e* /ology	
climatic /ally	
climax¹ /es	
climb¹* (go up) /er	
clime * (climate)	
clinch¹	
cling /ing	
clinic /al/ally	
clink¹	
clinker /-built	
cliontell	clientele
clip³ /per	
cliqu*e* /ish/y	
clitoris	
cloak /room	
clobber¹	
cloche	
clock¹ /wise/work	
clod /-hopper	
clog³	
cloister¹	
clorate	chlorate
clore	claw¹
cloride	chloride
clorinate	chlorinate²⁺
clorine	chlorine
clorofill	chlorophyll
cloroform	chloroform¹
clorophil	chlorophyll
cloroplast	chloroplast
clos*e*² /ure	
closet¹	
closher	closure
clot³	
cloth	
cloth*e*² /ier	

66

cloud ¹ /ier/less/y	
clout¹	
clove /n	
clover /-leaf	
clowd	cloud ¹⁺
clown ¹ /ish	
club ³ /bable	
cluch	clutch ¹
cluck ¹	
clue * (guide) /less	
clue	clew ¹*
clump ¹	
clumsi *ly* /ness	
clums *y* /ier/iest	
clung	
cluster ¹	
clutch ¹	
clutter ¹	
coach ¹ /ful/man	
coagulant	
coagulat *e* ² /ion/or	
coaks	coax ¹
coal /field/mine	
coala	koala
coalesans	coalescence
coalesce ² /nce/nt	
coalesent	coalescent
coaless	coalesce ²⁺
coalishun	coalition ⁺
coalition /ist	
coal-scuttle	
coarse * (rough) /ly/ness	
coarse	course *⁺
coarsen ¹	
coast ¹ /al	
coast *guard* /line	
coat ¹ /ee	
coax ¹	
cob	
cobalt	
cobble ² /r	
cobra	
cobul	cobble ²⁺
cobweb /bed	
coca	

cocaine	
cocane	cocaine
coccyx /es	
coch	coach ¹⁺
cochineal	
cock ¹ /crow/erel	
cockato	cockatoo
cockatoo	
cockchafer	
cocker	
cocket	coquette ⁺
cocketrey	coquetry
cock-eyed	
cockle	
cockney /ish/ism/s	
cockpit	
cockroach	
cockscomb	
cockshore	cocksure
cocksis	coccyx ⁺
cocksure	
cocktail	
cockul	cockle
cock *y* /ier/iest/ily	
coco * (palm tree)	
coco	cocoa *
cocoa * (cacao powder)	
coconut	
cocoon	
cocotte	
cod ³ /ling	
codak	Kodak
coddle ²	
code ²	
codecks	codex ⁺
codeine	
cod *ex* /ices (pl.)	
codger	
codicil	
codif *y* ⁴ /ication/ier	
codisil	codicil
codle	coddle ²
co-educate ²	
co-education /al	
coefficient	

coefishent	coefficient	coinidge	coinage
coegsist	coexist [1]+	coinside	coincide [2]
coequal /ity/ly		coinsidence	coincidence +
coerc e [2] /ible		coinsidens	coincidence +
coerc ion /ive		coinsident	coincident
coerse	coerce [2]+	coir ★ (coconut fibre)	
coershun	coercion +	coir	choir ★
coersive	coercive	coit us /ion	
coexist [1] /ence/ent		coke [2]	
cofee	coffee	coket	coquette +
cofer	coffer	cokoon	cocoon
cofey	coffee	col	
coff	cough [1]+	cola	koala
coffee		colaborate	collaborate [2]+
coffer		colage	collage
coffin		colander	
cog [3] /-wheel		colaps	collapse [2]+
cogen cy /t		colate	collate [2]+
coger	codger	cold /er/est/ly/ness	
cogitat e [2] /ion		cold-blooded	
cognac		cold-shoulder [1]	
cognate		cole	coal +
cognisabl e /y		colean	colleen
cognisan ce /t		colecshun	collection
cognishun	cognition +	colect	collect [1]+
cognition /al		colectabul	collectable +
cognitive		colection	collection
cognomen		colectiv	collective +
cohabit [1] /ation		coleeg	colleague
cohear	cohere [2]+	colege	college +
cohearent	coherent +	colegian	collegian
cohere [2] /nce		colegiate	collegiate
coherent /ly		coler	choler ★+
coheshun	cohesion +	coler	collar [1]★+
cohes ion /ive		colera	cholera
cohort		coleric	choleric
coifer	coiffeur ★+	colesterin	cholesterin +
coiffeu r ★† /se (fem.) †(hairdresser)		colesterol	cholesterol
coiffure ★ (hair style)		colic /ky	
coifur	coiffure ★	colide	collide [2]
coil [1]		colier	collier
coin [1] /age/er		colinder	colander
coincide [2]		colinear	collinear
coinciden ce /t		colishun	collision
		colision	collision

colitis
collaborat *e*² /ion/or
collage
collaps *e*² /ible
collar ¹*† /-bone
　†(seize, neckband)
collar　　　　　　choler *+
collat *e*² /ion/or
collateral
colleague
collect ¹ /ion/or
collect *able* /edly
collectiv *e* /ism/ist
colleen
colleg *e* /ian/iate
coller　　　　　　choler *+
coller　　　　　　collar ¹*+
collide²
collie
collier
collinear
collision
collocate²
colloid /al
colloquial /ism/ly
colloqu *y* /ies
collude²
collus *ion* /ive
colly　　　　　　collie
colokwey　　　　　colloquy +
colokwial　　　　　colloquial +
colon
colonade　　　　　colonnade
colonel * (officer)
colonial /ism
colonis *e*² /ation/er
colonnade
colon *y* /ies/ist
coloqual　　　　　colloquial +
coloquy　　　　　colloquy +
color　　　　　　colour ¹+
coloration
colorful　　　　　colourful +
colossal /ly
colossus /es

colour ¹ /less
colourful /ly
coloyd　　　　　colloid +
colt /ish
colude　　　　　collude²
colum　　　　　column +
columbine
column /ar/ist
colushun　　　　collusion +
colusion　　　　collusion +
coma * (deep sleep)
coma　　　　　comma *
comand　　　　command ¹+
comandment　　　commandment
comando　　　　commando +
comb ¹
combat ¹ /ant/ive
combinashun　　　combination
combin *e*² /ation
combuschun　　　combustion
combustib *le* /ility
combustibul　　　combustible +
combustion
com *e* /ing
come　　　　　comb ¹
comedi *an* /enne (fem.)
comed *y* /ies
comel *y* /ier/iest
comemorashun　　commemoration
comemorate　　　commemorate ²+
comence　　　　commence ²+
comend　　　　commend ¹+
comendabul　　　commendable +
comendashun　　　commendation
comendation　　　commendation
comens　　　　commence ²+
comenshurate　　commensurate
coment　　　　comment ¹+
comentater　　　commentator
comentrey　　　commentary +
comerce　　　　commerce
comercial　　　commercial +
comercialise　　　commercialise ²+
comercialism　　　commercialism
comerse　　　　commerce

69

comershal	commercial [+]	commit [3] /ment/tal	
comershalise	commercialise [2+]	committee ★ (body)	
comershalism	commercialism	commity	comity ★
comestibles		commod e /ious	
comet		commodit y /ies	
comfert	comfort [1+]	commodore	
comfort [1] /er/less		common /er/est/ly	
comfortabl e /y		Common Market	
comic /al/ally		commonplace	
comicalit y /ies		Commons	
comiserate	commiserate [2+]	Commonwealth	
comiserey	commissary [+]	commoshun	commotion
comishun	commission [1+]	commotion	
comission	commission [1+]	communal /ly	
comit	comet	communalise [2]	
comit	commit [3+]	commune [2]	
comital	committal	communicable	
comitey	comity ★	communicat e [2] /ion	
comitment	commitment	communicat ive /or	
comittal	committal	communikay	communiqué
comittey	committee ★	communi on /cant	
comit y ★(courtesy)		communiqué	
comma ★(punctuation)		communis m /t/tic	
comma	coma ★	communit y /ies	
command [1] /ant/er		commute [2] /r	
commandeer [1]		comode	commode [+]
commandment		comodious	commodious
commando /s		comodity	commodity [+]
commemorat e [2] /ion		comodius	commodious
commence [2] /ment		comodoor	commodore
commend [1] /ation		comon	common [+]
commendabl e /y		Comon Market	Common Market
commensurate		Comonwelth	Commonwealth
comment [1] /ator		comoshun	commotion
commentar y /ies		comotion	commotion
commentrey	commentary [+]	compact	
commerce		compair	compère [2]★
commercial /ism/ly		companion /ship	
commercialis e [2]/ation		compan y /ies	
commershal	commercial [+]	companyun	companion [+]
commershalise	commercialise [2+]	comparabl e /y	
commiserat e [2] /ion		comparabul	comparable [+]
commissar /iat		comparative /ly	
commissar y /ies		compare [2]★ (liken to)	
commission [1] /aire/er		compare	compère [2]★

comparison	
compartment	
compashonate	compassionate
compashun	compassion [+]
compass [1] /es	
compassion /ate/ately	
compatib le /ility	
compatibul	compatible [+]
compatriot	
compel [3]	
compendium	
compensat e [2] /ion	
compensator /y	
compère [2]* (presenter)	
competant	competent
compet e [2] /ition	
competen ce /t	
competit ive /or	
compil e [2] /ation	
complacenc e /y	
complacens	complacence [+]
complacent /ly	
complain [1] /ant/t	
complane	complain [1+]
complasense	complacence [+]
complasent	complacent [+]
complement [1*†] /ary	
† (balance)	
complete [2] /ly	
completion	
complex	
complexion /ed	
complexit y /ies	
complian ce /t	
complicat e [2] /ion	
complicity	
compliment [1*†] /ary	
† (praise)	
compl y [4] /iable	
component	
comport [1] /ment	
compose [2]	
composher	composure
composishun	composition
composite /ly	

composition	
compositor	
compost	
composure	
compot	compote
compote	
compound [1] /able	
comprehen d [1] /sible	
comprehens ion /ive	
compress [1] /ion/or	
compressib le /ility	
compris e [2] /able	
compromise [2]	
compulshun	compulsion [+]
compuls ion /ive	
compulsor y /ily	
compulsrey	compulsory [+]
compuncshun	compunction
compunction	
comput e [2] /ation/er	
computeris e [2] /ation	
comrad	comrade [+]
comrade /ly/ship	
comunal	communal [+]
comunalise	communalise [2]
comune	commune [2]
comunicable	communicable
comunicant	communicant
comunicashun	communication
comunicate	communicate [2+]
comunication	communication
comunikay	communiqué
comunion	communion[+]
comunism	communism [+]
comunist	communist
comunitey	community [+]
comunyun	communion[+]
comute	commute [2+]
con [3]	
concave	
concavit y /ies	
conceal [1] /ment	
concede [2]	
conceit /ed	
conceivabul	conceivable

conceiv e^2 /able/ably
concentrat e^2 /ion
concentric /ity
conception
concept /ual/ually
concern[1]
concert /ina
concerto /s
concession /ary
conch
concherto — concerto[+]
conciet — conceit[+]
concievabul — conceivable
concieve — conceive[2+]
conciliat e^2 /ion
conciliator /y
concise /ly/ness
conclave
conclude[2]
conclus ion /ive
concoct[1] /ion
concomitant
concord /ance/ant
concorse — concourse
concourse
concrete /ly/ness
concubine
concur[3]
concurren ce /t/tly
concuss[1] /ion
condemn[1] /ation
condens e^2 /ation/er
condescen d^1 /sion
condiment
condisend — condescend[1+]
condisenshun — condescension
condisension — condescension
condishun — condition[1+]
condit — conduit
condition[1] /al/ally
condole[2] /nce
condon e^2 /ation/er
conduc e^2 /ive
conduct[1] /ion
conductiv e /ity

conduct or /ress (fem.)
conduit
cone
conect — connect[1+]
conerbashun — conurbation
conerbation — conurbation
confabulat e^2 /ion
confection /er/ery
confederac y /ies
confederasey — confederacy[+]
confederat e^2 /ion
confer[3] /ment
conference
confeser — confessor
confess[1] /or
confession /al
confetti
confidant *† /e (fem.)
  †(trusted friend)
confide[2] /nce
confidenshal — confidential[+]
confident *† /ly
  †(self-assured)
confidential /ity/ly
configerashun — configuration
configuration
confine[2] /ment
confirm[1] /ation
confirmat ive /ory
confiscat e^2 /ion
conflagration
conflict[1]
conform[1] /able/ation
conform ist /ity
confound[1]
confownd — confound[1]
confurm — confirm[1+]
confus e^2 /ion
confut e^2 /ation
congeal[1]
congenial /ity/ly
congenital /ly
conger /-eel
congest[1] /ion/ive
conglomerat e^2 /ion

congratulat *e*² /ions/ory	
congregat *e*² /ion	
congregational /ist	
congress /ional	
conic /al/ally	
conifer /ous	
conjectcher	conjecture ²⁺
conjectur *e*² /al	
conjoin¹ /t	
conjucive	conducive
conjugal	
conjugat *e*² /ion	
conjuice	conduce ²⁺
conjuncshun	conjunction
conjunction	
conjunctiv *e* /itis	
conjur *e*² /ation/er	
conker*(horse chestnut)	
conker	conquer ¹*⁺
conkwest	conquest
connect¹ /ion/ive	
conneser	connoisseur
conning-tower	
conniv *e*² /ance/er	
connoisseur	
connot *e*² /ation	
connubial /ly	
conosseur	connoisseur
conote	connote ²⁺
conquer¹*(defeat) /or	
conquest	
consanguin *eous* /ity	
conscience	
conscienshus	conscientious ⁺
conscientious /ly	
conscious /ly/ness	
conscript¹ /ion	
conseal	conceal ¹⁺
conseat	conceit ⁺
consecrat *e*² /ion	
consecutive	
consekwence	consequence ⁺
consensus	
consent¹	
consequen *ce* /t	

consequential /ly	
conservancy	
conservansey	conservancy
conservashun	conservation
conservation	
conservat *ive* /ism	
conservatoire	
conservator *y* /ies	
conservatrey	conservatory ⁺
conserv *e*²	
consider¹ /able/ably	
considerat *e* /ion	
considrabul	considerable
consign¹ /ment	
consiliate	conciliate ²⁺
consine	consign ¹⁺
consise	concise ⁺
consist¹ /ence	
consistenc *y* /ies	
consistensey	consistency ⁺
consolabul	consolable
consolashun	consolation
consol *e*² /able/ation	
consolidat *e*² /ion	
consommé	
consonan *ce* /t	
consonans	consonance ⁺
consort¹ /ium	
conspicuous /ly/ness	
conspirac *y* /ies	
conspirasey	conspiracy ⁺
conspirater	conspirator ⁺
conspirator /y	
conspire²	
constable	
constabul	constable
constabular *y* /ies	
constan *cy* /t	
constansey	constancy ⁺
constelashun	constellation
constellation	
consternat *e*² /ion	
constipat *e*² /ion	
constituenc *y* /ies	
constituensey	constituency ⁺

73

constituent	
constitute [2]	
constitution /al/ally	
constrain [1] /t	
constrict [1] /ion	
construct [1] /ion	
constructive /ly	
constru *e* [2] /able	
consul /ar/ate	
consult [1] /ant	
consultat *ion* /ive	
consumashun	consummation
consum *e* [2] /able/er	
consummate [2] /ly	
consummation	
consumpt *ion* /ive	
consumshun	consumption [+]
consumtion	consumption [+]
contact [1] /or	
contag *ion* /ious	
contagus	contagious
contain [1] /er/ment	
contaminat *e* [2] /ion	
contemplat *e* [2] /ion	
contemplative /ly	
contemporaneous	
contemporar *y* /ies	
contempt /ible/uous	
contend [1]	
content [1] /ment	
content *ion* /ious	
contest [1] /able/ant	
context	
contigu *ous* /ity	
continence	
continens	continence
continent /al	
contingenc *y* /ies	
contingensey	contingency [+]
contingent	
continual /ly	
continua *nce* /tion	
continu *e* [2] /ity	
continuous /ly	
contorshun	contortion [+]

contort [1]	
contortion /ist	
contour	
contraband	
contracept *ion* /ive	
contract [1] /ion/or	
contractual /ly	
contradict [1] /ion/ory	
contralto /s	
contrapshun	contraption
contraption	
contrar *y* /ily/iness	
contrast [1]	
contraven *e* [2] /er/tion	
contribut *e* [2] /ion	
contributor /y	
contrit *e* /ion	
contriv *e* [2] /ance	
control [3] /lable/ler	
controvershal	controversial [+]
controversial /ly	
controvers *y* /ies	
contus *e* [2] /ion	
conurbation	
convalesce [2] /nce/nt	
convaless	convalesce [2+]
convalessence	convalescence
convect *ion* /ive/or	
convene [2] /r	
convenien *ce* /t	
conveniens	convenience [+]
convenshun	convention
convenshunal	conventional [+]
convent	
convention	
conventional /ism/ly	
converge [2] /nce/nt	
conversant	
conversation /al/alist	
converse [2] /ly	
conversion	
convert [1] /er/ible	
convex /ity	
convey [1]	
conveyanc *e* /ing	

conveyor belt	
convict [1] /ion	
convinc e [2] /ingly	
conviscate	confiscate [2+]
convivial /ity/ly	
convocashun	convocation
convocation	
convoke [2]	
convolut e [2] /ion	
convoy [1]	
convuls e [2] /ion	
convulsive /ly	
con y /ies	
conyac	cognac
coo [1]	
cooger	cougar
cook [1] /able	
cooker /y	
cool [1] /ant/est/ness	
coolie * (labourer)	
coolly * (calmly)	
coop [1]	
co-op	
cooper /age	
co-operat e [2] /ion/or	
co-operative /ly/ness	
co-opt [1] /ion	
co-ordinat e [2] /ion	
co-partner /ship	
cope [2]	
copeck	
Copernican system	
co-pilot	
copious /ly	
copiss	coppice
copper /plate	
coppice	
copra	
copse	
copulat e [2] /ion	
cop y [4] /ies/ier	
copyright	
copyrite	copyright
coquetry	
coquett e /ish	

coral * (sea life)	
coral	choral *+
coral	corral [3]*
corcus	caucus +
cord * (rope) /age	
cord	chord *
cordial /ity/ly	
cordite	
cordon [1]	
cordon bleu	
corduroy	
core * (centre)	
core	caw [1]*
core	corps *
corecshun	correction
corect	correct [1+]
corection	correction
corectiv	corrective
corespond	correspond [1+]
corespondence	correspondence
corespondens	correspondence
co-respondent	
coridoor	corridor
coriografey	choreography +
corispondence	correspondence
corispondens	correspondence
corister	chorister
cork /age/screw	
corm	
cormorant	
corn /flour	
cornea /l	
corner [1] /-stone	
cornet [1]	
cornia	cornea +
cornice	
cornucopia	
corny	
coroborate	corroborate [2+]
coroborativ	corroborative +
corode	corrode [2+]
corollary	
corona	
coronary	
coronashun	coronation

coronation		corterise	cauterise [2+]
coroner		cort *ex* /ices (pl.)	
coronet		cortion	caution [1+]
coroshun	corrosion [+]	cortious	cautious [+]
corosion	corrosion [+]	cortisan	courtesan
corosiv	corrosive	cortisone	
corporal		cortship	courtship
corporat *e* /ion		cortyard	courtyard
corporeal		corugate	corrugate [2+]
corps ★ (army)		corupt	corrupt [1+]
corpse ★ (body)		coruptible	corruptible [+]
corpulen *ce* /t		coruptibul	corruptible [+]
corpus		corus	chorus [1+]
corpusc *le* /ular		corvet	corvette
corpussel	corpuscle [+]	corvette	
corral [3] ★ (animal pen)		cosecant	
corral	coral ★	coset	cosset [1]
correct [1] /ion/ive/or		cosh [1]	
correlat *e* [2] /ion		cosi *er* /est/ly/ness	
correlative /ly		co-signator *y* /ies	
correspond [1] /ence/ent		cosine	
corridor		cosmetic /ian	
corrigend *um* /a (pl.)		cosmic /ally	
corrigible		cosmografey	cosmography [+]
corroborat *e* [2] /ion		cosmograph *y* /ic	
corroborative /ly		cosmolog *ý* /ical	
corrod *e* [2] /ible		cosmonaut	
corros *ion* /ive		cosmonort	cosmonaut
corrugat *e* [2] /ion		cosmopolitan /ism	
corrupt [1] /ive/ness		cosmos	
corruptib *le* /ility		cosmotron	
corsashun	causation [+]	co-sponsor	
corsation	causation [+]	Cossack	
corse	coarse ★[+]	cosset [1]	
corse	course ★[+]	cost [1] /ly	
corsen	coarsen [1]	cost	coast [1+]
corset /ed		costgard	coastguard [+]
corshun	caution [1+]	costive	
corshus	cautious [+]	costli *er* /est/ness	
corslet		costum *e* /ier	
corstic	caustic [+]	cosy	
cort	caught ★	cot	
cort	court [1★]	cotage	cottage [+]
cort marshal	court-martial [3+]	cotangent	
cortège		cote	coat [1+]

76

coterie
cotidge   cottage +
coton   cotton +
cottage /r
cotton /wool
cou dayta   coup d'état
couch¹ /es
cougar
cough¹ /er
could /n't
coulomb
council * (assembly)
councillor * (member of
    assembly)
counsel³* (advice)
counsellor * (adviser)
count¹ /ess (fem.) /less
countenance
counter¹ /foil
counteract¹ /ion
counter-attack¹
counterbalance²
counter-charge²
counter-claim¹
counter-clockwise
counterfeit¹ /er
countermand¹
countermine²
counterpane
counterpart
counterpoint
counterpoise²
countersign¹
countersine   countersign¹
counterway   counter-weigh¹
counter-weigh¹
countie   county +
country /ies
countryside
county /ies
coup d'état
couple² /t
coupon
courage /ous/ously
courier

cours e *† /ing
†(conduct, passage)
course   coarse *+
coursen   coarsen¹
court¹* (law)
court   caught*
courtesan
courtes y /ies
courtier
courtley   courtly +
courtl y /iness
court-martial³ /s
courtship
courtyard
cousin
covalent bond
cove
coven
covenant
Coventry
cover¹ /age/let
covert
covet¹ /er/ous
covey /s
cow
coward /ice
cowardl y /iness
cowboy
cowch   couch¹+
cower¹
cowerd   coward +
cowl /ing
cownt   count¹+
cowntenance   countenance
cowntenans   countenance
cownter   counter¹+
cownteract   counteract¹+
cowpox
cowslip
cox¹ /swain
coxcomb
coy /ly/ness
coyn   coin¹+
coyote
crab³ /-apple

crack¹ /er	
crackle²	
cracknel	
crackul	crackle²
cradel	cradle²
cradle²	
cradul	cradle²
craft /y	
crafti er /est/ly/ness	
craftsman /ship	
crag /gy	
crain	crane²⁺
cram³ /mer	
cramp¹ /on	
cranberie	cranberry⁺
cranberr y /ies	
crane² /-fly	
crani um /al	
crank¹ /case/shaft/y	
crann y /ies	
crape	
crash¹	
crash-land¹	
crass	
crate²	
crater	
cravat	
crave² /n	
crawl¹ /er	
crayfish	
crayon	
craz e² /y	
crazi er /est/ly/ness	
creacher	creature
creak¹★ (noise) /y	
creak	creek★
cream¹ /y	
creamer y /ies	
creami er /est/ness	
crease²	
creat e² /ion/or	
creativ e /ity	
creature	
crèche	
crecher	creature

credence	
credens	credence
credential	
credib le /ility/ly	
credibul	credible⁺
credit¹ /or	
creditabl e /y	
creditabul	creditable⁺
crediter	creditor
credul ity /ous	
creed	
creek★ (stream)	
creek	creak¹★⁺
creem	cream¹⁺
creep /er/ing/s/y	
creepi er /est/ly/ness	
cremat e² /ion	
crematorium	
Cremlin	Kremlin
crenellated	
creole	
crep	crêpe
crêpe	
crept	
crepuscular	
crescendo /s	
crescent	
cresent	crescent
cresh	crèche
creshendo	crescendo⁺
cresit	cresset
cresset	
crest /fallen	
cretin /ism/ous	
cretonne	
creture	creature
crevasse	
crevice	
crevis	crevice
crew¹ /s★ (sailors)	
crews	cruise²★⁺
crewsifix	crucifix⁺
crib³ /ber	
cribbage	
cribidge	cribbage

78

crick [1]
cricket /er
crime
criminal /ity/ly
criminolog ist /y
crimson
crincul crinkle [2+]
cringe [2]
crinkl e [2] /y
crinoline
cripple [2]
cript crypt [+]
criptograf cryptograph [+]
criptogram cryptogram
criptograph cryptograph [+]
cripul cripple [2]
crisalis chrysalis [+]
crisanthemum chrysanthemum
crisen christen [1+]
Crisendum Christendom
Crishna Krishna
cris is /es
Crismas Christmas [+]
crisp /iness/ly/y
criss-cross [1]
Crist Christ
cristal crystal [+]
cristaline crystalline
cristalise crystallise [2+]
cristalografer crystallographer [+]
Cristian Christian [+]
Cristianity Christianity
criteri on /a (pl.)
critic /al/ally
criticis e [2] /able
criticism
critisize criticise [2+]
criy cry [4+]
croak [1]
croch crotch
crochet [1]
crock /ery
crocodile
crocus /es
croft /er

croissant
crokay croquet
cromatic chromatic [+]
cromatin chromatin
cromatograf chromatograph [+]
cromatogram chromatogram
crome chrome [+]
cromic chromic
cromium chromium
crone * (hag)
crone krone *[+]
cronic chronic [+]
cronicul chronicle [2+]
cronie crony [+]
cronograf chronograph [+]
cronograph chronograph [+]
cronologey chronology [+]
cronological chronological [+]
cronometer chronometer
cron y /ies
crood crude [+]
crook
crooked /ly/ness
croon [1]
croop croup
croopier croupier
crop [3] /per
croquet
cross [1] /ly/ness
cross -breed /-bred
cross-country
cross-cut /ting
cross-examin e [2] /ation
cross-fertilis e [2] /ation
cross-fire
cross-legged
crosspatch
cross-purpose
cross-question [1]
cross-reference [2]
cross-road
crosswise
crossword
crotch
crotchet /y

crouch[1]
croup
croupier
crow[1]
crowbar
crowd[1]
crown[1]
crucial /ly
crucible
crucibul   crucible
crucifix /ion
crucify[4]
crude /ly/ness/st
cruditey   crudity +
crudit y /ies
cruel /ler/lest/ly
cruelt y /ies
cruet
cruise[2]* (voyage) /r
crum   crumb +
crumb /iness/y
crumbl e[2]*(break up)/y
crumbul   crumble[2]*+
crumpet
crumple[2]* (crease)
crumpul   crumple[2]*
crumy   crumby
crunch[1] /iness/y
cruper   crupper
crupper
crusade[2] /r
crush[1]
crushal   crucial +
crusible   crucible
crusibul   crucible
crust /y
crustace a /an/ous
crustasha   crustacea +
crutch
crux /es
cruze   cruise[2]*+
cr y[4] /ies/ier
crypt /ic/ically
cryptogram
cryptograph /ic

crysalis   chrysalis +
crystal /line
crystallis e[2] /ation
crystallograph er /y
cub
cubby-hole
cub e /age
cubical * (cube-shaped)
cubicle * (small room)
cubihole   cubby-hole
cubis m /t
cuboard   cupboard
cuckold[1]
cuckoo
cucumber
cuddle[2]
cudgel[3]
cudul   cuddle[2]
cue[2]* (billiards)
cue   queue[2]*
cuff[1]
cuisine
culcher   culture[2]+
cul-de-sac
culer   colour[1]+
culerashun   coloration
culinary
culinder   colander
culinrey   culinary
cull[1]
culminat e[2] /ion
culpab le /ility
culpabul   culpable +
culprit
cult
cultivat e[2] /ion/or
cultur e[2] /al/ist
culvert
cumbersome /ly/ness
cumbersum   cumbersome +
Cumbrian
cumfert   comfort[1]+
cumpas   compass[1]+
cumulative
cumulus

cuneiform		cursive /ly	
cuniform	cuneiform	cursory	
cunning		curt /ly/ness	
cuntreyside	countryside	curtail[1] /ment	
cup[3] /ful		curtain[1]	
cupboard		curtale	curtail[1+]
cupidity		curts *y*[4] /ies	
cupola		curv *e*[2] /ature	
cupro-nickel		curvilinear	
cur /rish		cushion[1]	
curab *le* /ility		cushon	cushion[1]
curabul	curable[+]	cusp	
curac *y* /ies		cuss[1] /edness	
curant	currant ★	custard	
curasey	curacy[+]	custod *y* /ial/ian	
curate		custom /er	
curater	curator[+]	customar *y* /ily	
curator /ship		cut /ter/ting	
curb[1]★ (chain in bit)		cute /ly/ness/r/st	
curb	kerb[1]★	cuticle	
curd		cuticul	cuticle
curdle[2]		cutlass /es	
curdul	curdle[2]	cutlery	
cur *e*[2] /ative		cutlet	
curent	current ★+	cuttle-fish	
curfew		cuvenant	covenant
curiculum	curriculum[+]	cuver	cover[1+]
curie		cuvet	covet[1+]
curio /s		cuvey	covey[+]
curiosit *y* /ies		cyanide	
curious /ly/ness		cybernetics	
curium		cyclamate	
curius	curious[+]	cyclamen	
curl[1] /er/iness/y		cycle[2]	
curlew		cyclic /al/ally	
curnel	colonel ★	cycl *ist* /ometer	
currage	courage[+]	cyclon *e* /ic	
curragus	courageous	Cyclops	
currant ★ (fruit)		cyclostyle	
currenc *y* /ies		cyclotron	
currensey	currency[+]	cygnet ★ (swan)	
current ★ (flow) /ly		cygnet	signet ★
curricul *um* /a (pl.)		cyle	chyle
curry[4] /comb		cylinder	
curse[2]		cylindrical /ly	

cymbal *† /ist	
†(musical instrument)	
cymbal	symbol *+
cynic /ism	
cynical /ly	
cynosure	
cypress	
cyst /itis	
cytology	
czar	tsar
Czech * (nationality)	
Czechoslovakian	

D

dab ³ /ber	
dabble ² /r	
dable	dabble ²+
dabul	dabble ²+
dabutant	débutant +
dace	
dachshund	
dactill	dactyl
dactyl	
daddy /-long-legs	
daffodil	
daft /er/est	
dagger	
dahlia	
dail	dale
dailie	daily +
dail y /ies	
daintie	dainty +
daint y /ier/iest/ily/iness	
dairie	dairy +
dairimade	dairymaid
dair y /ies	
dairymaid	
daisie	daisy +
dais y /ies	
daitee	deity +
dakshound	dachshund
dale	
dalia	dahlia

dalie	dally ⁴+
dall y ⁴ /ier	
dam ³* (water)	
dam	damn ¹*+
damage ² /able	
damask	
dame	
damidge	damage ²+
damn ¹* (curse) /ation	
damnabl e /y	
damnabul	damnable +
damp /er/est/ness	
dampen ¹	
damsel	
damson	
dance ² /r	
dandelion	
dandie	dandy +
dandifi	dandify ⁴
dandify ⁴	
dandilion	dandelion
dandruff	
dand y /ies	
Dane * (from Denmark)	
dane	deign ¹*
danger /ous/ously	
dangerus	dangerous
dangle ² /r	
dangul	dangle ²+
danjer	danger+
danjerus	dangerous
dank /ness	
danse	dance ²+
daper	dapper +
daple	dapple ²
dapper /ness	
dapple ²	
dapul	dapple ²
dare ² /-devil	
dark /er/est/ly/ness	
darken ¹	
darling	
darn ¹ /er	
darnel	
dart ¹	

dase — dace
dash [1] /board
dastard /ly
data
dat*e* [2] /able
dater — data
dative
daub [1] /er/y
daufin — dauphin
daughter /-in-law
daunt [1] /less
dauphin
dauter — daughter +
davenport
Davielamp — Davy lamp
davit
Davy lamp
dawb — daub [1]+
dawdle [2] /r
dawdul — dawdle [2]+
dawn [1]
dawnt — daunt [1]+
dawter — daughter +
day /-break/s * (dates)
daybu — début
day-dream /t/ing
dayify — deify [4]+
dayism — deism +
dayist — deist
dayity — deity +
daylight
daylite — daylight
day-nurser*y* /ies
daytant — détente
daze [2]* (stun)
dazle — dazzle [2]+
dazul — dazzle [2]+
dazzl*e* [2] /er/ingly
de luxe
deacon /ess (fem.)
deactivat*e* [2] /ion
dead /-beat/-line
deaden [1] /er
dead-heat [1]
deadlock

deadl*y* /ier/iest/iness
dead-nettle
deaf /-mute/ness
deafen [1] /ingly
deal /er/ing/t
deam — deem [1]
dean /ery
deap — deep +
dear * (loved)
dear — deer *
dear *er* /est/ly
dearth
death /-mask/-rate
death*ly* /less/like
death *-trap* /-watch
débâcle
debacul — débâcle
debar [3] /ment
debark [1] /ation
debase [2] /ment
debat*e* [2] /able/ably
debauch [1] /ery
debilitat*e* [2] /ion
debility
debit [1] /able
debonair /ness
deborch — debauch [1]+
debree — debris
debrief [1]
debris
debt /or * (owe money)
debunk [1] /er
début
débutant /e (fem.)
decade
decaden*ce* /t
decagon /al
deca*gram* /litre/metre
decamp [1] /ment
decant [1] /er
decapitat*e* [2] /ion
decapod
decarbonis*e* [2] /ation
decathlon
decay [1]

83

decease[2]
deceit /ful/fully/fulness
deceive[2] /r
decelerat e[2] /ion
December
decenc y /ies
decensey   decency[+]
decent ★ (good) /ly
decent   descent ★
decentralise[2]
decepshun   deception
deception
deceptive /ly/ness
decerus   decorous[+]
decibel
decide[2] /dly
deciduous
decifer   decipher[1+]
deci gram /litre/metre
decimal /ism
decimalis e[2] /ation
decimat e[2] /ion
decipher[1] /able
decision
decisive /ly/ness
deck[1] /-chair/-hand
declaim[1] /er
declamashun   declamation[+]
declamat ion /ory
declarat ion /ory
declare[2]
declassif y[4] /ication
declension
declin e[2] /able/ation
declivit y /ies
declutch[1]
decockshun   decoction
decoction
decode[2] /r
decoi   decoy[1]
décollet é /age
decompos e[2] /able/ition
decompress[1] /ion
decompress ive /or
decon   deacon[+]

decongestant
decontaminat e[2] /ion
decontrol[3]
décor
decorashun   decoration
decorat e[2] /ion/ive/or
decorous /ly/ness
decorum
decorus   decorous[+]
decoy[1]
decreas e[2] /ingly
decree /d/ing
decrepit /ude
decrese   decrease[2+]
decri   decry[4+]
decr y[4] /ier
ded   dead[+]
deden   deaden[1+]
dedheat   dead-heat[1]
dedicat e[2] /ion
dedlie   deadly[+]
dedlier   deadlier
dedlock   deadlock
dedly   deadly[+]
dednetle   dead-nettle
dednetul   dead-nettle
deduc e[2] /ible
deduct[1] /ible/ion
deed /-poll
deel   deal[+]
deem[1]
deen   dean[+]
deep /er
deepen[1]
deep-freez e /er/ing
deep-frozen
deep-fry[4]
deer ★ (animal)
deer   dear ★
de-escalat e[2] /ion
def   deaf[+]
deface[2] /ment
defamatory
defamatrey   defamatory
defam e[2] /ation

default¹ /er

defeat¹ /ism/ist

defecat e² /ion

defect¹ /ion/ive/or

defeet   defeat¹⁺

defen   deafen¹⁺

defence /less

defend¹ /able/ant

defens   defence⁺

defensib le /ility

defensibul   defensible⁺

defensive /ly/ness

defensless   defenceless

defer³★ (postpone)

deferen ce /tial

deferens   deference⁺

deferenshal   deferential

defesit   deficit

defi   defy⁴⁺

defian ce /t/tly

defians   defiance⁺

deficienc y /ies

deficient /ly

deficit

defile² /ment/r

defin e² /able/ition

definishun   definition

definit   definite⁺

definite /ly

definitive /ly

defishency   deficiency⁺

defishent   deficient⁺

defisit   deficit

deflashun   deflation

deflat e² /ion/ionary

deflecshun   deflection

deflect¹ /ion/ive/or

deflour   deflower¹

deflower¹

defmute   deaf-mute

deforest¹ /ation

deform¹ /ation

deformashun   deformation

deformit y /ies

defraud¹ /er

defray¹ /able/al

defreez e /ing

defrord   defraud¹⁺

defrost¹ /er

defrozen

deft /ly/ness

defunct /ive/ness

defy⁴

degeneracy

degenerat e² /ion

degrad e² /ation

degree

dehidrate   dehydrate²⁺

dehydrat e² /ion

de-ice² /r

deifi   deify⁴⁺

deif y⁴ /ier

deign¹★ (condescend)

de-ise   de-ice²⁺

deis m /t

deitee   deity⁺

deit y /ies

deject¹ /ion

dejeneracy   degeneracy

dejenerate   degenerate²⁺

dejeneration   degeneration

dekstrose   dextrose

dekstrus   dextrous

delay¹ /er

delectabl e /y

delectabul   delectable⁺

delegac y /ies

delegasey   delegacy⁺

delegat e² /ion

delet e² /ion

deleterious /ly

deliberat e² /ely/ion

delibratley   deliberately

delicac y /ies

delicate /ly/ness

delicatessen

delicious /ly/ness

deligacy   delegacy⁺

deligashun   delegation

deligate   delegate²⁺

85

delight [1] /ful/fully
delineat e [2] /ion
deliniashun   delineation
deliniate   delineate [2+]
delinkwasey   delinquency +
delinkwens   delinquence +
delinquen ce /t
delinquenc y /ies
delirious /ly/ness
delirium
delirius   delirious +
delishus   delicious +
delite   delight [1+]
deliteful   delightful
deliterius   deleterious +
deliver [1] /ance/er
deliver y /ies
delivrey   delivery +
dell
delouse [2]
delt   dealt
delta
delude [2]
deluge [2]
deluks   de luxe
delushun   delusion +
delusion /al
delus ive /ory
delve [2] /r
demagog   demagogue +
demagog ue /y
demand [1] /able/er
demarcat e [2] /ion
demarch   démarche
démarche
demean [1] /our
demeaner   demeanour
demented
demerara
demerit
demesne
demigod
demilitarise [2]
demis e [2] /able
demist [1] /er

demobilis e [2] /ation
democrac y /ies
democrasey   democracy +
democratic /ally
democratis e [2] /ation
demolish [1] /able
demolishun   demolition +
demolition /ist
demon /ic
demonstra ble /tive
demonstrashun   demonstration
demonstrat e [2] /ion/or
demoralise [2]
demot e [2] /ion
demur [3*] (object)
demure *(quiet, coy)/ly
denationalise [2]
dencher   denture
dendrology
deni   deny [4]
denial
denier
denigrat e [2] /ion/or
denim
denizen
denominat e [2] /or
denomination /al
denot e [2] /able/ation/ive
denounce [2] /ment
denownse   denounce [2+]
dense /ly/r
densitey   density +
densitie   density +
densit y /ies
dent [1]
dental
dentifrice
dentifriss   dentifrice
denti ne /tion
dentishun   dentition
dentist /ry
denture
denud e [2] /ation
denunciat e [2] /ion
deny [4]

deoderant	deodorant	deput *e* [2] /ation	
deoderise	deodorise [2+]	deputey	deputy [+]
deodorant		deputise [2]	
deodorise [2] /r		deput *y* /ies	
deparcher	departure	derail [1] /ment	
depart [1] /ure		derale	derail [1+]
department /al/ally		derange [2] /ment	
departmentalise [2]		derelicshun	dereliction
depen	deepen [1]	derelict /ion	
depend [1] /able/ence		derick	derrick
dependant * (n.)		deride [2] /r	
dependenc *y* /ies		derishun	derision
dependensey	dependency [+]	derision	
dependent * (adj.)		deris *ive* /ory	
depict [1] /ion		derivashun	derivation [+]
depilat *e* [2] /ion/or		derivat *ion* /ive	
depilatory		derivativ	derivative
deplet *e* [2] /ion		deriv *e* [2] /able/er	
deploi	deploy [1+]	dermatitis	
deplor *e* [2] /able/ably		dermatolog *y* /ist	
deploy [1] /ment		derogat *e* [2] /ive/ory	
depo	depot	derrick	
depopulat *e* [2] /ion		dert	dirt [+]
deport [1] /ment		derth	dearth
deportashun	deportation	derty	dirty [4+]
deportation		dervish	
depos *e* [2] /able		desalinat *e* [2] /ion	
deposishun	deposition	descant [1] /er	
deposit [1] /ion/or		descend [1] /er	
depositor *y* /ies		descendant * (n.)	
depositrey	depository [+]	descendent * (adj.)	
depot		descent * (go down)	
deprav *e* [2] /ity		describ *e* [2] /able	
deprecat *e* [2] /ion/ory		descript *ion* /ive	
depreciat *e* [2] /ion		descry [4]	
depredat *e* [2] /ion		deseat	deceit [+]
depresherise	depressurise [2]	deseave	deceive [2+]
depreshurise	depressurise [2]	desecrat *e* [2] /ion	
depresiv	depressive	desegregat *e* [2] /ion	
depress [1] /ion/ive		desel	diesel
depressant		deselerashun	deceleration
depressurise [2]		deselerate	decelerate [2+]
depricate	deprecate [2+]	Desember	December
depriv *e* [2] /ation		desency	decency [+]
depth		desend	descend [1+]

87

desensitise[2]	
desent	decent ★+
desent	descent ★
desentralise	decentralise[2]
desershun	desertion
desert[1]★ (abandon, dry land)	
desert	dessert ★
desert er /ion	
deserve[2] /dly	
desese	disease +
desibel	decibel
desiccat e[2] /ion	
desiduous	deciduous
design[1] /er	
designat e[2] /ion/or	
desimal	decimal +
desimalise	decimalise[2]+
desimate	decimate[2]+
desimation	decimation
desine	design[1]+
desirab le /ility	
desirabul	desirable +
desir e[2] /ous	
desist[1]	
desk	
deskant	descant[1]+
desolat e[2] /ion	
despair[1]	
desperado /es	
desperashun	desperation
desperate /ly/ness	
desperation	
despicabl e /y	
despise[2] /r	
despite	
despoil[1] /ment	
despoliation	
despond[1] /ent	
despondenc e /y	
despondens	despondence +
despot /ism	
despotic /ally	
dessert ★ (food)	
dessert	desert[1]★

destinashun	destination
destination	
destine[2]	
destin y /ies	
destitut e /ion	
destroy[1] /er	
destructib le /ility	
destructibul	destructible +
destruct ion /ive	
desultor y /ily	
det	debt +
detach[1] /ment	
detail[1]	
detain[1] /ment	
detale	detail[1]
detane	detain[1]+
detecshun	detection
detect[1] /ion/or	
detective	
détente	
detention	
deter[3]★ (hinder)	
deter	debtor ★
deterent	deterrent
detergent	
deteriorat e[2] /ion	
determinant	
determinashun	determination
determination	
determin e[2] /able	
deterrent	
detest[1] /able/ation	
deth	death +
dethrone[2] /ment	
detiriarate	deteriorate[2]+
detonat e[2] /ion/or	
detoor	detour
detour	
detract[1] /ion/or	
detriment /al	
detrishun	detrition
detrition	
deuce	
deuterium	
deuteron	

devalu *e*² /ation
devastat *e*² /ion/or
develop ¹ /er/ment
devian *ce* /t
deviat *e*² /ion
device ★ (scheme, means)
devil /ry
devilish /ly
devious /ly
devis *e*²★ (invent) /able
devitalis *e*² /ation
devius   devious ⁺
devoid
devolushun   devolution
devolution
devolve ²
devot *e*² /ee/ion
devour ¹
devout /ly/ness
dew ★ (moisture)
dew   due ★⁺
dew *y* /-drop
dext *erity* /rous
dextrose
dextrus   dextrous
dhoti
dhow
diabetes
diabetic
diabolic /al/ally
diadem
diafanous   diaphanous ⁺
diafanus   diaphanous ⁺
diafram   diaphragm ⁺
diagnose ²
diagnos *is* /es (pl.)
diagnostic /ian
diagnostishun   diagnostician
diagonal /ly
diagram
diagrammatic /ally
dial ³ /er
dialect /al/ally
dialectic /al/ally
dialisis   dialysis ⁺

dialog   dialogue
dialogue
dialy *sis* /tic
diamet *er* /ral
diametric /al/ally
diamond
diapason
diaper
diaphanous /ly
diaphragm /atic
diarea   diarrhoea
diarey   diary ⁺
diarrhoea
diar *y* /ies/ist
diatonic
diatribe

> *If you cannot find your word under* **di** *look under* **de**

dibase   debase ²⁺
dibate   debate ²⁺
dibble ² /r
dice ² (pl. of die)
dichotom *y* /ies
diciple   disciple
dicipul   disciple
dicotomey   dichotomy ⁺
dicotyledon
dicshun   diction
dicshunrey   dictionary ⁺
dictafone   dictaphone
dictaphone
dictat *e*² /ion
dictator /ial
diction
dictionar *y* /ies
dictum
didactic /ally/ism
diddle ² /r
didget   digit ⁺
didgitalis   digitalis
didn't (did not)
didnt   didn't
die ★ (sing. of dice)
die ★ (death) /d

die-hard		dignity	
dieing	dyeing ★	digress [1] /ion/ive	
dieing	dying ★	dike [2]	
diernal	diurnal +	dil	dill
diesel		dilapidat *e* [2] /ion	
diet [1] /ary		dilatashun	dilatation
dietetic /s		dilat *e* [2] /ation/or/ory	
dietician		dilemma	
dietishun	dietician	diletant	dilettante +
difer	differ [1]★	dilettant *e* /i (pl.)	
diference	difference +	dilidalie	dilly-dally [4]
diferens	difference +	diligen *ce* /t	
diferenshal	differential +	diligens	diligence +
diferenshiate	differentiate [2]+	dill	
diferent	different	dilly-dally [4]	
diferential	differential +	dilut *e* [2] /ion/or	
diferentiate	differentiate [2]+	diluvial	
differ [1]★ (disagree)		dim [3] /ly/ness	
differ	defer [3]★	dime	
differen *ce* /t		dimenshun	dimension +
differential /ly		dimension /al	
differentiat *e* [2] /ion		dimer	dimmer +
difficult		diminish [1] /able	
difficult *y* /ies		diminuendo	
diffiden *ce* /t		diminut *ive* /ion	
diffract /ion		dimm *er* /est	
diffus *e* [2] /ion/ive		dimpl *e* [2] /y	
dificult	difficult	dimpul	dimple [2]+
dificultey	difficulty +	dinamic	dynamic +
difidence	diffidence +	dinamite	dynamite [2]
difident	diffident	dinamo	dynamo +
difract	diffract +	dinastey	dynasty +
diftheria	diphtheria	dinastic	dynastic +
difthong	diphthong	dine [2]★ (eat) /r	
difuse	diffuse [2]+	dine	dyne ★
difushun	diffusion	diner	dinner
difusion	diffusion	dingh *y* /ies	
dig [3] /ger		dingie	dinghy +
digest [1] /ion/ive		ding *y* /ily/iness	
digestib *le* /ility		dinner	
digit /al/ally		dinosaur	
digitalis		dinosore	dinosaur
dignify [4]		dioces *e* /an	
dignitar *y* /ies		diode	
dignitrey	dignitary +	diokside	dioxide

90

diosees	diocese +	disarange	disarrange [2]+
dioxide		disaray	disarray
dip [3] /per		disarm [1] /ament	
diper	diaper	disarrange [2] /ment	
diphtheria		disarray	
diphthong		disasoshiate	disassociate [2]+
diploma /s		disassociat e [2] /ion	
diplomac y /ies		disast er /rous/rously	
diplomasey	diplomacy +	disastrus	disastrous
diplomat /ist		disatisfi	dissatisfy [4]+
diplomatic /ally		disavow [1] /al	
dipsomania /c		disband [1] /ment	
dire /ful/ly/r/st		disbar [3] /ment	
direcshun	direction	disbeleif	disbelief
direct [1] /ion/ive		disbeleive	disbelieve [2]+
director /ate		disbelief	
director y /ies		disbelieve [2] /r	
directrey	directory +	disberden	disburden [1]+
dirge /ful		disberse	disburse [2]+
dirigib le /ility		disbileaf	disbelief
dirigibul	dirigible +	disbileve	disbelieve [2]+
dirt /iness		disburden [1] /ment	
dirt y [4] /ier/iest/ily		disburse [2] /ment	
disabilit y /ies		disc /-brake/-jockey	
disable [2] /ment		discard [1]	
disabul	disable [2]+	discern [1] /ible/ment	
disabuse [2]		discernibul	discernible
disadvantage /ous		discharge [2]	
disadvantidge	disadvantage +	disciple	
disafecshun	disaffection	disciplinar y /ian	
disaffected		discipline [2]	
disaffection		discipul	disciple
disagreabul	disagreeable +	disclaim [1]	
disagree /d/ing/ment		disclaym	disclaim [1]
disagreeabl e /y		disclos e [2] /ure	
disagrement	disagreement	discolor	discolour [1]+
disallow [1]		discolo ur [1] /ration	
disapear	disappear [1]+	discomfert	discomfort [1]
disapearance	disappearance	discomfort [1]	
disapoint	disappoint [1]+	discompos e [2] /ure	
disapoynt	disappoint [1]+	disconcert [1]	
disappear [1] /ance		disconect	disconnect [1]+
disappoint [1] /ment		disconnect [1] /ion	
disapprov e [2] /al		disconsert	disconcert [1]
disaproval	disapproval	disconsolate /ly	

91

discontent [1]		disect	dissect [1+]
discontinu *e* [2] /ance		disembark [1] /ation	
discontinu *ity* /ous		disembarrass [1] /ment	
discord /ance/ant		disemble	dissemble [2+]
discorse	discourse [2]	disembodie	disembody [4+]
discotek	discotheque	disembod *y* [4] /iment	
discotheque		disembowel [3] /ment	
discount [1] /able/er		disembroil [1]	
discountenance [2]		disembul	dissemble [2+]
discourage [2] /ment		diseminashun	dissemination
discourse [2]		diseminate	disseminate [2+]
discourteous /ly/ness		disenchant [1] /ment	
discourtes *y* /ies		disengage [2] /ment	
discourtius	discourteous +	disenshent	dissentient
discover [1] /er		disenshun	dissension
discover *y* /ies		disentangle [2] /ment	
discownt	discount [1+]	disentient	dissentient
discowntenans	discountenance [2]	disentrey	dysentery
discredit [1] /able		disern	discern [1+]
discreet /ly/ness		disernible	discernible
discrepanc *y* /ies		disernibul	discernible
discrepansey	discrepancy +	disertashun	dissertation
discrepant		disertation	dissertation
discreshun	discretion +	diserviss	disservice
discretion /ary		disfaver	disfavour [1]
discribable	describable	disfavour [1]	
discribe	describe [2+]	disfiger	disfigure [2+]
discriminat *e* [2] /ion		disfigure [2] /ment	
discripshun	description +	disfranchise [2] /ment	
discriptiv	descriptive	disgise	disguise [2+]
disculer	discolour [1+]	disgorge [2] /ment	
discuridge	discourage [2+]	disgrace [2] /ful/fully	
discurs *ion* /ive		disgruntled	
discurtesey	discourtesy +	disguise [2] /r	
discurtius	discourteous +	disgust [1]	
discus *☆†* /es		dish /-cloth/ful	
†(heavy disc)		dishabille	
discushun	discussion	disharmoney	disharmony +
discuss [1]☆ (debate)		disharmon *y* /ious	
discussion		disharten	dishearten [1]
disdain [1] /ful/fully		dishearten [1]	
dise	dice [2]	dishevel [3]	
disease /d		dishonest /ly/y	
diseave	deceive [2+]	dishonour [1] /able/ably	
disecshun	dissection	dishonrabul	dishonourable

disidence	dissidence +	disobey [1]	
disidens	dissidence +	disoblige [2]	
disident	dissident	disoloot	dissolute +
disillusion [1] /ment		disoluble	dissoluble
disilushun	disillusion [1+]	disolute	dissolute +
disimilar	dissimilar +	disolution	dissolution
disimulashun	dissimulation	disolve	dissolve [2+]
disincentive		disonance	dissonance +
disinclinashun	disinclination	disonans	dissonance +
disinclin e [2] /ation		disonant	dissonant
disinfect [1] /ant/ion		disone	disown [1]
disinherit [1] /ance		disoner	dishonour [1+]
disinsentiv	disincentive	disonerabul	dishonourable
disintegrat e [2] /ion		disonest	dishonest +
disinter [3] /ment		disonist	dishonest +
disinterest [1]		disonrabul	dishonourable
disintigrate	disintegrate [2+]	disorder [1] /ly	
disipate	dissipate [2+]	disorganis e [2] /ation	
disiple	disciple	disorientate [2]	
disiplin	discipline [2]	disoshiate	dissociate [2+]
disiplinarey	disciplinary +	disown [1]	
disipul	disciple	disparage [2] /ment	
disjoint [1]		disparate /ly/ness	
diskwiet	disquiet [1+]	disparidge	disparage [2+]
diskwolification	disqualification	disparige	disparage [2+]
diskwolify	disqualify [4+]	disparitey	disparity +
dislik e [2] /able		disparit y /ies	
dislocat e [2] /ion		dispashonate	dispassionate +
dislodge [2] /ment		dispassionate /ly	
disloge	dislodge [2+]	dispatch [1] /er	
disloial	disloyal +	dispel [3] /ler	
disloialtey	disloyalty	dispensar y /ies	
disloyal /ly/ty		dispens e [2] /ation/er	
dismal /ly		dispepsia	dyspepsia +
dismantle [2]		dispeptic	dyspeptic
dismantul	dismantle [2]	dispers e [2] /al	
dismast [1]		dispershun	dispersion
dismay [1]		dispersion	
dismember [1] /ment		dispirit [1]	
dismisal	dismissal	displace [2] /ment	
dismiss [1] /al		displase	displace [2+]
dismount [1]		display [1]	
dismownt	dismount [1]	displeas e [2] /ure	
disobay	disobey [1]	displese	displease [2+]
disobedien ce /t		displesher	displeasure

disport [1]
dispos *e* [2] /able/al
disposeshun — dispossession
disposess — dispossess [1+]
disposishun — disposition
disposition
dispossess [1] /ion
disproof
disproov — disprove [2]
disproporshun — disproportion [+]
disproportion /ate
disprosium — dysprosium
disprove [2]
dispursal — dispersal
dispurse — disperse [2+]
dispurshun — dispersion
disputashun — disputation [+]
disputat *ion* /ious
disput *e* [2] /able
disqualif *y* [4] /ication
disquiet [1] /ude
disregard [1] /ful
disrepair
disreputabl *e* /y
disrepute
disrespect /ful/fully
disrigard — disregard [1+]
disripair — disrepair
disrispect — disrespect [+]
disrobe [2] /ment
disrupt [1] /ion/ive
dissapear — disappear [1+]
dissapoint — disappoint [1+]
dissaproov — disapprove [2+]
dissatisf *y* [4] /action
dissect [1] /ion/or
dissemble [2] /r
disseminat *e* [2] /ion/or
dissension
dissent [1]* (disagreement)
dissentient
dissentious
dissertation
disservice
dissiden *ce* /t

dissidens — dissidence [+]
dissimilar /ity/ities
dissimulat *e* [2] /ion
dissipat *e* [2] /ion
dissociat *e* [2] /ion
dissoluble
dissolute /ly/ness
dissolution
dissolve [2] /nt
dissonan *ce* /t
dissuade [2]
dissuas *ion* /ive
distaff
distance
distans — distance
distant /ly
distaste /ful/fully
distemper [1]
distend [1]
distenshun — distension
distens *ible* /ion
distensibul — distensible [+]
disterb — disturb [1+]
disterbance — disturbance
distil [3] /lation/ler
distiller *y* /ies
distinct /ive/ly
distinction
distinguish [1] /able
distingwish — distinguish [1+]
distorshun — distortion
distort [1] /ion
distracshun — distraction
distract [1] /ion
distrain [1] /t
distrane — distrain [1+]
distraught
distrawt — distraught
distress [1] /ful
distribut *e* [2] /ion
distribut *ive* /or
district /nurse
distrort — distraught
distrust [1] /ful
disturb [1] /ance

disunion	
disunit *e* [2] /y	
disurn	discern [1+]
disurnible	discernible
disuse [2]	
diswade	dissuade [2]
diswashun	dissuasion [+]
diswasion	dissuasion [+]
diswasiv	dissuasive
ditch [1] /er	
dither [1] /y	
ditie	ditty [+]
dito	ditto
ditto	
ditt *y* /ies	
dity	ditty [+]
diurnal /ly	
divan	
dive [2] /r	
diverge [2] /nce/nt	
divergens	divergence
divers	diverse [+]
diverse /ly	
divershun	diversion
diversifi	diversify [4+]
diversif *y* [4] /ication	
diversion	
diversitey	diversity [+]
diversity /ies	
divert [1] /er	
divest [1]	
divide [2] /r	
dividend	
divin *e* [2] /ation/ely/er	
divinitey	divinity [+]
divinit *y* /ies	
diviser	divisor
divishun	division [+]
divis *ible* /ive/ively	
divisibul	divisible [+]
division /al	
divisiv	divisive
divisor	
divorce [2] /é/ée (fem.)	
divorse	divorce [2+]

divulge [2] /nce/r	
dizier	dizzier [+]
dizmal	dismal [+]
dizolve	dissolve [2+]
dizy	dizzy
dizzi *er* /est/ly/ness	
dizzy	
do ★ (perform) /er/ing	
do ★ (music) /s ★ (pl.)	
do	doe ★+
docile /ly	
docility	
dock [1] /er/yard	
docket [1]	
dockit	docket [1]
docter	doctor [1+]
doctor [1] /ate/ial	
doctrin	doctrine [+]
doctrinair	doctrinaire
doctrin *e* /aire/al	
document [1] /ation	
documentar *v* /ies	
documentrey	documentary [+]
dodder [1] /er/y	
dodecagon	
doder	dodder [1+]
dodg *e* [2] /er/y	
dodgi *er* /est/ness	
doe ★ (deer) /s ★ (pl.)	
doe	do ★+
doe	dough ★+
does ★ (do-[verb])	
doesn't (does not)	
doff [1]	
dofin	dauphin
dog [3] /fight/fish	
dog-eared	
dogeared	dog-eared
dogeral	doggerel
dogfite	dogfight
doggerel	
dogma /tic/tically	
dogmatis *e* [2] /m	
doilie	doily [+]
doil *y* /ies	

95

doldrum	
dole [2]	
doleful /ly	
doler	dollar
dolerus	dolorous [+]
dolfin	dolphin
doll [1] /y	
dollar	
doller	dollar
dollop	
dolman	
dolomite	
dolorous /ly/ness	
dolorus	dolorous [+]
dolphin	
domain	
domane	domain
dome	
Domesday Book	
domestic /ally	
domesticate [2]	
domesticity	
domestisitey	domesticity
domicil e /iary	
dominan ce /t	
dominans	dominance [+]
dominat e [2] /ion/or	
dominear	domineer [1]
domineer [1]	
dominion	
domino /es	
dominyon	dominion
domisile	domicile [+]
don [3][*]† /nish	
†(put on, tutor)	
donat e [2] /ion/or	
done [*] (finished)	
doner	donor
donkey /s	
donky	donkey [+]
donor	
donut	doughnut
dooch	douche [2]
doodle [2] /r	
doodul	doodle [2+]

doom [1]	
doomsday book	Domesday Book
door /step/way	
door	dour
doordle	dawdle [2+]
doormouse	dormouse
doosh	douche [2]
dope [2] /y	
dophin	dauphin
dore	door [+]
dorman cy /t	
dormansey	dormancy [+]
dormice	
dormise	dormice
dormitor y /ies	
dormitrey	dormitory [+]
dormouse	
dorn	dawn [1]
dorsal /ly	
dorter	daughter [+]
dos e [2] /age	
dosidge	dosage
dosile	docile [+]
dosilitey	docility
dossier	
dot [3]	
dot age /ard	
dote [2] /r	
doti	dhoti
dotidge	dotage [+]
dotti er /est/ly/ness	
dotty	
double [2] /-barrelled	
double-bass	
double-cross [1]	
doublet	
doubloon	
doubly	
doubt [1] /er/less	
doubtful /ly/ness	
douche [2]	
dough [*] (bread) /nut/y	
dought y /ily	
dour	
douse [2][*] (shower) /r	

douse	dowse ²★	draftiness	draughtiness
dout	doubt ¹⁺	drafts	draughts ★
doutey	doughty ⁺	draftsman ★ (drafter	
doutful	doubtful ⁺	of documents)	
doutless	doubtless	draftsman	draughtsman ★
dove /-cot		drafty	draughty ⁺
dovetail ¹		drag ³ /ger	
dow	dhow	dragon	
dow	doe ★⁺	dragonfl y /ies	
dow	dough ★⁺	dragoon ¹	
dowager		drain ¹ /age/er	
dowdie	dowdy ⁺	drainidge	drainage
dowd y /ily/iness		drake	
dowey	doughy	dram	
down ¹ /cast/hill		drama /s/tist	
downey	downy	dramatic /ally	
downfall /en		dramatis e ² /ation	
downgrade ²		drank	
downharted	downhearted	drape ² /r	
downhearted		draper y /ies	
downie	downy	drastic /ally	
downpoor	downpour	draught ★† /s ★	
downpour		†(air current, game)	
downright		draughtiness	
downrite	downright	draughtsman ★†	
downstairs		†(drawer of plans)	
downtrodden		draught y /ier/iest	
downward		draw /ing/n	
downwerd	downward	drawback	
downy		drawbridge	
dowrie	dowry ⁺	drawer	
dowr y /ies		drawing-room	
dowse ²★ (divine with rod)		drawl ¹ /er	
dowse	douse ²★⁺	dray ★ (low cart)	
dowt	doubt ¹⁺	dray	drey ★
dowtey	doughty ⁺	dread ¹ /ful/fully	
dowtful	doubtful ⁺	dreadnort	dreadnought
doz e ²★ (sleep) /y		dreadnought	
doze	does ★	dream ¹ /ily/less/t/y	
dozen		drearey	dreary
dozi ly /ness		drearie	dreary
drab		dreari er /est/ly/ness	
draft ¹★ (bank, military)		dreary	
draft	draught ★⁺	dred	dread ¹⁺
draftey	draughty ⁺	dredful	dreadful

dredge² /r		dropper	
drednort	dreadnought	dropsey	dropsy⁺
dreem	dream¹⁺	dropsie	dropsy⁺
drege	dredge²⁺	drops y /ical/ied	
dregs		dross /iness	
dremt	dreamt	drought	
drench¹ /er		drout	drought
drerey	dreary	drove /r	
drerie	dreary	drown¹	
drerier	drearier⁺	drows e² /y	
dresage	dressage	drowsey	drowsy
dresie	dressy	drowsie	drowsy
dresmaker	dressmaker⁺	drowsi er /ly/ness	
dress¹ /er/es/iness/y		drowt	drought
dressage		dru	drew
dressmak er /ing		drub³ /ber	
dresy	dressy	drudge² /ry	
drew		drug³	
Drewid	Druid	druge	drudge²⁺
drey ★ (squirrel's nest)		drugery	drudgery
dri	dry⁴⁺	drugget	
dribble² /r		druggist	
driblet		Druid	
dribul	dribble²⁺	drum³ /mer/stick	
driclean	dry-clean¹	drumedarey	dromedary⁺
drift¹ /er/wood		drum-major	
dril	drill¹	drunk /ard/en/enness	
drill¹		dr y⁴ /ier/iest	
drily		dry-clean¹	
drink /able/er		dryer	drier
drip³ /-dry		dual ★ (two) /ism/ity	
driv e /en/er/ing		dual	duel³★
drivel³ /ler		dub³	
drizul	drizzle²⁺	dubbin	
drizzl e² /y		dubious /ly	
droll /ness		dubius	dubious⁺
droller y /ies		duble	double²⁺
dromedar y /ies		dublebareld	double-barrelled
drone²		dublet	doublet
Drooid	Druid	dublie	doubly
drool¹		dubloon	doubloon
droop¹ /y		dubly	doubly
drop³ /let		ducal	
droper	dropper	ducat	
drop-out		duce	deuce

duchess /es		dun * (colour)	
duchey	duchy +	dun	done *
duchie	duchy +	dunce	
duch y /ies		dune	
duck [1] /ling		dung /hill	
ducket	ducat	dungaree /s	
ducktile	ductile +	dungen	dungeon
duct /ing/less		dungeon	
ductil e /ity		dunjon	dungeon
du e *† /ly		duns	dunce
†(owing, expected)		dunse	dunce
due	dew *	duolog	duologue
duedrop	dew-drop	duologue	
duel [3]* (fight)		dup e [2] /able	
duel	joule *	dupleks	duplex +
dueler	dueller +	duplex /ity	
duelist	duellist	duplicat e [2] /ion/or	
duell er /ist		duplicity	
duet /tist		duplisitey	duplicity
duey	dewy +	durab le /ility/ly	
dufel	duffel	durabul	durable +
duffel		durashun	duration
duffer		duration	
dug /-out		duress	
dul	dull +	durge	dirge +
dulcet		during	
dulcimer		durt	dirt +
duler	duller +	durtie	dirty [4]+
dulie	duly	durtier	dirtier
dull /ard/y		durty	dirty [4]+
dull er /est/ish		dusbin	dustbin +
dulset	dulcet	duse	deuce
dulsimer	dulcimer	dusk /y	
dum	dumb +	dust [1] /er/y	
dumb /ly/ness		dust bin /man/pan	
dumb-bell		dusti er /est/ness	
dumbell	dumb-bell	Dutch /man/woman	
dumbfound [1]		dutie	duty +
dumfound	dumbfound [1]	dutifree	duty-free
dumfownd	dumbfound [1]	dutiful /ly	
dumm y /ies		dut y /ies	
dumness	dumbness	duty-free	
dump [1] /er/y		duv	dove +
dumpling		duvtail	dovetail [1]
dumy	dummy +	duvtale	dovetail [1]

duz	does ★
duzn	dozen
duznt	doesn't
dwarf[1] /ish	
dwell /er/ing	
dwelt	
dwindle[2]	
dwindul	dwindle[2]
dworf	dwarf[1+]
dye ★† /d ★† /ing ★†	
†(change colour)	
dye	die ★+
dyed	died ★
dyehard	die-hard
dying ★ (death)	
dying	dyeing ★
dynamic /ally	
dynamics	
dynamite[2]	
dynamo /s	
dynast	
dynastey	dynasty[+]
dynastic /ally	
dynast y /ies	
dyne ★ (unit of force)	
dysentery	
dysentrey	dysentery
dyspep sia /tic	
dysprosium	

E

each	
eager /ly/ness	
eagle /-eyed/t	
eal	eel
ear /-ache/-drum	
earie	eerie ★
earie	eyrie ★
earl /dom	
earli er /est	
early /ish	
earmark[1]	
earn[1]★ (gain) /ings	

earnest /ly/ness	
ear-ring	
earshot	
earth[1] /iness	
earthen /ware	
earthl y /iness	
earthquake	
earth work /worm	
earwig	
ease[2]	
easel	
east /erly/ward/wards	
easten	eastern +
Easter	
eastern /er	
eas y /ier/ily/iness	
easy-going	
eat /able/en/er/ing	
eau-de-cologne	
eaves	
eavesdrop[3] /per	
ebb[1]	
ebonie	ebony +
ebon y /ite	
ebulience	ebullience +
ebuliens	ebullience +
ebulient	ebullient
ebullien ce /t	
eccentric /ally/ity	
ecclesiastic /al/ally	
ecentric	eccentric +
ech	each
echelon	
echo[1] /es	
eclair	
eclare	eclair
eclectic	
eclesiastic	ecclesiastic +
eclipse[2]	
ecliptic	
ecolog	ecologue
ecologey	ecology +
ecological /ly	
ecologue	
ecolog y /ist	

economic /al/ally/s		efemeral	ephemeral +
economise [2]		efeminacy	effeminacy
economist		efeminasey	effeminacy
econom y /ies		efeminate	effeminate +
ecsema	eczema	efert	effort +
ecsentric	eccentric +	efervesence	effervescence
ecstas y /ies		efervesent	effervescent
ecstatic /ally		efervess	effervesce [2]+
ectoplasm		efface [2] /ment	
ecumenical		effect [1]	
eczema		effective /ly	
edd y [4] /ies		effectual	
edge [2] /ways/wise		effeminacy	
edgey	edgy +	effeminate /ly	
edgie	edgy +	effervesce [2] /nce/nt	
edg y /ily/iness		effervess	effervesce [2]+
edib le /ility		effete	
edibul	edible +	efficacious /ly/ness	
edict		efficacy	
edie	eddy [4]+	efficashus	efficacious +
edifice		efficienc y /ies	
edifiss	edifice	efficient /ly	
edif y [4] /ication		effigey	effigy +
edishun	edition	effig y /ies	
edit [1] /ion		efflorescen ce /t	
editer	editor +	effluen ce /t	
editor /ial/ially		effluvium	
educab le /ility		effort /less/lessly	
educashun	education +	effronter y /ies	
educat e [2] /ive/or		effulgen ce /t	
education /al/ally/ist		effulgens	effulgence +
edy	eddy [4]+	effus e [2] /ion/ive	
eeger	eager +	eficacious	efficacious +
eegle	eagle +	eficacy	efficacy
eel		eficasey	efficacy
eer	ear +	eficashus	efficacious +
eerie * (strange)		eficiency	efficiency +
eerie	eyrie *	eficient	efficient +
eeri er /est/ly/ness		efigey	effigy +
eermark	earmark [1]	efishency	efficiency +
eface	efface [2]+	efishensey	efficiency +
efect	effect [1]	efishent	efficient +
efectiv	effective +	efloresence	efflorescence +
efectual	effectual	efluence	effluence +
efeet	effete	efluens	effluence +

efluent	effluent
efluvium	effluvium
efort	effort +
efronterey	effrontery +
efulgence	effulgence +
efuse	effuse 2+
efusiv	effusive
eg	egg 1+
egalitarian /ism	
ege	edge 2+
egg 1 /-cup/-shell	
Egipshun	Egyptian
Egiptian	Egyptian
egis	aegis
ego /ism/tism	
egocentric /ity	
egoist /ic/ically	
egosentric	egocentric +
egotist /ical/ically	
egress 1	

If you cannot find your word under **egs** *look under* **ex**

egsact	exact 1+
egsamine	examine 2+
egsample	example
egsaust	exhaust 1+
egsecutive	executive
egsempt	exempt 1+
egsert	exert 1+
Egyptian	
eiderdown	
Eiffel	
eight * (number)	
eighteen /th	
eighth /ly	
eight y /ies	
einsteinium	
either	
ejaculat e 2 /ion/ory	
eject 1 /ion/or	
ejis	aegis
eke 2	
eko	echo 1+

If you cannot find your word under **eks** *look under* **ex**

ekscavate	excavate 2+
ekschange	exchange 2+
eksclaim	exclaim 1
eksite	excite 2+
ekumenical	ecumenical
ekwable	equable +
ekwabul	equable +
ekwal	equal 3+
ekwalise	equalise 2+
ekwalitey	equality +
ekwanimitey	equanimity
ekwashun	equation
ekwate	equate 2
ekwater	equator +
ekwation	equation
ekwerey	equerry +
ekwestrian	equestrian
ekwianguler	equiangular
ekwidistant	equidistant
ekwilateral	equilateral
ekwilibrium	equilibrium
ekwine	equine
ekwinox	equinox
ekwip	equip 3+
ekwitable	equitable +
ekwitabul	equitable +
ekwity	equity +
ekwivalence	equivalence +
ekwivocate	equivocate 2+
elaborat e 2 /ely/ion	
elapse 2	
elastic /ally/ity	
elat e 2 /ion	
elbow 1 /-room	
elder /ly	
elderberie	elderberry +
elderberr y /ies	
eldest	
elect 1 /ive/or/orate	
election /eering	
electoral /ly	
electric /al/ally	
electrician	

electricity	
electrif y⁴ /ication	
electrocut e² /ion	
electrode	
electrolight	electrolyte⁺
electrolite	electrolyte⁺
electrolysis	
electrolyt e /ic	
electromagnet /ic/ism	
electromotive	
electron /s	
electronic /ally/s	
electroplate²	
electroscope	
electrovalency	
elefant	elephant⁺
elegan ce /t	
elegans	elegance⁺
elegey	elegy⁺
eleg y /ies/iac	
element /al/ary	
elephant /ine	
elevat e² /ion/or	
eleven /th	
elf /in/ish	
elfs	elves
elicit¹★ (draw out)	
elicit	illicit★⁺
eli de² /sion	
elifant	elephant⁺
eligans	elegance⁺
eligant	elegant
eligib le /ility	
eligibul	eligible⁺
elikser	elixir
eliment	element⁺
elimental	elemental
elimentarey	elementary
elimentrey	elementary
eliminat e² /ion/or	
elips	ellipse
elipsis	ellipsis
eliptic	elliptic⁺
elishun	elision
élit e /ism/ist	

elivashun	elevation
elivate	elevate²⁺
elivater	elevator
elivation	elevation
elixir	
Elizabethan	
elk	
ellipse	
ellipsis	
elliptic /al/ally	
elocution /ary/ist	
elokwence	eloquence⁺
elokwens	eloquence⁺
elokwent	eloquent
elongat e² /ion	
elope² /ment/r	
eloquen ce /t	
eloquens	eloquence⁺
else /where	
elswere	elsewhere
elucidat e² /ion/or	
elude²★ (avoid)	
elude	allude²★
elushun	elusion★
elusidate	elucidate²⁺
elusion★ (escape)	
elusive★ (evasive) /ness	
elusive	illusive★
elver	
elves (pl. of elf)	
emaciat e² /ion	
emanat e² /ion/ive	
emancipat e² /ion/or	
emansipate	emancipate²⁺
emasculat e² /ion	
emasiate	emaciate²⁺
embalm¹ /er/ment	
embankment	
embarass	embarrass¹⁺
embargo¹ /es	
embark¹ /ation	
embarm	embalm¹⁺
embarrass¹ /ment	
embass y /ies	
embattle²	

embatul   embattle[2]
embed[3]
embellish[1] /ment
ember
embezul   embezzle[2+]
embezzle[2] /ment/r
embitter[1] /ment
emblazon[1]
emblem
emblematic /ally
embodie   embody[4+]
embod*y*[4] /iment
embolism
emboss[1]
embrace[2]
embrase   embrace[2]
embrio   embryo
embriologist   embryologist[+]
embrocashun   embrocation
embrocation
embroider[1] /y/ies
embroil[1] /ment
embryo /s/nic
embryolog*ist* /y
emend   amend[1+]
emerald
emerey   emery
emerge[2] /nce/nt
emergenc*y* /ies
emergensey   emergency[+]
emergent
emerie   emery
emershun   emersion
emersion
emery
emetic
emfasis   emphasis[+]
emfasise   emphasise[2]
emfatic   emphatic[+]
emigrant
emigrat*e*[2] /ion
emigray   émigré[+]
émigré /e (fem.)
eminen*ce* /t *†
   †(distinguished)

eminens   eminence[+]
eminent   imminent ★+
emisarey   emissary[+]
emishun   emission
emissar*y* /ies
emission
emit[3] /ter
emollient
emolument
emoshun   emotion[+]
emotion /al/ally
emotive
empanel[3]
emperer   emperor[+]
emp*eror* /ress (fem.)
emphas*is* /es (pl.)
emphasise[2]
emphatic /ally
empire ★ (dominion)
empire   umpire[2★]
empiric /ism/ist
empirical /ly
empirisist   empiricist
emplacement
emploi   employ[1+]
employ[1] /able/ee/er
emporium /s
empower[1]
empress   impress[1+]
emptie   empty[4]
empti*er* /est/ness
empt*y*[4]
emulashun   emulation
emulat*e*[2] /ion/ive/or
emulshun   emulsion
emulsif*y*[4] /ication
emulsion
en route
enable[2] /ment
enabul   enable[2+]
enact[1] /able/ment
enamel[3] /ler
enamer   enamour[1]
enamour[1]
encamp[1] /ment

encapsulat *e*² /ion	
encase² /ment	
encefalic	encephalic
encephalic	
enchant¹ /ment	
enchant *er* /ress (fem.)	
enciclical	encyclical
enciclopedia	encyclopedia⁺
encircle² /ment	
enclave	
enclos *e*² /ure	
encompass¹	
encore²	
encounter¹	
encourage² /ment	
encownter	encounter¹
encroach¹ /er/ment	
encrust¹	
encumb *er*¹ /rance	
encuridge	encourage²⁺
encurige	encourage²⁺
encyclical	
encyclopedi *a* /c	
end¹ /less/lessly	
endanger¹	
endear¹ /ment	
endeavour¹	
endeer	endear¹⁺
endever	endeavour¹
endive	
endocrine	
endorse² /ment/r	
endow¹ /ment	
end-product	
endur *e*² /able/ance	
enema /s	
enem *y* /ies	
energetic /ally	
energey	energy⁺
energise² /r	
energ *y* /ies	
enervat *e*² /ion	
enfebul	enfeeble²⁺
enfeeble² /ment	
enfold¹	

enforce² /ment	
enforceab *le* /ility	
enfors	enforce²⁺
enforsible	enforceable⁺
enforsibul	enforceable⁺
enfranchise² /ment	
engage² /ment	
engender¹	
engine /-driver	
enginear	engineer¹
engineer¹	
English /man/woman	
engraft¹ /ment	
engrain¹	
engrave² /r	
engrayn	engrain¹
engross¹	
engulf¹	
enhance² /ment	
enhans	enhance²⁺
eni	any
enibodie	anybody
enigma /tic/tically	
enihow	anyhow
enima	enema⁺
enithing	anything
eniware	anywhere
eniway	anyway
eniwhere	anywhere
eniwun	anyone
enjender	engender¹
enjin	engine⁺
enjineer	engineer¹
enjoi	enjoy¹⁺
enjoiable	enjoyable⁺
enjoiabul	enjoyable⁺
enjoiment	enjoyment
enjoin¹	
enjoy¹ /ment	
enjoyabl *e* /y	
enlace²	
enlarge² /able/ment/r	
enlase	enlace²
enlighten¹ /ment	
enlist¹	

enliten	enlighten [1+]	enterpris *e* /ing	
enliven [1]		entertain [1] /er/ment	
enmit *y* /ies		entertane	entertain [1+]
ennoble [2] /ment		enthral [3] /ment	
ennui		enthrone [2] /ment	
enobul	ennoble [2+]	enthuse [2]	
enormit *y* /ies		enthusias *m* /t	
enormous /ly/ness		enthusiastic /ally	
enormus	enormous [+]	entice [2] /ment/r	
enough		entire /ly/ty	
enquire [2] /r		entise	entice [2+]
enquir *y* /ies		entitey	entity [+]
enrage [2]		entitle [2] /ment	
enrap	enwrap [3]	entitul	entitle [2+]
enrapcher	enrapture [2]	entit *y* /ies	
enrapture [2]		entomb [1] /ment	
enrich [1] /ment		entomolog *y* /ical/ist	
enrol [3] /ment		entoom	entomb [1+]
enroot	en route	entrails	
ensconce [2]		entrain [1]	
enscons	ensconce [2]	entrales	entrails
ensefalic	encephalic	entrance [2] /ment	
ensemble		entrans	entrance [2+]
ensembul	ensemble	entrant	
ensercal	encircle [2+]	entrap [3]	
enshore	ensure [2★]	entreat [1] /ingly	
enshore	insure [2★+]	entreat *y* /ies	
enshrine [2]		entrée	
enshure	ensure [2★]	entreet	entreat [1+]
ensiclical	encyclical	entrench [1] /ment	
ensiclopedia	encyclopedia [+]	entreprener	entrepreneur [+]
ensign		entrepreneur /ial	
ensine	ensign	entrey	entry [+]
enslave [2] /ment		entrust [1]	
ensnare [2]		entr *y* /ies	
ensue [2]		entwine [2]	
ensure [2★] (make certain)		enuf	enough
ensure	insure [2★+]	enumerat *e* [2] /ion/or	
entail [1]		enunciat *e* [2] /ion/or	
entale	entail [1]	enunsiate	enunciate [2+]
entangle [2] /ment		envelop [1★†] /ment	
entangul	entangle [2+]	†(to surround)	
enteprise	enterprise [+]	envelope ★ (stationery)	
enter [1]		envenom [1]	
enteritis		envie	envy [4+]

envious /ly/ness
environ[1] /s
environment /al/ally
envisage[2]
envisidge   envisage[2]
envisige   envisage[2]
envius   envious[+]
envoi   envoy
envoy
env y[4] /iable/ier
enwrap[3]
enzime   enzyme
enzyme
epaulet
epawlet   epaulet
ephemeral /ly
epic /ally
epicenter   epicentre
epicentre
epicure /an/anism
epidemic
epiderm is /al
epidiascope
Epifaney   Epiphany
epiglottis
epigraf   epigraph[+]
epigram
epigrammatic /ally
epigraph /ic
epilep sy /tic
epilog   epilogue
epilogue
Epiphany
episcopacy
episcopal /ian
episcopasey   episcopacy
episod e /ic/ical
epist le /olary
episul   epistle[+]
epitaf   epitaph
epitaph
epithet
epitome
epitomise[2]
epoch /al

epok
eporlet
equab le /ility/ly
equal[3] /ly
equalis e[2] /ation/er
equalitey   equality[+]
equalit y /ies
equanimity
equashun   equation
equate[2]
equater   equator[+]
equation
equator /ial
equerr y /ies
equestrian
equiangular
equidistant
equilateral
equilibrium
equine
equinoks   equinox
equinox
equip[3] /ment
equitabl e /y
equitabul   equitable[+]
equit y /ies
equivalen ce /t
equivalens   equivalence[+]
equivocal /ly
equivocat e[2] /ion/or
equmenical   ecumenical
er   err[1]
era /s
eradicat e[2] /ion/or
erand   errand
erant   errant
eras e[2] /er/ure
erasher   erasure
erata   errata
eratic   erratic[+]
eratum   erratum[+]
erban   urban
erbane   urbane[+]
erbanise   urbanise[2+]
erbanitey   urbanity

epok   epoch[+]
    epaulet

107

erchin	urchin
ere * (before)	
erecshun	erection
erect [1] /ile/or	
erection	
erer	error
erge	urge [2+]
ergency	urgency
ergensey	urgency
ergent	urgent
erie	eerie *
erie	eyrie *
ering	ear-ring
erk	irk [1+]
erksome	irksome
erksum	irksome
erl	earl [+]
erlier	earlier [+]
erly	early [+]
ermine	
ern	earn [1*+]
ern	urn *
ernest	earnest [+]
erode [2]	
eroneous	erroneous [+]
eronius	erroneous [+]
eror	error
eroshun	erosion
erosion	
erotic /a/ally/ism	
err [1]	
errand	
errant	
erratic /ally	
errat um /a (pl.)	
erroneous /ly	
erronius	erroneous [+]
error	
erstwhile	
erstwile	erstwhile
erth	earth [1+]
erthen	earthen [+]
erthley	earthly [+]
erthquake	earthquake
erudishun	erudition

erudit e /ely/ion	
erupt [1] /ion/ive	
erwig	earwig
esay	essay [1+]
escalat e [2] /ion/or	
escallop [1]	
escapade	
escape [2] /ment	
escapis m /t	
escarpment	
eschew [1]	
eschu	eschew [1]
escort [1]	
esel	easel
esence	essence
esens	essence
esenshal	essential [+]
esential	essential [+]
eshelon	echelon
eshoo	eschew [1]
Eskimo /s (pl.)	
eskwire	esquire
esofagus	esophagus
esophagus	
esoteric /ally/ism	
especial /ly	
espeshal	especial [+]
espi	espy [4]
espionage	
esplanade	
esplanaid	esplanade
espous e [2] /al	
espowse	espouse [2+]
espresso	
esp y [4]	
esquire	
essay [1] /s/ist	
essence	
essens	essence
essenshal	essential [+]
essential /ly	
est	east [+]
establish [1] /able/ment	
estate	
esteam	esteem [1]

108

esteem [1]	
Ester	Easter
estern	eastern [+]
esthet	aesthete [+]
esthetic	aesthetic
estimable	
estimabul	estimable
estimat *e* [2] /ion/or	
estrange [2] /ment	
estuar *y* /ies	
et cetera	
etch [1] /er	
ete	eat [+]
eternal /ly	
eternit *y* /ies	
ether /eal	
ether	either
ethic /al/ally/s	
ethnic /ally	
ethnolog *y* /ical	
etholog *y* /ical	
ethos	
etiket	etiquette
etimology	etymology [+]
etiquet	etiquette
etiquette	
etsetera	et cetera
etymolog *y* /ical/ist	
eucalyptus /es	
Eucharist	
Euclid	
eufemism	euphemism
eufoney	euphony [+]
eufonious	euphonious
eufonius	euphonious
eufony	euphony [+]
euforia	euphoria [+]
euforic	euphoric
eugenic /ally/s	
Eukarist	Eucharist
Euklid	Euclid
eulogey	eulogy [+]
eulogis *e* [2] /m	
eulogistic /ally	
eulog *y* /ies	

eunuch	
euphemism	
euphemistic /ally	
euphon *y* /ious	
euphori *a* /c	
Eurashun	Eurasian
Eurasian	
eurhythmics	
eurithmics	eurhythmics
European	
euthanasia	
evacuashun	evacuation
evacuat *e* [2] /ion	
evacuee	
evad *e* [2] /able	
evaluat *e* [2] /ion	
evangelic /al/ally	
evangelis *e* [2] /m/t	
evanjelic	evangelic [+]
evaperate	evaporate [2+]
evaporat *e* [2] /ion/or	
evaquee	evacuee
evashun	evasion
evasion	
evasive /ly/ness	
eve	
even [1] /ly/ness	
even *song* /tide	
event /ful	
eventual /ly	
eventualit *y* /ies	
ever /green/lasting	
evermore	
every /body/day/one	
every *thing* /where	
eves	eaves
evesdrop	eavesdrop [3+]
evict [1] /ion	
eviden *ce* [2] /tial	
evidens	evidence [2+]
evident /ly	
evil /ly	
evince [2]	
evins	evince [2]
evocat *ion* /ive	

109

evoke²		excoriat *e* ² /ion	
evolushun	evolution +	excrement	
evolushunist	evolutionist	excrescence	
evolution /ary/ist		excresens	excrescence
evolve²		excreta	
evrie	every +	excret *e* ² /ion	
evry	every +	excruciating /ly	
ewe * (sheep)		excrushiating	excruciating +
ewe	yew *	excursion /ist	
ewe	you *	excus *e* ² /able/ably	
exacerbat *e* ² /ion		exebition	exhibition +
exacrabul	execrable	execrable	
exact¹ /itude/ly/ness		execrabul	execrable
exaggerat *e* ² /ion/or		execrat *e* ² /ion	
exalt¹ /ation		execut *e* ² /ant/or/rix (fem.)	
examination		execution /er	
examine² /r		executive	
example		exemplary	
exampul	example	exemplif *y* ⁴ /ication	
exaserbate	exacerbate ²+	exempt¹ /ion	
exasperat *e* ² /ion		exentric	eccentric +
excavat *e* ² /ion/or		exentricitey	eccentricity
exceed¹ /ingly		exercise²	
excel³		exert¹ /ion	
excellen *ce* /t		exhal *e* ² /ation	
excellenc *y* /ies		exhaust¹ /ion	
excellens	excellence +	exhaust *ible* /ive	
excellensey	excellency +	exhibit¹ /or	
excepshun	exception +	exhibition /er	
except¹		exhibitionis *m* /t	
exception /able/al/ally		exhilara *te* /nt/tion	
excerpt¹		exhort¹ /ation	
excess /ive/ively		exhum *e* ² /ation	
exchange² /able/r		exibition	exhibition +
exchequer		exigence	
excis *e* ² /able/ion		exigenc *y* /ies	
excitab *le* /ility		exigens	exigence
excitabul	excitable +	exigensey	exigency +
excite² /dly/ment		exigu *ous* /ity	
exclaim¹		exile²	
exclamashun	exclamation +	exist¹ /ence/ent	
exclamat *ion* /ory		existens	existence
exclu *de* ² /sion		exit¹	
exclusiv *e* /ely/ity		exkwisit	exquisite +
excommunicat *e* ² /ion		exonerat *e* ² /ion	

exorbitan *ce* /t
exorcise² /r
exorcis *m* /t
exorsism   exorcism⁺
exorst   exhaust¹⁺
exorstibul   exhaustible⁺
exort   exhort¹⁺
exortashun   exhortation
exoteric
exotic /ness
expand¹
expans *e* /ion
expanshun   expansion
expansive /ly/ness
expatriat *e*² /ion
expect¹ /ation
expectanc *e* /y
expectans   expectance⁺
expectant /ly
expedien *ce* /t
expedienc *y* /ies
expediens   expedience⁺
expedishun   expedition
expedishus   expeditious⁺
expedite² /r
expedition
expeditious /ly/ness
expel³
expend¹ /iture
expendab *le* /ility
expendabul   expendable⁺
expendicher   expenditure
expens *e* /ive
experience²
experiens   experience²
experiment¹ /ation
experimental /ly
expert /ise/ly
expiat *e*² /ion
expir *e*² /ation/y
explain¹ /able
explanashun   explanation⁺
explanat *ion* /ory
explane   explain¹⁺
explanetrey   explanatory

expletive
explicabl *e* /y
explicabul   explicable⁺
explicit /ly
explisit   explicit⁺
explode²
exploit¹ /ation/er
explorashun   exploration⁺
explorat *ion* /ory
explore² /r
exploshun   explosion⁺
explos *ion* /ive
exponent
export¹ /ation/er
expos *e*² /ure
exposher   exposure
expostulat *e*² /ion
expound¹
expreshun   expression⁺
expresibul   expressible⁺
expresive   expressive⁺
express¹
expressibl *e* /y
expression /less
expressive /ly
expresso   espresso
expropriat *e*² /ion/or
expulsion
expunge²
expurgate²
expurgat *ion* /ory
expurt   expert⁺
exquisite /ly/ness
exseed   exceed¹⁺
exsel   excel³
exselence   excellence⁺
exselens   excellence⁺
ex-service
exstravagans   extravagance⁺
exsurpt   excerpt¹
extant
extasey   ecstasy⁺
extatic   ecstatic⁺
extempor *e* /aneous
extemporis *e*² /ation

extend[1] /ible		eye[2]*† /ball/brow/s *†	
extenshun	extension	†(sight)	
extension		eyeglass /es	
extensive /ly		eyelash /es	
extent		eyelet * (hole for lace)	
extenuat e[2] /ion		eyelet	islet *
exterier	exterior	eye lid /sight	
exterior		eye-opener	
exterminat e[2] /ion/or		eye-witness	
external /ly		eyrie * (bird's nest)	
exterpate	extirpate [2]+	eyrie	eerie *
extinct /ion		eze	ease[2]
extinguish[1] /er		ezel	easel
extingwish	extinguish [1]+	ezier	easier
extirpat e[2] /ion		ezy	easy +
extol[3]			
extorshun	extortion +	**F**	
extort[1]			
extortion /ate/er/ist			
extra		fable /d	
extract[1] /ible/ion/or		fabric	
extradishun	extradition	fabricat e[2] /ion/or	
extradit e[2] /able/ion		fabul	fable +
extramural		fabulous /ly	
extraneous /ly/ness		fabulus	fabulous +
extranius	extraneous +	façade	
extraordinar y /ily		face[2] /less	
extra-sensory		faceshus	facetious +
extravagan ce /t/tly		facet /ed	
extravaganza		facetious /ly	
extrawdinrey	extraordinary +	facia * (shop-front)	
extream	extreme +	facia	fascia *
extreme /ly		facial /ly	
extremist		facile	
extremit y /ies		facilitat e[2] /ion	
extricable		facilit y /ies	
extricabul	extricable	facshun	faction +
extricat e[2] /ion		facshus	factious
extrordinary	extraordinary +	facsimile /s	
extrover t /sion		fact /ual/ually	
exuberan ce /t		factio n /us	
exuberans	exuberance +	factishus	factitious
exud e[2] /ation		factitious	
exult[1] /ant/ation		factor	
exume	exhume [2]+	factor y /ies	

facultative	
facult *y* /ies	
fad /dish/dy	
fade²	
faec *es* /al	
faeton	phaeton
fag³ /-end	
faggot /-stitch	
fagot	faggot⁺
Fahrenheit	
fail¹ /ure	
failier	failure
faim	fame²
faimus	famous⁺
fain ★ (glad)	
fain	feign¹★
faint¹★ (unconscious)	
faint	feint¹★
faint-hearted	
fair¹★ (beauty, just)	
fair	fare²★
fair *er* /est/way	
fairie	fairy⁺
fairwell	farewell
fair *y* /ies	
fairy *land* /tale	
fait	fate²★
faitful	fateful⁺
faith /ful/fully	
faithless /ly	
fake² /r★ (deceiver)	
fakir ★ (holy man)	
fal	fall⁺
falacious	fallacious
falacy	fallacy⁺
falanks	phalanx⁺
falanx	phalanx⁺
falasey	fallacy⁺
falashus	fallacious
falcon /er/ry	
fale	fail¹⁺
falibility	fallibility
falible	fallible⁺
falibul	fallible⁺
falic	phallic

fall /en/er/ing/-out	
fallacious	
fallac *y* /ies	
fallasey	fallacy⁺
fallib *le* /ility	
fallibul	fallible⁺
fallow¹	
fallus	phallus⁺
falout	fall-out
falow	fallow¹
fals	false⁺
false /hood/ly/r/st	
falsetto /s	
falsif *y*⁴ /ication/ier	
falsit *y* /ies	
falt	fault¹⁺
falter¹	
falure	failure
falus	phallus⁺
fam *e*²	
familey	family⁺
familiar /ity	
familiaris *e*² /ation	
familiaritey	familiarity
familier	familiar⁺
famil *y* /ies	
famine	
famish¹	
famous /ly/ness	
famus	famous⁺
fan³ /-belt	
fanatic /al/ally/ism	
fanatisism	fanaticism
fanci *er* /est/ly/ness	
fanciful /ly	
fanc *y*⁴ /ies	
fane	feign¹★
fanfair	fanfare
fanfare	
fansie	fancy⁴⁺
fansier	fancier⁺
fansiful	fanciful⁺
fansy	fancy⁴⁺
fant	faint¹★
fantasey	fantasy⁺

fantasia		fascia ★ (architecture)	
fantasm	phantasm	fascia	facia ★
fantasmagoria	phantasmagoria +	fascinat e ² /ion	
fantastic /ally		fascis m /t	
fantas y /ies		fase	face ²+
fantharted	faint-hearted	fase	phase ²
fantom	phantom	fasees	fasces
far /-fetched/-flung		fasen	fasten ¹+
farad /ay		fasener	fastener
farc e ² /ical/ically		faseshus	facetious +
fare ²★ (get along)		faset	facet +
fare	fair ¹★	fasetious	facetious +
Farenheight	Fahrenheit	fasha -	facia ★
Farenhite	Fahrenheit	fasha	fascia ★
farer	fairer +	fashal	facial +
farewell		fashion ¹ /able/ably	
fariland	fairyland +	fashism	fascism +
faringeal	pharyngeal +	fashist	fascist
faringitis	pharyngitis	fashon	fashion ¹+
farinks	pharynx	fashonable	fashionable
farinx	pharynx	fashonabul	fashionable
farisee	Pharisee +	fasile	facile
faritale	fairy-tale	fasilitate	facilitate ²+
farm ¹ /er/house		fasilitey	facility +
farmacist	pharmacist	fasinashun	fascination
farmacologey	pharmacology +	fasinate	fascinate ²+
farmacopea	pharmacopoeia	fasination	fascination
farmacy	pharmacy +	fast ¹	
farmasey	pharmacy +	fasten ¹ /er	
farmasist	pharmacist	fastidious /ly/ness	
farmasutic	pharmaceutic +	fastidius	fastidious +
farm stead /yard		fat ³ /ness/ter/test/ty	
faro	Pharaoh	fatal /ism/ly	
farse	farce ²+	fatalist /ic/ically	
farshal	farcical	fatalit y /ies	
far-sighted		fate ²★ (destiny)	
farth er ★† /est		fate	fête ²★
†(distant)		fateeg	fatigue ²
farther	father ¹★	fateful /ly	
farthing /gale		faten	fatten ¹
faryngeal	pharyngeal +	fath	faith +
faryngitis	pharyngitis	father ¹★ (parent)	
farynx	pharynx	father	farther ★+
fasade	façade	father hood /land	
fasces		father(s)-in-law	

father *less* /ly	
fathom¹ /able	
fatig	fatigue²
fatigue²	
faton	phaeton
fatten¹	
fatuous /ly	
fatuus	fatuous⁺
faty	fatty
faucet	
fault¹ /ily/less/y	
faun* (Roman god)	
faun	fawn¹*
fauna	
faux pas	
faver	favour¹⁺
faverable	favourable
faverabul ·	favourable
faverit	favourite⁺
faveritism	favouritism
favour¹ /able/ably	
favourit *e* /ism	
favrable	favourable
fawn¹* (young deer)	
fawn	faun*
fawna	fauna
fay* (fairy)	
fay	fey*
fayton	phaeton
fea	fee
feacher	feature²⁺
fealty	
fear¹ /less/some	
fearful /ly	
feasable	feasible⁺
feasib *le* /ility/ly	
feasibul	feasible⁺
feast¹	
feat* (act)	
feat	feet*
feather¹ /weight/y	
featherbed /ding	
feature² /less	
February	
Febuary	February

febus	Phoebus
feces	faeces⁺
fech	fetch¹
feckless	
fecund /ity	
fed /-up	
federal /ism/ist/ly	
federalis *e*² /ation	
federat *e*² /ion	
fee	
feeble /r/st	
feebul	feeble⁺
feed /back/er/ing	
feef	fief
feel /er/ing	
feeld	field¹⁺
feend	fiend⁺
feest	feast¹
feet* (pl. of foot)	
feet	feat*
feetle	foetal
feetus	foetus⁺
feif	fief
feign¹* (invent)	
feign	fain*
feild	field¹⁺
feildmarshal	field-marshal
feind	fiend⁺
feint¹* (pretend)	
feint	faint¹*
fekless	feckless
fekund	fecund⁺
fekunditey	fecundity
fel	fell
fela	fellah
felial	filial⁺
felicitat *e*² /ion	
felicit *y* /ous	
feline	
felisitate	felicitate²⁺
felisitey	felicity⁺
felisitus	felicitous
fell	
fellah	
fellow /ship	

felon /ious		fertil e /ity	
felon y /ies		fertilis e [2] /ation/er	
felow	fellow +	fertiv	furtive +
felt		ferule	ferrule
femail	female	ferus	ferrous
female		ferven cy /t	
femer	femur	ferver	fervour
feminin e /ity		fervour	
feminis m /t		fery	ferry [4]+
femur		fes	fez
fence [2] /r		fesant	pheasant
fenel	fennel	fesees	faeces +
feniks	phoenix	fesible	feasible+
fenix	phoenix	fesibul	feasible +
fennel		fester [1]	
fenobarbitone	phenobarbitone	festiv e /al	
fenol	phenol	festivit y /ies	
fenomenon	phenomenon +	festoon [1]	
fenomina	phenomena	fetch [1]	
fenominal	phenomenal +	fête [2]★ (festival)	
fense	fence [2]+	fête	fate [2]★
fer	fir ★	feter	fetter [1]
fer	fur ★	fether	feather [1]+
feret	ferret [1]	fetherbed	featherbed +
feric	ferric +	fetherwait	featherweight
ferie	ferry [4]+	fetid	
feris wheel	Ferris-wheel	fetish /ism/ist	
ferite	ferrite	fetlock	
ferl	furl [1]	fetter [1]	
ferlong	furlong	fettle [2]	
ferment [1] /ation		fetul	fettle [2]
fermium		feud [1]	
fern /ery		feudal /ism	
fernis	furnace	fever /ed/ish	
feroci ous /ty		few	
feroshus	ferocious +	fewdal	feudal +
ferositey	ferocity	fewdalism	feudalism
ferous	ferrous	fey ★ (fated to die)	
ferret [1]		fey	fay ★
ferr ic /ous		fez	
Ferris-wheel		fezant	pheasant
ferrite		fial	file [2]★+
ferrule		fial	phial ★
ferry [4] /ies		fiancé /e (fem.)	
ferthest	furthest	fiansay	fiancé +

116

fiasco /s	
fib [3] /ber	
fiber	fibre +
fibr e /ous	
fibreglass	
fibrus	fibrous
fibula	
fickle /ness	
ficshun	fiction +
fiction /al	
fictishus	fictitious +
fictitious /ly/ness	
ficul	fickle +
fiddl e [2] /er/y	
fiddlesticks	
fidelity	
fidget [1] /iness/y	
fidle	fiddle [2]+
fidul	fiddle [2]+
fie	
fief	
field [1] /-day/er	
field-marshal	
fiend /ish	
fierce /ly/ness/r/st	
fierey	fiery +
fierse	fierce +
fier y /ier/iest/ily	
fife	
fifteen /th	
fiftey	fifty +
fifth	
fift y /ies/ieth	
figer	figure [2]+
figerativ	figurative +
figerhead	figurehead
figerhed	figurehead
figet	fidget [1]+
fight /er/ing	
figment	
figurative /ly	
figure [2] /head	
fiks	fix [1]+
fiksashun	fixation +
fiksation	fixation +

fiksativ	fixative
fikscher	fixture
filament	
filander	philander [1]+
filanthropey	philanthropy +
filanthropic	philanthropic
filanthropist	philanthropist
filantropy	philanthropy +
filarmonic	philharmonic
filateley	philately +
filatelist	philatelist
filch [1]	
file [2]* (tool, folder) /r	
file	phial *
filet	fillet [1]
filharmonic	philharmonic
filial /ly	
filibuster [1]	
filie	filly +
filigree	
filip	fillip
filistine	Philistine
fill [1] /er	
fillet [1]	
fillip	
fill y /ies	
film [1] /y	
film-star	
film-strip	
filologey	philology +
filosofer	philosopher +
filosofey	philosophy
filosofical	philosophical +
filosofise	philosophise [2]
filosopher	philosopher +
filosophical	philosophical +
filosophise	philosophise [2]
filosophy	philosophy
filter [1]* (pass, strainer)	
filter	philtre *
filth /ier/iest/ily/iness/y	
filtrat e [2] /ion	
filum	phylum
fily	filly +
fin /ned/ny	

117

final ★ (at last)
finale ★ (the end)
finalis *e* ² /t
finalit *y* /ies
finally
financ *e* ² /ier
financial /ly
finans   finance ²⁺
finanshul   financial ⁺
finansier   financier
finch /es
find /er/ing
fine ² /r/ry/st
finerey   finery
finess   finesse
finesse
finger ¹ /print/tips
finicky
finikey   finicky
finish ¹ /er
finite
fiord
fir ★ (tree)
fir   fur ★
fire ² /arm/place/work
fire-brigade
fire-engine
fire-escape
fire-extinguisher
firefl *y* /ies
firm ¹ /er/est/ness
firmament
first /-aid/-class/-rate
firth
firy   fiery ⁺
fiscal /ism/ly
fiscul   fiscal ⁺
fiseek   physique ★
fish ¹ /ier/iest/iness/y
fisher   fissure
fisherm *an* /en (pl.)
fisher *y* /ies
fi•h- *hook* /monger
fishmunger   fishmonger
fishun   fission ⁺

fisic   physic ★
fisic   physique ★
fisical   physical ⁺
fisician   physician
fisicist   physicist
fisics   physics
fisile   fissile
fisiologey   physiology ⁺
fision   fission ⁺
fisionomey   physiognomy
fisiotherapey   physiotherapy
fisiotherapist   physiotherapist ⁺
fisique   physique ★
fisishun   physician
fisisist   physicist
fissile
fission /able
fissure
fit ³ /ment/ness/ter/test
fite   fight ⁺
fitful /ly
five /pence/r
fix ¹ /edly
fixat *ion* /ive
fixcher   fixture
fixture
fiy   fie
fizle   fizzle ²
fizul   fizzle ²
fizz ¹ /y
fizzle ²
fjord
flabbergast ¹
flabb *y* /ier/iest/iness
flabergast   flabbergast ¹
flabie   flabby ⁺
flaby   flabby⁺
flaccid /ity/ness
flag ³ /ship/staff
flagellate ²
flagon
flagrancy
flagransey   flagrancy
flagrant /ly
flail ¹

flair * (instinct)
flair | flare [2]*
flak *e* [2] /iness/y
flaks | flax [+]
flaksen | flaxen
flaksid | flaccid [+]
flamable | flammable
flamabul | flammable
flamboiant | flamboyant
flamboyan *ce* /cy/t
flamboyans | flamboyance [+]
flame [2]
flamingo /es
flammable
flammabul | flammable
flanel | flannel [3+]
flange [2]
flank [1]
flanle | flannel [3+]
flannel [3] /ette/graph
flanul | flannel [3+]
flap [3] /per
flare [2]* (light)
flare | flair *
flash [1] /ier/iest/ily/y
flash *back* /light
flask
flat /let/ly/test
flaten | flatten [1]
flater | flatter [1+]
flatten [1]
flatter [1] /er
flatulen *ce* /t
flatulens | flatulence [+]
flaunt [1]
flautist
flaver | flavour [1]
flavour [1]
flaw [1]* (blemish) /less
flaw | floor [1]*
flax /en
flay [1]
flea * (insect)
flea | flee *
flea-bite

fleat
flebitis | phlebitis
fled
fledgling
flee * (run) /ing
flee | flea *
fleec *e* [2] /y
flees | fleece [2+]
fleet /ing
flegling | fledgling
flegm | phlegm[+]
flegmatic | phlegmatic
fleks | flex [1]
fleksible | flexible [+]
fleksibul | flexible [+]
flem | phlegm [+]
Flemish
fler de lis | fleur-de-lis
flert | flirt [1+]
flesh /iness/y
fleur-de-lis
flew * (flight)
flew | flu *
flew | flue *
flex [1]
flexib *le* /ility/ly
flexibul | flexible [+]
fli | fly [+]
flick [1]
flicker [1]
flier | flyer
flight /iness/y
flimsie | flimsy [+]
flims *y* /ier/iest/ily/iness
flinch [1]
fling
flint /y
flipancy | flippancy [+]
flipansey | flippancy [+]
flipant | flippant
fliper | flipper
flippan *cy* /t
flipper
flirt [1] /ation/atious
flit [3]

fleet [+]
phlebitis

flea *

fleece [2+]

fledgling
phlegm+
phlegmatic
flex [1]
flexible [+]
flexible [+]
phlegm [+]

fleur-de-lis
flirt [1+]

flu *
flue *

flexible [+]
fly [+]

flyer

flimsy [+]

flippancy [+]
flippancy [+]
flippant
flipper

119

flite	flight +
flo	floe ★
flo	flow ¹★+
float ¹	
flock ¹ /s ★ (groups)	
flocks	phlox ★
floe ★ (ice)	
floem	phloem
flog ³	
flood ¹ /-gate/lit	
floodlight /ing	
flooid	fluid +
floor ¹★ (in room)	
floor	flaw ¹★+
flooride	fluoride
floorine	fluorine +
floot	flute
flop ³ /pily/py	
flora /l/lly	
Florentine	
florescen ce /t	
floresens	florescence +
floresent	florescent
florid	
floridate	fluoridate ²+
florin	
florist	
floss /y	
flotashun	flotation
flotation	
flote	float ¹
flotila	flotilla
flotilla	
flotsam	
flotsum	flotsam
flounce ²	
flounder ¹	
flouns	flounce ²
flour ¹★ (powder)	
flour	flower ¹★+
flourey	flowery
flourish ¹	
flout ¹	
flow ¹★ (to move) /n	
flow	floe ★

flower ¹★ (plant) /y	
flower	flour ¹★
flownder	flounder ¹
flownse	flounce ²
flowt	flout ¹
flox	phlox ★
flu ★ (cold)	
flu	flew ★
flu	flue ★
fluctuashun	fluctuation
fluctuat e ² /ion	
flud	flood ¹+
fludlight	floodlight +
fludlite	floodlight +
flue ★ (pipe)	
flue	flew ★
flue	flu ★
fluen cy /t	
fluff /iness/y	
fluid /ity	
fluke ²	
fluks	flux
flummox ¹	
flumuks	flummox ¹
flumux	flummox ¹
flung	
fluorescen ce /t	
fluoridat e ² /ion	
fluori ne /de	
flurie	flurry ⁴+
flurish	flourish ¹
flurr y ⁴ /ies	
flurt	flirt ¹+
flurtashun	flirtation
flurtation	flirtation
flury	flurry ⁴+
flush ¹	
fluster ¹	
flute	
flutter ¹	
fluvial	
flux	
fl y /ies/yer/ying	
flycatcher	
flylea f /ves (pl.)	

fly *weight* /wheel	
fo	foe +
foal¹	
foam¹	
fob³	
fobia	phobia
focal	
focus¹ /er	
fodder¹	
foder	fodder¹
foe /s	
foet *us* /al	
fog³ /horn	
fogg *y* /ier/iest/ily/iness	
foible	
foibul	foible
foier	foyer
foil¹	
foist¹	
foks	fox +
fold¹ /er	
fole	foal¹
foliage	
foliat *e*² /ion	
folie	folly +
foliidge	foliage
folio¹ /s	
folk /-dance/-song	
folklor *e* /ist	
follow¹ /er	
foll *y* /ies	
folow	follow¹+
foly	folly +
fome	foam¹
foment¹ /ation/er	
fon	phon *
fond /er/est/ly/ness	
fondant	
fondle²	
fondul	fondle²
fone	phone²*
fonetic	phonetic +
fonie	phony
fonograf	phonograph +
fonografic	phonographic
fonograph	phonograph +
fonographic	phonographic
fonologey	phonology +
font	
fony	phony
food /s	
fool¹ /proof	
foolhard *y* /iness	
foolscap	
foot¹ /fall/hold/note	
football /er	
foot *path* /print	
foot *sore* /step/stool	
fop /pish	
for * (on behalf of)	
for	fore *
for	four *+
for ever	
forage² /r	
foram *en* /ina (pl.)	
forarm	forearm¹
forbade	
forbarance	forbearance
forbare	forbear +
forbear /ance/ing	
forbid /den/ding	
forbode	forebode²+
forbore	
forcasel	forecastle
forcast	forecast¹+
forcastle	forecastle
forc *e*² /ible/ibly	
forceful /ly/ness	
forceps	
forclose	foreclose²+
ford¹ /able	
fore * (golf)	
fore	four *+
forearm¹	
forebode² /r	
forecast¹ /er	
forecastle	
foreclos *e*² /ure	
fored	forehead
forefathers	

121

forefinger	
forefoot	
forefront	
forego *(preceed)/ing*/ne*	
forego	forgo *+
foreground	
forehand	
forehead	
foreign /er/ness	
foreknowledge	
foreland	
foreleg	
forelock	
forem *an* /en (pl.)	
foremast	
foremost	
foren	foreign +
forener	foreigner
forenoledge	foreknowledge
forensic	
forerunner	
foresail	
foresaw	
foresee /able/ing/n	
foreshadow 1	
foreshorten 1	
foresight	
foresite	foresight
foreskin	
forest 1 /ation/er/ry	
forestall 1	
foretaste 2	
foretell	
forethought	
foretold	
forewarn 1	
foreword * (preface)	
foreword	forward 1*
forfathers	forefathers
forfeit 1 /ure	
forficher	forfeiture
forfinger	forefinger
forfit	forfeit 1+
forfiture	forfeiture
forfoot	forefoot

forfront	forefront
forfrunt	forefront
forgather 1	
forgave	
forge 2 /r	
forger *y* /ies	
forget /table/ting	
forgetful /ness	
forget-me-not	
forgiv *e* /able/eness/ing	
forgo *(waive)/ing*/ne*	
forgo	forego *+
forgot /ten	
forground	foreground
forhand	forehand
forhead	forehead
forhed	forehead
forige	forage 2+
forin	foreign +
fork 1	
forland	foreland
forleg	foreleg
forlock	forelock
forlorn	
form 1 /al/ation	
formalis *e* 2 /ation	
formalit *y* /ies	
formally *†	
†(conventionally)	
formally	formerly *
forman	foreman +
format	
formative	
former /ly *†	
†(before now)	
formerly	formally *
formic	
formidabl *e* /y	
formidabul	formidable +
formost	foremost
formula /e/s (pls.)	
formulat *e* 2 /ion	
forn	faun *
forn	fawn 1*
fornicat *e* 2 /ion	

fornolidge	foreknowledge
forruner	forerunner
forsable	forcible
forsail	foresail
forsak e /en/ing	
forsaw	foresaw
forse	force [2]+
forsee	foresee +
forseps	forceps
forsful	forceful +
forshadow	foreshadow [1]
forshorten	foreshorten [1]
forsible	forcible
forsite	foresight
forsithia	forsythia
forskin	foreskin
forsook	
forstall	forestall [1]
forsythia	
fort ★ (military)	
fort	fought ★
fortaste	foretaste [2]
forte ★ (strong point)	
forteen	fourteen +
fortel	foretell
forth ★ (forward)	
forth	fourth ★
forthcoming	
forthort	forethought
forth right /with	
fortie	forty +
fortif y [4] /ication/ier	
Fortin barometer	
fortissimo	
fortitude	
fortnight /ly	
fortnite	fortnight +
fortold	foretold
fortress	
fortuitous /ly	
fortuitus	fortuitous +
fortun e [2] /ate/ately	
fort y /ies/ieth	
forum	
forward [1]★ (advance)	

forward	foreword ★
forwarn	forewarn [1]
forwent	
forword	foreword ★
fosfate	phosphate
fosforesce	phosphoresce [2]+
fosforescent	phosphorescent
fosforess	phosphoresce [2]+
fosforus	phosphorous ★+
fosforus	phosphorus ★
fosil	fossil
fosilise	fossilise [2]+
fosphate	phosphate
fossil	
fossilis e [2] /ation	
foster [1] /-father/-mother	
foto	photo +
fotocopy	photocopy +
fotoelectric	photo-electric
fotofinish	photo-finish
fotogenic	photogenic
fotograf	photograph [1]+
fotografey	photography
fotograph	photograph [1]+
fotometer	photometer +
fotometrey	photometry
foton	photon
fotosinthesis	photosynthesis
fotostat	photostat
fototropism	phototropism
fought ★ (did fight)	
foul [1]★ (dirty) /ly/ness	
foul	fowl [1]★+
found [1] /ation/er/ling	
foundr y /ies	
fount	
fountain	
four ★ (number) /th ★	
four fold /some	
fourt	fort ★
fourt	fought ★
fourteen /th	
fourth	forth ★
fourty	forty +
fow	foe +

123

fowl [1]* (bird) /er	
fowl	foul [1]*+
fownd	found [1]+
fowndashun	foundation
fowndation	foundation
fowndrey	foundry +
fownt	fount
fowntain	fountain
fox-hunt /ing	
fox-terrier	
foyble	foible
foyer	
fracshun	fraction +
fracshus	fractious
fraction /al/ally	
fractious	
fracture [2]	
fraeltey	frailty
fragile /ly	
fragility	
fragment [1] /ary/ation	
fragran ce /t	
fragrans	fragrance +
frail /ty/ties	
frait	freight +
frame [2] /work	
franc * (money)	
franchise [2]	
francium	
frank [1]* (blunt) /ly/ness	
frankfurter	
frankincense	
frankium	francium
frantic /ally	
frase	phrase [2]*+
frasologey	phraseology
frate	freight +
fraternal /ly	
fraternis e [2] /ation	
fraternit y /ies	
fraud	
fraudulen ce /t	
fraudulens	fraudulence +
fraught	
fraut	fraught

frawd	fraud
frawdulence	fraudulence +
frawdulens	fraudulence +
frawdulent	fraudulent
frawt	fraught
fray [1] /s * (fights)	
frayl	frail +
frays	phrase [2]*+
freak [1] /ish	
freckle [2]	
frecul	freckle [2]
free /d/ing/ly/r/st	
freedom	
free-hand	
freehold /er	
freek	freak [1]+
freelance [2]	
freelans	freelance [2]
freemason /ry	
free-wheel [1]	
freez e * (cold) /er/ing	
freeze	frieze *
freight /age/er	
freind	friend +
frekwency	frequency +
frekwensey	frequency +
frekwent	frequent [1]+
French /man/woman	
frend	friend +
frendly	friendly +
frendship	friendship
frenetic	phrenetic
frenologey	phrenology +
frenologist	phrenologist
frenzie	frenzy +
frenz y /ies/ied	
frequenc y /ies	
frequensey	frequency +
frequent [1] /er/ly	
fresco /es	
fresh /er/ly/ness	
freshen [1]	
fresko	fresco +
fret [3] /ful/fully	
fret -saw /work	

124

Freudian		frostbit*e* /ten	
fri	fry[4]	froth[1] /iness/y	
friable		frown[1]	
friabul	friable	frowzie	frowzy[+]
friar		frowz*y* /ier/iest	
fricshun	friction[+]	froze /n	
friction /al		frugal /ity/ly	
friend /ship		fruishun	fruition
friendl*y* /ier/iest/iness		fruit[1] /ion	
frier	friar	fruiterer	
frieze * (ornament)		fruitful /ly/ness	
frigate		fruitless /ly/ness	
fright		fruit*y* /ier/iest/iness	
frighten[1]		frump /ish	
frightful /ly/ness		frunt	front[1+]
frigid /ity		fruntal	frontal
frill[1]		fruntier	frontier
fringe[2]		fruntispiece	frontispiece
fripper*y* /ies		frustrat*e*[2] /ion	
frisk[1] /ily/iness/y		frut	fruit[1+]
frite	fright	fruterer	fruiterer
friteful	frightful[+]	frutful	fruitful[+]
friten	frighten[1]	frutie	fruity[+]
friter	fritter[1+]	frutier	fruiterer
fritter[1] /er		fry[4]	
frivol[3] /ous		fu	few
frivolit*y* /ies		fucher	future[+]
frivolus	frivolous	fucherist	futurist[+]
frizul	frizzle[2+]	fucheristic	futuristic
frizz /y		fuchsia	
frizzl*e*[2] /y		fudal	feudal[+]
frock[1]		fudalism	feudalism
frog /man/men (pl.)		fuddle[2]	
froidian	Freudian	fude	feud[1]
frolic /some		fudge[2]	
frolick *ed* /ing		fudul	fuddle[2]
front[1] /age/al/ally		fuel[3]	
frontier		fug /gy	
frontispiece		fugitive	
froogal	frugal[+]	ful	full[+]
frooishun	fruition	fulblooded	full-blooded
frooition	fruition	fulbluded	full-blooded
froot	fruit[1+]	fulcrum	
frootful	fruitful[+]	fulfil[3] /ment	
frost[1] /ily/y		full /-blooded/er/-time	

fulscap	foolscap	furst	first +
fulsome /ly/ness		furstaid	first-aid
fulsum	fulsome +	furstrate	first-rate
fumble ² /r		furth	firth
fumbul	fumble ²+	further ¹ /more/most	
fume ²		furtherance	
fumigat e ² /ion/or		furtherans	furtherance
fun /nily/ny		furtive /ly	
funcshun	function ¹+	fur y /ies/ious	
funcshunrey	functionary	furze	
function ¹ /ary		fus	fuss ¹+
functional /ly		fus e ² /ion	
fund ¹		fuselage	
fundamental /ly		fusha	fuchsia
funel	funnel ³	fusib le /ility	
funer al /eal		fusibul	fusible +
fung us /i (pl.)		fusie	fussy
funicular		fusier	fussier +
funiculer	funicular	fusilade	fusillade
funily	funnily	fusilage	fuselage
funk ¹		fusilier	
funnel ³		fusilige	fuselage
funn y /ier/iest/ily		fusillade	
fur ★ (coat)		fuss ¹ /y	
fur	fir ★	fussie	fussy
furie	furry +	fussi er /est/ly/ness	
furie	fury +	fustie	fusty +
furier	furrier	fust y /ier/iest/ily/iness	
furious /ly		fusy	fussy
furius	furious +	futil e /ity	
furl ¹		futur e /ism/ity	
furlong		futurist /ic	
furm	firm ¹+	fuzz /ily/iness	
furmament	firmament	fwayay	foyer
furment	ferment ¹+	fyord	fiord
furmentashun	fermentation	fyord	fjord
furmentation	fermentation	fysical	physical +
furn	fern +	fysically	physically
furnace		fysician	physician
furnicher	furniture	fysicist	physicist
furnis	furnace	fysick	physic ★
furnish ¹ /er		fysick	physique ★
furniture		fysicks	physics
furrow ¹		fysicley	physically
furr y /ier/iest/iness		fysiologey	physiology +

126

fysionomey	physiognomy
fysiotherapey	physiotherapy
fysiotherapist	physiotherapist +
fysique	physique *
fysishun	physician
fysisist	physicist

G

gabardine	
gabble 2* (talk) /r	
gable 2* (on roof)	
gabul	gabble 2*+
gabul	gable 2*
gad 3 /about	
gadget /ry	
gadolinium	
gael	gale
Gaelic * (language)	
gaf	gaffe
gaffe	
gag 3	
gaga	
gage	gauge 2+
gagercounter	Geiger counter
gaget	gadget +
gaggle 2	
gagit	gadget +
gagul	gaggle 2
gai ety /ly	
gain 1 /er/ful/fully	
gait * (walk)	
gait	gate 2*+
gaiter /ed	
gaitey	gaiety +
gal	gall 1
gala	
galactic	
galaksey	galaxy +
galant	gallant +
galantrey	gallantry
galaw	galore
galax y /ies	
gale	

galery	gallery +
Galic	Gaelic *
Galic	Gallic *
galie	galley
galium	gallium
galivant	gallivant 1
gall 1	
gallant /ry	
galler y /ies	
galley	
Gallic *†	
†(of Gaul, French)	
gallic	Gaelic *
gallium	
gallivant 1	
gallon	
gallop 1 /er	
gallows	
galon	gallon
galop	gallop 1+
galore	
galoshes	
galows	gallows
galvanic	
galvanis e 2 /ation/m	
galvanometer	
galy	galley
gambit	
gamble 2* (games) /r	
gambol 3* (frolic)	
game /-bird/-cock	
gamekeeper	
gamesmanship	
gamie	game +
gaming	
gammon	
gamon	gammon
gamut	
gamy	game +
gander 1	
ganet	gannet
gang 1 /er	
gangling	
gang-plank	
gangreen	gangrene +

127

gangren *e* /ous		gash [1]	
gangrenus	gangrenous	gasha	geisha
gangster /ism		gasket	
gangway		gaslight	
gannet		gaslite	gaslight
gaol [1]★ (prison) /bird/er		gasoline	
gape [2]		gasometer	
garage [2]		gasp [1]	
garantee	guarantee ★+	gastley	ghastly +
garantor	guarantor +	gastri *c* /tis	
garb [1]		gastronom *y* /ic/ical	
garbage		gate [2]★ (entrance) /way	
garbige	garbage	gate	gait ★
garble [2]		gate-crash [1]	
garbul	garble [2]	gater	gaiter +
gard	guard [1+]	gather [1] /er	
garden [1] /er		gauche	
gardenia		gaudie	gaudy +
gardian	guardian +	gaud *y* /ily/iness	
gardroom	guard-room	gauge [2] /r	
gardsman	guardsman	gaunt /let	
garet	garret	gauze	
gargantuan		gave	
gargle [2]		gawdie	gaudy +
gargoil	gargoyle	gawk [1] /iness	
gargoyle		gawl	gall [1]
gargul	gargle [2]	gawnt	gaunt +
garish		gawntlet	gauntlet
garison	garrison [1]	gawse	gorse
garland [1]		gay /er/est	
garlic /ky		gayety	gaiety +
garment [1]		Gaylic	Gaelic ★
garner [1]		gayn	gain [1+]
garnet		gaysha	geisha
garnish [1]		gaze [2] /r	
garnit	garnet	gazel	gazelle
garot	garrotte [2]	gazelle	
garret		gazer	geyser
garrison [1]		gazet	gazette [2]
garrot	garrotte [2]	gazette [2]	
garrotte [2]		ge gaw	gew-gaw
garrulous /ly		gear [1] /box	
garter /ed		gees	geese
garulus	garrulous +	geese (pl. of goose)	
gas [3] /eous/es/-mask		Geiger counter	

geisha		genus	
gel ³		geny	genie
gelatin	gelatine ⁺	geocentric	
gelatin e /ous		geofisical	geophysical
gelatinus	gelatinous	geofisics	geophysics ⁺
geld ¹		geofysical	geophysical
gelignite		geofysics	geophysics ⁺
gem ³ /my		geografey	geography ⁺
Gemini		geografic	geographic
gendarme		geografical	geographical ⁺
gender ¹		geographical /ly	
gene		geograph y /er/ic	
genealog y /ist		geological /ly	
genee	genie	geolog y /ist	
general /ly		geometrey	geometry
generalis e ² /ation		geometric /al/ally	
generalit y /ies		geometry	
generat e ² /ion/or		geophysic s /al/ist	
generative		geosentric	geocentric
generic /ally		geranium /s	
generosity		gerd	gird ¹⁺
generous /ly/ness		gerder	girder
generus	generous ⁺	gerdle	girdle ²
genetic /ally/s		gerdul	girdle ²
geney	genie	geriatric /ian/s	
genial /ity/ly		gerilla	gorilla ★
genie		gerilla	guerrilla ★
geniologey	genealogy ⁺	gerkin	gherkin
genital /s		gerl	girl ⁺
genitive		gerlish	girlish
geni us /i/uses (pls.)		germ	
genocide		German	
genoside	genocide	germane	
genre		Germanic	
genteel /ism/ly		germanium	
gentile		germicid e /al	
gentility		germinat e ² /ion	
gentle ² /ness/r/st		germiside	germicide ⁺
gentlem an /en (pl.)		gerontology	
gentrey	gentry	gerth	girth
gentry		gerund /ive	
gentul	gentle ²⁺	gescher	gesture ²
gentulman	gentleman ⁺	gess	guess ⁺
genuin	genuine ⁺	gesswerk	guesswork
genuine /ly/ness		gesswork	guesswork

gest	guest ★	gilotine	guillotine [2]
gesticulat *e* [2] /ion		gilt ★ (gold leaf)	
gesture [2]		gilt	guilt ★
get /ting		gilt-edged	
getto	ghetto [+]	giltey	guilty [+]
gew-gaw		gilty	guilty [+]
geyser		gim	gym [+]
ghastl *y* /ier/iest/iness		gimick	gimmick [+]
gherkin		gimkana	gymkhana
ghetto /s		gimlet	
ghost [1] /ly		gimmick /ry/y	
ghoul /ish		gimnasium	gymnasium [+]
giant /ess (fem.)		gimnastics	gymnastics
gibber [1] /ish		gin [3]	
gibbet [1]		ginecologey	gynaecology [+]
gibbon		ginecologist	gynaecologist
gibe [2]★ (taunt)		gingam	gingham
gibe	gybe [2]★	ginger [1] /bread/ly	
giber	gibber [1][+]	gingham	
giberish	gibberish	ginie	guinea [+]
gibet	gibbet [1]	ginifowl	guinea-fowl
giblets		ginipig	guinea-pig
gibon	gibbon	ginjer	ginger [1][+]
gidance	guidance	ginjerbred	gingerbread
gidans	guidance	gipsey	gipsy [+]
gidd *y*/ier/iest/ily/iness		gipsie	gipsy [+]
gide	guide [2][+]	gipsum	gypsum
gidie	giddy [+]	gips *y* /ies	
gidily	giddily	giraf	giraffe
gidy	giddy [+]	giraffe	
gift /ed		girashun	gyration
gig		girate	gyrate [2][+]
gigantic /ally		giration	gyration
giggle [2] /r		gird [1] /er	
gigolo		girdle [2]	
gigul	giggle [2][+]	girdul	girdle [2]
gil	gill [1]	girl /hood/ish	
gild [1]★ (gold cover)		giro ★ (banking)	
gild	guild ★	giro	gyro ★[+]
gilder	guilder	girth	
Gildhall	Guildhall	gise	guise
gile	guile [+]	gist	
gileless	guileless	gitar	guitar [+]
gill [1]		gitarist	guitarist
giloteen	guillotine [2]	give /n/r	

giving	
Giy Forks	Guy Fawkes
gizerd	gizzard
gizzard	
glacia *l* /tion	
glacier	
glad /der/dest/ly	
gladden¹	
glade	
gladen	gladden¹
gladiater	gladiator
gladiator	
gladiol *us* /i (pl.)	
glamer	glamour
glamerus	glamorous⁺
glamoris *e*² /ation	
glamorous /ly/ness	
glamour	
glance²	
gland /ular	
glanduler	glandular
glans	glance²
glare²	
glas	glass⁺
glashal	glacial⁺
glasiashun	glaciation
glasiation	glaciation
glasier	glacier
glass /es/ily	
glassware	
glaswear	glassware
glaz *e*² /ier	
glea	glee⁺
gleam¹	
glean¹ /er	
glee /ful/fully	
gleem	gleam¹
gleen	glean¹⁺
glib /ber/best/ly	
glicerine	glycerine
glide² /r	
glimmer¹	
glimpse²	
glint¹	
glisen	glisten¹

gliserin	glycerine
glisten¹	
glitter¹	
glo	glow¹
gloaming	
gloat¹	
glob *e* /al/ally	
globe-trott *er* /ing	
globul *e* /ar	
globuler	globular
gloming	gloaming
gloo	glue²⁺
gloocose	glucose
glooie	gluey
gloom /y	
gloomi *er* /est/ly/ness	
glooten	gluten ★⁺
glorie	glory⁴⁺
glorif *y*⁴ /ication	
glorius	glorious
glor *y*⁴ /ies/ious	
glos	gloss¹⁺
glosarey	glossary⁺
gloss¹ /ier/iest/iness/y	
glossar *y* /ies	
glote	gloat¹
glotis	glottis⁺
glott *is* /al	
glove² /r	
glow¹	
glower¹	
glucose	
glue² /y	
glum /ly/mer/mest	
glut³	
glut *en* ★† /inous	
†(sticky substance)	
gluten	glutton ★⁺
glutinus	glutinous
gluton	glutton ★⁺
glutonus	gluttonous
glutony	gluttony
glutton ★† /ous/y	
†(greedy)	
glutton	gluten ★⁺

gluv	glove [2+]
glycerine	
gnarl [1]	
gnash [1]	
gnat	
gnaw [1]	
gnom e /ish	
gnu ★ (animal)	
go /er/es/ing	
goad [1]	
go -ahead /-kart	
goal ★† /ie/keeper/less	
†(an aim, sport)	
goal	gaol [1★+]
goat /ee	
goatherd	
gobble [2] /r	
go-between	
goblet	
goblin	
gobul	gobble [2+]
gocart	go-kart
god /child/like	
god -daughter /son	
goddess (fem.)	
gode	goad [1]
god father /mother	
god forsaken /head	
goggle [2]	
gogul	goggle [2]
goiter	goitre
goitre	
gold /en/finch/fish	
goldsmith	
gole	goal ★+
golf [1] /er	
golie	goalie
golliwog	
gon	gone +
gondol a /ier	
gone /r	
gong [1]	
gonoria	gonorrhoea
gonorrhoea	
good /ly/ness/will	

good-bye	
good-humered	good-humoured
good-humoured	
goodie	goody +
good-looking	
good y /ies	
gool	ghoul +
goolash	goulash
goolish	ghoulish
goord	gourd
goormand	gourmand +
goormay	gourmet
goose /flesh	
gooseberie	gooseberry +
gooseberr y /ies	
Gordian	
Gordyan	Gordian
gor e [2] /y	
gorge [2] /r	
gorgeous /ly/ness	
Gorgonzola	
gorgus	gorgeous
gorilla ★ (ape)	
gorilla	guerrilla ★
gorse	
gosamer	gossamer
gosip	gossip [1+]
gosling	
gospel /ler	
gossamer	
gossip [1] /er/y	
gost	ghost [1+]
gostly	ghostly
got /ten	
gote	goat +
goteherd	goatherd
Gothic	
gouge [2] /r	
goulash	
gourd	
gourmand /ism	
gourmet	
gout /y	
govern [1] /able/ance	
governer	governor +

government /al		granite	
govern or /ess (fem.)		grann y /ies	
govner	governor [+]	grant [1]	
gowge	gouge [2+]	granulat e [2] /ion	
gown		granul e /ar/arity	
gowt	gout [+]	grany	granny [+]
grab [3] /ber		grape /fruit/-shot	
grace [2] /less		graph [1]	
graceful /ly		graphic /al/ally	
gracious /ly/ness		graphite	
gradashun	gradation	grapholog y /ist	
grad e [2] /ation/er		graple	grapple [2]
gradient		grapnel	
gradual /ly		grapple [2]	
graduat e [2] /ion/or		grapul	grapple [2]
graf	graph [1]	gras	grass [1+]
graffiti		grase	grace [2+]
grafic	graphic [+]	grashus	gracious [+]
graficley	graphically	grasp [1]	
grafite	graphite	grass [1] /es/hopper	
grafiti	graffiti	grasshoper	grasshopper
grafologey	graphology [+]	grate [2*] (fire) /r	
grafologist	graphologist	grate	great [*+]
graft [1] /er		grateful /ly/ness	
grail		gratif y [4] /ication	
grain [1]		gratis	
graling	grayling	gratitude	
gramar	grammar [+]	gratuitey	gratuity [+]
gramatical	grammatical [+]	gratuitous /ly/ness	
gramefone	gramophone	gratuitus	gratuitous [+]
gramer	grammar [+]	gratuit y /ies	
grammar /ian		grave /ly/yard	
grammatical /ly		gravel [3] /ly	
gramophone		gravie	gravy
granar y /ies		gravitashun	gravitation [+]
grand /ee/eur/stand		gravitate [2]	
grandchild /ren (pl.)		gravitation /al	
grand- *daughter* /-son		gravity	
grand- *father* /-mother		gravy	
grandiloquen ce /t		gray	grey [+]
grandios e /ity		grayhound	greyhound
grane	grain [1]	grayhownd	greyhound
grange		grayl	grail
granie	granny [+]	grayling	
granit	granite	grayn	grain [1]

graz *e* ² /ier		griffin	
greas *e* ² /y		gril	grill ¹+
greasie	greasy	grill ¹ /-room	
greasi *er* /est/ly/ness		grim /ly/mer/mest/ness	
great ★ (big) /er/est		grimace ²	
great	grate ²★+	grimas	grimace ²
greatful	grateful +	grim *e* ² /ier/iest/iness/y	
grede	greed +	grin ³	
greed /y		grind ¹ /er	
greedi *er* /est/ly/ness		grip ³★ (hold)	
green /er/ery/ness		grip	gripe ²★
green *gage* /grocer		gripe ²★ (colic pain)	
green *horn* /house		grisel	gristle
Greenwich mean time		grisly ★ (ghastly)	
greese	grease ²+	grisly	gristly ★
greesie	greasy	grist	
greet ¹		gristle	
gref	grief	gristly ★ (full of gristle)	
gregarious /ly/ness		grisul	gristle
gregarius	gregarious +	grit ³ /tily/ty	
greif	grief	grizul	grizzle ²
greive	grieve ²+	grizzle ²	
greivus	grievous	gro	grow +
gremlin		groan ¹★ (moan)	
grenad *e* /ier		groan	grown ★+
grene	green +	grocer ★ (shop) /y/ies	
grenegage	greengage +	grocer	grosser ★
grengroser	greengrocer	grogg *ily* /iness/y	
grenich	Greenwich +	groin	
gresier	greasier +	grone	groan¹★
grete	greet ¹	grone	grown ★+
grevance	grievance	groo	grew
grevans	grievance	grooel	gruel ³
greve	grieve ²+	groom ¹	
grevus	grievous	groop	group ¹
grew		groosum	gruesome +
grey /er/est/hound		groov *e* ² /y	
grid		grope ²	
griddle ²		gros	gross ¹+
gridiron		groser	grocer ★+
gridul	griddle ²	groser	grosser ★
grief		groserey	grocery
grievance		gross ¹ /er ★ (fatter) /ly	
grievans	grievance	grotesk	grotesque +
griev *e* ² /ous/ously		grotesque /ly	

groto	grotto +	gufaw	guffaw [1]
grotto /es		guffaw [1]	
ground [1] /less		guid e [2] /ance	
ground -*swell* /work		guild ★ (association)	
group [1]		guild	gild [1]★
grouse [2] /r		guilder	
grove		Guildhall	
grovel [3] /ler		guile /ful/less	
grow /er/ing		guillotine [2]	
growl [1] /er		guilt ★ (law-breaking)	
grown ★† /-up		guilt y /ier/iest/ily	
†(matured)		guinea /-fowl/-pig	
grownd	ground [1]+	guise	
growndswell	ground-swell +	guitar /ist	
growse	grouse [2]+	gul	gull [1]
growth		gulash	goulash
grub [3] /by		gulet	gullet
grubbi er /est/ly/ness		gulf [1]	
grudge [2]		Gulf-stream	
gruel [3]		gulible	gullible +
gruesome /ly/ness		gulibul	gullible +
gruf	gruff +	gulie	gully [4]+
gruff /er/est		gull [1]	
gruge	grudge [2]	gullet	
grumble [2] /r		gullib le /ility	
grumbul	grumble [2]+	gull y [4] /ies	
grumpie	grumpy +	gulp [1]	
grump y /ily/iness		guly	gully [4]+
grunt [1] /er		gum [3] /boil/my/-tree	
grusome	gruesome +	gumption	
grusum	gruesome +	gumshun	gumption
gruyare	gruyère	gun [3] /powder	
gruyère		gunl	gunwale
guano		gunner /y	
guarantee ★ (pledge) /d/ing		gunwale	
guarant or /y ★ (undertaking)		gurgle [2]	
guard [1] /sman		gurgul	gurgle [2]
guardian /ship		gush [1]	
guard-room		gust [1]	
guava		gusto	
guerrilla ★ (war)		gut [3]	
guerrilla	gorilla ★	guter	gutter +
guess /ing/work		guteral	guttural +
guessed ★ (estimated)		gutersnipe	guttersnipe
guest ★ (visitor)		gutter /snipe	

guttural /ly		hacherey	hatchery +
guvern	govern ¹⁺	hachet	hatchet
guvernable	governable	hack ¹ /-saw	
guvernabul	governable	hackle ²	
guvernance	governance	hackney ¹	
guvernans	governance	hackul	hackle ²
guverner	governor +	had /n't	
guverness	governess	haddock	
guvernment	government +	Hades	
guvnable	governable	hadock	haddock
guy ¹ /s		haemofilia	haemophilia +
Guy Fawkes		haemoglobin	
guzul	guzzle ²⁺	haemophilia /c	
guzzle ² /r		haemoroids	haemorrhoids
gwano	guano	haemorrhage	
gwave	guava	haemorrhoids	
gybe ²★ (sailing)		haf	half +
gybe	gibe ²★	hafnium	
gym /nast/nastics		hafpenie	halfpenny +
gymkana	gymkhana	hafpeny	halfpenny +
gymkhana		hafway	half-way
gymnasium /s		hagerd	haggard
gynaecolog y /ist		haggard	
gypsum		haggis	
gyrat e ² /ion/ory		haggle ² /r	
gyro ★ /compass		hagis	haggis
gyro	giro ★	hagul	haggle ²⁺
gyroscop e /ic		hai	hay ★⁺
		haifever	hay fever
		hail ¹★ (salute, icy rain)	

H

		hail	hale ★
		hailo	halo ★⁺
habeas corpus		hailstone	
haberdasher /y		hair ★ (on head) /line/y	
habias corpus	habeas corpus	hair	hare ★⁺
habichual	habitual +	hair	heir ★
habichuate	habituate ²⁺	hairbreadth	
habitab le /ility		hairi er /est/ness	
habitabul	habitable +	hair-raising	
habitashun	habitation	hake	
habitat		halcion	halcyon
habitation		halcyon	
habitual /ly		hale ★ (hearty)	
habituat e ² /ion		hale	hail ¹★
hach	hatch ¹⁺	haleluya	hallelujah

halestone	hailstone	handkerchief /s	
half /ves (pl.)		handle ² /bar/r	
half -cast /-hearted		hand-made	
halfpenn y /ies		handriten	handwritten
half-wit /ted		handriting	handwriting +
halibut		handshake	
halilooya	hallelujah	handsome * (looks) /ly	
hall * (room)		handul	handle ²+
hall	haul ¹*+	handwrit ing /ten	
hallelujah		hand y /ier/iest/ily	
hall-mark ¹		hang ¹ /over	
hallo * (cry)		hangar * (shelter)	
hallow ¹* (make holy)		hanger * (for clothes)	
Hallowe'en		hangkerchif	handkerchief +
hallucinat e ² /ion/ory		hangman	
hallucinogen		hank	
halmark	hall-mark ¹	hanker ¹	
halo *(disc of light) /es		hankerchief	handkerchief +
halo	hallow ¹*	hankuf	handcuff ¹
halogens		hansom * (cab)	
halow	hallow ¹*	hansom	handsome *+
Haloween	Hallowe'en	hansum	handsome *+
halsiun	halcyon	hapen	happen ¹
halt ¹ /er/ingly		haphazard /ly/ness	
halusinate	hallucinate ²+	hapie	happy +
halusinogen	hallucinogen	hapier	happier +
halve ²		hapless	
halyard		happen ¹	
halyerd	halyard	happi er /est/ly/ness	
ham /burger		happy /-go-lucky	
hamer	hammer ¹+	hapy	happy +
ham-fisted		hara-kiri	
hamlet		harang	harangue ²
hammer ¹ /er		harangue ²	
hammock		haras	harass ¹+
hamper ¹		harass ¹ /ment	
hamster		harber	harbour ¹+
hamstring ¹		harbour ¹ /age	
hand ¹ /ful/fuls		hard /er/est/ly/ship	
handbag		harden ¹	
handcuff ¹		hard-hearted	
handicap ³		hardie	hardy +
handicraft		hardware	
handie	handy +	hardwear	hardware
handiwork		hard y /ier/iest/ily	

137

hare ★ (animal) /bell		hash¹	
hare	hair ★+	hashish	
hare-brained		hasock	hassock
harem		hassock	
harico	haricot	hast e /ily/iness/y	
haricot		hasten¹	
harier	hairier +	hat³ /ter	
hark¹		hatch¹ /es/way	
harlekwin	harlequin +	hatcherey	hatchery +
harlequin /ade		hatcher y /ies	
harlot /ry		hatchet	
harm¹ /ful/fully		hate² /ful/r	
harmless /ness		hatred	
harmonic /a/ally		hatrid	hatred
harmonious /ly/ness		haught y /ier/iest/ily	
harmonis e² /ation		haul¹★ (pull in) /age	
harmonium		haul	hall ★
harmonius	harmonious +	haulm	
harmon y /ies		haunch /es	
harness¹ /er		haunt¹	
harow	harrow¹	hav	have +
harp¹ /ist		Havana	
harpoon¹ /er		have /n't	
harpsichord		haven	
harpsicord	harpsichord	havent	haven't
harrier		haversack	
harrow¹		having	
harsh /ly/ness		havoc	
hart ★ (deer)		hawk¹ /er/ish	
hart	heart ★+	hawl	haul¹★+
hartbrake	heartbreak +	hawlidge	haulage
hartbroken	heartbroken	hawlige	haulage
hartburn	heartburn +	hawm	haulm
harten	hearten¹	hawnch	haunch +
harth	hearth	hawnet	hornet
hartie	hearty +	hawnpipe	hornpipe
hartless	heartless +	hawnt	haunt¹
harty	hearty +	hawser	
harum-scarum		hawthorn	
harve	halve²	hawticulcher	horticulture +
harvest¹ /er		hawticulture	horticulture +
harvist	harvest¹+	hawtie	haughty +
hary	hairy	hawtier	haughtier
has /-been/n't		hawty	haughty +
hasen	hasten¹	hay ★ (grass) /cock	

138

hay	hey *
hay fever	
hayday	heyday
hazard [1] /ous	
haz e /ier/iest/y	
hazel	
hazerd	hazard [1+]
hazerdus	hazardous
hazi ly /ness	
he /'ll * (he will)	
head [1] /ache/board	
head -dress /way	
head er /less/line/y	
head land /long/strong	
head master /mistress	
headquarters	
heal [1*] (to cure) /er	
heal	heel [1*]
health /y	
healthi er /est/ly/ness	
heap [1]	
hear * (sound) /er/ing	
hear	here *
hearabouts	hereabouts
hearafter	hereafter
heard * (sound)	
heard	herd [1*+]
hearken [1]	
hearsay	
hearse	
heart * (body) /broken	
heartbreak /ing	
heartburn /ing	
hearten [1]	
hearth	
heartless /ly/ness	
heart y /ier/iest/ily	
heat [1] /edly/er/-wave	
heath	
heathen /ish	
heather	
heave [2]	
heaven /ly	
heaviwait	heavyweight
heav y /ier/iest/ily	

heavyweight	
Hebrew	
hebroo	Hebrew
heckle [2] /r	
heckul	heckle [2+]
hectic /ally	
hecto gram /litre/metre	
hed	head [1+]
hedake	headache
heddress	head-dress +
heder	header +
hedge [2] /hog/row	
hedland	headland +
hedmaster	headmaster +
hedmistriss	headmistress
hedonis m /t	
hedquarters	headquarters
heed [1] /ful/less	
heel [1*] (of foot)	
heel	heal [1*+]
heep	heap [1]
heet	heat [1+]
heeth	heath
hefer	heifer
heftie	hefty +
heft y /ier/iest/ily/iness	
hege	hedge [2+]
heifer	
height	
heighten [1]	
heinous /ly/ness	
heinus	heinous +
heir * (inheritance)	
heir ess /loom	
hel	hell +
held	
helicks	helix +
helicopter	
heliocentric	
heliograf	heliograph
heliograph	
heliotrope	
heliport	
helium	
heli x /ces (pl.)	

hell /ish	
hello /s	
helm /sman	
helmet	
helo	hello+
help[1] /er	
helpful /ly/ness	
helpless /ness	
helpmate	
helter-skelter	
helth	health+
helthier	healthier+
hem[3] /stitch	
hemerige	haemorrhage
hemeroids	haemorrhoids
hemisfere	hemisphere+
hemispher e /ical	
hemlock	
hemofilia	haemophilia+
hemoglobin	haemoglobin
hemorige	haemorrhage
hemp /en	
hen /pecked	
hena	henna
hence /forth	
henceforward	
hench man /men (pl.)	
henna	
henrey	henry+
henry /s	
hens	hence+
hensforth	henceforth
hensforwerd	henceforward
henus	heinous+
hepatitis	
heptagon /al	
her /s/self	
herald[1] /ic/ry	
heraldrey	heraldry
herb /age	
herbaceous	
herbal /ist	
herbashus	herbaceous
herbicide	
herbiside	herbicide

herbivor e /ous	
herbivorus	herbivorous
herd[1]* (animals) /sman	
herd	heard*
here * (this place)	
here	hear *+
hereabouts	
hereafter	
here by /in/of	
heredit ary /y	
hereditey	heredity
hereditrey	hereditary+
heresay	hearsay
heresie	heresy+
heres y /ies	
heretic /al	
here to /upon/with	
hering	herring
heritage	
herita nce /ble	
heritans	heritance+
heritige	heritage
herl	hurl[1]
hermafrodite	hermaphrodite
hermaphrodite	
hermetic /ally	
hermit /age	
hernia	
hero /es/ic/ically/ism	
heroin * (drug)	
heroine * (fem. hero)	
heron /ry	
herring	
herse	hearse
hert	hurt+
hertle	hurtle[2]
hertul	hurtle[2]
hertz	
hesian	hessian
hesitan cy /t	
hesitansey	hesitancy+
hesitat e[2] /ion	
hessian	
heterodoks	heterodox+
hetero dox /sexual	

heterogeneous	
heterogenus	heterogeneous
heteroseksual	heterosexual
hethen	heathen +
hether	heather
heve	heave 2
heven	heaven +
hevenly	heavenly
hevie	heavy +
heviwait	heavyweight
heviweight	heavyweight
hevy	heavy +
hew 1★ (cut) /er/n	
hew	hue ★
hexagon /al	
hexahedr on /al	
hey ★ (call out)	
hey	hay ★+
heyday	

> If you cannot find your word
> under **hi** look under **hy**

hi ★ (call attention)	
hi	high ★+
hiasinth	hyacinth
hiatus /es	
hibernat e 2 /ion/or	
hibrid	hybrid
hiccup 1	
hich	hitch 1+
hichhike	hitch-hike 2+
hicup	hiccup 1
hid /den/ing	
hide /bound/-out	
hideous /ly/ness	
hidius	hideous +
hier	higher ★
hier	hire 2★+
hierarch /ical	
hierarch y /ies	
hierark	hierarch +
hierarkey	hierarchy +
hieroglif	hieroglyph +
hieroglyph /ic	
hi-fi	

higgledy-piggledy	
high ★ (tall) /est/ly	
higher ★ (taller)	
higher	hire 2★+
highfaluting	
highland	
highlight 1	
highness	
highway /man/men (pl.)	
hijack 1 /er	
hike 2 /r	
hil	hill +
hiland	highland
hilari ous /ty	
hilaritey	hilarity
hilarius	hilarious +
hilight	highlight 1
hilite	highlight 1
hill /ock	
hill y /ier/iest/iness	
him ★ (he) /self	
him	hymn ★+
hind /sight	
hinder 1	
hindoo	Hindu +
hindrance	
hindrans	hindrance
hindsite	hindsight
Hindu /ism	
hiness	highness
hinge 2	
hint 1	
hinterland	
hipie	hippy +
hipodrome	hippodrome
hipopotamus	hippopotamus
hippodrome	
hippopotamus	
hipp y /ies	
hipy	hippy +
hire 2★ (employ) /ling	
hire	higher ★
hiroglif	hieroglyph +
hiss 1	
histerey	history +

141

histeria	hysteria +	holie	holly *+
histerical	hysterical +	holie	holy *
historian		holi er /est/ness	
historic /al/ally		holihock	hollyhock
histor y /ies		hollow [1]	
histrey	history +	holly * (tree) /hock	
histrionic /s		holly	holy *
hit /ter/ting		holly	wholly *
hitch [1] /es		holm * (river islet)	
hitch-hike [2] /r		holmium	
hite	height	holocaust	
hither /to		holocorst	holocaust
hive [2]		holow	hollow [1]
hiway	highway +	holster [1]	
ho * (surprise)		holy * (sacred)	
ho	hoe [2]*+	holy	holey *
hoaks	hoax [1]+	holy	holly *+
hoard [1] * (collect) /er		holy	wholly *
hoard	horde [2]*	homage	
hoarse * (voice)		home [2] * /ward/work	
hoarse	horse [2]*	home	holm *
hoarse ly /ness/st		home ly /less	
hoax [1] /es/er		homesick /ness	
hobble [2]		homicid e /al	
hobb y /ies		homige	homage
hobie	hobby +	homiley	homily
hobnob [3]		homily	
hobul	hobble [2]	homiopath	homoeopath +
hoby	hobby +	homisidal	homicidal
hochpoch	hotchpotch	homiside	homicide +
hock		homoeopath /ic	
hockey		homogene ity /ous	
hockie	hockey	homogenius	homogeneous
hocus-pocus		homonim	homonym +
hoe [2]* (dig) /s *		homonym /ic	
hoes	hose [2]*	homoseksual	homosexual +
hog [3] /gish		homosexual /ity	
hogshead		hone [2]	
hogshed	hogshead	honest /ly/y	
hoist [1]		honey /dew	
hold /-all/er/ing		honeycomb [1]	
hole [2]* (cavity) /y *		honeymoon [1] /er	
hole	whole *	honeysuckle	
holey	wholly *	honie	honey +
holiday /er/ing		honorari um /a/ums (pls.)	

honorary
honorific
honour [1] /able/ably
hony — honey [+]
hood [1]
hoodwink [1]
hoo *f* [1] /fs/ves (pls.)
hook [1] /-up
hooligan /ism
hoop [1]★ (circle)
hoop — whoop [1]★
hooping coff — whooping cough
hoot [1] /er
hoover [1]
hop [3] /per/scotch
hope [2] /ful/fully
hopeless /ness
horde [2]★ (swarm)
horde — hoard [1]★[+]
hore — whore [2][+]
horer — horror
horible — horrible [+]
horibul — horrible [+]
horid — horrid [+]
horific — horrific [+]
horify — horrify [4]
horizon
horizontal /ly
hormone
horn [1] /beam/y
hornet
hornpipe
horology
horor — horror
horoscope
horribl *e* /y
horribul — horrible [+]
horrid /ness
horrific /ally
horrify [4]
horror
hors-d'oeuvre
horse [2]★ (animal)
horse — hoarse ★
horse *back* /-chestnut

horsely — hoarsely [+]
horse *power* /radish
horseshoe /s
horsewhip [3]
horswip — horsewhip [3]
horthorn — hawthorn
horticulcher — horticulture [+]
horticultur *e* /al/ist
hortie — haughty [+]
horty — haughty [+]
hose [2]★ (stockings, water
  down)
hose — hoes ★
hosier /y
hospitabl *e* /y
hospitabul — hospitable [+]
hospital
hospitalis *e* [2] /ation
hospitality
host [1] /ess (fem.)
hostage
hostel
hostelr *y* /ies
hostige — hostage
hostile /ly
hostilit *y* /ies
hot /ly/-plate/ter/test
hotchpotch
hotel /ier
hoter — hotter
hotest — hottest
hotheaded
hotheded — hotheaded
hound [1]
hour ★ (time) /ly
hour — our ★
house [2] /boat/ful
household /er
house *keeper* /master
housewi *fe* /ves (pl.)
hovel
hover [1] /craft
how /ever
howl [1] /er
hownd — hound [1]

howse	house ² ⁺	humock	hummock
howsekeeper	housekeeper ⁺	humorist /ic	
howsewife	housewife ⁺	humorous ★ (funny)	
howshold	household ⁺	humorous	humerus ★
hu	hew ¹★⁺	humour ¹	
hu	hue ★	hump ¹ /back	
hubbub		humus	
huch	hutch ⁺	hunch ¹ /back/es	
huddle ²		hundred /fold/th	
hudul	huddle ²	hundredwait	hundredweight
hudwink	hoodwink ¹	hundredweight	
hue ★ (tint, pursuit)		huney	honey ⁺
hue	hew ¹★⁺	hung	
huf	huff ¹⁺	hunger ¹	
huff ¹ /ily/iness/y		hungrie	hungry
hug ³		hungri er /est/ly/ness	
huge /ly/r/st		hungry	
Hugeno	Huguenot	huni	honey ⁺
Huguenot		hunk	
hul	hull	hunt ¹ /er/ress (fem.)	
hulabaloo	hullabaloo	huntsman	
hulk /ing		hura	hurrah
hull		huray	hurray
hullabaloo		hurd	heard ★
hum ³		hurd	herd ¹★⁺
human ★ (person) /ly		hurdigurdie	hurdy-gurdy
humane ★ (kindly) /ly		hurdle ²	
humanis e ² /ation		hurdul	hurdle ²
humanis m /t/tic		hurdy-gurdy	
humanitarian /ism		huricane	hurricane
humanit y /ies		hurie	hurry ⁴
humble ² /ness		hurl ¹	
humbly		hurmit	hermit ⁺
humbug ³		hurnia	hernia
humbul	humble ² ⁺	hurrah	
humdrum		hurray	
humer	humour ¹	hurricane	
humerist	humorist ⁺	hurry ⁴	
humerus ★ (bone)		hurse	hearse
humerus	humorous ★	hurt /ful/ing	
humid /ity		hurtle ²	
humidif y ⁴ /ier		hurtul	hurtle ²
humiliat e ² /ion		hurtz	hertz
humility		hury	hurry ⁴
hummock		husband ¹ /ry	

husel	hustle ² +
hush ¹ /-hush	
nusie	hussy +
husk ¹ /ily/iness	
huskie	husky +
husk y /ies	
huss y /ies	
hustle ² /r	
husul	hustle ² +
husy	hussy +
hutch /es	
hyacinth	
hybrid	
hydra	
hydrangea	
hydranja	hydrangea
hydrant	
hydraulic /ally/s	
hydrocarbon	
hydrochloric	
hydro-electric	
hydrofobia	hydrophobia
hydrofoil	
hydrogen	
hydrografey	hydrography
hydrography	
hydrokside	hydroxide
hydrolysis	
hydromet er /ry	
hydropath /ic/y	
hydrophobia	
hydroplane	
hydrostat /ic	
hydrotherapy	
hydrous	
hydroxide	
hydrus	hydrous
hyena	
hygene	hygiene +
hygien e /ic/ically	
hygromet er /ric	
hygroscopic	
hym	hymn * +
hymen	
hymn * (song) /al	

hyperbola * (curve)	
hyperbole * (exaggerate)	
hyperbolical /ly	
hypermarket	
hyphenate ²	
hypnosis	
hypnoti c /sm/st	
hypnotise ²	
hypochondria /c	
hypocris y /ies	
hypocrit e /ical	
hypodermic	
hypotenuse	
hypothermia	
hypothes is /es (pl.)	
hypothetical	
hysteri a /cs	
hysterical /ly	

I

I /'ll * (I will)	
I	eye ² * +
iambic	
ice ² /-apron/berg	
ice -*bucket* /-rink	
ich	itch ¹ +
icicle	
iclesiastic	ecclesiastic +
iclips	eclipse ²
icliptic	ecliptic
icon	
iconomey	economy +
iconomist	economist
icy	
idea /s	
ideal /ism	
idealise ²	
identical	
identif y ⁴ /ication	
identit y /ies	
ideological /ly	
ideolog y /ies	
iderdown	eiderdown

idilic	idyllic
idill	idyll +
idioc y /ies	
idiologey	ideology +
idiological	ideological +
idiom /atic	
idiosincrasy	idiosyncrasy +
idiosincratic	idiosyncratic
idiosyncra sy /tic	
idiot /ic	
idium	idiom +
idle ²★ (lazy) /ness/r	
idol ★ (worship)	
idol	idle ²★+
idolatr y /ous	
idolise ²	
idyl	idyll +
idyll /ic	
iface	efface ²+
ifect	effect ¹
ifectiv	effective +
ifectual	effectual
Ifel	Eiffel
ifeminate	effeminate +
ificiency	efficiency +
ificient	efficient +
ifishensey	efficiency +
ifishent	efficient +
ifrunterey	effrontery +
igalitarian	egalitarian +
igloo	
igneous	
ignishun	ignition
ignit e ² /ion	
ignius	igneous
ignoble	
ignominious /ly	
ignominius	ignominious +
ignominy	
ignor	ignore ²
ignoramus	
ignoran ce /t	
ignorans	ignorance +
ignore ²	
iguana	

igwana	iguana
ijaculashun	ejaculation
ijaculate	ejaculate ²+
ijaculation	ejaculation
ijecshun	ejection
iject	eject ¹+
ijection	ejection
ikon	icon
ikwip	equip ³+
ikwivocal	equivocal +
ikwivocate	equivocate ²+
il	I'll ★
ilaberate	elaborate ²+
ilaborashun	elaboration
ilaborate	elaborate ²+
iland	island +
ilapse	elapse ²
ilash	eyelash +
ilashun	elation
ilastic	elastic +
ilasticity	elasticity
ilastisitey	elasticity
ilate	elate ²+
ilation	elation
ile	aisle ★
Ile	I'll ★
ile	isle ★
ilect	elect ¹+
ilection	election +
ilectoral	electoral +
ilectorate	electorate
ilectrocute	electrocute ²+
ilectron	electron
ilectronic	electronic +
ilectroplate	electroplate ²
ilegal	illegal +
ilegalitey	illegality
ilegible	illegible +
ilegibul	illegible +
ilegitimacy	illegitimacy +
ilegitimasey	illegitimacy +
ilegitimate	illegitimate
ilet	islet ★
ileven	eleven +
ilicit	elicit ¹★

ilikser	elixir
iliminashun	elimination
iliminate	eliminate [2+]
ilimination	elimination
ilips	ellipse
iliptic	elliptic [+]
iliptical	elliptical
ilisit	elicit [1*]
iliteracy	illiteracy [+]
iliterasey	illiteracy [+]
iliterat	illiterate
ilixir	elixir
il	
llegal /ity	
llegib *le* /ility	
llegibul	illegible [+]
llegitima *cy* /te	
llicit * (illegal) /ly	
llicit	elicit [1*]
llitera *cy* /te	
llogical /ity	
lluminat *e* [2] /ion	
llusion * (false idea)	
llusion	allusion *
llusion	elusion *
llusive * (deceptive)	
llusive	allusive *[+]
llusive	elusive *[+]
llustrat *e* [2] /ion	
llustrious	
logical	illogical [+]
lope	elope [2+]
lucidate	elucidate [2+]
lude	elude [2*]
luminashun	illumination
luminate	illuminate [2+]
lumination	illumination
lusidate	elucidate [2+]
lusion	illusion *
lusive	elusive *[+]
lusive	illusive *
lustrate	illustrate [2+]
lustration	illustration
lustrius	illustrious
I'm (I am)	

imaciate	emaciate [2+]
imaculate	immaculate
image [2]	
imagin	imagine [2+]
imaginashun	imagination
imagin *e* [2] /ation	
imancipate	emancipate [2+]
imansipashun	emancipation
imansipate	emancipate [2+]
imansipation	emancipation
imasculate	emasculate [2+]
imashiate	emaciate [2+]
imaterial	immaterial
imature	immature [+]
imaturitey	immaturity
imbalance	
imbalans	imbalance
imbecil *e* /ity	
imbesile	imbecile [+]
imbibe [2]	
imbue [2]	
imediacy	immediacy
imediasey	immediacy
imediate	immediate [+]
imense	immense [+]
imensitey	immensity
imerge	emerge [2+]
imergence	emergence
imergency	emergency [+]
imergens	emergence
imergent	emergent
imerse	immerse [2+]
imershun	immersion
imersion	immersion
imesurable	immeasurable [+]
imesurabul	immeasurable [+]
imetic	emetic
imige	image [2]
imigrant	immigrant
imigrashun	immigration
imigrate	immigrate [2+]
imigration	immigration
iminent	imminent *[+]
imishun	emission
imission	emission

147

imit
imitat *e*² /ion
immaculate
immaterial
immatur *e* /ity
immeasurabl *e* /y
immediacy
immediasey   immediacy
immediate /ly
immens *e* /ely/ity
immers *e*² /ion
immigrant
immigrat *e*² /ion
imminent *† /ly
   †(about to happen)
imminent   eminent *
immobil *e* /ity
immobilis *e*² /ation
immoderate /ly
immodest /ly/y
immoral /ity/ly
immortal /ity/ly
immortalis *e*² /ation
immovabl *e* /y
immun *e* /ity
immunis *e*² /ation
immunology

emit ³+

imobile   immobile +
imoderate   immoderate +
imodest   immodest +
imodestey   immodesty
imolient   emollient
imolument   emolument
imoral   immoral +
imoralitey   immorality
imortal   immortal +
imortalise   immortalise 2+
imortalitey   immortality
imoshun   emotion +
imoshunal   emotional
imotion   emotion +
imotional   emotional
imotiv   emotive
imovable   immovable +
imovabul   immovable +

imp /ish/ishness
impact ¹ /ion
impair ¹ /ment
impalpabl *e* /y
imparshal   impartial +
imparshialitey   impartiality
impart ¹
impartial /ity/ly
impas   impasse
impasabul   impassable
impashence   impatience
impashens   impatience
impashent   impatient +
impashund   impassioned
impasioned   impassioned
impasiv   impassive +
impassable
impasse
impassioned
impassive /ness
impassivity
impatience
impatient /ly
impeach ¹ /able/ment
impecabul   impeccable +
impeccabl *e* /y
impecunio *us* /sity
impecunius   impecunious +
impede ²
impediment /a
impeech   impeach ¹+
impel ³ /ler
impend ¹
impenetrab *le* /ility
impeniten *ce* /t
impenitens   impenitence +
imperative /ly/ness
imperceptibl *e* /y
imperfect /ion
imperial /ism/ly
imperialist /ic
imperil ³ /ment
imperious /ly/ness
imperishable
imperius   imperious +

impermeable		imposter	impostor
impermiabul	impermeable	impostor	
imperseptible	imperceptible [+]	imposture	
imperseptibul	imperceptible [+]	impoten *ce* /t	
impersonal /ly		impotens	impotence [+]
impersonat *e* [2] /ion/or		impound [1]	
imperterbable	imperturbable	impoverish [1] /ment	
impertinen *ce* /t		impownd	impound [1]
impertinens	impertinence [+]	impracticab *le* /ility	
imperturbab *le* /ility		impracticabul	impracticable [+]
impervious /ly/ness		imprecat *e* [2] /ion	
impervius	impervious [+]	imprecise /ly	
impetuosity		impregnab *le* /ility	
impetuous /ly/ness		impregnat *e* [2] /ion	
impetus /es		impres	impress [1+]
impetuus	impetuous [+]	impresario /s	
impiety		impreshun	impression [+]
impinge [2] /ment		impreshunism	impressionism [+]
impious /ly		impresible	impressible
impius	impious [+]	impresibul	impressible
implacabl *e* /y		impresionism	impressionism [+]
implacabul	implacable [+]	impresionist	impressionist
implant [1] /ation		impresise	imprecise [+]
implement [1] /ation		impresiv	impressive [+]
impli	imply [4+]	impress [1] /ible	
implicat *e* [2] /ion		impression /able	
implicit /ly/ness		impressionis *m* /t/tic	
implisit	implicit [+]	impressive /ly/ness	
implore [2]		imprint [1]	
impl *y* [4] /ication		imprison [1] /ment	
impolite /ly/ness		improbab *le* /ility/ly	
impolitic		improbabul	improbable [+]
imponderable /s		impromptu	
impondrabul	imponderable [+]	impromtoo	impromptu
import [1] /able/ation		improper /ly	
importan *ce* /t/tly		impropriet *y* /ies	
importans	importance [+]	improve [2] /ment	
importunate /ly		improviden *ce* /t/tly	
importun *e* [2] /ity		improvidens	improvidence [+]
imposcher	imposture	improvis *e* [2] /ation	
impos *e* [2] /able/ition		impruden *ce* /t/tly	
imposible	impossible [+]	imprudens	imprudence [+]
imposibul	impossible [+]	impruve	improve [2+]
imposishun	imposition	impuden *ce* /t/tly	
impossib *le* /ility/ly		impudens	impudence [+]

impugn[1]
impuls e /ion/ive/ively
impune   impugn[1]
impunity
impure /ly
impurit y /ies
imput e[2] /able/ation
imulshun   emulsion
imulsion   emulsion
imune   immune[+]
imunise   immunise[2+]
imunitey   immunity
imunologey   immunology
imurge   emerge[2+]
in ★ (on inside)
in   inn ★[+]
inability
inaccessib le /ility
inaccurac y /ies
inaccurate /ly
inacsesible   inaccessible[+]
inacsesibul   inaccessible[+]
inacshun   inaction
inaction
inactive /ly
inactivit y /ies
inacuracy   inaccuracy[+]
inacurasey   inaccuracy[+]
inacurate   inaccurate[+]
inadekwacy   inadequacy[+]
inadekwasey   inadequacy[+]
inadekwat   inadequate[+]
inadequac y /ies
inadequate /ly
inadmisibul   inadmissible[+]
inadmissib le /ility
inadverten ce /t
inadvertens   inadvertence[+]
inalienab le /ility
inalienabul   inalienable[+]
inane /ly
inanimate
inanit y /ies
inaplicable   inapplicable[+]
inapplicabl e /y

inapplicabul   inapplicable[+]
inappropriate /ly
inapropriat   inappropriate[+]
inaptitude
inarticulate /ly
inasmuch
inate   innate[+]
inatenshun   inattention[+]
inatention   inattention[+]
inatentiv   inattentive
inattent ion /ive
inaudib le /ility
inaugural
inaugurat e[2] /ion/ive
inauspicious /ly
inawmus   enormous[+]
inawspicious   inauspicious[+]
inawspishus   inauspicious[+]
inborn
inbred
inbreeding
incalculab le /ility
incandescen ce /t
incandesence   incandescence[+]
incant[1] /ation
incapab le /ility/ly
incapabul   incapable[+]
incapacitat e[2] /ion
incapacity
incapasitate   incapacitate[2+]
incapasitey   incapacity
incarcerat e[2] /ion
incarnat e[2] /ion
incarserate   incarcerate[2+]
incendiar y /ies
incense[2]
incentive
incept ion /ive
incertitude
incessant /ly
incest /uous
inch[1] /es
incidence ★ (bearing)
incident /al/ally
incidents ★ (events)

incinerat *e*² /ion/or
incipient
incis *e*² /ion
incisive /ly/ness
incisor
incite ²★ (stir up)
incite   insight ★
incivilit *y* /ies
inclemen *cy* /t
inclemensey inclemency ⁺
inclin *e*² /ation
inclose   enclose ²⁺
inclu *de*² /sion
inclusive /ly
incognito
incoheren *ce* /t
incoherens incoherence ⁺
incombustible
income /tax
incomensurat incommensurate
incoming
incommensurate
incommod *e*² /ious
incommunicado
incomparabl *e* /y
incompatib *le* /ility
incompatibul incompatible ⁺
incompeten *ce* /t/tly
incompetens incompetence ⁺
incomplete
incomprehensible
incomunicado incommunicado
inconceivabl *e* /y
inconclusive /ly
incongru *ent* /ous
incongruit *y* /ies
incongruus incongruous
inconseavable inconceivable ⁺
inconsiderable
inconsiderate /ly
inconsistenc *y* /ies
inconsistensey inconsistency ⁺
inconsistent /ly
inconsolable
inconsolabul inconsolable

inconspicuous /ly
inconstan *cy* /t
incontestabl *e* /y
incontestabul incontestable ⁺
incontinen *ce* /t
incontinens incontinence ⁺
incontrovertibl *e* /y
inconvenien *ce*² /t
inconveniens inconvenience ²⁺
incorect incorrect ⁺
incorigible incorrigible ⁺
incorigibul incorrigible ⁺
incorporat *e*² /ion/or
incorrect /ly
incorrigib *le* /ility
incorruptib *le* /ility
increase ²
incredibl *e* /y
incredibul incredible ⁺
incredul *ity* /ous
incredulus incredulous
increment /al
increse increase ²
incriminat *e*² /ion
incrust encrust ¹
incubat *e*² /ion/or
inculcat *e*² /ion
inculpat *e*² /ion
incum income ⁺
incumbenc *y* /ies
incumbensey incumbency ⁺
incumbent
incur ³
incurab *le* /ility/ly
incurabul incurable ⁺
incurshun incursion ⁺
incurs *ion* /ive
indebted /ness
indecenc *y* /ies
indecensey indecency ⁺
indecent /ly
indecipherable
indecishun indecision
indecision
indecisive /ly

151

indecorous /ness	
indecorum	
indecorus	indecorous +
indeed	
indefatigabl e /y	
indefatigabul	indefatigable +
indefensibl e /y	
indefensibul	indefensible +
indefinable	
indefinabul	indefinable
indefinite /ly	
indeks	index ¹+
indelibl e /y	
indelibul	indelible +
indelicac y /ies	
indelicasey	indelicacy +
indelicate /ly	
indemnifi	indemnify ⁴+
indemnif y ⁴ /ication	
indemnit y /ies	
indencher	indenture
indent ¹ /ation/ure	
independen ce /t	
independens	independence +
indescribabl e /y	
indescribabul	indescribable +
indesency	indecency +
indesensey	indecency +
indesent	indecent +
indesiferable	indecipherable
indestructib le /ility	
indestructibul	indestructible +
indeted	indebted +
indeterminate /ly	
ind ex ¹ /exes/ices (pls.)	
Indian	
indicat e ² /ion/ive/or	
indict ¹*(accuse)/ment	
indiference	indifference +
indiferens	indifference +
indiferent	indifferent
indifferen ce /t	
indigen ce /t	
indigenous	
indigens	indigence +
indigenus	indigenous
indigeschun	indigestion +
indigestibl e /y	
indigestibul	indigestible +
indigest ion /ive	
indignant /ly	
indignashun	indignation
indignation	
indignit y /ies	
indigo	
indipendence	independence +
indipendens	independence +
indipendent	independent
indirect /ly	
indiscre et /tion	
indiscreshun	indiscretion
indiscriminate	
indisishun	indecision
indisision	indecision
indisisiv	indecisive +
indispensabl e /y	
indispensabul	indispensable +
indispos e ² /ition	
indisputabl e /y	
indisputabul	indisputable +
indistinct	
indistinguishable	
indite ²* (compose)	
indite	indict ¹*+
indium	
individual /ity/ly	
individualis m /t	
indivisibl e /y	
indivisibul	indivisible +
indoctrinat e ² /ion	
indolen ce /t/tly	
indolens	indolence +
indomitabl e /y	
indomitabul	indomitable +
indoor /s	
indubitabl e /y	
indubitabul	indubitable +
induce ² /ment	
inducshun	induction +
inductance	

inductans	inductance	inequity * (injustice)	
induct *ion* /ive/ively		inequity	iniquity *
indulge ² /nce/nt		iner	inner +
indulgens	indulgence	ineradicabl *e* /y	
induse	induce ²+	ineradicabul	ineradicable +
industrey	industry +	inersha	inertia
industrial /ism/ist/ly		inert /ia/ly/ness	
industrialis *e* ² /ation		inescapabl *e* /y	
industrious /ly		inescapabul	inescapable +
industrius	industrious +	inesenshal	inessential
industr *y* /ies		inesential	inessential
inebriat *e* ² /ion		inessential	
inedib *le* /ility		inestimabl *e* /y	
inedibul	inedible +	inestimabul	inestimable +
inefectiv	ineffective +	inestinium	einsteinium
inefectual	ineffectual +	inevitability	
ineffective /ly/ness		inevitabl *e* /y	
ineffectual /ly		inevitabul	inevitable +
inefficienc *y* /ies		inexact /itude	
inefficient /ly		inexcusabl *e* /y	
ineficiency	inefficiency +	inexhaustibl *e* /y	
ineficient	inefficient +	inexorabl *e* /y	
inefishensey	inefficiency +	inexpedient /ly	
inefishent	inefficient +	inexpensive /ly	
inegsact	inexact +	inexperience /d	
inegsactitude	inexactitude	inexperiens	inexperience +
inegsawstible	inexhaustible +	inexplicabl *e* /y	
inekscusable	inexcusable +	inexpressibl *e* /y	
inekserable	inexorable +	inextinguishable	
inekspedient	inexpedient +	inextingwishabul	inextinguishable
inekspensive	inexpensive +	inextricabl *e* /y	
ineksperience	inexperience +	infalible	infallible +
ineksplicable	inexplicable +	infalibul	infallible +
inekspresible	inexpressible +	infallib *le* /ility/ly	
inekstricable	inextricable +	infamey	infamy
inekwitable	inequitable +	infamous /ly	
inekwity	inequity *	infamus	infamous +
inelegan *ce* /cy/t		infamy	
inelegens	inelegance +	infancy	
ineligib *le* /ility		infansey	infancy
ineligibul	ineligible +	infant /icide/ile	
inept /itude/ly		infantrey	infantry +
inequalit *y* /ies		infantr *y* /ies	
inequitabl *e* /y		infatuat *e* ² /ion	
inequitabul	inequitable +	infecshun	infection

infecshus	infectious +	influx	
infect [1] /ion		inform [1] /ative/er	
infectious /ness		informal /ity/ly	
infer [3] /ence		informant	
inferens	inference	informashun	information
inferier	inferior +	information	
inferior /ity		infracshun	infraction
inferm	infirm	infraction	
infermarey	infirmary +	infra-red	
infermitey	infirmity +	infrastructure	
infernal /ly		infrekwency	infrequency +
inferno /s		infrekwent	infrequent
infertil e /ity		infrequen cy /t/tly	
infest [1] /ant/ation		infringe [2] /ment	
infidel		infuriate [2]	
infidelit y /ies		infus e [2] /er/ion	
infiltrat e [2] /ion/or		ingenious /ly	
infinite /ly		ingenius	ingenious +
infinitesimal /ly		ingenuity	
infinitey	infinity +	ingenuous /ly/ness	
infinitive		ingenuus	ingenuous +
infinit y /ies		ingle-nook	
infirm		Inglish	English +
infirmar y /ies		inglorious /ly	
infirmit y /ies		inglorius	inglorious +
inflamable	inflammable +	ingot	
inflamabul	inflammable +	ingrained	
inflamashun	inflammation	ingrashiate	ingratiate [2]
inflamatrey	inflammatory	ingratiate [2]	
inflame [2]		ingratitude	
inflamma ble /tion		ingredient	
inflammatory		ingrowing	
inflashun	inflation +	ingulnook	ingle-nook
inflat e [2] /able		inhabit [1] /able/ant	
inflation /ary		inhal e [2] /ant/ation	
inflect [1] /ion		inherent /ly	
inflexib le /ility		inherit [1] /ance/or	
inflict [1] /ion		inheritans	inheritance
inflooenza	influenza	inhibishun	inhibition
influence [2]		inhibit [1] /ion/or/ory	
influens	influence [2]	inhospitabl e /y	
influenshal	influential +	inhospitabul	inhospitable +
influential /ly		inhuman /ity/ly	
influenza		inikwalitey	inequality +
influks	influx	inikwitey	iniquity *

154

inikwitous	iniquitous
inikwitus	iniquitous
inimical	
inimitabl e /y	
inimitabul	inimitable +
inings	innings
iniquitey	iniquity *
iniquitous	
iniquitus	iniquitous
iniquity * (badness)	
iniquity	inequity *
inishal	initial 3+
inishativ	initiative
inishiashun	initiation
inishiate	initiate 2+
inishiation	initiation
initial 3 /ly	
initiat e 2 /ion/ive	
inject 1 /ion/or	
injer	injure 2+
injunction	
injunkshun	injunction
injur e 2 /ious	
injurey	injury +
injurius	injurious
injur y /ies	
injustice	
injustis	injustice

If you cannot find your word under **ink** *look under* **inc**

---

ink 1 /-pot/-well	
inkalculable	incalculable +
inkeeper	innkeeper
inkling	
inkrement	increment +
inkwest	inquest
inkwire	enquire 2+
inkwisitiv	inquisitive +
inkwisitor	inquisitor
inlade	inlaid
inland	
in-law	
inla y /id	
inlet	

inmate	
inmost	
inn * (tavern) /keeper	
innate /ly	
inner /most	
innings	
innocen ce /t/tly	
innocuous /ly	
innovat e 2 /ion/ive	
innuendo /es	
innumerabl e /y	
inocence	innocence +
inocens	innocence +
inocent	innocent
inoculat e 2 /ion	
inocuous	innocuous +
inocuus	innocuous +
inofensiv	inoffensive +
inoffensive /ly/ness	
inoperative /ness	
inoportune	inopportune +
inopportune /ly	
inordible	inaudible +
inordinate /ly	
inorganic	
inorgural	inaugural
inorgurate	inaugurate 2+
inormitey	enormity +
inormous	enormous +
inormus	enormous +
inorspicious	inauspicious +
inorspishus	inauspicious +
inosent	innocent
inough	enough
inovashun	innovation
inovate	innovate 2+
inovation	innovation
inovativ	innovative
input	
inquest	
inquisitive /ly/ness	
inquisitor	
inroad	
inrode	inroad
insan e /ely/ity	

155

insanitar y /iness	
insanitey	insanity
insanitrey	insanitary +
insashable	insatiable +
insashabul	insatiable +
insatiabl e /y	
inscribe 2	
inscripshun	inscription
inscription	
inscrutab le /ility	
insect /icide	
insectiside	insecticide
insecure /ly	
insecurity	
inseminat e 2 /ion	
insendiarey	incendiary +
insense	incense 2
insensib le /ility/ly	
insensibul	insensible +
insensitive /ly	
insensitivity	
insentiv	incentive
inseparabl e /y	
inseprabul	inseparable +
insepshun	inception +
inseption	inception +
insermountable	insurmountable +
insert 1 /ion	
insertitude	incertitude
insesant	incessant +
insest	incest +
insestuous	incestuous
insestuus	incestuous
inset 3	
inshorance	insurance
inshorans	insurance
inshore	ensure 2★
inshore	insure 2★+
inside /r	
insidence	incidence ★
insidens	incidence ★
insidens	incidents ★
insident	incident +
insidental	incidental
insidious /ly/ness	

insidius	insidious +
insight ★ (keen understanding)	
insight	incite 2★+
insignia	
insignifican ce /t/tly	
insincere /ly	
insincerity	
insinerate	incinerate 2+
insinerater	incinerator
insinsere	insincere +
insinseritey	insincerity
insinuat e 2 /ion/or	
insipid /ly/ness	
insipient	incipient
insiser	incisor
insishun	incision
insision	incision
insisiv	incisive +
insist 1 /ence/ent/ently	
insite	incite 2★
insite	insight ★
insivilitey	incivility +
insolen ce /t/tly	
insolens	insolence +
insolub le /ility/ly	
insolubul	insoluble +
insolven ce /cy/t	
insolvens	insolvence +
insomnia /c	
insomuch	
inspecshun	inspection
inspect 1 /ion	
inspecter	inspector +
inspector /ate	
inspir e 2 /ation	
instability	
instal	install 1+
install 1 /ation	
instalment	
instance 2	
instans	instance 2
instant /ly	
instantaneous /ly	
instantanius	instantaneous +

instead		intangibl *e* /y	
insted	instead	intangibul	intangible +
instep		integer	
instigat *e* ² /ion/or		integral /ly	
instigater	instigator	integrashun	integration
instill ¹		integrat *e* ² /ion/or	
instinct /ive/ively		integrity	
institushun	institution +	intelect	intellect
institut *e* ² /or		intelectual	intellectual +
institution /al		inteligence	intelligence +
institutionalis *e* ² /m		inteligens	intelligence +
instrement	instrument +	inteligensia	intelligentsia
instruct ¹ /ion/ive/or		inteligent	intelligent +
instrument /ation		inteligible	intelligible +
instrumental /ist		intellect	
insubordinashun	insubordination	intellectual / ly	
insubordinat *e*/ely/ion		intelligen *ce* /tsia	
insufferabl *e* /y		intelligent /ly	
insufficien *cy* /t/tly		intelligibl *e* /y	
insuficiency	insufficiency +	intelligibul	intelligible +
insuficient	insufficient	intemperance	
insufishensey	insufficiency +	intemperans	intemperance
insufishent	insufficient	intemperate /ly	
insufrable	insufferable +	intend ¹	
insular /ity		intense /ly	
insulat *e* ² /ion/or		intenshun	intention +
insulin		intensif *y* ⁴ /ication	
insult ¹		intensit *y* /ies	
insuperabl *e* /y		intensive /ly/ness	
insuprabul	insuperable +	intent	
insurance		intention /al/ally	
insurans	insurance	inter ³ /ment	
insure ²★(insurance)/r		interbred	
insure	ensure ²★	interbreeding	
insurecshun	insurrection	intercede ²	
insurection	insurrection	intercept ¹ /ion/or	
insurgen *ce* /t		interceshun	intercession +
insurgens	insurgence +	intercess *ion* /or	
insurmountabl *e* /y		interchange ² /able	
insurrection		interconnect ¹ /ion	
insurshun	insertion	intercorse	intercourse
insurt	insert ¹+	intercourse	
insurtion	insertion	interelate	interrelate ²
intact		interest ¹	
intake		interfere ² /nce	

interier	interior	intervenshun	intervention
interim		interview¹	
interior		intervue	interview¹
interject¹ /ion		interweav e /ing	
interlock¹		interwoven	
interloper		intestin e /al	
interlude		intiger	integer
intermarie	intermarry⁴	intigral	integral⁺
intermarry⁴		intigrashun	integration
intermediar y /ies		intigrate	integrate²⁺
intermediate		intigration	integration
interment		intijer	integer
interminable		intimacy	
interminabul	interminable	intimasey	intimacy
intermingle²		intimate /ly	
intermingul	intermingle²	intimidashun	intimidation
intermishun	intermission	intimidat e² /ion	
intermission		intoksicant	intoxicant
intermittent		intoksicate	intoxicate²⁺
intern¹ /ment		intolerabl e /y	
internal		intoleran ce /t	
internashunal	international⁺	intolerans	intolerance⁺
international /ly		intolrabul	intolerable⁺
internecine		intonashun	intonation
internisine	internecine	intonation	
interogashun	interrogation	intoxicant	
interogate	interrogate²⁺	intoxicat e² /ion	
interogation	interrogation	intractable	
interplanetary		intractabul	intractable
Interpol		intramuscular	
interpolat e² /ion		intransigen ce /t	
interpret¹ /ation		intransigens	intransigence⁺
interrelate²		intransitive	
interrogat e² /ion/or		intreeg	intrigue²⁺
interrupt¹ /ion		intrepid /ly	
intersect¹ /ion		intricac y /ies	
interseed	intercede²	intricasey	intricacy⁺
intersepshun	interception	intricate /ly	
intersept	intercept¹⁺	intrigue² /r	
intersepter	interceptor	intrinsic /ally	
interseshun	intercession⁺	introduc e²	
interupshun	interruption	introducshun	introduction⁻
interuption	interruption	introduct ion /ory	
interval		introduse	introduce²
interven e² /tion		introod	intrude²⁺

introoshun	intrusion +	invenshun	invention
introosion	intrusion +	invent [1] /ion/or	
introosiv	intrusive	inventer	inventor
introspect [1] /ion /ive		inventive /ness	
introver t [1] /sion		inventor y /ies	
intrude [2] /r		inventrey	inventory +
intrushun	intrusion +	invers e /ion	
intrus ion /ive		invershun	inversion
intuishun	intuition	invert [1] /er	
intuition		invertebrate	
intuitive /ly		invest [1] /ment	
inturn	intern [1]+	investicher	investiture
inturnal	internal	investigashun	investigation
inuendo	innuendo +	investigat e [2] /ion	
inuf	enough	investiture	
inumerable	innumerable +	inveterate	
inumerashun	enumeration	invidious /ly	
inumerate	enumerate [2]+	invidius	invidious +
inumerater	enumerator	invigilat e [2] /ion/or	
inumeration	enumeration	invigilater	invigilator
inumrabul	innumerable +	invigorat e [2] /ion	
inunciashun	enunciation	invincibl e /y	
inunciate	enunciate [2]+	invinsible	invincible +
inunciation	enunciation	inviolate	
inundat e [2] /ion		invisib le /ility/ly	
inunsiate	enunciate [2]+	invisibul	invisible +
inure [2]		invitashun	invitation
inursha	inertia	invit e [2] /ation	
inurt	inert +	invoice [2]	
invade [2] /r		invois	invoice [2]
invalid /ity		invoke [2]	
invalidate [2]		involuntar y /ily	
invaluable		involuntrey	involuntary +
invaluble	invaluable	involve [2] /ment	
invalubul	invaluable	invulnerab le /ility	
invariabl e /y		invulnerabul	invulnerable +
invariabul	invariable +	invurs	inverse +
invashun	invasion	invurt	invert [1]+
invasion		invurtebrate	invertebrate
invay	inveigh [1]	inward /ly/ness/s	
invaygul	inveigle [2]	inwud	inward +
invective		iodene	iodine
inveigh [1]		iodine	
inveigle [2]		iodise [2]	
inveigul	inveigle [2]	ion /ic	

159

ionis *e* ² /ation	
ionosfere	ionosphere
ionosphere	
iota	
ira	era +
iradiate	irradiate ²+
iradicate	eradicate ²+
irascib *le* /ility	
irascibul	irascible +
irase	erase ²+
irasher	erasure
irashonal	irrational +
irasible	irascible +
irate	
irational	irrational +
ire	
ireclaimable	irreclaimable
ireconcilable	irreconcilable +
ireconcilabul	irreconcilable +
irecoverable	irrecoverable +
irect	erect ¹+
irecuvrable	irrecoverable +
irefutable	irrefutable +
iregular	irregular +
iregularitey	irregularity +
ireguler	irregular +
irelegious	irreligious
irelevance	irrelevance +
irelevans	irrelevance +
irelevansey	irrelevancy +
irelevant	irrelevant
ireligus	irreligious
iremediable	irremediable +
iremediabul	irremediable +
iremovable	irremovable +
iremovabul	irremovable +
ireplacable	irreplaceable
ireplasable	irreplaceable
ireprable	irreparable
ireprabul	irreparable
irepressible	irrepressible
iresolute	irresolute +
irespectiv	irrespective +
iresponsible	irresponsible +
iresponsibul	irresponsible +

ireverence	irreverence +
ireverens	irreverence +
ireverent	irreverent
ireversible	irreversible +
irevocable	irrevocable +
irevocabul	irrevocable +
irideemable	irredeemable +
irideemabul	irredeemable +
iridium	
irigashun	irrigation
irigate	irrigate ²+
irigation	irrigation
iris	
Irish	
irisistible	irresistible +
irisistibul	irresistible +
iritable	irritable +
iritant	irritant
iritashun	irritation
iritate	irritate ²+
iritation	irritation
iriversible	irreversible +
irk ¹ /some	
irode	erode ²
iron ¹ /monger	
ironeous	erroneous +
ironey	irony +
ironic /al/ally	
ironie	irony +
ironius	erroneous +
iron *y* /ies	
iroshun	erosion
irosion	erosion
irotic	erotic +
irradiat *e* ² /ion	
irrational /ly	
irreclaimable	
irreclaimabul	irreclaimable
irreconcilabl *e* /y	
irreconcilabul	irreconcilable +
irrecoverabl *e* /y	
irrecoverabul	irrecoverable +
irredeemabl *e* /y	
irredeemabul	irredeemable +
irrefutabl *e* /y	

irrefutabul	irrefutable +	ishuans	issuance
irregular /ly		ishue	issue ²+
irregularit y /ies		isicle	icicle
irrelevan ce /t		isight	eyesight
irrelevanc y /ies		isinglass	
irrelevansey	irrelevancy +	isite	eyesight
irreligious		island /er	
irreligus	irreligious	isle * (island)	
irremediabl e /y		isle	aisle *
irremediabul	irremediable +	islet * (small island)	
irremovabl e /y		islet	eyelet *
irremovabul	irremovable +	isn't (is not)	
irreparable		isnt	isn't
irreplacabul	irreplaceable	isobar	
irreplaceable		isolashun	isolation +
irreprabul	irreparable	isolate ²	
irrepresibul	irrepressible	isolation /ist	
irrepressible		isometric /ally	
irresistibl e /y		isosceles	
irresolute /ly/ness		isosilese	isosceles
irrespective /ly		isotherm	
irresponsibility		isotope	
irresponsibl e /y		Israeli	
irresponsibul	irresponsible +	Isralie	Israeli
irretrievabl e /y		issuans	issuance
irretrievabul	irretrievable +	issu e ² /ance	
irreveren ce /t/tly		isthmus	
irreverens	irreverence +	Italian	
irreversibl e /y		italic /s	
irreversibul	irreversible +	italicise ²	
irrevocabl e /y		italisize	italicise ²
irrevocabul	irrevocable +	Italyun	Italian
irrigat e ² /ion/or		itch ¹ /y	
irrisistable	irresistible +	item	
irritab le /ility/ly		itemise ²	
irritabul	irritable +	iternal	eternal +
irritant		iternally	eternally
irritashun	irritation	iternitey	eternity +
irritat e ² /ion		ither	either
irrupt ¹ /ion/ive		itinerant	
irupshun	irruption	itinerar y /ies	
irupt	irrupt ¹+	itinerey	itinerary +
iruption	irruption	it's * (it is)	
ise	ice ²+	its * (possessive)	
ishuance	issuance	iun	iron ¹+

iunmunger	ironmonger	jackdaw	
ivacuashun	evacuation	jackdoor	jackdaw
ivacuate	evacuate [2+]	jacket [1]	
ivacuation	evacuation	jack-kni*fe* [2] /ves (pl.)	
ivacuee	evacuee	Jacobean	
ivade	evade [2+]	Jacobi*n* /te	
ivaluashun	evaluation	jade [2]	
ivaluate	evaluate [2+]	jaffa	
ivaluation	evaluation	jaffer	jaffa
ivangelise	evangelise [2+]	jag [3]	
ivangelist	evangelist	jaguar	
ivaperator	evaporator	jail [1] /bird/er	
ivaporashun	evaporation	jam [3]★ (preserve) /my	
ivaporate	evaporate [2+]	jamb ★ (side post)	
ivaporation	evaporation	jamboree	
ivashun	evasion	jambori	jamboree
ivasion	evasion	jangle [2]	
ivasiv	evasive [+]	jangul	jangle [2]
I've (I have)		janiter	janitor
Ive	I've	janitor	
ivent	event [+]	January	
iventful	eventful	Janurey	January
iventual	eventual [+]	Japanese	
iventualitey	eventuality [+]	jar [3]	
ivicshun	eviction	jargon	
ivict	evict [1+]	jasmin	jasmine
iviction	eviction	jasmine	
ivie	ivy	jasper	
ivocashun	evocation [+]	jaundice [2]	
ivocation	evocation [+]	jaundis	jaundice [2]
ivocativ	evocative	jaunt [1] /ily/iness/y	
ivoke	evoke [2]	jauntie	jaunty
ivolve	evolve [2]	javelin	
ivory		jaw /bone	
ivry	ivory	jawndice	jaundice [2]
ivy		jawndis	jaundice [2]
		jawnt	jaunt [1+]
		jawntey	jaunty
J		jay /-walker	
		jaz	jazz [1+]
jab [3]		jazz [1] /y	
jabber [1] /er		jealous /ly/y	
jabot		jeans	
jack [1] /boot/pot		jeep	
jackal		jeer [1]	
jackass /es			

Jehovah		jingo /es/ism	
jelie	jelly +	jingul	jingle ²
jell y /ies		jirashun	gyration
jelous	jealous +	jirate	gyrate ²+
jelus	jealous +	jiration	gyration
jely	jelly +	jiro	giro ⋆
jemie	jemmy +	jiro	gyro ⋆+
jemm y /ies		jiroscope	gyroscope +
jemy	jemmy +	jist	gist
jenes	jeans	jiter	jitter ²+
jeopard ise ² /y		jitter ² /y	
jepadise	jeopardise ²+	jive ²	
jepardy	jeopardy	job ³ /less	
jeribilt	jerry-built	jockey ¹ /s	
jerie	jerry +	jockie	jockey ¹+
jerk ¹ /ily/iness/y		jocky	jockey ¹+
jerkin		jocose /ly	
jerry /-building/-built		jocular /ity/ly	
jersey /s		jocund /ity	
jersie	jersey +	jodhpurs	
jersy	jersey +	jodpers	jodhpurs
jery	jerry +	jodpurs	jodhpurs
jest ¹ /er		jog ³	
jet ³ /-propelled		joggle ²	
jetie	jetty +	jogul	joggle ²
jetison	jettison ¹	joi	joy +
jetsam		joiful	joyful
jettison ¹		join ¹ /er/ery	
jett y /ies		joint ¹ /er/ly	
jety	jetty +	joiride	joy-ride +
Jew /ish/ry		joist ¹	
jewel ³⋆ (gem)		joius	joyous +
jewel	duel ³⋆	jok e ² /er/ingly	
jewel	joule ⋆	joll y ⁴ /ier/iest/ily/ity	
jeweler	jeweller +	jolt ¹ /y	
jeweller /y		joly	jolly ⁴+
jewelrey	jewellery	jonkwil	jonquil
jib ³		jonquil	
jiffy		Joo	Jew +
jifie	jiffy	Jooish	Jewish
jify	jiffy	jool	joule ⋆
jig ³ /saw		joon	June
jilt ¹		joopiter	Jupiter
jim	gym +	joos	juice +
jingle ²		joosey	juicy

163

joot	jute	jugle	juggle ²⁺
jostle ²		jugular ★ (vein)	
josul	jostle ²	juic *e* /ier/iest/ily/y	
jot ³		Juish	Jewish
joule ★ (unit of energy)		jujoob	jujube
joule	duel ³★	jujube	
joule	jewel ³★	juke-box	
journal /ism/ist		jukstapose	juxtapose ²⁺
journey ¹ /s		jukstaposition	juxtaposition
jovial /ity/ly		Juli	July
jowl		July	
joy /ful/fully		jumble ²	
joyous /ly		jumbo	
joy-rid *e* /ing		jumbul	jumble ²
joyus	joyous ⁺	jump ¹ /er/iness/y	
ju	Jew ⁺	junkcher	juncture
jubilant /ly		junction	
jubilashun	jubilation	juncture	
jubilation		June	
jubilee		jungle	
jubili	jubilee	jungul	jungle
juce	juice ⁺	junier	junior
jucy	juicy	junior	
Judas		juniper	
judder ¹		junk	
judge ² /ment		junket ¹	
judicacher	judicature	junta	
judicature		Jupiter	
judicial /ly		jurer	juror
judiciar *y* /ies		juri	jury ⁺
judicious /ly		juridical /ly	
judishal	judicial ⁺	juriman	juryman ⁺
judisharey	judiciary ⁺	jurisdicshun	jurisdiction ⁺
judishus	judicious ⁺	jurisdiction /al	
judo		jurispruden *ce* /t	
juel	duel ³★	jurisprudens	jurisprudence ⁺
juel	jewel ³★	jur *ist* /or	
juel	joule ★	jurnal	journal ⁺
jueller	jeweller ⁺	jurnalism	journalism
juelrey	jewellery	jurnalist	journalist
jug ³		jurnie	journey ¹⁺
juge	judge ²⁺	jurny	journey ¹⁺
jugernawt	juggernaut	jur *y* /ies	
juggernaut		jury *man* /men (pl.)	
juggle ² /r ★ (conjurer)		juse	juice ⁺

jusie	juicy
just	
justice	
justifiabl *e* /y	
justifiabul	justifiable +
justificashun	justification
justif*y* ⁴ /ication	
justis	justice
jut ³	
jute	
juvenil *e* /ity	
juwel	jewel ³★
juweller	jeweller +
juwellrey	jewellery
juxtapos *e* ² /ition	
jym	gym +
jymkana	gymkhana
jymnasium	gymnasium +
jymnast	gymnast
jymnastics	gymnastics
jyroscope	gyroscope +

K

> *If you cannot find your word*
> *under* **k** *look under* **c**

kacao	cacao
kaen	cayenne
Kaiser	
kaison	caisson
kakey	khaki
kakie	khaki
kale	
kaleidoscop *e* /ic	
kalidascope	kaleidoscope +
kameliun	chameleon
kangaroo	
kaolin	
kaos	chaos +
kaotick	chaotic
karate	
karicter	character
karicterisashun	characterisation
karicterise	characterise ²+

karicteristic	characteristic +
karizma	charisma
kayak	
kedgeree	
keel ¹ /age	
keelige	keelage
keen ¹ /ly/ness	
keep /er/ing/sake	
keg	
kegeree	kedgeree
kejery	kedgeree
kelp	
kelsius	Celsius
kelt	Celt +
keltic	Celtic
kemical	chemical +
kemist	chemist +
kemistrey	chemistry
ken ³	
kenl	kennel
kennel	
kept	
kerb ¹★ (stone edging)	
kerb	curb ¹★
kerchief	
kernel ★ (seed)	
kernel	colonel ★
keropodie	chiropody +
keropody	chiropody +
keroseen	kerosene
kerosene	
kestrel	
ketch /es	
ketchup	
ketle	kettle +
kettle /drum	
ketul	kettle +
kew	cue ²★
kew	queue ★+
key ¹★† /hole/stone †(with lock)	
key	quay ★
khaki	
khan	
khrist	Christ

165

khristianity	Christianity	kiropodey	chiropody +
kiak	kayak	kiropodist	chiropodist
kibbutz		kiropody	chiropody +
kick [1] /er		kiser	Kaiser
kick-off		kiss [1] /er/es	
kid [3]		kit [3]	
kidd *y* /ies		kitchen	
kidie	kiddy +	kite	
kidnap [3] /per		kiten	kitten
kidney		kith	
kidy	kiddy +	kitie	kitty
kile	chyle	kitn	kitten
kill [1] /er		kitten	
kiln		kitty	
kilo		kity	kitty
kilocycle		kiyak	kayak
kilogram		klorate	chlorate
kilohertz		kloride	chloride
kiloliter	kilolitre	klorinashun	chlorination
kilolitre		klorinate	chlorinate [2]+
kilometer	kilometre	klorination	chlorination
kilometre		klorine	chlorine
kilotonne		klorofil	chlorophyll
kilotun	kilotonne	kloroform	chloroform [1]
kilowatt		klorophill	chlorophyll
kilowhat	kilowatt	knack /er	
kilt		knapsack	
kime	chyme	knave * (rascal) /ry	
kimono		knead [1]* (press)	
kin /dred/ship		knee /-cap/d *†/ing	
kinaesthesis		† (touch with knee)	
kind /ly/ness		kneel [1]	
kindergarten		knell [1]	
kindle [2]		knelt	
kindrid	kindred	knew * (did know)	
kindul	kindle [2]	knew	gnu *
kinesthesis	kinaesthesis	knew	new *+
kinetic		knickerbockers	
king /ly/-pin/-size		knickers	
kink /ier/iest/y		knick-knack	
kins *man* /woman/folk		kni *fe* [2] /ves (pl.)	
kiosk		knight * (rank)	
kipper [1]		knit [3]* (with needles)	
kirk		knob [3]* (handle) /by	
		knob	nob *

knock[1] /er/-kneed
knoll[1]
knot[3]* (what you tie) /ty
know *† /ing/ingly/s *†
  †(understand)
knowledge /able
knuckle[2] /duster
koala
Kodak

kola	koala
koolom	coulomb
kopeck	copeck
koral	choral *+
koral	coral *
koral	corral[3]*
kord	chord *
kord	cord *+
Kremlin	
kresh	crèche
krisalis	chrysalis +
krisanthimum	chrysanthemum
Krishna	
kroisant	croissant
kromate	chromate
kromatic	chromatic +
kromatin	chromatin
kromatograf	chromatograph +
kromatogram	chromatogram
krome	chrome +
kromic	chromic
kromium	chromium
kromosome	chromosome
krone*(money)/r(pl.)	
krone	crone *
kronicul	chronicle[2]+
kronie	crony +
kronik	chronic +
kronologey	chronology +
kuisine	cuisine
Ku-Klux-Klan	
kul de sac	cul-de-sac
kurb	curb[1]*
kurb	kerb[1]*
kurchif	kerchief
kurd	curd

kurdle	curdle[2]
kurdul	curdle[2]
kurk	kirk
kurl	curl[1]+
kurlew	curlew
kurlu	curlew
kurly	curly
kurnel	colonel *
kurnel	kernel *

> *If you cannot find your word under* **kw** *look under* **qu**

kwack	quack[1]
kwaff	quaff[1]
kwafur	coiffeur *+
kwafur	coiffure *
kwagmire	quagmire
kwail	quail[1]
kwaint	quaint +

L

label[3]	
laber	labour[1]+
labernum	laburnum
labirinth	labyrinth +
labium	
labor	labour[1]+
laborator *y* /ies	
laboratrey	laboratory +
laborious /ly	
laborius	laborious +
labour[1] /er	
Labrador	
labrum	
laburnum	
labyrinth /ine	
lac *e*[2] /y	
lacerat *e*[2] /ion	
lach	latch[1]+
lachrym *al* /ose	
lack[1] /-lustre	
lackadaisical	
lackadaysical	lackadaisical
lacker	lacquer[1]

167

lackey /s		lakrimal	lachrymal +
lacky	lackey +	lakross	lacrosse
laconic /ally		laks	lax +
lacquer [1]		laksativ	laxative
lacrimal	lachrymal +	lama * (Tibetan monk)	
lacros	lacrosse	lama	llama *
lacrosse		lamb /'s-wool	
lactashun	lactation	lame [2] /ly/ness	
lactation		lament [1] /ation	
lactic		lamentabl e /y	
lad /die		lamentabul	lamentable +
ladder [1]		lamentashun	lamentation
lad e *† /en/ing		laminate [2]	
†(load cargo)		lamp /light/shade	
lade	laid *	lampoon [1] /er/ist	
lader	ladder [1]	lampray	lamprey
ladie	lady +	lamprey	
ladilike	ladylike +	lance [2] /r/t	
ladiship	ladyship	land [1] /lord	
ladle [2]		landau	
ladul	ladle [2]	landaw	landau
lad y /ies		landing /-place	
lady like /ship		landlad y /ies	
laer	lair *	landlocked	
laer	layer [1]*	landlubber /ly	
laerd	laird	landmark	
laf	laugh [1]+	landoner	landowner
laffing stock	laughing-stock	landowner	
lafter	laughter	landscape [2]	
lag [3]		landsli de /p	
lagard	laggard	lane * (path)	
lager		lane	lain *
laggard		langger	languor +
lagoon		language	
laid * (lay)		languid /ly/ness	
laid	lade *+	languish [1]	
lain * (did lie on)		languor /ous	
lain	lane *	langwid	languid +
lair * (den)		langwidge	language
lair	layer [1]*	langwige	language
laird		langwish	languish [1]
laitie	laity	lanjerie	lingerie
laity		lank /iness/y	
lake		lanladie	landlady +
laker	lacquer [1]	lanlord	landlord

lanolin	
lans	lance [2+]
lanset	lancet
lantern	
lanthanum	
lanyard	
lap [3]	
lapel /led	
lapidary	
lapis lazuli	
lapse [2]	
larcen y /ies/ous	
larch /es	
larconic	laconic [+]
lard [1] /er	
large /ly/r/sse/st	
lariat	
laringitis	laryngitis
larinks	larynx [+]
larinx	larynx [+]
lark [1] /er	
larseny	larceny [+]
larva *† /e (pl.)/l †(of insects)	
larva	lava *
laryn x /gitis	
lascivious /ly/ness	
lase	lace [2+]
laser	
laserashun	laceration
laserate	lacerate [2+]
laseration	laceration
lasitude	lassitude
lasivious	lascivious [+]
lasivius	lascivious [+]
lasoo	lasso [1+]
lassitude ◄	
lasso [1] /es	
last [1] /ly	
latch [1] /key	
late /ly/st	
laten cy /t	
latensey	latency [+]
later * (afterwards)	
later	latter *[+]

lateral	
lath * (wooden strip)	
lathe * (machine)	
lather [1]	
Latin	
latis	lattice [+]
latitude	
latrine	
latter * (last) /ly	
lattice /d	
lattis	lattice [+]
laud [1*] (praise)	
laud	lord [1*+]
lauda ble /bly/tory	
laugh [1] /ter	
laughing-stock	
launch [1] /er/es	
laund er [1] /erette/ress	
laundrey	laundry [+]
laundr y /ies	
laureate	
laurel [3]	
lava * (of volcano)	
lava	larva *[+]
lavator y /ies	
lavatrey	lavatory [+]
lavender	
lavish [1] /ly/ness	
law * (rule) /-abiding	
law	lore *
law court /suit/yer	
lawd	laud [1*]
lawd	lord *[+]
Lawd Maer	Lord Mayor
lawdable	laudable [+]
lawdabul	laudable [+]
lawdatorey	laudatory
lawditrey	laudatory
lawful /ly	
lawless /ness	
lawn	
lawnch	launch [1+]
lawnder	launder [1+]
lawnderet	launderette
lawndress	laundress

169

lawndrey	laundry +
lax /ity/ly/ness	
laxative	
lay /by/ing/-out	
laybie	layby
laybye	layby
layer ¹★ (thickness)	
layer	lair ★
layman	
laz e ² /y	
lazi er /est/ly/ness	
lea ★ (open ground)	
lea	lee ★+
leach ¹★ (purge)	
leach	leech ★
lead ★ (direct) /er/ing	
lead ★ (element) /en	
lea f /flet/ves (pl.)	
leaf y /iness	
league	
leak ¹★ (hole) /age/y	
leak	leek ★
lean ¹	
leant ★ (inclined)	
leant	Lent ★
leant	lent ★
leap /ing/t	
leap -*frog* /-year	
learn ¹ /er/t	
lease ²	
leash ¹	
least /ways/wise	
leather /iness/n/y	
leav e /er/ing	
leaven ¹	
lebra	libra
lecher /ous/y	
lecherus	lecherous
lectern	
lecture ² /r/ship	
led ★ (did guide)	
led	lead ★+
ledge	
ledger	
ledo	lido

lee ★† /ward/way †(shelter)	
lee	lea ★
leech ★ (worm) /es	
leech	leach ¹★
leed	lead ★+
leef	leaf +
leeflet	leaflet
leeg	league
leege	liege
leek ★ (vegetable)	
leek	leak ¹★+
leen	lean ¹
leep	leap +
leep yeer	leap-year
leer ¹ /y	
leesh	leash ¹
left /ist/ward	
leftenancy	lieutenancy +
leftenansey	lieutenancy +
leftenant	lieutenant
left-hand /ed	
leg ³ /gy	
legac y /ies	
legal /ly	
legalis e ² /ation	
legalit y /ies	
legasey	legacy +
legashun	legation
legation	
legend /ary	
legendrey	legendary
leger	ledger
legib le /ility/ly	
legibul	legible +
legion /ary/aries	
legislacher	legislature
legislashun	legislation
legislat e ² /ion/or	
legislature	
legitima cy /te/tely	
legitimasey	legitimacy +
legitimis e ² /ation	
legonrey	legionary
leisure /ly	

lejun	legion +	lest	least +
lejunrey	legionary	lesure	leisure +
leksicografer	lexicographer +	let /table/ting	
leksicographer	lexicographer +	leter	letter 1
leksicon	lexicon	lethal /ly	
lemon /ade		lethargey	lethargy +
lemur		letharg y /ic	
lend /er/ing		lether	leather +
length /wise/y		letice	lettuce
lengthen 1		letis	lettuce
lenienc e /y		letre	litre
leniens	lenience +	letter 1	
lenient /ly		lettuce	
lens /es		letus	lettuce
Lent * (40 days)		leucocytes	
lent * (did lend)		leukaemia	
lent	leant *	Levant	
lenth	length +	leve	leave +
lenthen	lengthen 1	level 3 /ler/ly	
lenticel		level-headed	
lentil		levelheded	level-headed
Leo		leven	leaven 1
leopard		lever 1 /age	
leotard		leves	leaves
lep er /rous		leviathan	
leperd	leopard	levie	levy 4+
lepidopterous		levitashun	levitation
leprosy		levitat e 2 /ion	
lept	leapt	levity	
lerch	lurch 1+	levy 4 /ies	
lerk	lurk 1	lewd /ly/ness	
lern	learn 1+	lexicografer	lexicographer +
les	less +	lexicograph er /y	
Lesbian		lexicon	
lese	lease 2	lezbian	Lesbian
lesen	lessen 1*	li	lie *
lesher	leisure +	li	lye *
leshon	lesion	lia	liar *
lesion		liabilit y /ies	
leson	lessen 1*	liable	
leson	lesson *	liabul	liable
less /ee/er * (minor)		liaise 2	
lessen 1* (to belittle)		liaison 1	
lesson * (learnt)		liar * (tells lies)	
lessor * (grants lease)		liar	lyre *+

171

libel [3] /ler/lous	
libelus	libellous
liberal /ity/ly	
liberalis e [2] /ation	
liberashun	liberation
liberat e [2] /ion/or	
libertey	liberty +
libertine	
libert y /ies	
libid o /inal/inous	
libra	
libralise	liberalise [2+]
librar y /ies/ian	
lice	
licee	lycée
licence * (n.)	
license [2*] (v.) /e/r	
licenshiate	licentiate
licenshus	licentious +
licentiate	
licentious /ness	
lichen /ed	
lick [1]	
licoriss	liquorice
lid /ded	ˊ
lido	
lie * (untruth)	
lie	lye *
liege	
lieu * (place)	
lieutenan cy /t	
li fe /ves (pl.)	
life belt /blood/less/long	
life-size	
lift [1] /-off	
ligacher	ligature
ligament	
ligature	
light /er/ing	
lighten [1]	
light est /ly/ness	
lighthouse	
lightning	
light-weight	
light-year	

lignin	
lignite	
likable	
likabul	likable
like [2] /ly/ness	
likelihood	
liken [1]	
liker	liqueur [1*]
liker	liquor [1*]
likewise	
likoris	liquorice
likwefi	liquefy [4+]
likwid	liquid +
likwidashun	liquidation
likwidate	liquidate [2+]
likwidation	liquidation
likwiditey	liquidity
lilac	
lilak	lilac
lile	lisle
lilie	lily +
Lilipushun	Lilliputian
Lilliputian	
lilt [1]	
lil y /ies	
limb [1] /less	
limber [1]	
limbo /s	
lime /-kiln/light	
limelite	limelight
limerick	
limestone	
limf	lymph +
limfatic	lymphatic
limit [1] /ation	
limoosene	limousine
limousine	
limp [1] /er/ness	
limpet	
limph	lymph +
limphatic	lymphatic
limpid	
linage *†	
†(number of lines)	
linch	lynch [1]

172

line ² /r		lire	lyre ★+
lineage ★ (ancestry)		lirical	lyrical
lineament ★ (features)		lisay	lycée
lineament	liniment ★	lise	lice
linear /ity/ly		lisen	listen ¹+
linet	linnet	lisence	licence ★
linger ¹		lisence	license ²★+
lingerie		lisener	listener
lingo /es		lisensee	licensee
lingual		lisenshiat	licentiate
linguist /ic/ics		lisenshus	licentious +
lingwal	lingual	lisentiate	licentiate
lingwist	linguist +	lisentious	licentious +
liniament	lineament ★	lisle	
linier	linear +	lisp ¹	
liniige	lineage ★	lissom	
liniment ★ (salve)		list ¹	
liniment	lineament ★	listen ¹ /er	
link ¹ /age		listless /ly/ness	
links ★ (joins)		lisum	lissom
links	lynx ★	lit	
linnet		litan y /ies	
lino /cut/leum		lite	light +
linolium	linoleum	litehowse	lighthouse
linseed		litely	lightly
lint		liten	lighten ¹
lintel /led		liter	litre
lintul	lintel +	liter	litter ¹
linx	lynx ★+	literacher	literature
lio	Leo	litera cy /te	
lion /ess (fem.)		literal /ly	
lion-hearted		literar y /ily	
liotard	leotard	literasey	literacy +
lip ³ /stick		literat	literate
lip-read /er/ing		literature	
liquef y ⁴ /action		litergic	liturgic +
liquer	liquor ¹★	litergy	liturgy +
liqueur ¹★†		litewait	light-weight
†(sweet liquor)		lithe /ly/some	
liquid /ity		lithium	
liquidat e ² /ion/or		lithograf	lithograph +
liquor ¹★ (drink)		lithografey	lithography
liquor	liqueur ¹★	lithograph /ic/y	
liquorice		litig ant /ious	
liquoris	liquorice	litigashun	litigation

173

litigat *e* ² /ion		loby	lobby ⁴⁺
litijus	litigious	local ★ (of place)	
litle	little	locale ★ (locality)	
litmus paper		localis *e* ² /ation	
litning	lightning	localit *y* /ies	
litracher	literature	locashun	location
litre		locat *e* ² /ion/or	
litter ¹		loch ★ (lake)	
little		lock ¹★ (door) /er/jaw	
litul	little	locket	
liturgey	liturgy ⁺	locksmith	
liturgic /al		lockwacious	loquacious ⁺
liturg *y* /ies		lockwacity	loquacity
liv	live ²⁺	lockwashus	loquacious ⁺
livable		locomoshun	locomotion ⁺
livabul	livable	locomot *ion* /ive	
live ² /lihood/ly		locum	
liveli *er* /est/ness		locust	
liven ¹		lode ★ (mineral) /stone	
liver /ish		lode	load ¹★⁺
liver *y* /ies		lodge ² /ment/r	
livid		lof	loaf ¹⁺
living-room		loft ¹ /ier/iest/ily/iness	
livlie	lively	log ³ /ger	
livlier	livelier ⁺	loganberie	loganberry ⁺
livrey	livery ⁺	loganberr *y* /ies	
liying	lying	logarithm /ic	
lizard		log-book	
lizerd	lizard	loge	lodge ²⁺
llama ★ (animal)		logerhed	loggerhead
lo	low ⁺	loggerhead	
load ¹ ★† /er		logic /al/ally/ian	
†(heavy weight)		logishun	logician
load	lode ★⁺	logistics	
loa *f* ¹ /ves (pl.)		loial	loyal ⁺
loam /y		loialist	loyalist
loan ¹★ (lending)		loialtey	loyalty ⁺
loan	lone ★⁺	loier	lawyer
loath ★ (reluctant)		loin	
loath *e* ²★ (hate) /some		loiter ¹ /er	
lob ³		lokust	locust
lobby ⁴ /ist		lol	loll ¹
lobe		lolipop	lollipop
lobie	lobby ⁴⁺	loll ¹	
lobster		lollipop	

lom	loam +	lorgnette	
lone ★ (lonely) /r		loriat	laureate
lone	loan ¹★	lorie	lorry +
loneliness		lornch	launch +
lonesome		lornderet	launderette
lonesum	lonesome	lornyet	lorgnette
long ¹ /er/est/wise		lorr y /ies	
longevity		lory	lorry +
longitud e /inal/inally		los	loss +
loo ¹★ (card game)		los e ★† /ing/er/t	
loo	lieu ★	†(fail to win)	
loobricant	lubricant	lose	loose ²★+
loobricashun	lubrication	loshun	lotion
loobricate	lubricate ²+	loss +	
loocrativ	lucrative	lotery	lottery +
loodicrous	ludicrous +	lothe	loathe ²★+
loodicrus	ludicrous +	lothsum	loathsome
look ¹		lotion	
lookemia	leukaemia	lotter y /ies	
looker	lucre +	lotus	
looking-glass		loud /er/ly/ness	
lookwarm	lukewarm	loud-speaker	
loom ¹		lounge ² /r	
loominus	luminous +	lous e /y	
loona	luna	lout /ish	
loop ¹		lov e ² /able/ely/er	
loose ²★† /ly/ness/r/st		loveli er /est/ness	
†(not tight)		loves	loaves
loose	lose ★+	low ¹ /est/liness/ly	
loosen ¹		lowd	loud +
loosing	losing	lower ¹	
loot ¹★ (booty) /er		lownge	lounge ²+
loot	lute ★	lowse	louse +
lop ³		lowt	lout +
lope ²		loyal /ism/ist/ly	
loquacious /ly/ness		loyalt y /ies	
loquacity		lozenge	
loquashus	loquacious +	lozinge	lozenge
lord ¹★ (noble) /ly/ship		lu	lieu ★
lord	laud ¹★	lu	loo ¹★
lord(s) justice(s)		lubber /ly	
Lord Mayor		luber	lubber +
lore ★ (teaching)		lubricant	
lore	law ★+	lubricat e ² /ion	
lorel	laurel ³	lucer	lucre +

lucid /ity/ly/ness	
luck /ier/iest/ily/y	
lucr e /ative	
lude	lewd +
ludicrous /ly	
luff[1]	
lug[3] /ger	
luggage	
lugige	luggage
lugsuriant	luxuriant
lugubrious	
lukemia	leukaemia
lukewarm	
luksurey	luxury +
luksuriant	luxuriant
luksuriate	luxuriate[2]
luksurious	luxurious +
luksurius	luxurious +
lul	lull[1]
lulabie	lullaby +
lull[1]	
lullab y /ies	
lumbago	
lumbar * (back)	
lumber[1]* (wood)	
lumberjack	
luminary	
lumino us /sity	
luminus	luminous +
lump[1] /iness/y	
luna	
luna cy /tic	
lunasey	lunacy +
lunch[1] /eon/es	
lung	
lunge[2]	
lurch[1] /er	
lure[2]	
lurid /ly	
lurk[1]	
lurn	learn[1+]
lurner	learner
lurnt	learnt
luscious	
lushus	luscious

lusid	lucid +
lust[1] /ful	
luster	lustre +
lustie	lusty +
lustr e /ous	
lust y /ily/iness	
lute * (instrument)	
lute	loot[1*+]
lutetium	
Lutheran	
luv	love[2+]
luver	lover
luvley	lovely
luvlier	lovelier +
luxurey	luxury +
luxurian ce /t/tly	
luxuriate[2]	
luxurious /ly	
luxur y /ies	
lycée	
lye * (chemical)	
lye	lie *
lying	
lymph /atic	
lynch[1]	
lynx * (animal) /es	
lynx	links *
lyre *† /-bird †(instrument)	
lyre	liar *
lyric /al/ism/ist	

M

ma'am	
mac * (macintosh)	
mac	mach *
macabre	
macadam /ise[2]	
macaroni	
macaroon	
mace	
macerat e[2] /ion	
mach * (speed ratio)	

mach	match [1+]	magnificens	magnificence [+]
machate	machete	magnifisence	magnificence [+]
machete		magnifisent	magnificent
machiage	maquillage	magnif y [4] /ication	
Machiavellian		magnitude	
machination		magnolia	
machine [2] /ry		magnum	
machinist		magot	maggot [+]
mackerel		magpie	
mackintosh /es		Magyar	
macrocosm		mahara ja /nee (fem.)	
macroscopic		mahem	mayhem
mad /der/dest/ly/ness		mahjong	
madam /e (French)		mahogany	
madden [1]		maid * (girl) /en/enly	
made * (built)		maid	made *
made	maid *[+]	mail [1]* (letters)	
Madeira		mail	male *
mademoiselle		maim [1]	
mademwoisel	mademoiselle	main *† /land/ly	
maden	madden [1]	†(most important)	
madera	Madeira	main	mane *
madonna		maintain [1]	
madrigal		maintenance	
maelstrom		maintenans	maintenance
maer	mayor [+]	maisonette	
magazine		maize * (corn)	
magenta		maize	maze [2]*
maggot /y		majenta	magenta
Magi		majer	major [1+]
magic /al/ally/ian		majestey	majesty [+]
magishun	magician	majestic /ally	
magisterial /ly		majest y /ies	
magistrac y /ies		majong	mahjong
magistrat e /ure		major [1] /ette	
magnanim ity /ous		majorit y /ies	
magnanimus	magnanimous	mak	mac *
magnate *†		mak	mach *
†(prominent person)		makaber	macabre
magnesi a /um		makadam	macadam [+]
magnet *† /ic/ism		makaroon	macaroon
†(attracts iron)		mak e /ing/er/eshift	
magnetis e [2] /ation		Makiavelian	Machiavellian
magneto /s		makination	machination
magnificen ce /t/tly		maksila	maxilla [+]

maksim	maxim	malnutrishun	malnutrition
maksimise	maximise [2]	malnutrition	
maksimum	maximum [+]	malodorous	
malachite		Malpighian (layer)	
maladey	malady [+]	malstrom	maelstrom
maladjust *ed* /ment		malt [1] /ose	
maladministration		Maltese	
maladroit /ness		maltreat [1] /ment	
malad *y* /ies		maltreet	maltreat [1+]
malaise		mam	ma'am
malakite	malachite	mamal	mammal [+]
malaprop *ism* /os		mamarey	mammary
malard	mallard	mame	maim [1]
malaria		mammal /ian	
malase	malaise	mammary	
malcontent		mammon	
male [*] (man)		mammoth	
male	mail [1*]	mamon	mammon
maledicshun	malediction	mamoth	mammoth
malediction		man [3] /fully/ly/-of-war	
malefactor		mana	manna [*]
malet	mallet	manacle [2]	
maleus	malleus	manacul	manacle [2]
malevolen *ce* /t		manage [2] /able/ment	
malevolens	malevolence [+]	manager /ial	
malform [1] /ation		mandarin	
malformashun	malformation	mandat *e* [2] /ary [*] (law)	
malfuncshun	malfunction [1]	mandatory [*](command)	
malfunction [1]		mandatrey	mandatory [*]
maliable	malleable [+]	mandible	
malice		mandibul	mandible
malicious /ly/ness		mandolin	
malign [1] /er/ity		mane [*] (hair)	
malignanc *y* /ies		mane	main [*+]
malignansey	malignancy [+]	maner	manner [*+]
malignant		maner	manor [*+]
maline	malign [1+]	manganese	
malinger [1] /er		mang *e* /y	
malis	malice	mangel-wurzel	
malishus	malicious [+]	manger	
mallard		mangle [2]	
malleab *le* /ility		mango /es	
malleabul	malleable [+]	mangrove	
mallet		mangul	mangle [2]
malleus		manhandle [2]	

178

nanhandul	manhandle [2]
manhole	
manhood	
mania /c/cal	
manicur e [2] /ist	
manidge	manage [2]+
manie	many
manifest [1] /ation	
manifesto /s	
manifold [1]	
manige	manage [2]+
manikin	mannequin
manila	manilla
manilla	
manipulashun	manipulation
manipulat e [2] /ion	
manipulat ive /or	
manjer	manger
manliness	
manna * (food)	
mannequin	
manner *† /ed/ism/ly	
†(method)	
manoeuvr e [2] /able	
manoover	manoeuvre [2]+
manoovrable	manoeuvrable
manoovrabul	manoeuvrable
manor * (estate) /ial	
manshun	mansion
mansion	
manslaughter	
manslorter	manslaughter
mantel *† /piece	
†(shelf at fireplace)	
mantilla	
mantle [2]* (cloak)	
mantul	mantle [2]*
manual /ly	
manufaccher	manufacture [2]+
manufactur e [2] /er	
manure [2]	
manuscript	
many	
maonaise	mayonnaise
map [3]	

maple	
mapul	maple
maquillage	
mar [3]	
marathon	
maraud [1] /er	
marawd	maraud [1]+
marble [2]	
marbul	marble [2]
march [1] /er/es	
marchioness (fem.)	
Marconi	
mare	
mareen	marine +
margarine	
margerit	marguerite
margin /al/ally	
marguerite	
mariage	marriage +
marie	marry [4]
marige	marriage +
marigold	
marijuana	
marina	
marinade	
marinate [2]	
marine /r	
marionet	marionette
marionette	
marital	
maritime	
maritul	marital
mariwana	marijuana
marjoram	
mark [1] /edly/er	
market [1] /ability	
markey	marquee *
markey	marquis *+
markoni	Marconi
marksism	Marxism +
marksman	
markwis	marquis *+
marline-spike	
marmalade	
marmoreal	

179

marmorial	marmoreal
marmoset	
marmot	
maroon [1]	
marow	marrow
marquee * (tent)	
marquis * (noble)	
marriage /able	
marrow	
marry [4]	
Mars	
Marseillaise	
Marselase	Marseillaise
marsh /-mallow/y	
marshal [3]*†	
†(arrange in order)	
marshal	martial *+
marshoness	marchioness
marshun	Martian
marsupial	
marten * (animal)	
marten	martin *
marter	martyr [1]+
marterdom	martyrdom
marterise	martyrise [2]
martial *† /ly	
†(relating to war)	
martial	marshal [3]*
Martian	
martin * (bird)	
martin	marten *
martinet	
martyr [1] /dom	
martyrise [2]	
marvel [3] /lous/lously	
Marxis m /t	
marv	marry [4]
marzipan	
mas	mass [1]+
masacer	massacre [2]
masacre	massacre [2]
masage	massage [2]
mascot	
masculin e /ity	
mase	mace

maserate	macerate [2]+
mash [1]	
mashene	machine [2]+
mashenerey	machinery
mashenist	machinist
mashine	machine [2]+
mashinerey	machinery
mashinist	machinist
masiv	massive +
mask [1]* (cover)	
mask	masque *
maskerade	masquerade [2]
masoch ism /ist/istic	
masocism	masochism +
masocist	masochist
mason /ic/ry	
masonet	maisonette
masque * (ball)	
masque	mask [1]*
masquerade [2]	
mass [1] /es	
massacer	massacre [2]
massacre [2]	
massage [2]	
masseu r /se (fem.)	
massive /ly/ness	
massur	masseur +
master [1] /ly	
masterbate	masturbate [2]+
masterful /ly/ness	
masterpeace	masterpiece
masterpiece	
masticat e [2] /ion	
mastiff /s	
masturbat e [2] /ion	
mat [3]* (rug)	
mat	matt *
matador	
match [1] /es/less	
mate [2]	
mater	matter [1]
material /ism/ist/ly	
materialis e [2] /ation	
maternal /ly	
maternit y /ies	

180

mathematic s /al/ian	
mathematishun	mathematician
maths	
matinay	matinée
matinée	
mating	matting
matins	
matress	mattress +
matriarch /al/y	
matriculat e ² /ion	
matriks	matrix +
matrikulate	matriculate ²+
matrimon y /ial	
matri x /ces/xes (pls.)	
matron /ly	
matt * (dull surface)	
matter ¹	
matting	
mattress /es	
mature ² /ly	
maturity	
maul ¹	
mausoleum	
mauve	
maverick	
mawgage	mortgage ²+
mawkish /ness	
mawl	maul ¹
mawsoleum	mausoleum
maxilla /e (pl.)	
maxim	
maximise ²	
maxim um /a (pl.)	
may /be	
May /day/-fly	
mayhem	
mayonnaise	
mayor /al/alty	
maypole	
maze ²*†	
†(confusing paths)	
maze	maize *
mazurka	
mead	
meadow	

meager	meagre +
meagre /ly	
meak	meek +
meal /time/y	
mean * (nasty) /ing/t	
mean	mien *
meander ¹	
mean er /est/ly/ness	
meaning /ful/fully/less	
means	
meantime	
meanwhile	
measl es /y	
measuls	measles +
measurable	
measure ² /less/ment	
meat * (flesh)	
meat	meet *+
meat	mete ²*
mecanic	mechanic +
mecanise	mechanise ²+
mecanism	mechanism
mechanic /al/ally	
mechanis e ² /ation/m	
medal * (award) /list	
medal	meddle ²*+
medallion	
medalyon	medallion
medcine	medicine +
meddle ²*† /some/r *	
†(interfere /r)	
meddler	medlar *
medeval	medieval
medi an /al/ally	
medical /ly	
medicament	
medicat e ² /ion	
medicin e /al	
medieval	
mediocer	mediocre
mediocre	
mediocrit y /ies	
medisinal	medicinal
meditat e ² /ion/ive/or	
Mediterranean	

181

medi *um* /a/ums (pls.)	
medlar * (fruit)	
medle	meddle [2]*+
medler	meddler *
medler	medlar *
medley	
medly	medley
medow	meadow
medsin	medicine +
medul	meddle [2]*+
medulla	
meed	mead
meek /ly/ness	
meel	meal +
meeltime	mealtime
meen	mean *+
meener	meaner +
meening	meaning +
meeningful	meaningful
meens	means
meentime	meantime
meenwile	meanwhile
meerschaum	
meershum	meerschaum
meesels	measles +
meesley	measly
meet *(encounter)/ing	
meet	meat *
meet	mete [2]*
megacycle	
megafone	megaphone
megalith /ic	
megalomania /c	
megaphone	
meger	meagre +
megohm	
megom	megohm
mekanic	mechanic +
mekanical	mechanical
mekanise	mechanise [2]+
mekanism	mechanism
melanchol *y* /ia/ic	
melay	mêlée
mêlée	
melifluous	mellifluous

melifluus	mellifluous
mellifluous	
mellow [1]	
melodey	melody +
melodic /ally	
melodius	melodious
melodrama /tic	
melod *y* /ies/ious	
melon	
melow	mellow [1]
melt [1]	
member /ship	
membrain	membrane +
membran *e* /ous	
memento /es	
memo /s	
memoir	
memorabl *e* /y	
memorand *um*/a/ums(pls.)	
memorey	memory +
memorial	
memorise [2]	
memor *y* /ies	
memrable	memorable +
men (pl. of man)	
menace [2]	
menagerie	
menajerey	menagerie
menas	menace [2]
mend [1]	
mendacious /ly	
mendacity	
mendashus	mendacious +
mendasitey	mendacity
mendelevium	
mendicity	
menial /ly	
meningitis	
meninjitis	meningitis
menopause	
menopaws	menopause
menshun	mention [1]
menstrooal	menstrual
menstrooate	menstruate [2]+
menstrual	

menstruat *e* ² /ion	
ment	meant
mental /ity/ly	
mentalitey	mentality
menthol	
mention ¹	
mentor	
menu /s	
merang	meringue
mercantil *e* /ism	
mercenar *y* /ies	
mercenrey	mercenary +
merchandise	
merchant	
mercur *y* /ial	
merc *y* /iful/ifully/iless	
mere /ly/st	
meretricious	
meretrishus	meretricious
merge ² /r	
meridian	
meridional	
merie	merry +
meriment	merriment
meringue	
merit ¹	
meritorious	
meritorius	meritorious
mermade	mermaid
mermaid	
merr *y* /ier/ily/iment	
merry-go-round	
merry-making	
mersenrey	mercenary +
mersie	mercy +
mersiful	merciful
mersy	mercy +
mery	merry +
mesenger	messenger
mesh ¹	
Mesia	Messiah +
mesidge	message
mesie	messy
mesige	message
mesmeris *e* ² /m	

mesofill	mesophyll
mesophyll	
mess ¹ /ier/iest/ily/y	
message	
messenger	
Messia *h* /nic	
mesur	monsieur
mesurable	measurable
mesurabul	measurable
mesure	measure ²+
metabol *ic* /ism	
metacarpals	
metafisical	metaphysical +
metafisics	metaphysics
metafor	metaphor
metaforical	metaphorical +
metal ³★ (material)	
metal	mettle ★
metalic	metallic
metalise	metallise ²+
metallic	
metallis *e* ² /ation	
metallurg *y* /ical/ist	
metalurgey	metallurgy +
metamorfose	metamorphose ²+
metamorfosis	metamorphosis
metamorphos *e* ² /is/es (pl.)	
metaphor	
metaphorical /ly	
metaphysical /ly	
metaphysics	
metatarsals	
mete ²★ (measure)	
mete	meat ★
mete	meet ★+
meteor /ic/ite	
meteorolog *y* /ical	
meter ¹★ (machine)	
meter	metre ★+
methane	
methilate	methylate ²
method /ical/ically	
methylate ²	
meticulous /ly	
meticulus	meticulous +

183

metior	meteor +
metiorite	meteorite
metiorologey	meteorology +
metiorological	meteorological
metr e * (measure) /ic	
metre	meter ¹*
metricashun	metrication
metricat e ² /ion	
metronome	
metropoli s /tan	
mettle * (spirit)	
mettle	metal ³*
metul	mettle *
mew ¹ /s *†	
†(cat's cry, stable)	
mezanin	mezzanine
mezzanine	
mi	my +
miander	meander ¹
miaow	
mica	
mice (pl. of mouse)	
Michaelmas	
microb e /ial	
microbiolog y /ist	
microcosm	
microfilm	
microfone	microphone +
micrometer	
micron	
micro-organism	
microphon e /ic	
micropyle	
microscop e /ic/ical/y	
microwave	
mid-brain	
midday	
middle /-weight	
middling	
midge /t	
Midlands	
midling	middling
midnight	
midnite	midnight
midriff	

midshipman	
midst	
midsummer	
midul	middle +
midwi fe /ves (pl.)/fery	
mien * (bearing)	
mige	midge +
might * (strength, may)	
might	mite *
might ier /iest/ily/y	
migit	midget
migraine	
migrane	migraine
migrant	
migrat e ² /ion/or	
mika	mica
miklmas	Michaelmas
miks	mix ¹+
miksamatosis	myxomatosis
mikscher	mixture
mikser	mixer
miksture	mixture
mil	mill ¹+
milch-cow	
mild /ly/ness	
mildew /y	
mildu	mildew +
mile /age/stone	
milenium	millennium +
milet	millet
miligram	milligram +
milileter	millilitre
milimeter	millimetre
miliner	milliner +
milinerey	millinery
milinrey	millinery
milion	million +
milionair	millionaire
milipede	millepede
milisha	militia
militan cy /t	
militansey	militancy +
militarey	military +
militar y /ily/ism/ist	
militate ²	

militia	
milivolt	millivolt +
miliwot	milliwatt
milk [1] /er/iness/y	
milkmade	milkmaid +
milk *maid* /sop	
mill [1] /er	
millenni *um* /a (pl.)	
millepede	
millet	
milli *gram* /litre/metre	
milliner /y	
million /aire/th	
milli *volt* /watt	
milyun	million +
milyunair	millionaire
mime [2]	
mimeograph [1]	
mimic /ry	
mimick *ed* /ing	
mimiograf	mimeograph [1]
mimosa	
minaret	
mince [2] /meat/-pie/r	
mind [1] /er/ful/less	
mine [2] /sweeper	
miner *†	
†(works in a mine)	
miner	minor *
mineralog *y* /ical/ist	
minestrone	
minestrony	minestrone
mingle [2]	
mingul	mingle [2]
mini /skirt	
miniatur *e* /ist	
minicher	miniature +
minim /al/um/a (pl.)	
minimise [2]	
minion	
miniscule	minuscule
minister [1]	
ministerial /ly	
ministra *tion* /nt	
ministrey	ministry +

ministr *y* /ies	
minit	minute [2]+
mink	
minks	minx
minnow	
minor * (lesser)	
minor	miner *
minorit *y* /ies	
minow	minnow
minse	mince [2]+
minsmeat	mincemeat
minspie	mince-pie
minster	
minstrel	
mint [1]	
minuet	
minus /sign	
minuscule	
minushia	minutia +
minute [2] /ly	
minutia /e (pl.)	
minx	
minyouet	minuet
minyun	minion
miopia	myopia +
miow	miaow
mirac *le* /ulous	
miracul	miracle +
miraculus	miraculous
mirage	
mir *e* /y	
mirer	mirror [1]
miriad	myriad
mirror [1]	
mirth /ful/fully	
mis	miss [1]+
misadvencher	misadventure
misadventure	
misal	missal *
misal	missile *
misaliance	misalliance
misalians	misalliance
misalliance	
misanthrop *e* /ic/ist/y	
misapli	misapply [4]+

185

misappl*y*⁴ /ication
misapprehen*d*¹ /sion
misappropriat*e*² /ion
misaprehend — misapprehend¹⁺
misaprehenshun — misapprehension
misaprehension — misapprehension
misapropriate — misappropriate²⁺
misbehav*e*² /iour
misbehavier — misbehaviour
misbihave — misbehave²⁺
miscalculat*e*² /ion
miscariage — miscarriage
miscarie — miscarry⁴⁺
miscarige — miscarriage
miscarr*y*⁴ /iage
miscast
miscelanius — miscellaneous
miscellaneous
miscellan*y* /ies
mischance
mischans — mischance
mischie*f* /vous
mischif — mischief⁺
mischivus — mischievous
miscible
misconceive²
misconception
misconcieve — misconceive²
misconduct¹
misconsepshun — misconception
misconstru*e*² /ction
miscount¹
miscownt — miscount¹
miscreant
misdeed
misdemeanour
misdemener — misdemeanour
mise — mice
miselaneous — miscellaneous
miselaney — miscellany⁺
miselanius — miscellaneous
miself — myself
miselium — mycelium
miser /liness/ly
miserabl*e* /y

miserabul — miserable⁺
miser*y* /ies
misfire²
misfit
misfortune
misgave
misgidance — misguidance
misgidans — misguidance
misgide — misguide²⁺
misgiv*e* /en/ing
misgovern¹ /ment
misguid*e*² /ance
misguven — misgovern¹⁺
mishandle²
mishandul — mishandle²
mishap
mishun — mission
mishunarey — missionary
mishunrey — missionary
misile — missile ★
misinform¹ /ation
misinterpret¹ /ation
misiv — missive
misjudge² /ment
misjuge — misjudge²⁺
miskwotashun — misquotation
miskwotation — misquotation
miskwote — misquote²⁺
mislade — mislaid
mislaid
mislay /ing
misle — missal ★
misle — missile ★
mislead /ing
misled
misleed — mislead⁺
misnomer
misogyn*y* /ism/ist
misojinist — misogynist
misojiny — misogyny⁺
mispell — misspell⁺
mispelt — misspelt
mispend — misspend⁺
mispent — misspent
misplace² /ment

misplase	misplace [2+]	misultoe	mistletoe
misprint [1]		misunderstand /ing	
mispronounce [2]		misunderstood	
mispronownce	mispronounce [2]	misuse [2]	
misquot e [2] /ation		mite * (very small)	
misrable	miserable +	mite	might *
misrabul	miserable +	miten	mitten
misread /ing		miter	mitre [2]
misred	misread +	mith	myth +
misrepresent [1] /ation		mithical	mythical
misrool	misrule [2]	mithologey	mythology +
misrule [2]		mitie	mighty
miss [1] /es		mitigat e [2] /ion	
missal *(prayer book)		mitre [2]	
missal	missile *	mitten	
missellaneous	miscellaneous	mix [1] /er/ture	
missellany	miscellany +	mixamatosis	myxomatosis
missel-thrush		mixcher	mixture
misshapen		mnemonic	
missible	miscible	mo	mow [1+]
missile * (weapon)		moan [1] /er	
mission /ary/aries		moat [1]	
missive		mob [3]	
misspell /ing		mobil e /ity	
misspelt		mobilis e [2] /ation	
misspend /ing		mobilitey	mobility
misspent		moca	mocha
misstate [2] /ment		moccasin	
mist /ily/iness/y		mocha	
mistak e /able/en/ing		mock [1] /ery	
misterey	mystery +	mod e /ish	
misterious	mysterious +	model [3]	
misterius	mysterious +	moderashun	moderation
mistic	mystic *+	moderat e [2] /ion/or	
mistic	mystique *	modern /ism/ity	
mistifi	mystify [4+]	modernis e [2] /ation	
mistime [2]		modest /y	
mistisism	mysticism	modicum /s	
mistletoe		modifi	modify [4+]
mistook		modificashun	modification
mistress /es		modif y [4] /ication	
mistrust [1] /ful		modul	model [3]
misul	missal *	modulat e [2] /ion/or	
misul	missile *	modul us /i (pl.)	
misul thrush	missel-thrush	mohair	

mohare	mohair
moischer	moisture
moisen	moisten[1]
moist /ness/ure	
moisten[1]	
moka	mocha
mokasin	moccasin
molar	
molasses	
mold	mould[1+]
molder	moulder[1]
moldey	mouldy
mole	
molecul e /ar	
molest[1] /ation	
molicodle	mollycoddle[2]
molicodul	mollycoddle[2]
mollify[4]	
mollusc	
mollycoddle[2]	
molt	moult[1]
molten	
molusk	mollusc
molybdenum	
moment /arily/ary	
momentous	
momentum	
monak	monarch[+]
monakey	monarchy[+]
monarch /al/ical	
monarch y /ies	
monaster y /ial/ies	
monastic /ism	
monastrey	monastery[+]
Monday	
mone	moan[1+]
monetar y /ism/ist	
money /s (pl.)/ed	
Mongol /ian	
Mongol ism /oid	
mongoose /s	
mongrel	
moniter	monitor[1]
monitor[1]	
monk /ish	
monkey /s	
monochord	
monochrom e /atic/ic	
monocle	
monocotyledon	
monocul	monocle
monogamus	monogamous
monogam y /ist/ous	
monograf	monograph[1]
monogram	
monograph[1]	
monokord	monochord
monokrome	monochrome[+]
monokside	monoxide
monolith /ic	
monolog	monologue
monologue	
monomania /c	
monophonic	
monoplane	
monopoley	monopoly[+]
monopolis e[2] /ation	
monopolist /ic	
monopol y /ies	
monorail	
monosilabic	monosyllabic
monosilable	monosyllable[+]
monosyllab le /ic	
monothaism	monotheism[+]
monotheis m /t/tic	
monotipe	Monotype
monoton e /ic	
monoton ous /y	
monotonus	monotonous[+]
Monotype	
monoxide	
monsieur	
monsoon	
monst er /rous	
monstrosit y /ies	
monstrus	monstrous
month /ly	
monument /al/ally	
moo[1]	
mooch[1]	

mood /ily/iness/y	
moon[1] /beam/lit/y	
moonlight	
moor[1]*† /age	
†(waste ground)	
moor	more *+
moose * (animal)	
moose	mousse *
moot[1]	
moov	move[2]+
moovable	movable
moovabul	movable
mop[3]	
mope[2]	
moped	
moraine	
moral /e/ity/ly	
moralise[2]	
moralitey	morality
morass	
moratorium /s	
morbid /ity	
mordant	
more *† /over	
†(greater quantity)	
more	moor[1]*+
morfia	morphia +
morfine	morphine
morg	morgue
morgage	mortgage[2]+
morganatic /ally	
morgige	mortgage[2]+
morgue	
moribund	
morn * (morning)	
morn	mourn[1]*+
mornful	mournful +
moron /ic	
morose /ly	
morover	moreover
morow	morrow
morphi a /ne/nism	
morrow	
Morse	
morsel	

mortal /ity/ly	
mortar[1] /-board	
mortary	mortuary +
mortgag e[2] /ee/or	
mortifi	mortify[4]+
mortif y[4] /ication	
mortise[2]	
mortuar y /ies	
mos	moss +
mosaic	
moshun	motion[1]+
mosk	mosque
moskito	mosquito +
Moslem	
mosque	
mosquito /es	
moss /es/y	
most	
mote	
moteef	motif *+
motel	
moter	motor[1]+
moterboat	motorboat
motercycle	motorcycle
moterise	motorise[2]+
moterist	motorist
moterway	motorway
moth /-eaten	
mother[1] /ly	
mother-tongue	
motif * (ornament) /s	
motion[1] /less	
motivat e[2] /ion	
motive * (movement)	
motled	mottled
motley	
motlie	motley
motly	motley
moto	motto +
motor[1]/boat/cycle/way	
motoris e[2] /t	
mottled	
motto /es	
mould[1] /iness/y	
moulder[1]	

189

moult [1]	
mound [1]	
mount [1]	
mountain /eer/ous	
mountebank	
mountenus	mountainous
mourn [1]★ (grieve) /er	
mournful /ly	
mous e ★ (rodent) /er/y	
mouse	moose ★
mousse ★ (pudding)	
moustache	
mouth [1] /ful/piece	
movable	
movabul	movable
move [2] /ment	
move	mauve
mow [1] /er/n	
mownd	mound [1]
mownt	mount [1]
mowntain	mountain [+]
mowntbank	mountebank
mownten	mountain [+]
mowntenear	mountaineer
mowntenus	mountainous
mowse	mouse ★[+]
mowth	mouth [1+]
mowthful	mouthful
mu	mew [1+]
much	
muchooal	mutual [+]
mucilag e /inous	
muck [1] /y	
mucous ★ (adj.)	
mucus ★ (n.)	
mud /dy/guard	
muddid	muddied [+]
muddi ed /er/est	
muddle [2] /r	
mudid	muddied [+]
mudie	muddy
mudul	muddle [2+]
muff [1]	
muffin	
muffle [2] /r	

mufin	muffin
mufti	
muful	muffle [2+]
mug [3] /gy	
mukus	mucous ★
mukus	mucus ★
mulatto /s	
mulberie	mulberry [+]
mulberr y /ies	
mulch [1]	
mulct [1]	
mul e /eteer/ish	
mulkt	mulct [1]
mullion	
multifarious	
multifarius	multifarious
multiform	
multilateral /ly	
multiple	
multipleks	multiplex
multiplex	
multipli	multiply [4+]
multiplicashun	multiplication
multiplicity	
multipl y [4] /ication	
multipul	multiple
multiracial	
multirashul	multiracial
multitud e /inous	
multitudinus	multitudinous
mulyun	mullion
mumble [2]	
mumbo-jumbo	
mumbul	mumble [2]
mumie	mummy [+]
mumifi	mummify [4]
mummify [4]	
mumm y /ies	
mumy	mummy [+]
munch [1]	
mundane	
Munday	Monday
munetarey	monetary [+]
munetrey	monetary [+]
mungrel	mongrel

municipal /ity/ities	
munie	money +
munificen ce /t	
munifisens	munificence +
munifisent	munificent
munishun	munition [1]
munisipal	municipal +
munisipalitey	municipality
munition [1]	
munk	monk +
munky	monkey +
munth	month +
muny	money +
mur	myrrh
mural /ly	
murder [1] /er/ess/ous	
murk /ily/iness/y	
murmer	murmur [1]
murmur [1]	
murth	mirth +
murtle	myrtle
mus	mews *
mus	muse [2]*
muscat /el	
muscle [2]* (in body)	
muscle	mussel *
muscular /ity	
muse [2]* (think)	
muse	mews *
musel	muscle [2]*
musel	mussel *
museum /s	
mush /y	
mushroom [1]	
music /al/ally/ian	
musilage	mucilage +
musishun	musician
musk	
musket /eer/ry	
muskwash	musquash
musquash	
mussel * (shellfish)	
mussel	muscle [2]*
must /n't	
mustach	moustache

mustang	
mustard	
muster [1]	
mustie	musty +
must y /iness	
mutashun	mutation
mutation	
mute [2] /ly	
muter	mutter [1]
mutilat e [2] /ion/or	
mutinear	mutineer +
mutin eer /ous	
mutinus	mutinous
mutin y [4] /ies	
muton	mutton
mutter [1]	
mutton	
mutual /ly	
muzie	muzzy +
muzul	muzzle [2]
muzzle [2]	
muzz y /ily/iness	
my /self	
mycelium	
myopi a /c	
myriad	
myrrh	
myrtle	
mysterious /ly/ness	
mysterius	mysterious +
myster y /ies	
mystic *† /al/ism	
†(spiritual)	
mystif y [4] /ication	
mystique * (mystery)	
myth /ical/ology	
myxomatosis	

N

nab [3]	
naber	neighbour +
nabob	
nabour	neighbour +

nacher	nature	nascen *ce* /t	
nacheral	natural +	nasel	nasal +
nacheralise	naturalise ²+	nash	gnash ¹
nachural	natural +	nashanality	nationality +
nack	knack +	nashnalism	nationalism +
nacker	knacker	nashun	nation +
nader	nadir	nastie	nasty +
nadir		nast *y* /ier/iest/ily/iness	
naftha	naphtha	nat	gnat
nag ³ /ger		natal	
nail ¹		natie	natty
naive /té/ty		nation /al/ally	
naked /ness		nationalis *e* ² /ation	
nakid	naked +	nationalis *m* /t/tic	
nale	nail ¹	nationalit *y* /ies	
namby-pamby		native	
name ² /less/ly		Nativity	
nanie	nanny +	natle	natal
nann *y* /ies		natsi	Nazi
nany	nanny +	natty	
nap ³		natul	natal
napalm		natural /ism/ist/ly	
naparm	napalm	naturalis *e* ² /ation	
nape		nature	
naphtha		naty	natty
napie	nappy +	naught	
napkin		naughtie *r* /st	
napp *y* /ies		naught *y* /ily/iness	
napsack	knapsack	nause *a* /ous	
narate	narrate ²+	nauseate ²	
narativ	narrative	nautical	
narcissis *m* /t/tic		naval ★ (navy)	
narcissus		nave ★ (of church)	
narcosis		nave	knave ★+
narcotic		navel ★ (stomach)	
nar-do-well	ne'er-do-well	naverey	knavery
narl	gnarl ¹	navie	navvy ★+
narow	narrow ¹+	navie	navy ★+
narrat *e* ² /ion/or		navigab *le* /ility	
narrative		navigabul	navigable +
narrow ¹ /er/ly/ness		navigashun	navigation
narsissism	narcissism +	navigat *e* ² /ion/or	
narsissist	narcissist	navul	naval ★
narsisus	narcissus	navv *y* ★ (labourer) /ies	
nasal /ly		nav *y* ★ (warships) /ies	

naw	gnaw [1]	négligé	
nay * (no)		negligen ce /t	
nay	neigh [1]*	negligens	negligence [+]
naybour	neighbour [+]	negligibl e /y	
nayl	nail [1]	negligibul	negligible [+]
Nazi		neglijay	négligé
nead	knead [1]*	negoshable	negotiable
nead	need [1]*[+]	negoshabul	negotiable
neadle	needle [2]	negoshiate	negotiate [2+]
neadless	needless [+]	negotiable	
Neapolitan		negotiat e [2] /ion/or	
near /-by/ly/ness		negr o /oes/ess (fem.)	
neat /er/est/ly/ness		negroid	
nebul a /ous		neice	niece
nebulus	nebulous	neigh [1]* (horse's cry)	
necesarey	necessary [+]	neighber	neighbour [+]
necesitate	necessitate [2]	neighberhood	neighbourhood
necesitey	necessity [+]	neighbour /ing/ly	
necessar y /ily		neighbourhood	
necessitate [2]		neither	
necessit y /ies/ous		nek	neck [+]
neck /lace/tie		neklace	necklace
necksus	nexus	necklis	necklace
necrofilia	necrophilia	nekrofilia	necrophilia
necrophilia		nekropolis	necropolis
necropolis		nekst	next [+]
nectar /y		neksus	nexus
nee	knee [+]	nell	knell [1]
need [1]* (lack) /ful/y		nelt	knelt
need	knead [1]*	Nemesis	
need	kneed *	nemisis	Nemesis
needle [2]		nemonic	mnemonic
needless /ly		neodimium	neodymium
needul	needle [2]	neodymium	
neel	kneel [1]	neolithic	
neer	near [+]	neon	
ne'er-do-well		nephew	
neet	neat [+]	nepotism	
nefarious /ly		Neptune	
nefarius	nefarious [+]	neptunium	
nefew	nephew	nerv e [2] /y	
negashun	negation	nervous /ly/ness	
negation		nervus	nervous [+]
negative /ly		nesesarey	necessary [+]
neglect [1] /ful		nesesitate	necessitate [2]

nesesitey	necessity [+]	next /-of-kin	
neslin	nestling	nexus	
nest [1] /ling		ni	nigh
net [3] /ball		nibble [2]	
netha	neither	nibul	nibble [2]
nether		nice /ly/ness/r/st	
nettle [2] /rash		nicet y /ies	
netul	nettle [2+]	nich	niche
network		niche	
neumatick	pneumatic	nick [1]	
neural /gia		nickel	
neuritis		nickerbockers	knickerbockers
neurologist		nickers	knickers
neuron		nickle	nickel
neuro sis /tic		nicknack	knick-knack
neuter		nickname [2]	
neuton	newton	nicotine	
neutral /ity		niece	
neutralis e [2] /ation		niether	neither
neutron /s		nifarious	nefarious [+]
neva	never [+]	nifarius	nefarious [+]
never /more/theless		nife	knife [2+]
nevu	nephew	niftie	nifty [+]
new ★ (not old) /er/est		nift y /iness	
new	gnu ★	nigerd	niggard [+]
new	knew ★	niggard /ly	
newclear	nuclear	niggl e [2] /y	
newcleus	nucleus [+]	nigh	
new comer /fangled		night ★† /dress/gown	
new ly /ness		† (the dark)	
newmatic	pneumatic	night	knight ★
newmonia	pneumonia	night fall /jar	
newral	neural [+]	nightingale	
newritis	neuritis	nightmar e /ish	
newrologist	neurologist	night -shift /-time	
newron	neuron	night-watch /man	
newrosis	neurosis [+]	nigle	niggle [2+]
newrotic	neurotic	niglect	neglect [1+]
news /agent/-flash		nigul	niggle [2+]
news paper /print/y		niks	nix
newt		nilon	nylon
newter	neuter	nimble /ness	
newton		nimblie	nimbly
newtralise	neutralise [2+]	nimbly	
newtron	neutron	nimbul	nimble [+]

nimbus /es	
nimf	nymph
nimph	nymph
nincompoop	
nin e /th/thly	
nineteen /th	
ninet y /ies/ieth	
ningcumpoop	nincompoop
ninie	ninny +
ninn y /ies	
niobium	
nion	neon
nip 3 /per/py	
nipie	nippy
nipple	
nipul	nipple
nipy	nippy
nise	nice +
nisitey	nicety +
niss	niece
nit * (insect)	
nit	knit 3*
nite	knight *
nite	night *+
niter	nitre
nither	neither
nitrate	
nitre	
nitric	
nitrifi	nitrify 4
nitrify 4	
nitrite	
nitrogen /ous	
nitrogliserine	nitroglycerine
nitroglycerine	
nitrojen	nitrogen +
nitrous /oxide	
nitrus	nitrous +
nitwit	
nives	knives
nix	
no * (negative reply)	
no	know *+
nob * (cribbage)	
nob	knob 3*+

nobie	knobby
nobility	
noble /man/men(pl.)/r/st	
noblie	nobly
nobly	
nobul	noble +
nock	knock 1+
nocker	knocker
nockneed	knock-kneed
nodes	
nodule	
noes * (negative)	
noes	knows *
noes	nose *+
noledge	knowledge +
nolidge	knowledge +
noll	knoll 1
nome	gnome +
nomon	gnomon
none * (not any)	
none	nun *+
nor	gnaw 1
norsia	nausea +
norsiate	nauseate 2
nort	naught
nortey	naughty +
nortickle	nautical
nortie	naughty +
Norwegian	
nose * (on face) /y	
nose	knows *
nose	noes *
nostril	
not * (no)	
not	knot 3*+
notie	knotty
notty	knotty
nova	
nowing	knowing
nowledge	knowledge +
nu	gnu *
nu	knew *
nu	new *+
nuance	
nuans	nuance

nuckle	knuckle [2]+	nuspaper	newspaper +
nuclear		nut /cracker/shell	
nucle *us* /i (pl.)		nuta	neuter
nud *e* /ist/ity		nuter	neuter
nudge [2]		nutie	nutty
nuge	nudge [2]	nutmeg	
nugget		nuton	newton
nulifi	nullify [4]+	nutralise	neutralise [2]+
nulitey	nullity	nutrishun	nutrition
null		nutrition	
nullif *y* [4] /ication		nutron	neutron
nullity		nutty	
numatic	pneumatic	nuty	nutty
numb [1] /ness		nuzul	nuzzle [2]
number [1] /-plate		nuzzle [2]	
numer *able* /acy/al		nylon	
numerabul	numerable +	nymf	nymph
numerasey	numeracy	nymph	
numerat *e* [2] /ion			
numerical			
numerous /ly/ness			
numerus	numerous +		
numismatic /s			

O

numonia	pneumonia	O ★ (addressing)	
numrable	numerable +	o	oh ★
numrabul	numerable +	o	owe [2]★
numskull		oaf /ish	
nun ★ (religious) /nery		oak /en	
nun	none ★	oakum	
nupshal	nuptial	oar ★ (of a boat)	
nuptial		oar	ore ★
nural	neural +	oas *is* /es (pl.)	
nuralgia	neuralgia	oast	
nurcher	nurture [2]	oat /meal	
nuritis	neuritis	oath	
nurologist	neurologist	obay	obey [1]
nuron	neuron	obduracy	
nurosis	neurosis +	obdurasey	obduracy
nurotic	neurotic	obdurate /ly	
nurse [2]		obedien *ce* /t	
nurser *y* /ies		obediens	obedience +
nursrey	nursery +	obelisk	
nurture [2]		obes *e* /ity	
nurv	nerve [2]+	obey [1]	
nus	news +	obituar *y* /ies	
		objecshun	objection +

object [1] /or	
objection /able	
objectiv e /ely/ity	
obligashun	obligation +
obligat ion /ory	
obligatrey	obligatory
oblige [2]	
oblik	oblique +
oblique /ly/ness	
obliterashun	obliteration
obliterat e [2] /ion	
obliv ion /ious	
oblivius	oblivious
oblivyun	oblivion +
oblokwey	obloquy +
oblong	
obloqu y /ies	
obnokshus	obnoxious +
obnoxious /ly	
obo	oboe +
obo e /ist	
obscene /ly	
obscure [2] /ly	
obscurit y /ies	
obseen	obscene +
obsekwies	obsequies
obsekwius	obsequious +
obsequies	
obsequious /ly	
observable	
observabul	observable
observan ce /t	
observashun	observation
observator y /ies	
observatrey	observatory +
observ e [2] /ation/er	
observence	observance +
observens	observance +
obseshun	obsession
obsess [1] /ion/ive	
obsolescen ce /t	
obsolesens	obsolescence +
obsolesent	obsolescent
obsolete	
obstacle	

obstacul	obstacle
obstetric /ian/s	
obstetrishun	obstetrician
obstinacy	
obstinasey	obstinacy
obstinate /ly	
obstreperous	
obstreperus	obstreperous
obstrucshun	obstruction
obstruct [1] /ion/ive	
obtain [1] /able	
obtane	obtain [1]+
obtroode	obtrude [2]+
obtrooshun	obtrusion +
obtroosion	obtrusion +
obtroosiv	obtrusive
obtrude [2] /r	
obtrus ion /ive	
obtuse /ly/ness	
obverse	
obviate [2]	
obvious /ly	
obvius	obvious +
ocasion	occasion[1]+
ocasional	occasional
occashun	occasion [1]+
occasion [1] /al/ally	
occident /al	
occlu de [2] /sion	
occlushun	occlusion
occult [1] /ation	
occupan cy /t	
occupation /al	
occupi	occupy [4]+
occup y [4] /ier	
occur [3] /rence	
occurens	occurrence
ocean	
ocell us /i (pl.)	
ocelot	
ochre	
o'clock	
oclude	occlude [2]+
oclusion	occlusion
ocsident	occident +

197

octagon /al	
octane	
octav e /o	
octet	
October	
octogenarian	
octopus /es	
ocul ar /ist	
ocult	occult [1+]
ocupancy	occupancy +
ocupant	occupant
ocupashun	occupation +
ocupation	occupation +
ocupi	occupy [4+]
ocur	occur [3+]
ocurence	occurrence
ocurens	occurrence
od	odd +
odd /er/est/ly/ment	
oddit y /ies	
ode	
odecolone	eau-de-cologne
oder	odour +
oderiferus	odoriferous
oderous	odorous
oderus	odorous
odiferus	odoriferous
odious /ly	
oditey	oddity +
odium	
odius	odious +
odontology	
odoriferous	
odorous	
odour /less	
oesofagus	oesophagus
oesophagus	
of * (belonging to)	
of	oaf +
of	off *+
ofal	offal
ofence	offence
ofend	offend [1+]
ofens	offence
ofensiv	offensive +

ofer	offer [1]
off * (away from) /ing	
offal	
offence	
offend [1] /er	
offens	offence
offensive /ly/ness	
offer [1]	
offhand /ed/edness	
office /r	
official /ly	
officiate [2]	
officious /ly/ness	
offis	office +
offishal	official +
offishus	officious +
offprint	
offset /ting	
offshoot	
offside	
ofhand	offhand +
oficial	official +
oficiate	officiate [2]
oficious	officious +
ofing	offing
ofis	office +
ofiser	officer
ofishal	official +
ofishiate	officiate [2]
ofishus	officious +
ofprint	offprint
ofset	offset +
ofshoot	offshoot
ofside	offside
oft /en	
ofthalmia	ophthalmia +
ofthalmologist	ophthalmologist +
oger	ogre +
ogle [2] /r	
ogre /ss (fem.)	
ogul	ogle [2+]
oh * (exclaim)	
oh	O *
ohm /ic/meter	
oil [1] /y	

ointment	
oister	oyster
oiyay	oyez
ok	oak +
oks	ox +
oksalic	oxalic
oksbridge	Oxbridge
oksbrige	Oxbridge
oksen	oxen
oksiasetilene	oxy-acetylene
oksidashun	oxidation
oksidation	oxidation
okside	oxide +
oksident	occident +
oksidise	oxidise 2+
oksigen	oxygen
oksigenate	oxygenate 2+
oksigenise	oxygenise 2
oksihemoglobin	oxyhaemoglobin
oksonian	Oxonian
okstail	oxtail
okstale	oxtail
okstung	ox-tongue
okum	oakum
old /en/er	
olfacshun	olfaction +
olfact ion /ory	
olfactrey	olfactory
oligarch y /ies	
oligarkey	oligarchy +
olimpic	Olympic +
oliv	olive
olive	
Olympi c /an	
om	ohm +
ombudsman	
omega	
omelet	omelette
omelette	
omen 1	
ominous /ly	
ominus	ominous +
omishun	omission
omission	
omit 3	

omlet	omelette
omnibus /es	
omnipoten ce /t	
omnipotens	omnipotence +
omnipresent	
omniscien ce /t	
omnisiens	omniscience +
omnisient	omniscient
omnivorous /ly	
omnivorus	omnivorous +
on	own 1
once	
oncoming	
oncore	encore 2
one * (single) /self	
oner	honour 1+
oner	owner +
onerable	honourable
onerabul	honourable
onerous	
onership	ownership
onerus	onerous
oniks	onyx
onion	
onist	honest +
onistey	honesty
onley	only
onlook er /ing	
only	
onomatipea	onomatopoeia +
onomatopoei a /c	
onorarey	honorary
onorarium	honorarium +
onrable	honourable
onrabul	honourable
onrush	
onset	
onslaught	
onslawt	onslaught
onslort	onslaught
onto	
ontray	entrée
ontreprener	entrepreneur +
onus	
onward /s	

199

onyx	
oolit e /ic	
ooze ² /y	
opacity	
opake	opaque +
opal /ine	
opalescen ce /t	
opalesens	opalescence +
opaque /ly	
opasitey	opacity
open ¹ /er	
open sesame	
opera /tic/tically	
operab le /ility	
operabul	operable +
operashun	operation +
operat e ² /ive/or	
operater	operator
operation /al	
operetta	
ophthalmi a /c	
ophthalmolog ist /y	
opiate	
opine ²	
opinion /ated	
opinyun	opinion +
opium	
oponent	opponent
oportune	opportune +
oportunism	opportunism +
oportunist	opportunist
oportunitey	opportunity +
opose	oppose ²+
oposishun	opposition
oposit	opposite +
oposition	opposition
opossum	
oposum	opossum
opponent	
opportune /ly/ness	
opportun ism /ist	
opportunit y /ies	
oppose ² /r	
opposishun	opposition
opposit e /ion	

oppress ¹ /ion/ive	
oprable	operable +
oprabul	operable +
opreshun	oppression
opresiv	oppressive
opress	oppress ¹+
opshun	option +
opshunal	optional
opt ¹ /ative	
opthalmia	ophthalmia +
opthalmic	ophthalmic
opthalmologist	ophthalmologist +
opthalmology	ophthalmology
optic /al/ally	
optician	
optimise ²	
optimism	
optimistic /ally	
optimum	
option /al/ally	
optishun	optician
opulen ce /t	
opulens	opulence +
opus	
or * (alternative)	
or	awe ²*+
or	oar *
or	ore *
ora	aura
orac le /ular	
oracul	oracle +
oral * /ly (verbal)	
oral	aural *+
orangatang	orang-outang
orange /ade	
orang-outang	
orashun	oration +
orater	orator
orat ion /or	
oratorio /s	
orator y /ies	
oratrey	oratory +
orb ¹	
orbit ¹ /al	
orcestra	orchestra

orcestrate	orchestrate $^{2+}$	original /ity/ly	
orchard		originat e^2 /ion/or	
orchestra		oringe	orange $^+$
orchestrat e^2 /ion/or		oriole	
orchid		orkestrate	orchestrate $^{2+}$
ordain ^{1}		orkid	orchid
ordane	ordain ^{1}	orlder	alder
ordeal		ornament ^{1} /al/ation	
ordenrey	ordinary $^+$	ornate /ly	
order ^{1} /liness/ly		orning	awning
ordinal		ornitholog y /ist	
ordinance $\star$ (rule)		orphan ^{1} /age	
ordinance	ordnance $\star$	orspishus	auspicious
ordinar y /ily		orstralian	Australian
ordinat e^2 /ion		orstruck	awestruck
ordinrey	ordinary $^+$	orsum	awesome
orditer	auditor	ort	aught $\star$
orditorey	auditory	ort	ought $\star$
orditrey	auditory	orthedoks	orthodox
ordnance $\star$ (survey, guns)		orthodox	
ordure		orthografey	orthography $^+$
ore $\star$ (mineral)		orthograph y /ic/ical	
ore	awe $^{2\star+}$	orthopaedic	
ore	oar $\star$	orthopeadic	orthopaedic
orfan	orphan $^{1+}$	orthoritarian	authoritarian $^+$
orfanage	orphanage	ortolan	
orfanige	orphanage	oscilashun	oscillation $^+$
orful	awful $^+$	oscilation	oscillation $^+$
organ /ist		oscillate ^{2*} (swing)	
organic		oscillat ion /or/ory	
organis e^2 /ation/er		oscillogra m /ph	
organism		oscilloscope	
orgasm		osculate ^{2*} (contact)	
orger	auger $\star$	oselot	ocelot
orger	augur ^{1*}	oshun	ocean
orgey	orgy $^+$	osicul	ossicle
org y /iastic/ies		osier	
orical	auricle $^+$	osifi	ossify $^{4+}$
oriel		osius	osseous
orient /al/ally		osler	ostler
orientashun	orientation	osmium	
orientat e^2 /ion		osmosis	
orifice		ospray	osprey $^+$
orifis	orifice	osprey /s	
origin		osseous	

osseus	osseous	outbid /ding	
ossicle		outbilding	outbuilding
ossifi	ossify [4+]	outboard	
ossif *y* [4] /ication		outbound	
ossilate	oscillate [2★]	outbownd	outbound
ossilation	oscillation [+]	outbrake	outbreak
ossilograf	oscillograph	outbreak	
ossilogram	oscillogram [+]	outbuilding	
ossiloscope	oscilloscope	outburst	
ost	oast	outcase	
ostensibl *e* /y		outclass [1]	
ostensibul	ostensible [+]	outcome	
ostentashun	ostentation [+]	outcri	outcry [+]
ostentashus	ostentatious	outcrop	
ostentat *ion* /ious		outcr *y* /ies	
osteo-arthritis		outdate [2]	
osteology		outdistance [2]	
osteopath /y		outdo /ing/ne	
ostintashun	ostentation [+]	outdoor /s	
ostioarthritis	osteo-arthritis	outer /most	
ostiologey	osteology	outface	
ostler		outfall	
ostracis *e* [2] /m		outfit /ter	
ostrasism	ostracism	outflank [1]	
ostrasize	ostracise [2+]	outflow	
ostrich /es		outgoing /s	
ote	oat [+]	outgrow /n/th	
oter	otter	outhouse	
oth	oath	outhowse	outhouse
other /wise		outlandish /ness	
otoman	ottoman	outlast [1]	
otter		outlaw [1] /ry	
ottoman		outlay	
ought ★ (should)		outlet	
ought	aught ★	outliing	outlying
ouija		outline [2]	
ounce		outlive [2]	
ouns	ounce	outlook	
our ★ (belonging to us)		outlying	
our	hour ★+	outmanoeuvre [2]	
ourly	hourly	outmanoover	outmanoeuvre [2]
ourselves		outmatch [1]	
oust [1]		outmoded	
out [1]		outnumber [1]	
outback		outpace [2]	

outpashent	out-patient
out-patient	
outpoor	outpour [1]
outpost	
outpour [1]	
output	
outrage [2] /ous/ously	
outragus	outrageous
outran	
outreach [1]	
outrid e /den/ing/er	
outright	
outrite	outright
outrun /ning	
outset	
outshin e /ing	
outshone	
outside /r	
outsize	
outskirts	
outspoken /ness	
outstanding /ly	
outstare [2]	
outstay [1]	
outstretch [1]	
outstrip [3]	
outvote [2]	
outward /ly/s	
outwit [3]	
outworn	
ov	of *
oval	
ovarey	ovary [+]
ovarian	
ovar y /ies	
ovashun	ovation
ovation	
oven	
over	
overact [1]	
overall /s	
overan	overran
overarm	
overate * (overeat)	
overate	overrate [2]*

overawe [2]	
overawl	overall [+]
overbalance [2]	
overbalans	overbalance [2]
overbaring	overbearing
overbearing	
overberden	overburden [1]
overblown	
overboard	
overbord	overboard
overburden [1]	
overcame	
overcast	
overcharge [2]	
overcoat	
overcom e /ing	
overcrowd [1]	
overdew	overdue
overdo /ing/ne	
overdose [2]	
overdraft	
overdraw /n	
overdrive	
overdu	overdue
overdue	
overdun	overdone
overeach	overreach [1]
overeat /en/ing	
overeet	overeat [+]
overestimate [2]	
overflow [1]	
overground	
overgrow /n/th	
overgrownd	overground
overhand	
overhang /ing	
overhaul [1]	
overhawl	overhaul [1]
overhead /s	
overhear /ing	
overheard	
overheat [1]	
overhed	overhead [+]
overheet	overheat [1]
overherd	overheard

203

overhere	overhear +	overstate² /ment	
overhung		overstep³	
overide	override +	overstock¹	
overjoi	overjoy +	overstrung	
overjoy /ed		overt /ly	
overladen		overtak e /en/ing	
overland		overtaks	overtax¹
overlap³		overtax¹	
overla y /id		overtern	overturn¹
overleaf		overthrow /n	
overleef	overleaf	overtime	
overload¹		overtire²	
overlode	overload¹	overtone	
overlook¹		overtook	
overmuch		overture	
overnight		overturn¹	
overnite	overnight	overwate	overweight
overore	overawe²	overweight	
overought	overwrought	overwelm	overwhelm¹⁺
overpass		overwerk	overwork¹
overpower¹		overwhelm¹ /ingly	
overproduc e² /tion		overw ind /ound	
overproducshun	overproduction	overwork¹	
overran		overwownd	overwound
overrate²★ (overvalue)		overwrought	
overrate	overate ★	oviduct	
overrawt	overwrought	ovine	
overreach¹		oviparous	
overreech	overreach¹	oviparus	oviparous
overrid e /den/ing		ovipositor	
overrool	overrule²	ovoid	
overrule²		ovoyd	ovoid
overrun /ning		ovulashun	ovulation
oversaw		ovulat e² /ion	
oversea ★ (abroad) /s ★		ovule	
oversee ★† /ing/n/r/s ★†		ov um /a (pl.)	
†(supervise)		owe²★ (in debt)	
overshadow¹		ower	hour ★⁺
overshoot		ower	our ★
overshot		owerselves	ourselves
oversight		owl /ish	
oversite	oversight	own¹	
oversle ep /pt		ownce	ounce
oversore	oversaw	owner /less/ship	
overspill¹		owns	ounce

204

owst	,oust [1]
owt	out [1]
owtbilding	outbuilding
owtbord	outboard
owtbound	outbound
owtbownd	outbound
owtbreak	outbreak
owtlaw	outlaw [1+]
ox /en (pl.)	
oxalic	
Oxbridge	
oxbrige	Oxbridge
oxidashun	oxidation
oxid *e* /ation	
oxidis *e* [2] /ation	
oxigenate	oxygenate [2+]
oxigenise	oxygenise [2]
oxihemoglobin	oxyhaemoglobin
Oxonian	
oxtail	
oxtale	oxtail
ox-tongue	
oxy-acetylene	
oxygen	
oxygenat *e* [2] /ion	
oxygenise [2]	
oxyhaemoglobin	
oyez	
oyster	
ozier	osier
ozone layer	

P

pace [2] /-maker	
pach	patch [1+]
pachwerk	patchwork
pachwork	patchwork
pachyderm /atous	
pacific /ally	
pacifis *m* /t	
pacif *y* [4] /ication/ier	
pack [1] /-horse/-ice	
package [2]	

packet	
packiderm	pachyderm [+]
packidge	package [2]
packing-case	
pact	
pad [3]	
paddle [2] /r/-wheel	
paddock	
paddy /-field	
pade	paid [+]
padie	paddy [+]
padlock [1]	
padock	paddock
padray	padre
padre	
padul	paddle [2+]
pady	paddy [+]
pagan /ism	
pag *e* [2] /ination	
pageant /ry	
pagentrey	pageantry
paginashun	pagination
pagoda	
paid /-up	
pail ★ (bucket)	
pail	pale [2★]
pain [1★] (suffering) /less	
pain	pane ★
painful /ly	
pain-killer	
painstaking	
paint [1] /er	
pair [1★] (two)	
pair	pare [2★]
pair	pear ★+
pakiderm	pachyderm [+]
pakidurm	pachyderm [+]
pal /ly	
pala *ce* /tial	
paladium	palladium
palankwin	palanquin
palanquin	
palas	palace [+]
palashul	palatial
palatabl *e* /y	

205

palatabul	palatable +	pamphlet /eer	
palat e /al		pan ³ /cake	
palatinate		panacea	
palaver		panache	
pale ²★ (whitish)		pan-African	
pale	pail ★	Panama	
paleografey	paleography	pan-American	
paleography		panasea	panacea
paleolithic		panash	panache
paleontolog y /ist		panchromatic	
paleozoic		pancrea s /tic	
pale r /ly/ness/st		pancromatic	panchromatic
palet	pallet ★	panda ★ (animal)	
palet	palette ★+	pandemonium	
palette ★† /-knife		pander ¹★ (indulge)	
†(artist's board)		pane ★ (of glass)	
palfrey		pane	pain ¹★+
paliass	palliasse	paneful	painful +
paliate	palliate ²+	panegyric	
palid	pallid +	panekiller	pain-killer
palindrome		panel ³ /list	
palis	palace +	panestaking	painstaking
palisade		pang	
pall ¹ /-bearer		panic /-stricken/-struck	
palladium		panick ed /ing/y	
pallet ★ (bed)		panickt	panicked +
pallet	palette ★+	panier	pannier
palliasse		panigiric	panegyric
palliat e ² /ive		panikey	panicky
pall id /or		panikstriken	panic-stricken
palm ¹ /ist/istry		pannier	
palmie	palmy	panopl y /ied	
palmy		panorama /s	
palor	pallor	panoramic /ally	
palpabl e /y		pansie	pansy +
palpabul	palpable +	pansnay	pince-nez
palpitashun	palpitation	pans y /ies	
palpitat e ² /ion		pant ¹	
palsie	palsy +	pantaloon	
pals y /ied		pantechnicon	
paltrie	paltry +	panteknicon	pantechnicon
paltr y /iness		pantheis m /t/tic	
pamflet	pamphlet +	pantheon	
pampas		panther	
pamper ¹ /er		panthiism	pantheism +

206

panthion	pantheon
pantile	
pantograf	pantograph +
pantograph /y	
pantomime	
pantrey	pantry +
pantr *y* /ies	
papa *cy* /l	
papasey	papacy +
\per [1] /back/-chase	
paperwait	paperweight
paperweight	
papier-mâché	
papirus	papyrus +
papist /ical	
papoose	
paprika	
papyamashay	papier-mâché
papyr *us* /i (pl.)	
parable	
parabol *a* /ic	
parabul	parable
parachut *e* [2] /ist	
parade [2]	
paradigm	
paradim	paradigm
paradise	
paradoks	paradox +
paradox /ical/ically	
parafernalia	paraphernalia
paraffin	
parafrase	paraphrase [2]
paragon	
paragraf	paragraph
paragraph	
parakeet	
paralaks	parallax
paralax	parallax
paralel	parallel [1]+
paralelogram	parallelogram
paralise	paralyse [2]+
paralisis	paralysis
paralitic	paralytic
parallax	
parallel [1] /ogram/ism	

paraly *se* [2] /sis/tic	
parameter	
paramilitary	
paramilitrey	paramilitary
paramiter	parameter
paramoor	paramour
paramount	
paramour	
paramownt	paramount
paranoi *a* /c/d	
parapet	
paraphernalia	
paraphrase [2]	
paraplegi *a* /c	
parapleja	paraplegia +
paraselene	
parashoot	parachute [2]+
parashootist	parachutist
parasilene	paraselene
parasit *e* /ic/ical	
parasol	
paratifoid	paratyphoid
paratroop /er	
paratyphoid	
parboil [1]	
parcel [3]	
parch [1] /ment	
pardon [1] /able/er	
pardonabul	pardonable
pare [2]★ (trim)	
pare	pair [1]★
pare	pear ★+
parent /age/al/ally	
parenthes *is* /es (pl.)	
parenthesise [2]	
parenthetic /ally	
parentige	parentage
pariah	
parie	parry [4]
parish /es/ioner	
parishoner	parishioner
Parisi *an* /enne (fem.)	
pariside	parricide +
parisidul	parricidal
parit *y* /ies	

207

park¹ /er		part¹ /ly/-time	
parket	parquet	partak e /en/er/ing	
parking-meter		partial /ly	
parlament	parliament⁺	partialit y /ies	
parlance		participant	
parlans	parlance	participat e² /ion/or	
parlay¹★ (bet)		particip le /ial	
parlay	parley¹★	participul	participle⁺
parlementarey	parliamentary	particle	
parlementarian	parliamentarian	particul	particle
parler	parlour⁺	particular /ity/ly	
parlermade	parlour-maid	particularis e² /ation	
parley¹★ (discuss)		partie	party⁺
parley	parlay¹★	partisan /ship	
parliament /arian/ary		partishun	partition¹⁺
parlour /-maid		partisipant	participant
parlous		partisipashun	participation
parlus	parlous	partisipate	participate²⁺
parm	palm¹⁺	partisipation	participation
Parmesan		partisipul	participle⁺
parmist	palmist	partit ion¹ /ive	
parochial /ism/ly		partly	
parod y⁴ /ies		partner¹ /ship	
parokial	parochial⁺	partook	
paroksism	paroxysm	partridge	
parole²		partrige	partridge
parot	parrot¹⁺	part y /ies	
paroxysm		parvenew	parvenu
parquet		parvenu	
parricid e /al		pary	parry⁴
parrot¹ /-fish		pas	pass⁺
parry⁴		pasable	passable⁺
parse²		pasabul	passable⁺
parsec		pascher	pasture⁺
parsel	parcel³	pase	pace²⁺
parshal	partial⁺	pasemaker	pace-maker
parshialitey	partiality⁺	pasenger	passenger
parsimon ious /y		paserbie	passer-by
parsimonius	parsimonious⁺	paserby	passer-by
parsley		pasha	
parslie	parsley	pashence	patience★
parsly	parsley	pashens	patience★
parsnip		pashent	patient⁺
parson /age/ic		pashonat	passionate
parsonige	parsonage	pashun	passion⁺

208

pasidge	passage	pasturn	pastern
pasific	pacific +	past y /ies	
pasifier	pacifier	paswerd	password
pasifism	pacifism +	pasword	password
pasifist	pacifist	pat ³ /ly/ness	
pasify	pacify ⁴+	patay	pâté
pasige	passage	patch ¹ /es/work/y	
pasiv	passive +	pâté	
pasivitey	passivity	patella	
pasover	passover	paten	pattern ¹
paspartoo	passe-partout	patency	
pasport	passport	patensey	patency
pass /book/es/ing/key		patent ¹ /able/ee/ly	
passabl e /y		pater	patter ¹+
passage		patern	pattern ¹
passed * (did pass)		paternal /ism/ly	
passed	past *	paternalist /ic	
passenger		paternity	
passe-partout		path /way	
passer /-by		pathetic /ally	
passige	passage	pathological /ly	
passion /ate/ately		patholog y /ist	
passive /ly		pathos	
passivity		patie	patty +
passover		patience *†	
passport		†(forbearance)	
password		patient /s * (under	
past * (just over)		doctor's care)	
past	passed *	patina	
pasta		patio /s	
paste ² /board		patiserey	pâtisserie
pastel		pâtisserie	
paster	pastor +	patois	
pasterise	pasteurise ²+	patriarch /al/y	
pastern		patriark	patriarch +
pasteuris e ² /ation		patrician	
pastie	pasty +	patricide	
pastil	pastille	patrimon y /ies	
pastille		patriot /ism	
pastime		patriotic /ally	
pastmaster		patrishun	patrician
pastor /al/ate		patriside	patricide
pastrey	pastry +	patrol ³	
pastr y /ies		patron /ess (fem.)	
pastur e /age		patron age /al	

patronige	patronage +	pay /able/ee/ing/ment	
patronise² /r		payabul	payable
patten		paynt	paint¹+
patter¹ /er		pe	pea+
pattern¹		pea /nut	
patt y /ies		peace * (calm)	
paturnal	paternal +	peace	piece²*+
paturnitey	paternity	peaceabl e /y	
patwa	patois	peaceabul	peaceable +
paucity		peaceful /ly/ness	
paunch /y		peace-offering	
pauper /ism		peach /es	
pauperis e² /ation		pea cock /fowl/hen	
pause²* (stop)		peak¹* (top)	
pause	paws*	peak	pique *
pave² /ment		peal¹* (of bells)	
pavier	paviour	peal	peel¹*
pavilion		peap	peep¹
pavilyun	pavilion	pear * (fruit) /-shaped	
paviour		pear	pare²*
paw¹* (foot, feet) /s *		pear	peer¹*+
paw	pore²*	pear	pier *
pawcelain	porcelain	pearage	peerage +
pawch	porch +	pearce	pierce²
pawferey	porphyry	pearl * (gem) /y	
pawk	pork +	pearl	purl¹*+
pawkupine	porcupine	peasant /ry	
pawl	pall¹+	peat	
pawlbarer	pall-bearer	pebbl e /y	
pawlfrey	palfrey	pebul	pebble +
pawltrey	paltry +	pecadillo	peccadillo
pawlzid	palsied	pecan	
pawlzy	palsy +	peccadillo	
pawn¹ /broker/shop		peck¹ /er/ish	
pawnch	paunch +	pecock	peacock +
pawnografey	pornography +	pectin	
pawnography	pornography +	pectoral	
pawper	pauper +	peculat e² /ion/or	
pawperise	pauperise²+	peculiar /ly	
pawpus	porpoise	peculiarit y /ies	
paws	pause²*	pecuniary	
pawselane	porcelain	pedagog	pedagogue +
pawselin	porcelain	pedagogic /al	
pawshun	portion¹	pedagog ue /y	
pawsitey	paucity	pedal³* (of bicycle)	

pedant /ic/ry		pelt [1]	
peddle [2]★ (sell)		pelusid	pellucid
pedestal		pelvi s /c	
pedestrian crossing		pemmican	
pediatric s /ian		pen [3] /-friend/-name	
pediatrishun	pediatrician	penal	
pedi cure /gree/ment		penalis e [2] /ation	
pedlar		penalt y /ies	
pedler	pedlar	penance ★ (repentance)	
pedometer		penance	pennants ★
pedul	pedal [3]★	penans	penance ★
pedul	peddle [2]★	penant	pennant +
peech	peach +	pence	
peel [1]★ (remove skin)		pencil [3]	
peel	peal [1]★	pendant ★ (ornament)	
peep [1]		pendent ★ (hanging)	
peer [1]★† /ess (fem.)		pending	
†(look, noble)		pendulous	
peer	pier ★	pendulum /s	
peer age /less/lessly		pendulus	pendulous
peet	peat	penetrab le /ility	
peev ed /ish/ishness		penetrabul	penetrable +
peg [3]		penetrashun	penetration
pehen	peahen	penetrat e [2] /ion/ive	
peice	piece [2]★+	penguin	
peiceofring	peace-offering	pengwin	penguin
pejorative		penicillin	
pekancy	piquancy +	penie	penny +
pekanese	pekinese	peniless	penniless +
pekansey	piquancy +	peninsula ★(n.) /r ★(adj.)	
pekant	piquant	penis	
peek	peak [1]★	penisilin	penicillin
peek	pique ★	peniten ce /t	
pekinese		penitens	penitence +
pekish	peckish	penitensharey	penitentiary +
pektin	pectin	penitentiar y /ies	
pektoral	pectoral	penkni fe /ves (pl.)	
pelican		pennant /s ★ (flags)	
pelit	pellet	pennife	penknife +
pellet		penniless /ness	
pell-mell		pennives	penknives
pellucid		pennon	
pelmel	pell-mell	penn y /ies	
pelmet		penon	pennon
pelota		pens	pence

211

penshun	pension ¹⁺	perchance	
penshunabul	pensionable	perchans	perchance
penshuner	pensioner	perchase	purchase ²⁺
pensil	pencil ³	percolat *e* ² /ion/or	
pension ¹ /able/er		percushun	percussion ⁺
pensive /ly/ness		percuss *ion* /ive	
pentagon /al		perda	purdah
pentameter		perdishun	perdition
pentathlon		perdition	
Pentecost		peregrin *e* /ation	
penthouse		peremptor *y* /ily/iness	
penthows	penthouse	peremtrey	peremptory ⁺
penticost	Pentecost	perenial	perennial ⁺
penultimate /ly		perennial /ly	
penumbra		perfecshun	perfection ⁺
penurey	penury ⁺	perfect ¹ /ible	
penurius	penurious	perfection /ist	
penur *y* /ious		perfidey	perfidy ⁺
penut	peanut	perfidius	perfidious
peonie	peony ⁺	perfid *y* /ious	
peon *y* /ies		perforashun	perforation
people ²		perforat *e* ² /ion/or	
peper	pepper ¹⁺	perforce	
pepercorn	peppercorn	perform ¹ /ance/er	
peperey	peppery	performans	performance
pepper ¹ /corn/mint/y		perfors	perforce
pepsin /ogen		perfume ² /ry/ries	
pep-talk		perfunctor *y* /ily	
peptic		perfunctrey	perfunctory ⁺
peptides		pergative	purgative ⁺
pepul	people ²	pergatrey	purgatory
per	purr ¹	perge	purge ²⁺
per annum		perhaps	
per capita		pericarp	
peradvencher	peradventure	periferal	peripheral
peradventure		periferey	periphery ⁺
perambulat *e* ² /ion/or		periferic	peripheric
perblind	purblind	perifery	periphery ⁺
perceiv *e* ² /able		perigee	
percentage		peril /ous/ously	
percepshun	perception ⁺	perilus	perilous
perceptibl *e* /y		perimeter	
perceptibul	perceptible ⁺	period	
percept *ion* /ive		periodic /al/ally	
perch ¹ /es		periosteum	

peripatetic	
peripher *y* /al/ic	
periscope	
perish [1] /able/ables	
peristalsis	
periton *eum* /itis	
periwinkle	
periwinkul	periwinkle
perjur *e* [2] /y	
perk [1] /iness/s/y	
perkushun	percussion +
perkusiv	percussive
perl	pearl *+
perl	purl [1]*+
perloin	purloin [1]
perlu	purlieu
perm [1]	
permanenc *e* /y	
permanens	permanence +
permanent /ly	
permanganate	
permeab *le* /ility	
permeabul	permeable +
permeat *e* [2] /ion	
permishun	permission +
permisibul	permissible
permisiv	permissive +
permiss *ion* /ible	
permissive /ness	
permit [3]	
permutashun	permutation
permut *e* [2] /ation	
pernicious /ly/ness	
pernickety	
pernikitey	pernickety
pernishus	pernicious +
perokside	peroxide
peroxide	
perpechooal	perpetual +
perpechooate	perpetuate [2]+
perpechual	perpetual +
perpechuate	perpetuate [2]+
perpendicular /ity	
perpetrashun	perpetration
perpetrat *e* [2] /ion/or	

perpetrater	perpetrator
perpetual /ly	
perpetuat *e* [2] /ion	
perpetuity	
perple	purple
perpleks	perplex [1]+
perplex [1] /ity/ities	
perport	purport [1]
perpose	purpose +
perse	purse [2]+
persecut *e* [2] /ion/or	
persepshun	perception +
perseptible	perceptible +
perseption	perception +
perseptiv	perceptive
perseve	perceive [2]+
persever *e* [2] /ance	
pershun	Persian
Persian	
persist [1] /ent/ently	
persistenc *e* /y	
persistens	persistence +
person /able/age	
persona /(non) grata	
personal * (private) /ly	
personal	personnel *
personalit *y* /ies	
personat *e* [2] /ion/or	
personel	personal *+
personel	personnel *
personifi	personify [4]+
personif *y* [4] /ication/ier	
personnel * (employees)	
personnel	personal *+
perspective	
perspeks	perspex
perspektiv	perspective
perspex	
perspicaci *ous* /ty	
perspicashus	perspicacious +
perspicu *ous* /ity	
perspicuus	perspicuous +
perspirashun	perspiration
perspir *e* [2] /ation	
persuad *e* [2] /able/er	

213

persuashun	persuasion	pestle	
persuasion		pesul	pestle
persuasive /ly/ness		pet³ /-name	
perswadable	persuadable	petal³	
perswadabul	persuadable	peteat	petite
perswade	persuade²⁺	peter¹ /sham	
perswasion	persuasion	peticoat	petticoat
perswasiv	persuasive⁺	petie	petty⁺
pert /ly/ness		petiole	
pertain¹		petish	pettish
pertane	pertain¹	petishun	petition¹⁺
pertinaci ous /ty		petite	
pertinashus	pertinacious⁺	petition¹ /er	
pertinen ce /t		petrel ★ (sea bird)	
pertinens	pertinence⁺	petrel	petrol ★⁺
perturb¹ /ation		petrifacshun	petrifaction
perva de² /sive		petrifaction	
perverse /ly/ness		petrifi	petrify⁴⁺
pervershun	perversion⁺	petrif y⁴ /ication	
pervers ion /ive		petrol ★ (gasoline) /eum	
pervert¹ /er		petrol	petrel ★
pervious		petrolog y /ist	
pervius	pervious	petrul	petrel ★
pervurs	perverse⁺	petrul	petrol ★⁺
pervurshun	perversion⁺	petticoat	
pervursiv	perversive	pettish	
pervurt	pervert¹⁺	pett y /ier/iest/ily/iness	
pesable	peaceable⁺	petul	petal³
pesabul	peaceable⁺	petulan ce /t	
pesant	peasant⁺	petulans	petulance⁺
pesarey	pessary⁺	petunia	
pese	peace ★	peved	peeved⁺
pese	piece²★⁺	pevish	peevish
peseful	peaceful⁺	pew	
peseofring	peace-offering	pewit	
peseta		pewter	
pesimism	pessimism⁺	phaeton	
pesimist	pessimist	phalanks	phalanx⁺
pesimistic	pessimistic	phalan x /ges/xes (pls.)	
pessar y /ies		phall ic /us	
pessimis m /t/tic		phantasm	
pest /icide		phantasmagori a /c	
pester¹		phantom	
pestilen ce /t/tial		Pharaoh	
pestilens	pestilence⁺	pharingeal	pharyngeal⁺

214

pharinx	pharynx
Pharis *ee* /aic	
pharmaceutic /al	
pharmacist	
pharmacolog*y* /ist	
pharmacopoeia	
pharmac*y* /ies	
pharmasey	pharmacy +
pharmasist	pharmacist
pharmasutical	pharmaceutical
pharo	Pharaoh
pharyng *eal* /itis	
pharynx	
phase ²	
phayton	phaeton
pheasant	
phebus	Phoebus
pheniks	phoenix
phenix	phoenix
phenobarbitone	
phenol	
phenomenal /ly	
phenomen *on* /a (pl.)	
phesant	pheasant
phial * (bottle)	
philander ¹ /er	
philanthrop*y* /ic/ist	
philarmonic	philharmonic
philatel*y* /ist	
philharmonic	
philip	fillip
Philistine	
philolog*y* /ical/ist	
philosofer	philosopher
philosofey	philosophy +
philosofical	philosophical +
philosofise	philosophise ²
philosoph *er* /y	
philosophical /ly	
philosophise ²	
philter	philtre *
philtre * (love potion)	
phisic	physic *
phisical	physical +
phisician	physician

phisicist	physicist
phisics	physics
phisik	physique *
phisiologey	physiology +
phisionomey	physiognomy
phisiotherapist	physiotherapist
phisiotherapy	physiotherapy +
phisique	physique *
phlebitis	
phlegm /atic	
phlem	phlegm +
phloem	
phloks	phlox *
phlox * (flower)	
phobia	
Phoebus	
phoenix	
phon * (unit of sound)	
phone ²* (telephone)	
phonetic /ally	
phonograf	phonograph +
phonograph /ic	
phonolog*y* /ical	
phony	
phosfate	phosphate
phosforesence	phosphorescence
phosforesent	phosphorescent
phosforous	phosphorous *+
phosforus	phosphorus *
phosphate	
phosphoresce ² /nce/nt	
phosphor *ous* * (adj.) /ic	
phosphorus * (n.)	
photo /-electric/stat	
photocopie	photocopy +
photocop*y* /ies	
photo-finish	
photogenic	
photograf	photograph ¹+
photograph ¹ /ic/y	
photomet *er* /ric/ry	
photon	
photosynthesis	
phototropism	
phrase ²* (words) /ology

215

phrenetic
phrenolog*y* /ist
phthisis
phylum
physic ★ (remedy)
physic   physique ★
physical /ly
physician
physicist
physics
physiognomy
physiolog*y* /ical/ist
physiotherap *ist* /y
physique ★ (body)
pi ★ (maths)
pi   pie ★+
pianist
piano /forte
piatsa   piazza
piazza
pibald   piebald
picador
picalilli   piccalilli
picancy   piquancy +
picaniny   piccaninny
picant   piquant
piccalilli
piccaninny
piccolo /s
pich   pitch [1]+
pichfork   pitchfork [1]
pick [1] /axe/pocket
pickcher   picture [2]+
picket [1]
pickle [2]
picnic /ked/ker/king
Pict /ish
pictorial /ly
picture [2] /sque
picturesk   picturesque
pidgin ★ (jargon)
pidgin   pigeon ★
pie ★ (food) /crust
pie   pi ★
piebald

piece [2]★ (part) /meal
piece   peace ★
piece-work
pier ★ (jetty)
pier   peer [1]★+
pierce [2]
piers   pierce [2]
piety
pig [3] /-iron/let
pigeon ★ (bird)
pigeon   pidgin ★
pigeon-hole [2]
pigerey   piggery +
pigger*y* /ies
piggyback
pigheaded /ness
pigheded   pigheaded +
pigiback   piggyback
pigin   pidgin ★
pigin   pigeon ★
pigment [1] /ation
pig *skin* /tail
pigsti   pigsty +
pigst*y* /ies
pigtale   pigtail
pijamas   pyjamas
pikaxe   pickaxe
pike [2] /staff
piks   pyx [1]
piksy   pixie +
pil   pill +
pilage   pillage [2]+
pilchard
pile [2]
piler   pillar +
pilerbox   pillar-box
pilfer [1] /age/er
pilgrim /age
pilgrimige   pilgrimage
pilige   pillage [2]+
pilion   pillion
pill /-box
pillage [2] /r
pillar /-box
pillion

pillor y⁴ /ies	
pillow	
pilon	pylon
pilorey	pillory⁴⁺
pilot¹ /age	
pilow	pillow
pilyun	pillion
pimento	
pimpernel	
pimpl e /y	
pimpul	pimple⁺
pin³ /-prick/-up	
pinacle	pinnacle²
pinacul	pinnacle²
pinafore	
pince-nez	
pincers	
pinch¹ /er/es	
pincushion	
pincushun	pincushion
pine² /-cone	
pineapple	
pineapul	pineapple
ping-pong	
pinion¹	
pink¹	
pinnacle²	
pinpoint¹	
pinsers	pincers
pint	
pinyun	pinion¹
pionear	pioneer¹
pioneer¹	
pious /ly	
pip³ /-squeak	
pipe² /line/r	
pipe -clay /dream	
pipet	pipette
pipette	
pippin	
piquan cy /t	
pique* (anger)	
piracy	
piramid	pyramid⁺
pirasey	piracy

pirat e² /ical	
pire	pyre
piric	Pyrrhic
pirite	pyrite
pirooet	pirouette²
pirotecnic	pyrotechnic⁺
pirouette²	
pirric	Pyrrhic
pistachio /s	
pistil* (flower)	
pistol* (gun)	
piston	
pit³ /fall/man	
pitance	pittance
pitans	pittance
pit-a-pat /ter	
pitch¹ /blende/er/es	
pitchfork¹	
pitch-pine	
piteous /ly/ness	
pith /ily/iness/y	
pithon	python
pitiabl e /y	
pitiabul	pitiable⁺
pitie	pity⁴⁺
pitiful /ly	
pitius	piteous⁺
pitsicato	pizzicato
pittance	
pittans	pittance
pituitary	
pituitrey	pituitary
pit y⁴ /iless	
pius	pious⁺
pivot¹ /al	
pix	pyx¹
pixie /s	
pixy	pixie⁺
pizzicato	
placab le /ility	
placabul	placable⁺
placard¹	
placat e² /ion	
place²* (position)	
place	plaice*

217

placenta /l
placid /ity/ly
placket
plagarise   plagiarise [2]+
plage   plague [2]
plagiaris *e* [2] /m/t
plague [2]
plaice ★ (fish)
plaid
plain ★ (flat land)
plain   plane [2]★
plain *er* /ness/song
plaintiff ★ (legal)
plaintive ★ (sad) /ly
plait [1]
plait   plate [2]+
plajarise   plagiarise [2]+
plak   plaque
plaket   placket
plan [3] /ner
plane [2]★ (smooth,
   aircraft)
plane   plain ★
planet /arium/ary
planetrey   planetary
plank
plankton
plant [1] /ain/ation/er
plantashun   plantation
plantif   plaintiff ★
plantin   plantain
plantiv   plaintive ★+
plaque
plase   place [2]★
plase   plaice ★
plasenta   placenta +
plasid   placid +
plasma
plasmolysis
plaster [1] /cast/er
plastic /ally/ity
plasticine
plastiseen   plasticine
plastisine   plasticine
plate [2] /ful/-glass

plate   plait [1]
plateau /x (pl.)
platelet
plater   platter
platform
platichood   platitude +
platinum
platipus   platypus +
platitud *e* /inous
platitudinus   platitudinous
plato   plateau +
platonic /ally
platoon
platter
platypus /es
plaudit
plausib *le* /ility/ly
plausibul   plausible +
plawdit   plaudit
plawsible   plausible +
play [1] /er/ing/mate
playfellow
playful /ly/ness
playground
playgrownd   playground
playrite   playwright
playwright
ple   plea +
plea /s ★ (appeal)
plead [1] /er
pleasant /ly/ry
please [2]★ (request)
pleasur *e* /able/ably
pleat [1]
plebean   plebeian
plebeian
plebian   plebeian
plebiscite
plebisit   plebiscite
plectrum
pledge [2]
pleed   plead [1]+
pleet   pleat [1]
plege   pledge [2]
plenary

plenipotensharey	plenipotentiary	plumage	
plenipotentiary		plumb [1]★ (weight) /line	
plenitude		plumbago	
plentie	plenty +	plumber	
plentiful /ly/ness		plume [2]	
plentius	plenteous	plumer	plumber
plent y /eous		plumet	plummet [1]
plesant	pleasant +	plumige	plumage
plese	pleas ★	plumline	plumbline
plese	please [2]★	plummet [1]	
plesurable	pleasurable	plump [1] /er/est/ness	
plesurabul	pleasurable	plunder [1] /er	
plesure	pleasure +	plunge [2] /r	
plethor a /ic		pluperfect	
pleural ★ (membrane)		plural ★ (a few) /ism/ity	
pleural	plural ★+	plural	pleural ★
pleurisy		plurisey	pleurisy
pli	ply [4]+	plus	
pliab le /ility		plush /y	
pliabul	pliable +	Pluto	
plian cy /t		plutocrac y /ies	
pliansey	pliancy +	plutocrasey	plutocracy +
pliers		plutocrat /ic	
plight /ed		plutonium	
Plimsoll /line/mark		pluvial	
plimsolls		ply [4] /wood	
plinth		pnemonic	mnemonic
plite	plight +	pneumatic	
pliwood	plywood	pneumonia	
plod [3] /der		poach [1] /er	
ploi	ploy	poch	poach [1]+
plooto	Pluto	pock /-marked	
plootocracy	plutocracy +	pocket [1] /-book/-knife	
plootocrat	plutocrat +	pocket-money	
plootonium	plutonium	podgy	
ploovial	pluvial	podium	
plot [3] /ter		poem	
plough [1] /man/share		poet /ess (fem.)	
plover		poetic /al/ally	
plow	plough [1]+	poetry	
ploy		pogo-stick	
pluck [1] /ier/iest/ily/y		poignan cy /t/tly	
plug [3] /ger		poim	poem
plum ★ (fruit)		poinancy	poignancy +
plum	plumb [1]★+	poinansey	poignancy +

poinant	poignant	polip	polyp
point [1] /edly/er/less		polisey	policy +
point -*blank* /-duty		polish [1]	
poise [2]		polisilable	polysyllable +
poisenous	poisonous	polite /ly/ness	
poisenus	poisonous	politecnic	polytechnic
poison [1] /er/ous		politey	polity
pok *e* [2] /er/y		politheism	polytheism +
poker-face /d		polithene	polythene
pokey	poky	politic /ian/s	
pokmarked	pock-marked	political /ly	
poks	pox	politishun	politician
pol	poll [1]★+	polity	
polar /ity		polka /dot	
polar bear		poll [1]★ (vote) /-tax	
polard	pollard +	poll	pole ★+
Polaris		pollard /ed	
polaris *e* [2] /ation/er		pollen	
pole ★ (tall staff) /cat		pollinat *e* [2] /ion	
pole	poll [1]★+	pollster	
pole-jump [1]		pollut *e* [2] /ion	
polemic /al		polonaise	
polen	pollen	polonase	polonaise
poler	polar +	polo-neck	
polerbare	polar bear	polonium	
polerbear	polar bear	poltax	poll-tax
polese	police [2]+	poltegist	poltergeist
pole-star		polterer	poulterer
pole-vault [1]		poltergeist	
poliandrey	polyandry +	poltice	poultice
poliandrus	polyandrous	poltis	poultice
polianthus	polyanthus	poltrey	poultry
police [2] /man/woman		polushun	pollution
polic *y* /ies		polute	pollute [2]+
poligamey	polygamy +	polution	pollution
poligamus	polygamous	polyandrey	polyandry +
poliglot	polyglot	polyandr *y* /ous	
poligon	polygon	polyanthus	
polihedron	polyhedron +	polygam *y* /ous	
polimer	polymer	polyglot	
polinashun	pollination	polygon	
polinate	pollinate [2]+	polyhedr *on* /al	
polination	pollination	polymer	
polinesian	Polynesian	polymeris *e* [2] /ation	
polio /myelitis		polyneshun	Polynesian ¬

Polynesian	
polyp	
polysyllab le /ic	
polytechnic	
polytheis m /t/tic	
polythene	
pomace * (pulp)	
pomade 2	
pomegranate	
pomegranit	pomegranate
pomel	pommel 3
Pomeranian	
pomfret /cake	
pomfrit	pomfret +
pomiculcher	pomiculture
pomiculture	
pommel 3	
pomology	
pomp /osity/ous	
pompus	pompous
ponder 1 /able	
ponderous /ly	
ponderus	ponderous +
pondrabul	ponderable
poney	pony +
poniard	
ponie	pony +
ponitale	pony-tail
pontiff	
pontificate 2	
pontoon	
pon y /ies /y-tail	
ponyard	poniard
poo	pooh 1+
poodle	
poodul	poodle
poof	pouffe
pooh 1 /-pooh	
pool	
pooley	pulley
poolit	pullet
poop 1	
poor * (needy)	
poor	pore 2*
poor	pour 1*

poor er /est/ly	
pop 3 /corn/gun	
pop e /ery/ish	
popet	poppet
pop-eyed	
popicock	poppycock
popie	poppy +
popinjay	
poplar * (tree)	
poplar	popular *+
poplin	
poppet	
popp y /ies	
poppycock	
populace	
popular *† /ity/ly	
†(well known)	
popularis e 2 /ation	
popularitey	popularity
populas	populace
populashun	population
populat e 2 /ion	
populer	popular *+
populous	
populus	populous
popy	poppy +
por	paw 1*+
por	pore 2*
porcelain	
porch /es	
porcupine	
pore 2* (of skin)	
pore	poor *
pore	pour 1*
porer	poorer +
porfrey	porphyry
poridge	porridge
porige	porridge
poringer	porringer
pork /er/y	
porkupine	porcupine
pornografey	pornography +
pornograph y /ic	
poro us /sity	
porphyry	

porpoise	
porpus	porpoise
porridge	
porringer	
porselin	porcelain
porshun	portion [1]
porslin	porcelain
port /age/-hole	
portab *le* /ility	
portabul	portable +
portal	
portcullis	
portend [1]	
portent /ous	
portentus	portentous
porter /house	
portfolio	
portico	
portion [1]	
portkulis	portcullis
portl *y* /iness	
portmanteau	
portrait /ure	
portray [1] /al	
portrit	portrait +
portul	portal
porus	porous +
poscher	posture [2]
pose [2]	
poseshun	possession
posess	possess [1+]
posession	possession
posessiv	possessive
posey	posy +
posh	
poshun	potion
posibilitey	possibility
posible	possible +
posibul	possible +
posie	posy +
posishun	position +
position /al	
positive /ly/ness	
positivism	
positron	

posse	
possess [1] /ion/ive/or	
possi	posse
possib *le* /ility/ly	
possibul	possible +
possum	
post [1] /-card	
post office	
postage /-stamp	
postal	
post-date [2]	
poster	
posterier	posterior
posterior	
posterity	
postern	
post-graduate	
post-haste	
posthumous /ly	
posthumus	posthumous +
postige	postage +
postilion	
postilyon	postilion
post-impressionist	
post *man* /mark	
post *master* /mistress	
post-meridiem	
post-mortem	
postofiss	post office
postpone [2] /ment	
postulant	
postulate [2]	
postumus	posthumous +
posture [2]	
post-war	
posum	possum
pos *y* /ies	
potash	
potasium	potassium
potassium	
potato /es	
pot-bell *y* /ied	
poteen	
poten *cy* /t	
potene	poteen

potensey	potency [+]	praer	prayer [+]
potenshul	potential [+]	pragmati *c* /sm	
potentate		prairey	prairie
potential /ity/ly		prairie	
poter	potter [1]	praise [2] /worthy	
poterey	pottery [+]	prance [2]	
pot-hol *e* /er/ing		prank	
pot-hook		prans	prance [2]
potie	potty	prarey	prairie
potion		prase	praise [2+]
pot-pourri		prasee	précis [1]
potter [1]		praseworthey	praiseworthy
potter *y* /ies		prate [2]	
potty		prattle [2]	
pouch [1] /es		pratul	prattle [2]
pouffe		prawn [1]	
poulterer		pray [1]* (say prayers)	
poultice		pray	prey [1]*
poultry		prayer /book/ful	
pounce [2]		preach [1] /er	
pound [1] /age		preamble [2]	
pour [1]* (to flow)		preambul	preamble [2]
pour	poor *	prearrange [2]	
pour	pore [2]*	precarious /ly/ness	
pout [1]		precarius	precarious [+]
poverty /-stricken		precaution /ary	
powch	pouch [1+]	precawshun	precaution [+]
powder [1] /y		precede [2]* (go before)	
power [1] /less/-station		precede	proceed [1]*+
powerful /ly/ness		precedence * (priority)	
pownce	pounce [2]	precedent *† /s *†	
pownd	pound [1+]	†(previous law[s])	
powns	pounce [2]	precedent	president *+
powt	pout [1]	precentor	
pow-wow [1]		precept /or	
pox		preceshun	procession
practicab *le* /ility		prech	preach [1+]
practicabul	practicable [+]	precinct	
practical /ity/ly		precious /ly	
practice * (n.)		precipice	
practician		precipis	precipice
practise [2]* (v.)		precipitanc *e* /y	
practishun	practician	precipitans	precipitance [+]
practishuner	practitioner	precipitat *e* [2] /ion/or	
practitioner		precipitous /ly	

223

precipitus	precipitous [+]	preferens	preference
précis [1]		preferenshal	preferential [+]
precise /ly		preferential /ly	
preclu *de* [2] /sion/sive		preferment	
preclushun	preclusion	prefiks	prefix [1]
precocious /ness		prefis	preface [2+]
precocity		prefix [1]	
preconceive [2]		pregnanc *y* /ies	
preconception		pregnansey	pregnancy [+]
preconsepshun	preconception	pregnant	
preconseve	preconceive [2]	prehensile	
precoshus	precocious [+]	prehistor *ic* /y	
precositey	precocity	pre-ignition	
precursor /y		prejudge [2]	
predater	predator [+]	prejudice [2]	
predator /y		prejudicial /ly	
predecessor		prejudis	prejudice [2]
predesesor	predecessor	prejudishal	prejudicial [+]
predestinashun	predestination	prejuge	prejudge [2]
predestin *e* [2] /ation		prelate	
predetermine [2]		prelim	
predicament		preliminar *y* /ies	
predicate [2]		preliminrey	preliminary [+]
predicshun	prediction	prelude [2]	
predict [1] /able/ion		premature /ly	
predictabul	predictable	premeditat *e* [2] /ion	
predilecshun	predilection	premier *† /ship	
predilection		†(Prime Minister)	
predispos *e* [2] /ition		première *†	
prediturmine	predetermine [2]	†(first performance)	
predominance		premise [2*] (postulate)	
predominans	predominance	premises (house)	
predominant /ly		premiss * (logic)	
predominate [2]		premium /s	
preegsist	pre-exist [1+]	premonishun	premonition [+]
pre-eminen *ce* /t		premonit *ion* /ory	
pre-empt [1] /ion		prenatal	
preemshun	pre-emption	prene	preen [1]
preen [1]		preoccupi	preoccupy [4+]
pre-exist [1] /ence		preoccup *y* [4] /ation	
prefabricat *e* [2] /ion		preocupashun	preoccupation
prefa *ce* [2] /tory		preocupy	preoccupy [4+]
prefect /orial/ure		prepade	prepaid
prefer [3] /able/ably		prepaid	
preference		preparashun	preparation

preparatrey	preparatory
prepar *e*² /ation/atory	
prepay /ing/ment	
preponder *ance* /ant	
preponderate²	
preposess	prepossess ¹⁺
preposishun	preposition ⁺
preposition /al	
prepossess ¹ /ion	
preposterous /ly	
preposterus	preposterous ⁺
prerekwisit	prerequisite
prerequisite	
prerogative	
pres	press ¹⁺
presage ²	
presbiterian	Presbyterian
Presbyterian	
prescribe ²*†	
†(give directions)	
prescribe	proscribe ²*
prescripshun	prescription ⁺
prescript *ion* /ive	
presede	precede ²*
presedence	precedence *
presedence	precedents *
presedent	precedent *⁺
presedent	president *⁺
preseed	precede ²*
presence	
presens	presence
present ¹ /ation/ly	
presentabl *e* /y	
presentashun	presentation
presentiment	
presentor	precentor
presept	precept ⁺
preservashun	preservation
preservative	
preserv *e* ² /ation	
preseshun	procession
presession	procession
presher	pressure ²⁺
presherise	pressurise ²⁺
preshus	precious ⁺

presid *e* ² /ial	
presidency	
presidensey	presidency
presidenshal	presidential
president *† /ial/s *†	
†(elected head[s])	
president	precedent *⁺
presidial	
presige	presage ²
presinct	precinct
presipice	precipice
presipis	precipice
presipitance	precipitance ⁺
presipitans	precipitance ⁺
presipitate	precipitate ²⁺
presipitation	precipitation
presipitous	precipitous ⁺
presipitus	precipitous ⁺
presise	precise ⁺
press ¹ /er	
press-stud	
pressure ² /-cooker	
pressuris *e* ² /ation	
prest	priest ⁺
prestege	prestige ⁺
presthood	priesthood
prestig *e* /ious	
prestigus	prestigious
presto	
presum *e* ² /ably	
presumpt *ion* /ive/uous	
presumshun	presumption ⁺
presumshus	presumptuous
presumtuous	presumptuous
presuppos *e* ² /ition	
pretekst	pretext
pretence	
pretend ¹ /er	
pretens	pretence
pretenshun	pretension
pretenshus	pretentious ⁺
pretension	
pretentious /ly/ness	
preterite	
pretext	

pretie	pretty +	principal ★ (chief) /ly	
pretty /ily/iness		principal	principle ★
prety	pretty +	principality /ies	
prevail [1]		principle ★†	
prevalence /t		†(moral code)	
prevalens	prevalence +	principle	principal ★+
prevaricate [2] /ion/or		prins	prince +
prevayl	prevail [1]	prinsess	princess
prevenshun	prevention	prinsipal	principal ★+
prevent [1] /able/ion/ive		prinsipality	principality +
preview		print [1] /er	
previous /ly		prior /ess (fem.)/y	
previus	previous +	priority /ies	
prevue	preview	prise [2]★ (lever)	
pre-war		prise	price [2]+
prey [1]★ (devour)		prise	prize [2]★
prey	pray [1]★	prisie	prissy
prezbiterian	Presbyterian	prism /atic	
pri	pry [4]	prison /er	
price [2] /less		prissy	
prick [1]		pristene	pristine
prickle [2] /y		pristine	
pricul	prickle [2]+	prithee	
pride [2]		prity	pretty +
prier	prior +	privacy	
prierey	priory	privaricate	prevaricate [2]+
priest /hood/ly		privasey	privacy
prig /gish		privashun	privation
prim /ly/mer/mest/ness		private /ly	
prima donna		privateer	
prima facie		privation	
primacy /te		privet	
primary /ies/ily		privie	privy
primasey	primacy +	privilege [2]	
prime [2] /r		privilige	privilege [2]
Prime Minister		privit	private +
primeval		privy	
primitive /ism		prize [2]★ (award)	
primogenital /or/ure		prize	prise [2]★
primordial		prizm	prism +
primrey	primary +	probable /ility/ly	
primrose		probabul	probable +
primula		probashun	probation +
primus		probate	
prince /ly/ss (fem.)		probation /ary/er	

probe [2]		profet		prophet [+]
problem		profetical		prophetical
problematic /al/ally		proffer [1]		
proboscis		proficien *cy* /t		
procedure		profilactic		prophylactic [+]
proceed [1]* (go on) /s		profile		
proceed	precede [2]*	profishency		proficiency [+]
proceshun	procession	profishensey		proficiency [+]
process [1] /ion/ional		profishent		proficient
proclaim [1]		profit [1] /less		
proclamashun	proclamation	profitab *le* /ility/ly		
proclamation		profitabul		profitable [+]
proclaym	proclaim [1]	profiteer [1]		
procrastinat *e* [2] /ion		profliga *cy* /te		
procreat *e* [2] /ion		profound /ly		
proctor /ial		profownd		profound [+]
procura *ble* /tion/tor		profundity		
procurabul	procurable [+]	profus *e* [2] /ion		
procurater	procurator	profushun		profusion
procure [2] /ment		progenitor		
prod [3]		progeny		
prodigal /ity		prognos *is* /es (pl.)/tic		
prodigey	prodigy [+]	prognosticat *e* [2] /ion		
prodigious /ly/ness		program [3]* (computer)		
prodigus	prodigious [+]	programme *†		
prodig *y* /ies		†(list of events)		
produc *e* [2] /er/ible		progreshun		progression
product /ion/ive		progress [1] /ion/ional		
produse	produce [2+]	progressive /ly		
produser	producer	prohibishun		prohibition
profan *e* [2] /ation		prohibit [1] /ion/ive/ory		
profanit *y* /ies		proibit		prohibit [1+]
profecy	prophecy *	projecshun		projection
profecy	prophesy [4]*	project [1] /ile/ion/or		
profer	proffer [1]	projeney		progeny
profeser	professor [+]	projeniter		progenitor
profesey	prophecy *	proksey		proxy [+]
profeshonal	professional [+]	proksimate		proximate [+]
profeshun	profession [+]	proksimitey		proximity
profesi	prophesy [4]*	prolapse [2]		
profesor	professor [+]	proletaria *n* /t		
profess [1] /edly		proliferashun		proliferation
profession /alism		proliferat *e* [2] /ion		
professional /ly		prolific /ally		
professor /ial		prolog		prologue [2]

prologue [2]	
prolong [1]	
prolongat *e* [2] /ion	
promenade [2] /r	
promethium	
prominen *ce* /t	
prominens	prominence [+]
promiscu *ous* /ity	
promiscuus	promiscuous [+]
promis *e* [2] /sory	
promoshun	promotion [+]
promote [2] /r	
promotion /al	
prompt [1] /er/ness	
promulgat *e* [2] /ion	
prone /ly/ness	
prong [1]	
pronoun	
pronounce [2] /ment	
pronown	pronoun
pronowns	pronounce [2+]
pronunciation	
pronunsiashun	pronunciation
prood	prude [+]
proof [1] /-reader	
proon	prune [2]
proov	prove [2+]
prop [3]	
propaganda	
propagashun	propagation
propagat *e* [2] /ion	
propane	
propel [3] /ler	
propell *ant* (n.) /ent (adj.)	
propensit *y* /ies	
proper /ly	
propert *y* /ies	
prophecy * (n.)	
prophesy [4]* (v.)	
prophet /ess (fem.)/ical	
prophilactic	prophylactic [+]
prophyl *actic* /axis	
propishiate	propitiate [2+]
propishous	propitious [+]
propishus	propitious [+]

propitiat *e* [2] /ion/or	
propitious /ly	
propolis	
proporshonal	proportional [+]
proporshonate	proportionate
proporshun	proportion [1+]
proportion [1] /ate	
proportional /ly	
proposal	
propos *e* [2] /ition	
proposishun	proposition
propound [1]	
propownd	propound [1]
proprietary	
proprieter	proprietor
proprietey	propriety [+]
proprietor	
proprietrey	proprietary
propriet *y* /ies	
propulshun	propulsion [+]
propuls *ion* /ive	
prorog	prorogue [2+]
prorog *ue* [2] /ation	
prosaic /ally	
proscribe [2]* (outlaw)	
proscribe	prescribe [2]*
proscripshun	proscription [+]
proscript *ion* /ive	
prose	
prosecushun	prosecution
prosecut *e* [2] /ion/or	
prosedure	procedure
proseed	proceed [1]*[+]
proselight	proselyte [2]
proselyte [2]	
proselytise [2] /r	
prosess	process [1+]
prosicushun	prosecution
prosilite	proselyte [2]
prosilitise	proselytise [2+]
prosody	
prospect [1] /ive/or	
prospectus /es	
prosper [1] /ity/ous	
prosperus	prosperous

228

prostate * (gland)	
prostitushun	prostitution
prostitut *e* ² /ion	
prostrat *e* ²* (lay flat)	
protactinium	
protagonist	
protecshun	protection
protect ¹ /ion/ive/or	
protectorate	
proteen	protein
protégé /e (fem.)	
protein	
protejay	protégé +
protene	protein
protest ¹ /ation	
Protestant /ism	
protocol	
proton	
protoplasm	
prototipe	prototype +
prototyp *e* /al/ical	
protract ¹ /ion/or	
protrood	protrude ²
protrooshun	protrusion +
protrude ²	
protrus *ion* /ive	
protuberan *ce* /t	
protuberans	protuberance +
proud /ly/ness	
prov *e* ² /able	
provenance	
provenans	provenance
provender	
proverb /ial	
provide ² /r	
providence	
providens	providence
providenshul	providential
provident/ial/ially	
provijun	provision +
provijunal	provisional
provinc *e* /ial	
provins	province +
provinshal	provincial
provishun	provision +

provision /al/ally	
proviso /ry	
provocat *ion* /ive	
provok *e* ² /able	
provost	
prow	
prowd	proud +
prowess	
prowibishun	prohibition
prowibition	prohibition
prowl ¹ /er	
proximate /ly	
proximity	
prox *y* /ies	
prozaic	prosaic +
prud *e* /ery/ish	
pruden *ce* /t	
prudens	prudence +
prudenshal	prudential +
prudential /ly	
prune ²	
prurien *ce* /t	
pruriens	prurience +
prushan	Prussian
Prussian	
pry ⁴	
psalm /ist	
psalter /y	
pseudo /nym	
psycedelic	psychedelic
psyche	
psychedelic	
psychiatr *ist* /y	
psychic /al	
psychoanal *yse* ² /ysis/yst	
psychological /ly	
psycholog *y* /ist	
psychopath /ic	
psycho *sis* /tic	
psychosomatic	
psychotherap *ist* /y	
psycoanalise	psychoanalyse ²+
psycologey	psychology +
psycological	psychological +
psycopath	psychopath +

229

psycosis	psychosis [+]	pulie	pulley
psycosomatic	psychosomatic	pulkritude	pulchritude
psycotherapist	psychotherapist [+]	pull [1]	
psykey	psyche	pullet	
psykick	psychic [+]	pulley	
ptarmigan		Pullman	
pterodactyl		pullover	
Ptolemaic system		pulman	Pullman
ptomaine		pulmonary	
ptyalin		pulmonrey	pulmonary
pu	pew	pulover	pullover
pub /lican		pulp [1] /y	
puberty		pulpit	
pubescen *ce* /t		pulsar	
pubesens	pubescence [+]	pulsashun	pulsation
pubesent	pubescent	pulsat *e* [2] /ion	
pubic		pulse [2] /less	
pubis		pulser	pulsar
public /ation/ly		pulveris *e* [2] /ation	
publicis *e* [2] /t		puma	
publicity		pumel	pummel [3]
publish [1] /er		pumice [2]★ (lava) /-stone	
publisitey	publicity	pumice	pomace ★
publisize	publicise [2+]	pumis	pomace ★
puce		pumis	pumice [2★+]
puck		pumkin	pumpkin
pucker [1]		pummel [3]	
pudding		pump [1] /er	
puddle [2]		pumpernickel	
puding	pudding	pumpkin	
pudul	puddle [2]	pumy	pumice [2★+]
pueril *e* /ity		pun [3] /ner/nist	
puff [1] /iness/y		punch [1] /eon/es	
puffin		punchun	puncheon
pufin	puffin	punctilious /ly/ness	
pug		punctilius	punctilious [+]
pugilis *m* /t/tic		punctual /ity/ly	
pugnaci *ous* /ty		punctuat *e* [2] /ion	
pugnashus	pugnacious [+]	puncture [2]	
pugnasitey	pugnacity	pundit	
puka	pucker [1]	pungen *cy* /t	
puke [2]		pungensey	pungency [+]
puker	pucker [1]	punie	puny [+]
pulchritude		punish [1] /able/ment	
pulcritude	pulchritude	punitive /ly	

punjency	pungency +
punjensey	pungency +
punjent	pungent
punt [1] /er	
pun*y* /ier/iest/ily	
pupa /e (pl.)	
pupat*e* [2] /ion	
pupie	puppy +
pupil	
pupit	puppet +
puppet /eer/ry	
pupp*y* /ies	

*If you cannot find your word under **pur** look under **per***

pur anum	per annum
puray	purée
purblind	
purceive	perceive [2]+
purcentige	percentage
purchas*e* [2] /able	
purchis	purchase [2]+
purda	purdah
purdah	
pure /ly/r/st	
purée	
purgat*ive* /ory	
purgatrey	purgatory
purg*e* [2] /ation	
purifi	purify [4]+
purif*y* [4] /ication	
purile	puerile +
purist	
puritan /ical	
purity	
purje	purge [2]+
purjer	perjure [2]+
purjerey	perjury
purl [1]* (knitting) /y	
purl	pearl *+
purlieu	
purloin [1]	
purlu	purlieu
puroolence	purulence +

purple	
purport [1]	
purpose /ful/fully/ly	
purpul	purple
purr [1]	
purse [2] /r	
pursuan*ce* /t	
pursue [2] /r	
pursuit	
pursute	pursuit
purulen*ce* /t	
purvay	purvey [1]+
purvey [1] /ance/or	
puse	puce
push [1] /-chair/y	
pusillanim*ity* /ous	
puss /y	
pussy-willow	
put [3]	
putative	
puter	pewter
putie	putty [4]
putrefi	putrefy [4]+
putref*y* [4] /action	
putrid	
putrifi	putrefy [4]+
putt [1] /er	
putty [4]	
puty	putty [4]
puzle	puzzle [2]+
puzzle [2] /ment	
pyatsa	piazza
pye	pie *+
pygmy	
pyjamas	
pylon	
pyramid /al	
pyre	
pyrenoid	
pyric	Pyrrhic
pyrite	
pyrotechnic /als/s	
Pyrrhic victory	
python	
pyx [1]	

231

Q

quack [1]
quad
quadrang *le* /ular
quadrangul   quadrangle [+]
quadrant
quadratic
quadrennial
quadrenyal   quadrennial
quadril   quadrille
quadrilateral
quadrille
quadruped
quadruple [2] /t/x
quadruplicat *e* [2] /ion
quadrupul   quadruple [2+]
quaff [1]
quagmire
quail [1]
quaint /er/est/ly/ness
quake [2]
Quaker /ism
qualifactory
qualifi   qualify [4+]
qualif *y* [4] /ication
qualitative
qualit *y* /ies
qualm
quandar *y* /ies
quandrey   quandary [+]
quantifi   quantify [4+]
quantif *y* [4] /ication
quantitative
quantit *y* /ies
quant *um* /a (pl.)
quarantine [2]
quarel   quarrel [3+]
quarey   quarry [+]
quarrel [3] /some
quarr *y* /ies
quart
quarter [1] /ly/master
quartern
quartet

quarto /s
quarts * (fluid measure)
quartz * (mineral) /ite
quasar
quash [1]
quaternary
quatrain
quaver [1]
quay * (by sea)
que   cue [2*]
que   queue [2*]
queas *y* /iness
queen /ly
queer [1] /er/est/ly/ness
quell [1]
quench [1] /able/less
querey   query [4+]
quern
querulous /ly/ness
querulus   querulous [+]
quer *y* [4] /ies
queschun   question [1+]
quest [1]
question [1] /able/ably/naire
quetzal
queue [2*] (line)
quibble [2] /r
quibul   quibble [2+]
quich   quitch
quick /er/est/ly/ness
quicken [1]
quick *sand* /silver
quid
quid pro quo
quiescen *ce* /t
quiesense   quiescence [+]
quiet [1] /er/est/ly
quieten [1]
quietude
quiff
quill [1]
quilt [1]
quin
quince
quincentenary

quinine	
quins	quince
quinsy	
quintesence	quintessence +
quintessen *ce* /tial	
quintet	
quintupl *e* /et/icate	
quintupul	quintuple +
quip [3]	
quire ★ (of paper)	
quire	choir ★
quirk	
quisling	
quit [3] /ter	
quitch	
quite	
quits	
quiver [1]	
quixot *ic* /ry	
quiz [3]	
quizzical /ly	
quod	quad
quodrangul	quadrangle +
quodrant	quadrant
quodratic	quadratic
quodrenial	quadrennial
quodril	quadrille
quodrilateral	quadrilateral
quodrooped	quadruped
quodruplicate	quadruplicate [2+]
quóf	quaff [1]
quogmire	quagmire
quoit	
quolitativ	qualitative
quolitey	quality +
quontify	quantify [4+]
quontitativ	quantitative
quontitey	quantity +
quontum	quantum +
quorantine	quarantine [2]
quorrel	quarrel [3+]
quorrey	quarry +
quorum	
quoshent	quotient
quota	

quot *e* [2] /able/ation	
quotidian	
quotient	

R

rabbi /s	
rabbit [1]★ (animal)	
rabbit	rarebit ★
rabble	
rabes	rabies
rabi	rabbi +
rabid /ly	
rabies	
rabit	rabbit [1]★
rabit	rarebit ★
rable	rabble
rabul	rabble
race /-course/-horse	
rachit	ratchet
racial /ism/ist/ly	
racis *m* /t	
rack [1]★ (shelf)	
rack	wrack ★
racket [1] /eer	
racoon	
rac *y* /ily	
radar	
raddle [2]	
rade	raid [1+]
radial /ly	
radian *ce* /t	
radians	radiance +
radiashun	radiation
radiat *e* [2] /ion/or	
radiater	radiator
radical ★ (political) /ly	
radicle ★ (rootlet)	
radio [1] /wave	
radioactiv *e* /ity	
radio-astronomy	
radiografer	radiographer +
radiogram	
radiographʼer /y	

233

radioisotope		ramifi	ramify [4+]
radiolog *y* /ist		ramificashun	ramification
radiotherapy		ramif *y* [4] /ication	
radish /es		ramp [1]	
radium		rampage [2] /ous	
radi *us* /i (pl.)		rampagus	rampageous
radon		rampan *cy* /t	
radul	raddle [2]	rampart	
radyal	radial [+]	rampige	rampage [2+]
raffia		ramshackle	
raffish		ramshacul	ramshackle
raffle [2]		ranch [1] /er/es	
rafia	raffia	rancid /ity	
rafish	raffish	rancor	rancour [★+]
raft [1] /er		ranco *ur* ★ (hate) /rous	
raful	raffle [2]	random	
rag [3] /ger/time/wort		randum	random
ragamuffin		rane	rain [1★+]
ragamufin	ragamuffin	ranee	
rage [2]		ranefall	rainfall
raglan		range [2] /finder/r	
raid [1] /er		rangle	wrangle [2+]
rail [1] /road/way		rangul	wrangle [2+]
raillery		rank [1] /er ★ (soldier)	
raiment		ranker	rancour [★+]
rain [1★] (water) fall/y		rankle [2]	
rain	reign [1★]	rankul	rankle [2]
rain	rein ★	ransack [1]	
raindeer	reindeer	ransid	rancid [+]
raise [2★] (lift)		ransom [1] /er	
raise	rays ★	ransum	ransom [1+]
raise	raze [2★]	rant [1] /er	
raisin		raon	rayon
raith	wraith	rap [3★] (knock) /per ★	
raja		rap	wrap [★+]
rak *e* [2] /ish		rapaci *ous* /ty	
rakoon	racoon	rapashus	rapacious [+]
rale	rail [1+]	rapasitey	rapacity
ralerey	raillery	rapcher	rapture [+]
ralie	rally [4+]	rap *e* [2] /er/ine/ist	
rall *y* [4] /ies		rapid /ity/ly	
ram [3] /mer/rod		rapier	
ramble [2] /r		rapper	wrapper ★
rambul	ramble [2+]	rapscallion	
rament	raiment	rapscalyon	rapscallion

rapsodey	rhapsody +
rapsodise	rhapsodise [2]
rapt * (absorbed)	
rapt	wrapped *
raptur e /ous	
rapturus	rapturous
rare /ly/r/st	
rarebit * (food)	
raref y [4] /ication	
rarifi	rarefy [4+]
rarit y /ies	
rasberie	raspberry +
rasbery	raspberry +
rascal /ity/ly	
rase	raise [2*]
rase	raze [2*]
rasecorse	race-course
rasehorse	race-horse
rash /er/est/ly/ness	
rashal	racial +
rashalism	racialism
rashalist	racialist
rashio	ratio +
rashul	racial +
rashun	ration [1]
rashunal	rational +
rashunalise	rationalise [2+]
rashunalitey	rationality
rashyo	ratio +
rasie	racy +
rasin	raisin
rasism	racism +
rasist	racist
raskal	rascal +
rasp [1]	
raspberr y /ies	
rat [3] /-race/ter	
ratable	rateable
ratabul	rateable
ratafia	
ratchet	
rate [2] /able/payer	
rath	wrath +
rather	
ratifi	ratify [4+]

ratif y [4] /ication/ier	
ratio /s	
ration [1]	
rational * (adj.) /ity/ly	
rationale * (n.)	
rationalis e [2] /ation/m	
rattle [2] /snake	
ratul	rattle [2+]
raucous /ly	
raucus	raucous +
ravage [2] /r	
rave [2]	
ravel [3]	
raven	
ravene	ravine
ravenous /ly/ness	
ravenus	ravenous +
ravige	ravage [2+]
ravine	
ravioli	
ravish [1]	
raw /er/est/ness	
rawcus	raucous +
rayon	
rays * (light beams)	
raze [2*] (demolish)	
raze	raise [2*]
razer	razor +
razor /-bill/-blade	
reach [1]	
reacshun	reaction +
react [1] /ive/or	
reaction /ary	
read *† /able/er/ing †(book)	
read	red [*+]
read	reed [1*]
readdress [1]	
readi ly /ness	
readmishun	readmission
readmission	
readmit [3] /tance	
readress	readdress [1]
ready /-made	
reaf	reef [1+]

reagent	
reak	reek [1]★
reak	wreak [1]★
real ★ (actual) /ly	
real	reel [1]★
realey	really
realisashun	realisation
realis e [2] /able/ation	
realis m /t	
realistic /ally	
realit y /ies	
realm	
realter	realtor
realtor	
ream	
reanimat e [2] /ion	
reap [1] /er	
reapear	reappear [1]+
reapearance	reappearance
reappear [1] /ance	
rear [1] /guard	
rear-admiral	
rearange	rearrange [2]+
reargard	rearguard
rearm [1] /ament	
rearrange [2] /ment	
reasemble	reassemble [2]
reasembul	reassemble [2]
reasershun	reassertion
reasert	reassert [1]+
reasertion	reassertion
reasess	reassess [1]+
reashorance	reassurance
reashorans	reassurance
reashore	reassure [2]+
reason [1] /able/ably	
reassemble [2]	
reassembul	reassemble [2]
reassert [1] /ion	
reassess [1] /ment	
reassur e [2] /ance	
reath	wreath ★
reath	wreathe [2]★
rebate [2]	
rebel [3] /lion	

rebellious /ly/ness	
rebelyun	rebellion
rebelyus	rebellious +
reberth	rebirth
rebild	rebuild +
rebilt	rebuilt
rebirth	
rebound [1]	
rebownd	rebound [1]
rebuff [1]	
rebuild /ing	
rebuilt	
rebuk e [2] /ingly	
rebut [3] /tal	
rebutal	rebuttal
recalcitran ce /t	
recall [1]	
recalsitrance	recalcitrance +
recant [1] /ation	
recap [3]	
recapcher	recapture [2]
recapitulat e [2] /ion	
recapture [2]	
recast [1]	
recede [2]	
receipt [1]★ (document)	
receit	receipt [1]★
receiv e [2] /able/er	
recent ★ (of late) /ly	
recepshun	reception +
recepshunist	receptionist
receptacle	
receptacul	receptacle
reception /ist/-room	
receptive /ly/ness	
receptivity	
receptor	
receshun	recession +
recess [1] /ive	
recession /al	
rech	retch [1]★
rech	wretch ★
recharge [2] /able	
recicle	recycle [2]
recidivis m /t	

recieve	receive ²⁺
recipe	
recipi	recipe
recipient	
reciproc *al* /ally/ity	
reciprocat *e* ² /ion	
recita *l* /tion/tive	
recitashun	recitation
recite ²	
reck	wreck ¹⁺
reckage	wreckage
reckidge	wreckage
reckless /ly/ness	
reckon ¹	
reclaim ¹	
reclamashun	reclamation
reclamation	
reclaym	reclaim ¹
recline ²	
recluse	
recognis *e* ² /able/ably	
recognishun	recognition
recognition	
recoil ¹	
recolect	recollect ¹⁺
recollect ¹ /ion	
recomence	recommence ²⁺
recomend	recommend ¹⁺
recomens	recommence ²⁺
recommence ² /ment	
recommend ¹ /ation	
recommendabl *e* /y	
recompense ²	
reconcil *e* ² /able/iation	
reconcilement	
recondishun	recondition ¹
recondite	
recondition ¹	
reconker	reconquer ¹
reconnoitre ²	
reconoiter	reconnoitre ²
reconquer ¹	
reconsider ¹ /ation	
reconsile	reconcile ²⁺
reconstitut *e* ² /ion	

reconstruct ¹ /ion/ive	
recoop	recoup ¹⁺
record ¹ /er/-player	
recorse	recourse
recount ¹★ (tell)	
re-count ¹★†	
†(count again)	
recoup ¹ /ment	
recourse	
recover ¹ /y	
recownt	recount ¹★
recownt	re-count ¹★
recreant /ly	
recreashun	recreation
recreat *e* ²★ (entertain) /ion	
re-create ²★ (form anew)	
recriminat *e* ² /ion	
recriminat *ive* /ory	
recruit ¹	
rectang *le* /ular	
rectangul	rectangle ⁺
recter	rector ⁺
rectifi	rectify ⁴⁺
rectifi *able* /er	
rectifiabul	rectifiable ⁺
rectif *y* ⁴ /ication	
rectilinea *r* /l	
rectilinier	rectilinear ⁺
rectitude	
recto	
rector /y/ies	
rect *um* /al	
recumben *cy* /t	
recuperat *e* ² /ion/ive	
recur ³ /rence/rent	
recurens	recurrence
recycle ²	
recycul	recycle ²
red ★† /-handed	
†(colour)	
red	read ★⁺
redbreast	
redbrest	redbreast
redbrick	
redden ¹	

redd *er* /est/ish		reel	real ★+
redeem [1] /able/er		re-elect [1] /ion	
redempt *ion* /ive		reem	ream
redemshun	redemption +	re-enter [1]	
reden	redden [1]	re-entr *y* /ies	
redeploi	redeploy [1+]	reep	reap [1+]
redeploy [1] /ment		reer	rear [1+]
reder	redder +	reer admiral	rear-admiral
redevelop [1] /ment		reergard	rearguard
redie	ready +	re-establish [1] /ment	
rediffusion		reeve [2]	
redifushun	rediffusion	re-examin *e* [2] /ation	
redifusion	rediffusion	re-export [1] /ation	
rediley	readily +	refashion [1]	
redimade	ready-made	refashun	refashion [1]
rediploi	redeploy [1+] ,	refector *y* /ies	
rediploy	redeploy [1+]	refer [3] /able/ence	
redirecshun	redirection	referee /d/ing	
redirect [1] /ion		referend *um* /a/ums (pls.)	
redistribut *e* /ion		referens	reference
redivelop	redevelop [1+]	refewel	refuel [3]
redolen *ce* /t		refill [1] /able	
redouble [2]		refine [2] /ment	
redoubt /able		refiner *y* /ies	
redound [1]		refit [3]	
redress [1] /ment		reflashun	reflation +
redskin		reflate [2]	
reduble	redouble [2]	reflation /ary	
reduc *e* [2] /ible/tion		reflect [1] /ion/ive/or	
reducshun	reduction	refleks	reflex +
redundanc *y* /ies		refleksiv	reflexive
redundansey	redundancy +	reflex /ive	
redundant		refloat [1]	
reduplicat *e* [2] /ion		reflote	refloat [1]
redwood		reform [1] /ation/er	
re-echo [1]		reformashun	reformation
reed [1]★ (water-plant)		reformator *y* /ies	
reed	read ★+	reformatrey	reformatory +
reef [1] /er/-knot		refracshun	refraction
reegsamin	re-examine [2+]	refract [1] /able/ion/ive	
reek [1]★ (smell)		refractor *y* /iness	
reek	wreak [1]★	refrain [1]	
reeko	re-echo [1]	refresh [1] /er/ment	
reeksport	re-export [1+]	refrigerat *e* [2] /ion/or	
reel [1]★ (wind in)		refuel [3]	

refuge * (shelter) /e *†	
†(fugitive)	
refulgen *ce* /t	
refulgens	refulgence +
refund [1]	
refurbish [1]	
refus *e* [2] /al	
refutashun	refutation
refut *e* [2] /able/al/ation	
regain [1]	
regal *† /ia/ly	
†(of a king)	
regale [2]* (to feast)	
regane	regain [1]
regard [1] /less	
regatta /s	
regen *cy* /t	
regenerat *e* [2] /ion/ive/or	
regicid *e* /al	
regime /n	
regiment [1] /al/ation	
region /al/alism/ally	
regiside	regicide +
regist *er* [1] /ration	
registrar	
registrashun	registration
registr *y* /ies	
regreshun	regression
regress [1] /ion/ive	
regret [3] /ful/fully	
regretabul	regrettable +
regrettabl *e* /y	
regular /ity/ly	
regularis *e* [2] /ation	
regularitey	regularity
regulashun	regulation
regulat *e* [2] /ion/or	
reguler	regular +
regurgitat *e* /ion	
rehabilitat *e* [2] /ion	
rehash [1]	
rehears *e* [2] /al	
rehersal	rehearsal
reherse	rehearse [2]+
Reich	

reign [1]* (rule)	
reimburse [2] /ment	
rein * (of horse)	
rein	reign [1]*
reincarnashun	reincarnation
reincarnat *e* [2] /ion	
reindeer	
reinforce [2] /able/ment	
reinfors	reinforce [2]+
reinshore	re-insure [2]+
reinstate [2] /ment	
re-insur *e* [2] /ance	
reinvest [1] /ment	
reiterashun	reiteration
reiterat *e* [2] /ion	
rejecshun	rejection
reject [1] /ion	
rejeme	regime +
rejoic *e* [2] /ingly	
rejoin [1] /der	
rejoise	rejoice [2]+
rejoovenate	rejuvenate [2]+
rejuvenat *e* [2] /ion	
rekindle [2]	
rekindul	rekindle [2]
rekwest	request [1]
rekwiem	requiem
rekwisishun	requisition
rekwisit	requisite +
rekwisition	requisition
rekwite	requite [2]+
relaks	relax [1]+
relaksashun	relaxation
relaksation	relaxation
relapse [2]	
relashun	relation
relat *e* [2] /ion	
relative /ly	
relativity	
relax [1] /ation	
relay [1]	
releaf	relief
release [2]	
relegashun	relegation
relegat *e* [2] /ion	

releif	relief
relent [1] /less/lessly	
relese	release [2]
relevan ce /t	
relevans	relevance +
releve	relieve [2]+
reli	rely [4]
reliabilitey	reliability
reliab le /ility/ly	
reliabul	reliable +
relian ce /t	
relians	reliance +
relic	
relief	
reliev e [2] /able	
religion	
religious /ly/ness	
religun	religion
religus	religious +
relinkwish	relinquish [1]+
relinquish [1] /ment	
relish [1] /able	
relm	realm
reluctan ce /t/tly	
reluctans	reluctance +
rely [4]	
remain [1] /der/s	
remand [1]	
remaridge	remarriage
remarie	remarry [4]+
remarige	remarriage
remark [1] /able/ably	
remarr y [4] /iage	
remed y [4] /ies	
rememb er [1] /rance	
remembrans	remembrance
remind [1] /er	
reminisce [2] /nce/nt	
reminisence	reminiscence
reminisens	reminiscence
reminisent	reminiscent
reminiss	reminisce [2]+
remishun	remission
remiss /ion/ly	
remit [3] /tal/tance	

remitans	remittance
remnant	
remonstran ce /t	
remonstrans	remonstrance +
remõnstrat e [2] /ion/ive	
remoov	remove [2]+
remooval	removal
remorse /ful/fully	
remorseless /ly/ness	
remote /ly/r/st	
remount [1]	
removal	
remov e [2] /able/ability	
remownt	remount [1]
remunerat e [2] /ion/ive	
ren	wren
Renaissance *†	
†(historic period)	
renal	
renascen ce *† /t	
†(rebirth)	
rench	wrench [1]
rend [1]	
render [1]	
rendezvous [1]	
renegade [2]	
renew [1] /able/al	
renit	rennet
renium	rhenium
rennet	
renounce [2] /ment	
renouns	renounce [2]+
renovashun	renovation
renovat e [2] /ion/or	
renown /ed	
renowns	renounce [2]+
rent [1] /al/er	
rentul	rental
renue	renew [1]+
renunciat e [2] /ion	
reorganis e [2] /ation	
re-orientat e [2] /ion	
repade	repaid
repaid	
repair [1] /er	

repara*ble* /tion	
reparashun	reparation
repartee /s	
repast	
repatriashun	repatriation
repatriat*e*[2] /ion	
repay /able/ing/ment	
repeal[1]	
repeat[1] /able/edly	
repel[3] /lent	
repent[1] /ance/ant	
repentans	repentance
repercushun	repercussion
repercussion	
repertoire	
repertory	
repetishun	repetition +
repetishus	repetitious
repetiti*on* /ous/ve	
repetitiv	repetitive
repetrey	repertory
repine[2]	
replace[2] /able/ment	
replase	replace[2+]
replay[1]	
replenish[1] /ment	
replet*e* /ion	
repli	reply[4+]
replica	
repl*y*[4] /ies	
report[1] /able/er	
repose[2] /ful	
repositor*y* /ies	
repositrey	repository +
reprable	reparable +
reprabul	reparable +
reprehend	
reprehenshun	reprehension +
reprehensibul	reprehensible
reprehensi*on* /ble	
represent[1] /ation	
representashun	representation
representative	
represhun	repression
repress[1] /ible/ion/ive	
reprieve[2]	
reprimand[1]	
reprint[1]	
reprisal	
reproach[1] /ful/fully	
reprobate[2]	
reproduc*e*[2] /ible	
reproducshun	reproduction
reproduction	
reproof /s	
reprov*e*[2] /al/ingly	
reptil*e* /ian	
republic /an	
repudiat*e*[2] /ion/or	
repugnan*ce* /t	
repugnans	repugnance +
repuls*e*[2] /ion	
repulshun	repulsion
repulsive /ly/ness	
reputashun	reputation
reput*e*[2] /able/ation	
reputedly	
request[1]	
requiem	
require[2] /ment	
requisishun	requisition
requisit*e* /ion	
requit*e*[2] /al	
rerite	rewrite +
reritten	rewritten
rerote	rewrote
rescind[1]	
rescue[2] /r	
research[1] /er	
reseat ★ (seat again)	
reseat	receipt[1★]
resede	recede[2]
reseed	recede[2]
reseipt	receipt[1★]
resembl*e*[2] /ance	
resembul	resemble[2+]
resent[1★] (peeve) /ment	
resent	recent ★+
resentful /ly	
resepshonist	receptionist

resepshun	reception [+]	resistans	resistance [+]
reseptacul	receptacle	resit /ting	
reseption	reception [+]	resitashun	recitation
reseptionist	receptionist	resitation	recitation
reseptiv	receptive [+]	resite	recite [2]
reseptor	receptor	resle	wrestle [2+]
reserch	research [1+]	resler	wrestler
reservashun	reservation	resole [2]	
reserv e [2] /ation/ist		resoloot	resolute [+]
reservoir		resolushun	resolution
reseshun	recession [+]	resolute /ly/ness	
resess	recess [1+]	resolution	
resession	recession [+]	resolve [2]	
resessiv	recessive	reson	reason [1+]
reset /ting		resonable	reasonable
reseve	receive [2+]	resonabul	reasonable
reshuffle [2]		resonan ce /t/tly	
reshuful	reshuffle [2]	resonans	resonance [+]
resicle	recycle [2]	resonat e [2] /or	
reside [2] /nce		resorce	resource [+]
residenc y /ies		resort [1]	
residens	residence	resound [1]	
residensey	residency [+]	resource /ful/fully	
residenshal	residential	respect [1] /ful/fully	
resident /ial		respectab le /ility/ly	
residivism	recidivism [+]	respectabul	respectable [+]
residivist	recidivist	respective /ly	
residu e /al/ary/um		respirashun	respiration
resign [1] /ation		respirater	respirator
resignashun	resignation	respir e [2] /ation/ator	
resilien ce /t/tly		respite	
resiliens	resilience [+]	resplenden ce /t	
resin /ous		respond [1] /ence/ent	
resind	rescind [1]	respons e /ive/iveness	
resinus	resinous	responsib le /ility/ly	
resipe	recipe	responsibul	responsible [+]
resipie	recipe	rest [1*] (repose)	
resipient	recipient	rest	wrest [1*]
resiprocal	reciprocal [+]	restaurant	
resiprocate	reciprocate [2+]	resterant	restaurant
resiprositey	reciprocity	restful /ly/ness	
resist [1] /er/ive		restitushun	restitution
resistab le /ility/ly		restitution	
resistabul	resistable [+]	restive /ness	
resistan ce /t		restle	wrestle [2+]

restler	wrestler
restless	
restorashun	restoration
restor e² /ation/ative	
restrain¹ /t	
restrict¹ /ion/ive	
restruccher	restructure²
restructure²	
resul	wrestle²⁺
result¹ /ant	
resumay	résumé ★
resume²★ (restart)	
résumé ★ (summary)	
resumption	
resurecshun	resurrection
resurection	resurrection
resurgen ce /t	
resurgens	resurgence⁺
resurrect¹ /ion	
resus	rhesus
resuscitat e² /ion	
resusitashun	resuscitation
resusitate	resuscitate²⁺
resusitation	resuscitation
retail¹ /er	
retain¹ /er	
retale	retail¹⁺
retaliat e² /ion/ory	
retard¹ /ation/er	
retayn	retain¹⁺
retch¹★ (vomit)	
retch	wretch ★
retenshun	retention⁺
retent ion /ive	
reticen ce /t	
retina	
retinew	retinue
retinue	
retire² /ment	
retisens	reticence⁺
retisent	reticent
retoric	rhetoric⁺
retorical	rhetorical
retort¹	
retrace²	

retract¹ /able/ile/ion	
retrase	retrace²
retread ★ (walk again)	
re-tread¹★ (tyre)	
retreat¹	
retred	retread ★
retred	re-tread¹★
retreive	retrieve²⁺
retrench¹ /ment	
retribushun	retribution
retribut e² /ion	
retriev e² /able/al/er	
retroactive	
retrograde	
retrogress¹ /ion/ive	
retrospect¹ /ion/ive	
return¹ /able	
reunion	
reunite²	
reunyun	reunion
rev³	
revali	reveille
revaluashun	revaluation
revalu e² /ation	
reve	reeve²
reveal¹	
reveille	
revel³ /ler/ry	
revelashun	revelation
revelation	
revelrey	revelry
revenew	revenue
revenge² /ful/fully	
revenue	
reverberat e² /ion/or	
revere² /nce	
reverend ★ (priest)	
reverens	reverence
reverent ★† /ly †(respectful)	
reverey	reverie
reverie	
revers e² /al/ible/ion	
revershun	reversion
revert¹ /ible	

243

review ¹★ (survey) /er		rice ★ (food)	
review	revue ★	rich /er/es/est/ly/ness	
revijun	revision	ricital	recital ⁺
revile ²		ricite	recite ²
revis e ² /ion		rick ¹ /ety	
revishun	revision	rickets	
reviv e ² /al		rickshaw	
revocabl e /y		ricline	recline ²
revokashun	revocation	ricluse	recluse
revo ke ² /cation		ricochet ¹	
revolt ¹		ricooperate	recuperate ²⁺
revolushun	revolution	ricroot	recruit ¹
revolushunise	revolutionise ²	ricshore	rickshaw
revolushunrey	revolutionary ⁺	ricumbent	recumbent
revolution		ricur	recur ³⁺
revolutionar y /ies		ricuver	recover ¹⁺
revolutionise ²		rid /dance	
revolve ² /r		ridance	riddance
revue ★ (entertainment)		ridans	riddance
revue	review ¹★⁺	riddle ²	
revulshun	revulsion	rid e /den/er/ing	
revulsion		rideem	redeem ¹⁺
reward ¹		rideemable	redeemable
rewrit e /ten/ing		rideemabul	redeemable
rewrote		rideemer	redeemer
rhapsodise ²		ridemshun	redemption⁺
rhapsod y /ies		ridge ²	
rhenium		ridicule ²	
rhesus		ridiculous /ly/ness	
rhetoric /al		ridiculus	ridiculous ⁺
rheumat ic /ism		ridownd	redound ¹
rhinoceros /es		ridowt	redoubt ⁺
rhizome		ridress	redress ¹⁺
rhizomorph		riduce	reduce ²⁺
rhodium		riducshun	reduction
rhododendron		ridul	riddle ²
rhomb us /oid		ridundansey	redundancy ⁺
rhubarb		ridundant	redundant
rhyme ²★ (poetry)		riduse	reduce ²⁺
rhythm		ridusible	reducible
rhythmic /al/ally		ridusibul	reducible
rib ³		rie	rye ★
ribald /ry		rie	wry ★⁺
ribbon		rife	
ricalsitrant	recalcitrant	riff-raff	

rifinerey	refinery +	rikwest	request 1
rifle 2 /-range		rikwire	require 2+
riflecshun	reflection	rikwite	requite 2+
riflect	reflect 1+	rile 2	
riflecter	reflector	riluctance	reluctance +
riflectiv	reflective	riluctans	reluctance +
riform	reform 1+	riluctant	reluctant
rifract	refract 1+	rim 3	
rifrane	refrain 1	rimainder	remainder
rifresh	refresh 1+	rimand	remand 1
rifrigerate	refrigerate 2+	rimane	remain 1+
rifrigerater	refrigerator	rimark	remark 1+
rift /-valley		rimarkable	remarkable
rifulgens	refulgence +	rime 2★ (frost)	
rifulgent	refulgent	rime	rhyme 2★
rifusal	refusal	rimember	remember 1+
rifuse	refuse 2+	rimembrance	remembrance
rifutal	refutal	rimembrans	remembrance
rifute	refute 2+	rimind	remind 1+
rig 3 /ger		riminder	reminder
rigard	regard 1+	rimishun	remission
rigardless	regardless	rimiss	remiss +
rigata	regatta +	rimit	remit 3+
rige	ridge 2	rimitance	remittance
riger	rigor ★	rimitans	remittance
riger	rigour ★	rimonstrativ	remonstrative
riggle	wriggle 2	rimoov	remove 2+
right 1★ (correct)		rimorse	remorse +
right	rite ★	rimorsless	remorseless +
right	write ★+	rimote	remote +
righteous /ly/ness		rimunerate	remunerate 2+
rightful /ly		rimuneration	remuneration
rigid /ity/ly		rinasance	Renaissance ★
rigmarole		rinasance	renascence ★+
rigor ★ (stiffness)		rinasant	renascent
rigour ★ (severity)		rind	
rigreshun	regression	rinew	renew 1+
rigresiv	regressive	rinewable	renewable
rigress	regress 1+	rinewabul	renewable
rigret	regret 3+	rinewal	renewal
rigretable	regrettable +	ring 1★ (circle, bell)	
rigretabul	regrettable +	ring	wring 1★
rigretful	regretful	ring er ★† /leader/let	
rigul	wriggle 2	†(horse)	
rike	Reich	ringer	wringer ★

245

rink	
rinkle	wrinkle [2]
rinkul	wrinkle [2]
rinoceros	rhinoceros [+]
rinoserus	rhinoceros [+]
rinounce	renounce [2+]
rinownse	renounce [2+]
rinse [2]	
rinuable	renewable
rinuabul	renewable
rinual	renewal
rinue	renew [1+]
rinunsiashun	renunciation
rinunsiate	renunciate [2+]
rinunsiation	renunciation
riot [1] /ous/ously	
riotus	riotous
rip [3] /per	
ripair	repair [1+]
ripare	repair [1+]
ripe /r/st/ly/ness	
ripeel	repeal [1]
ripeet	repeat [1+]
ripel	repel [3+]
ripen [1]	
ripent	repent [1+]
ripentance	repentance
ripentans	repentance
ripentant	repentant
ripine	repine [2]
riple	ripple [2]
riplete	replete [+]
ripli	reply [4+]
riport	report [1+]
ripose	repose [2+]
ripositrey	repository [+]
ripple [2]	
ripreshun	repression
ripress	repress [1+]
ripreve	reprieve [2]
riprisal	reprisal
riproch	reproach [1+]
riprochful	reproachful
riproof	reproof [+]
riproov	reprove [2+]

ripublic	republic [+]
ripublican	republican
ripudiate	repudiate [2+]
ripugnance	repugnance [+]
ripugnans	repugnance [+]
ripugnant	repugnant
ripul	ripple [2]
ripulse	repulse [2+]
ripulshun	repulsion
ripulsiv	repulsive [+]
ripute	repute [2+]
riquest	request [1]
riquire	require [2+]
riquite	requite [2+]
ris *e* *(get up)/en/er/ing	
rise	rice *
risemblans	resemblance
risemble	resemble [2+]
risembul	resemble [2+]
risent	resent [1*+]
risentful	resentful [+]
riserch	research [1+]
riserve	reserve [2+]
riservist	reservist
riside	reside [2+]
risign	resign [1+]
risilience	resilience [+]
risilient	resilient
risilyant	resilient
risilyens	resilience [+]
risist	resist [1+]
risistable	resistable [+]
risistabul	resistable [+]
resistance	resistance [+]
risistans	resistance [+]
risistant	resistant
risital	recital [+]
risite	recite [2]
risk [1] /ier/iest/y	
riski *ly* /ness	
risolve	resolve [2]
risorce	resource [+]
risorceful	resourceful
risort	resort [1]
risotto	

risound	resound [1]	riter	writer
risource	resource [+]	rithe	writhe [2]
risourceful	resourceful	rithm	rhythm
risownd	resound [1]	rithmic	rhythmic [+]
rispect	respect [1+]	riting	writing
rispectable	respectable [+]	ritire	retire [2+]
rispectful	respectful	ritort	retort [1]
rispectiv	respective [+]	ritracshun	retraction
rispire	respire [2+]	ritract	retract [1+]
rispite	respite	ritraction	retraction
risplendence	resplendence [+]	ritreet	retreat [1]
risplendens	resplendence [+]	retrevable	retrievable
risplendent	resplendent	retreval	retrieval
rispond	respond [1+]	ritreve	retrieve [2+]
rispondence	respondence	ritten	written
rispondens	respondence	ritual /ism/ist	
responsible	responsible [+]	riturn	return [1+]
responsibul	responsible [+]	rityoual	ritual [+]
risponsiv	responsive	rival [3] /ry	
rissole		riveal	reveal [1]
rist	wrist [+]	rivenge	revenge [2+]
ristband	wristband	rivengeful	revengeful
ristlet	wristlet	river	
ristore	restore [2+]	rivere	revere [2+]
ristrain	restrain [1+]	rivet [1]	
ristraint	restraint	rivijun	revision
ristrict	restrict [1+]	rivile	revile [2]
ristwatch	wrist-watch	rivise	revise [2+]
risult	result [1+]	rivishun	revision
risultant	resultant	rivision	revision
risume	resume [2*]	rivival	revival
risurgence	resurgence [+]	rivive	revive [2+]
risurgens	resurgence [+]	rivocable	revocable [+]
risurgent	resurgent	rivocabul	revocable [+]
rit	writ	rivoke	revoke [2+]
ritaliate	retaliate [2+]	rivolt	revolt [1]
ritard	retard [1+]	rivolv	revolve [2+]
ritchus	righteous [+]	rivolver	revolver
		rivue	review [1*+]
rite * (ceremony)		rivue	revue *
rite	right [1*]	rivulet	
rite	write [*+]	rivulshun	revulsion
riteful	rightful [+]	rivulsion	revulsion
ritenshun	retention [+]	rivursal	reversal
ritention	retention [+]	rivurse	reverse [2+]
ritentiv	retentive		

247

rivurt	revert [1+]	roli poli	roly-poly
riward	reward [1]	rolick	rollick [1+]
ro	roe *[+]	roll [1*] (move) /-call/er	
ro	row [1*+]	roller-skate [2]	
roach [1] /es		rollick [1] /er	
road * (highway)		rolling-pin	
road	rode *	roly-poly	
roadworth y /iness		Roman Catholic	
roam [1]		romance [2]	
roan		romans	romance [2]
roar [1] /er		romantic /ally/ism	
roast [1]		Romany	
rob [3] /ber		romboid	rhomboid
robber y /ies		rombus	rhombus [+]
robe [2]		rome	roam [1]
roberey	robbery [+]	romp [1] /er	
robin redbreast		rondayvoo	rendezvous [1]
robot		rondo /s	
robust /ly/ness		rone	roan
roch	roach [1+]	rong	wrong [1+]
rock [1] /er/y		rongful	wrongful [+]
rock -cake /garden		roo	rue [2+]
rocker y /ies		roobarb	rhubarb
rocket [1] /eer/ry		rooble	rouble
rocking -chair /-horse		roobul	rouble
rococo		rood * (church)	
rode *(did ride)		rood	rude *[+]
rode	road *	roodiment	rudiment [+]
rodedendron	rhododendron	roodimentrey	rudimentary
rodent		roof [1] /less	
rodeo /s		rooful	rueful
rodeworthey	roadworthy [+]	rooge	rouge [2]
rodio	rodeo [+]	rooin	ruin [1+]
rodium	rhodium	rooinashun	ruination
roe * (deer) /buck		rooination	ruination
roe	row [1*+]	rooinous	ruinous [+]
rog	rogue [+]	rooinus	ruinous [+]
rogish	roguish	rook [1] /ery/eries	
rogu e /ery/ish		rool	rule [2+]
roial	royal [+]	roolet	roulette
roialtey	royalty	room /ful/iness/y	
rol	role *	roomatic	rheumatic [+]
rol	roll [1*+]	roomatism	rheumatism
rolcall	roll-call	roomer	rumour [1]
role * (of an actor)		roomey	roomy

roon	rune	rough-and-tumble	
roopee	rupee	roughen[1]	
rooral	rural[+]	rough er /est/ly/ness	
roose	ruse	rough-shod	
roost[1] /er		rought	wrought[+]
root[1]* /-crop/less		roulette	
root	route *	round[1] /er/est/ly/ness	
roothless	ruthless[+]	roundabout	
rootine	routine	Roundhead	
rootstock		round -table /-up	
rop e[2] /iness/y		rous e[2] /ingly	
rope-ladder		rout[1]* (defeat)	
ropey	ropy	route * (way)	
ror	roar[1+]	routeen	routine
rort	wrought[+]	routine	
rosarey	rosary[+]	rove[2] /r	
rosar y /ies		row[1]* (boat) /er	
rose * /-bud/-tree		rowdie	rowdy[+]
rose	rows *	rowd y /ies/ily/iness	
roset	rosette	rownd	round[1+]
rosette		rowndabout	roundabout
rosewood		rowndhed	Roundhead
rosie	rosy[+]	rowndup	round-up
rost	roast[1]	rows * (lines)	
roster		rowse	rouse[2+]
rostrum /s		rowt	rout[1]*
ros y /ily/iness		rowze	rouse[2+]
rot[3] /ter		royal /ly/ty	
rota /s		royaltey	royalty
rotarey	rotary[+]	rub[3] /ber	
rotar y /ies		rubarb	rhubarb
rotashun	rotation	rubbish /y	
rotat e[2] /able/ion		rubble	
rote * (repetition)		rubicund	
rote	wrote *	rubie	ruby[+]
roten	rotten[+]	rubish	rubbish[+]
roter	rotor	rubric	
roth	wrath[+]	rubul	rubble
rotor		rub y /ies	
rotten /ly/ness		rucksack	
rotund /a/ity		rudder	
rouble		rudd y /iness	
rouge[2]		rude *(offensive)/ly/r/st	
rough * (coarse) /age		rude	rood *
rough-and-ready		ruder	rudder

rudie	ruddy +	run /ner/ning/way	
rudiment /ary		runaway	
rue ² /ful/fully		rune	
ruf	rough *+	runerup	runner-up
ruf	ruff *	rung *†	
ruf and redy	rough-and-ready	†(step, did ring)	
ruf and tumbul	rough-and-tumble	rung	wrung *
ruff * (collar, bird)		runner-up	
ruff	rough *+	runt	
ruffage	roughage	rupcher	rupture ²
ruffen	roughen ¹	rupea	rupee
ruffian /ism/ly		rupee	
ruffle ²		rupture ²	
ruffley	roughly	rural /ly	
rufidge	roughage	ruse	
rufige	roughage	rush ¹	
rufle	ruffle ²	rushun	Russian
rufshod	rough-shod	rusit	russet
ruful	rueful	rusk	
rufyan	ruffian +	rusler	rustler
rugbe	Rugby	russet	
Rugby		Russian	
rugged /ly/ness		rust ¹ /less/y	
rugid	rugged +	rustic /ity	
ruin ¹ /ation		rusticat e ² /ion	
ruinashun	ruination	rusti er /est/ly/ness	
ruinous /ly		rustle ² /r	
ruinus	ruinous +	rust-proof	
ruksac	rucksack	rusul	rustle ²+
rule ² /r		rut ³	
rum /ba/my		ruthenium	
rumatic	rheumatic +	ruthless /ly/ness	
rumatism	rheumatism	rye * (grain)	
rumble ²		rye	wry *+
rumbul	rumble ²	ryly	wryly
rumer	rumour ¹	rythm	rhythm
rumidge	rummage ²	rythmic	rhythmic +
rumige	rummage ²		
ruminat e ² /ion/ive			
rummage ²			
rumour ¹			
rump /steak			
rumple ²		saans	seance
rumpul	rumple ²	sabath	sabbath +
rumpus /es		sabatical	sabbatical
		sabbat h /ical	

S

saber	sabre +	sail	sale *+
sable		sailsman	salesman
sabotage ²		saint /hood/ly	
sabre /-toothed		sake	
sabul	sable	sakshorn	saxhorn
sacarin	saccharin	saksofone	saxophone +
saccharin		sakson	Saxon +
sacerdotal		saksophone	saxophone +
sachel	satchel	salar y ⁴ /ies	
sachet		sale *† /ability/able	
sack ¹ /ful		†(of goods)	
sackarin	saccharin	sale	sail ¹*+
sacrament		salesman	
sacred /ly/ness		salie	sally ⁴+
sacrement	sacrament	salien ce /t	
sacrific e ² /ial		saliens	salience +
sacrifise	sacrifice ²+	salin e /ity	
sacrifishal	sacrificial	saliva /ry/tion	
sacrileg e /ious		sallow /ness	
sacrilige	sacrilege +	sall y ⁴ /ies	
sacriligus	sacrilegious	salm	psalm +
sacrosanct		salmon	
sacsophone	saxophone +	salon	
sad /der/dest/ly/ness		saloon	
sadden ¹		saloot	salute ²+
saddle ² /r/ry		salow	sallow +
saden	sadden ¹	salsify	
sadis m /t		salt ¹ /iness/y	
sadul	saddle ²+	salt -cellar /-lick	
safari /s		salter	psalter +
safe /ly/r/st/ty		saltpeter	saltpetre
safegard	safeguard ¹	saltpetre	
safeguard ¹		salubri ous /ty	
saffron		salubrius	salubrious +
safire	sapphire	salutar y /iness	
saftie	safety	salutashun	salutation
sag ³		salut e ² /ation	
saga /s		salvage ²	
sagaci ous /ty		salvashun	salvation
sagashus	sagacious +	salvation	
sagasitey	sagacity	salv e ² /able	
sage /ly/ness		salver	
sago		salvidge	salvage ²
said		salvige	salvage ²
sail ¹* (of boat) /or		salvo /s	

251

samaritan		sap³	
samarium		saper	sapper
same /ness		sapien ce /t	
samon	salmon	sapiens	sapience +
samovar		sapling	
sample² /r		sapper	
sampul	sample²+	sapphire	
sanatorium /s		sarcasm	
sancshun	sanction¹	sarcastic /ally	
sanctifi	sanctify⁴+	sarcofagus	sarcophagus +
sanctif y⁴ /ication		sarcophag us /i (pl.)	
sanctimonious /ly		sardine	
sanctimonius	sanctimonious +	sardonic /ally	
sanction¹		sargant	sergeant +
sanctity		sari	
sanctuar y /ies		sarjent	sergeant +
sanctum /s		sarm	psalm +
sand¹ /y		sartorial	
sandal /-wood		sary	sari
sandle	sandal +	saserdotle	sacerdotal
sandpaper¹		sash /es	
sandwhich	sandwich¹+	sashable	satiable
sandwich¹ /es		sashabul	satiable
sane * (not mad) /ly/ness		sashay	sachet
sane	seine²*	sashiate	satiate²
sang-froid		Satan /ic	
sanguin e /ary		satchel	
sangwin	sanguine +	sate²	
sanitary		sateen	
sanitashun	sanitation	satelight	satellite
sanitation		satellite	
sanitey	sanity	saten	sateen
sanitrey	sanitary	saterday	Saturday
sanity		satiable	
sankshun	sanction¹	satiabul	satiable
sanktify	sanctify⁴+	satiate²	
sanktimonius	sanctimonious +	satin	
sanktitey	sanctity	satir e /ist	
sanktuarey	sanctuary +	satirical /ly	
sanktum	sanctum +	satirise²	
Sanskrit		satisfacshun	satisfaction
sant	saint +	satisfactor y /ily	
Santa Claus		satisfactrey	satisfactory +
Santa klaws	Santa Claus	satisfiabul	satisfiable
santeem	centime	satisf y⁴ /iable/action	

saturashun	saturation	say /ing	
saturat *e* ² /ion		sayance	seance
Saturday		scab ³ /by	
Saturn		scabbard	
sauce * (liquid) /boat/pan		scabees	scabies
sauce	source *	scabies	
saucer		scaffold	
saucerer	sorcerer +	scald ¹	
saucerey	sorcery	scal *e* ² /y	
sauci *er* /est/ly/ness		scaliwag	scallywag
saucy		scallop	
sauna		scallywag	
saunter ¹		scalp ¹ /er	
sausage		scalpel	
sausie	saucy	scamp ¹	
savage ² /ly/ry		scamper ¹	
savana	savannah	scampi	
savannah		scan ³ /ner	
save ²		scandal /ous/ously	
saver	savour ¹+	scandalise ²	
savier	saviour	scandium	
savige	savage ²+	scanshun	scansion
savigrey	savagery	scansion	
saviour		scant /ily/iness/y	
savorey	savoury	scapegoat	
savour ¹ /iness/y		scapula /r	
savyer	saviour	scar ³	
saw * (cut) /n		scarab	
saw	soar ¹*	scarce /ly/ness/r	
saw	sore *+	scarcit *y* /ies	
sawcer	saucer	scare ² /crow/y	
sawcy	saucy	scaremonger	
sawdid	sordid +	scar *f* /ves (pl.)	
sawdust		scarf-pin	
sawna	sauna	scarif *y* ⁴ /ication	
sawnter	saunter ¹	scarlatina	
saws	sauce *+	scarlet	
saws	source *	scarsitey	scarcity +
sawser	saucer	scathe ² /less	
sawsey	saucy	scatter ¹ /-brain	
sawsier	saucier +	scavenge ² /r	
saxhorn		scavinge	scavenge ²+
saxofone	saxophone +	sceme	scheme ²+
Saxon /y		scenario /s	
saxophon *e* /ist		scene * (of a play) /ry	

253

scenic /ally	
scent ¹* (smell)	
scepter	sceptre
sceptic /al/ally/ism	
sceptre	
scerge	scourge ²
scermish	skirmish ¹⁺
schedule ²	
schematic /ally	
scheme ² /r	
scherzo /s	
schism /atic	
schist	
schizofrenia	schizophrenia ⁺
schizoid	
schizophreni a /c	
schnaps	
scholar /ly/ship	
scholastic /ism	
school ¹ /boy/girl	
schooner	
sciatic /a	
scien ce /tist	
scientific /ally	
scintillat e ² /ion	
scion	
scission	
scissors	
scitsofrenia	schizophrenia ⁺
sclerosis	
sclerotic	
scoff ¹ /er	
scolar	scholar ⁺
scolarship	scholarship
scolastic	scholastic ⁺
scold ¹ /er	
scone	
scool	school ¹⁺
scoop ¹	
scoot ¹ /er	
scorch ¹ /er/ingly	
score ² /r	
scorn ¹ /ful/fully	
scorpion	
scorpyun	scorpion

scot /ch/-free/tish	
Scots man /woman	
scoundrel /ism/ly	
scour ¹ /er	
scourge ²	
scout ¹	
scower	scour ¹⁺
scowl ¹	
scowndrel	scoundrel ⁺
scowt	scout ¹
scrabble ²	
scrabul	scrabble ²
scrag ³ /gy	
scram ³	
scramble ²	
scrambul	scramble ²
scrap ³ /-book/-heap	
scrape ² /r	
scrapie	scrappy ⁺
scrapp y /ily/iness	
scrapy	scrappy ⁺
scratch ¹ /es	
scrawl ¹	
scrawny	
scream ¹ /er	
scree	
screech ¹ /es/-owl	
screed	
screen ¹	
screw ¹ /driver/y	
screwtinise	scrutinise ²
scribble ² /r	
scribe ²	
scribul	scribble ²⁺
scrimige	scrimmage
scrimmage	
scrimp ¹ /y	
scripcher	scripture ⁺
script /-writer	
scriptur e /al	
scroful a /ous	
scroll	
scroo	screw ¹⁺
scrotum	
scrounge ² /r	

scrownge	scrounge ²⁺	seam	seem ¹★
scrub ³ /ber/by		seaman /ship	
scruff /ier/iest/y		seamstress	
scrum half		seam y /ier/iest	
scrummage		sean	scene ★⁺
scrumptious /ly/ness		sean	seen ★
scrumshus	scrumptious ⁺	seance	
scrunch ¹ /es		seans	seance
scruple ²		sear ¹★ (scorch)	
scrupul	scruple ²	sear	seer ★
scrupulous /ly/ness		search ¹ /es/er	
scrutinise ²		sea *shore* /side/weed	
scrutiny y /ies/eer		seasick /ness	
scud ³		season ¹ /able/ably	
scuffle ²		seasonal /ly	
scuful	scuffle ²	seasor	seesaw ¹
scul	scull ¹★⁺	seat ¹	
scul	skull ★⁺	seaworth y /iness	
sculerey	scullery ⁺	sebaceous	
scull ¹★ (boat) /er		sebashus	sebaceous
sculler y /ies		secaters	secateurs
sculpcher	sculpture ²	secateurs	
sculpt *or* /ress (fem.)		secede ²	
sculpture ²		seceshun	secession
scum ³ /my		secession	
scupper ¹		seclu *de* ² /sion	
scurf /iness/y		second ¹ /ly/-rate	
scurge	scourge ²	secondar y /ily	
scurie	scurry ⁴	secondrey	secondary ⁺
scurilus	scurrilous ⁺	secrecy	
scurrilous /ly		secresey	secrecy
scurry ⁴		secret /ive/ly	
scurv y /ily		secretaria *l* /t	
scury	scurry ⁴	secretar y /ies	
scuttle ²		secret *e* ² /ion	
scutul	scuttle ²	sect /arian	
scythe ²		section /al/ally	
sea ★ (water) /-gull		sector	
sea	see ★⁺	secular /ism	
seafar *er* /ing		secularis *e* ² /ation	
seal /ed/er/ing ★ (fasten)		secur *e* ² /able/ely	
sea -*level* /-lion		securitey	security ⁺
sealing	ceiling ★	securit y /ies	
sealskin		sed	said
seam ★ (join in cloth)		sedashun	sedation ⁺

255

sedate /ly/ness	
sedat *ion* /ive	
sedentary	
sedentrey	sedentary
seder	cedar
sedge	
sedila	cedilla
sediment /ation	
sedishun	sedition +
sedishus	seditious
sedit *ion* /ious	
seduce [2] /r	
seducshun	seduction
seduction	
seductive /ly	
sedulous /ly	
sedulus	sedulous +
seduse	seduce [2]+
see *† /ing/n *†	
†(with eyes)	
see	sea *+
seed [1]* (of plants)	
seed	cede [2]*
seed *iness* /ling/y	
seefarer	seafarer +
seege	siege
seek /er/ing	
seel	seal +
seeling	ceiling *
seeling	sealing *
seem [1]* (appear)	
seem	seam *
seeman	seaman +
seemey	seamy +
seeml *y* /ier/iest/iness	
seemstress	seamstress
seen	scene *+
seenerey	scenery
seenic	scenic +
seep [1] /age	
seepige	seepage
seer * (prophet)	
seer	sear [1]*
seesaw [1]	
seese	cease [2]+

seesfire	cease-fire
seesher	seizure
seeshore	seashore +
seesick	seasick +
seeside	seaside
seet	seat [1]
seeth	seethe [2]
seethe [2]	
seeworthey	seaworthy +
seeze	seize [2]
sefalic	cephalic +
sefalitis	cephalitis
sege	sedge
segment /ation	
segregashun	segregation
segregat *e* [2] /ion/ive	
seige	siege
seine [2]* (fishing net)	
seism *ic* /ometer	
seismograph /ic	
seismolog *y* /ist	
seize [2]	
seizure	
sekaters	secateurs
sekstant	sextant
sekstet	sextet
sekston	sexton
seksual	sexual +
sekt	sect +
sekwel	sequel
sekwence	sequence +
sekwens	sequence +
sekwester	sequester [1]
sekwestrate	sequestrate [2]+
sekwin	sequin
selandine	celandine
selcius	Celsius
seldom /ly	
selebritey	celebrity +
select [1] /ion/or	
selective /ly	
selenium	
seler	cellar *
seler	seller *
selerey	celery

256

seleritey	celerity		semi-final	
self /ish/ishness			semikwaver	semiquaver
self-assured			semilunar	
self-centred			seminal	
self-confiden ce /t			seminar /y	
selfconfidens	self-confidence +		semi-precious	
self-conscious /ly/ness			semipreshus	semi-precious
selfconshus	self-conscious +		semiquaver	
self-contained			Semit e /ic	
self-control			semitone	
self-respect /ing			semitrey	cemetery +
self-righteous /ly/ness			semolena	semolina
self-service			semolina	
selibacy	celibacy +		sena	senna
selibasey	celibacy +		senario	scenario +
selibat	celibate		senat	senate +
selibrant	celebrant		senat e /or	
selibrate	celebrate 2+		senater	senator
sell * (goods) /er *			send /er	
sell	cell *		senil e /ity	
seller	cellar *		senilitey	senility
Sellotape			senior /ity	
selofane	cellophane		senna	
selsius	Celsius		senotaf	cenotaph
selt	Celt +		sensashun	sensation
seltic	Celtic		sensashunal	sensational +
selular	cellular		sensation	
selule	cellule		sensational /ism/ly	
seluloid	celluloid		sense 2 /less	
selulose	cellulose		senser	censer *
selvage			senser	censor 1*+
selvige	selvage		sensher	censure 2+
semafor	semaphore		senshience	sentience +
semantic /s			senshooal	sensual +
semaphore			sensib le /ility/ly	
semblance			sensibul	sensible +
semblans	semblance		sensitise 2	
semen			sensitiv e /ely/ity	
semester			sensitivitey	sensitivity
semibreve			sensorey	sensory
semicercul	semicircle +		sensorious	censorious
semicirc le /ular			sensorius	censorious
semicolon			sensory	
semi-conductor			sensual /ist/ity/ly	
semi-detached			sensus	census +

sent * (did send)		septer	sceptre
sent	cent *	septic	
sent	scent [1]*	septicaemia	
sentenarey	centenary +	septisemia	septicaemia
sentenarian	centenarian	sepulchr *e* /al	
sentence [2]		sepulker	sepulchre +
sentenial	centennial +	sequel	
sentens	sentence [2]	sequen *ce* /tial	
sentenshus	sententious +	sequester [1]	
sententious /ly		sequestrat *e* [2] /ion/or	
sentenyal	centennial +	sequin	
senter	centre [2]+	ser	sir
senter forwud	centre-forward	seraf	seraph +
sentien *ce* /t		serafic	seraphic
sentigrade	centigrade	seramic	ceramic +
sentigram	centigram	seraph /s/ic	
sentileter	centilitre	serch	search [1]+
sentiment		serebral	cerebral +
sentimental /ist/ity/ly		serees	series
sentimentalise [2]		serenade [2]	
sentimeter	centimetre	serendipity	
sentinel		seren *e* /ely/ity	
sentipede	centipede	serenitey	serenity
sentor	centaur	seres	series
sentral	cențral +	sereze	cerise
sentralise	centralise [2]+	serf * (slave) /dom	
sentralitey	centrality	serf	surf [1]*+
sentrey	sentry +	sergeant /-major	
sentrifugal	centrifugal +	serial *† /ly	
sentrifuge	centrifuge	†(part of a story)	
sentripetal	centripetal	serial	cereal *
sentr *y* /ies		serialis *e* [2] /ation	
sentuple	centuple	seribelum	cerebellum
senturey	century +	seribrum	cerebrum
senturion	centurion	serid	serried
senyor	senior +	series	
senyoritey	seniority	serimonial	ceremonial +
separashun	separation	serimonius	ceremonious +
separat *e* [2] /ion/ist/or		serimuney	ceremony +
sephalic	cephalic +	serious /ly/ness	
sephalitis	cephalitis	serius	serious +
sepia		serlier	surlier +
sepoi	sepoy	serloin	sirloin
sepoy		serly	surly *
September		sermise	surmise [2]

sermon		sesmic	seismic +
sermonise ²		seson	season ¹+
sermownt	surmount ¹	sesonable	seasonable
sername	surname	sesonabul	seasonable
serpass	surpass ¹	sesonal	seasonal +
serpent /ine		sespit	cesspit
serplis	surplice *	sespool	cesspool
serplus	surplus *	sessashun	cessation
serprise	surprise ²	sessesion	secession
serrated		session * (period)	
serried		session	cession *
sertaks	surtax +	set /ting/-square	
sertax	surtax +	setea	settee
sertifi	certify ⁴+	seter	setter
sertifiable	certifiable +	setle	settle ²+
sertificat	certificate ²+	settee	
sertify	certify ⁴+	setter	
sertintey	certainty +	settle ² /ment/r	
sertitude	certitude	setul	settle ²+
serum		setulment	settlement
servant		seudo	pseudo +
servay	survey ¹+	seudonim	pseudonym
servaylans	surveillance	sevear	severe +
serve ² /r		seven /teen/teenth/th	
servical	cervical	seventy /ies/ieth	
service ² /ability/able		sever ¹ /ance˙	
serviet	serviette	several /ly	
serviette		severans	severance
serviks	cervix +	sever e /ely/ity	
servil e /ity		severitey	severity
servitude		sew *† /er *† /ing/n *†	
servival	survival	†(with a needle)	
servive	survive ²+	sew er ¹*† /age/erage	
serviver	survivor	†(public drain)	
servix	cervix +	sewn	sown *
sesashun	cessation	sex /ed/iness/less	
sese	cease ²+	sextant	
seseed	secede ²	sextet	
seseshun	secession	sexton	
seshun	cession *	sexual /ity/ly	
seshun	session *	sezarian	Caesarean
sesion	cession *	Sezer	Caesar
sesion	session *	sfere	sphere ²+
sesium	caesium	sferical	spherical
sesless	ceaseless	sferoid	spheroid

259

sfincter	sphincter	shan't (shall not)	
sfinks	sphinx +	shant	shan't
sfinx	sphinx +	shant y /ies	
sha	shah	shape ² /liness/ly	
shabbi ly /ness		shaperon	chaperon ¹⁺
shabb y /ier/iest		sharad	charade
shaby	shabby +	share ² /holder/r	
shack		shark	
shackle ²		sharlot	charlotte
shad e ² /y		sharp /er/est/ly/ness	
shadervre	chef-d'oeuvre	sharpen ¹ /er	
shadow ¹ /y		sharpshooter	
shaft		shasee	chassis
shagay da fare	chargé-d'affaires	shater	shatter ¹
shagg y /iness		shatow	chateau +
shagie	shaggy +	shatter ¹	
shagrin	chagrin +	shave ² /n/r	
shah		shawl	
shak	shack	shea f ¹ /ves (pl.)	
shake *† /down/n/r		shear * (clip) /s	
†(agitate)		shear	sheer ¹*
shake	sheik *	sheath * (n.)	
shakey	shaky +	sheathe ²* (v.)	
shak y /ily/ing/iness		shed ³	
shal	shall	shedule	schedule ²
shalaton	charlatan	sheef	sheaf ¹⁺
shalay	chalet	sheek	chic *
shale		sheek	sheik *
shalet	chalet	sheen	
shall		sheep /-dog/skin	
shallot		sheepish /ly/ness	
shallow /er/est/ness		sheer ¹* (thin, steep)	
sham ³ /mer		sheer	shear *⁺
shamble ²		sheet ¹	
shambul	shamble ²	shef	chef
shame ² /-faced/less		sheik * (Arab chief)	
shameful /ly		sheik	chic *
shampane	champagne	sheild	shield ¹
shampoo ¹		shel	shell ¹⁺
shamrock		shelac	shellac +
shamwa	chamois	sheld	shield ¹
shandeleer	chandelier	shel f /ves (pl.)	
shandie	shandy +	shelfish	shellfish
shand y /ies		shell ¹ /fish	
shank		shellac /ked/king	

shelter¹ /er
shelve²
shemeez — chemise
sheperd — shepherd¹⁺
sheperds pie — shepherd's pie
shepherd¹ /ess (fem.)
shepherd's pie
sherbet
sherie — sherry⁺
sherif — sheriff⁺
sheriff /s
sheroot — cheroot
sheropodey — chiropody⁺
sherr y /ies
shery — sherry⁺
sheth — sheath ★
sheth — sheathe²★
shevaler — chevalier
sheves — sheaves
shevron — chevron
shi — shy⁴⁺
shic — chic★
shic — sheik★
shicanerey — chicanery
shield¹
shifon — chiffon
shift¹ /ily/iness/less/y
shiling — shilling
shilling
shilly-shall y⁴ /ier
shily shaly — shilly-shally⁴⁺
shimeric — chimeric⁺
shimmer¹ /y
shin³
shin e² /er/y
shingle²
shingles
shingul — shingle²
shinguls — shingles
ship³ /ment/per
shipreck — shipwreck¹
ship shape /wright
shipwreck¹
shire
shirk¹ /er

shirt /ing/y
shivalrey — chivalry⁺
shivalrous — chivalrous
shivalrus — chivalrous
shiver¹ /y
shnaps — schnaps
shoal¹
shock¹ /-absorber/er
shoddi ly /ness
shodd y /ier/iest
shodie — shoddy⁺
shody — shoddy⁺
shoe /lace/string
shofer — chauffeur
sholder — shoulder¹
shole — shoal¹
shoo — shoe⁺
shood — should⁺
shook
shoolace — shoelace
shoostring — shoestring
shoot ★ (gun) /er
shoot — chute ★
shooting /-brake
shop³ /keeper/per
shoplift¹ /er
shop-soiled
shop-steward
shore²★ (prop up)
shore — sure★⁺
shoretey — surety⁺
shorley — surely
shorn
short /age/ly
short bread /cake
short-circuit¹
shorten¹
shorthand
short-sighted /ness
short sited — short-sighted⁺
shot
should /n't
shoulder¹
shout¹ /er
shove²

shovel³ /ler		siatic	sciatic⁺
shovinism	chauvinism⁺	sibernetics	cybernetics
shovinist	chauvinist	sibilant	
show /down/ily/ing/n/y		sibling	
shower¹ /-bath/y		sicamore	sycamore
showt	shout¹⁺	sicedelic	psychedelic
shrank		siciatrey	psychiatry
shrapnel		sicick	psychic⁺
shred³ /der		sick /ly/ness	
shreek	shriek¹	sicken¹	
shrew /ish/ishly		sickle	
shrewd /er/est/ly/ness		siclamate	cyclamate
shriek¹		siclamen	cyclamen
shrift		siclic	cyclic⁺
shrike		siclist	cyclist⁺
shrill¹ /er/est/ness/y		siclometer	cyclometer
shrimp		siclone	cyclone⁺
shrine²		siclops	Cyclops
shrink /age/ing		siclostile	cyclostyle
shrivel³		siclotron	cyclotron
shroo	shrew⁺	sicoanalise	psychoanalyse²⁺
shrood	shrewd⁺	sicofant	sycophant⁺
shroud¹		sicologey	psychology⁺
Shrovetide		sicological	psychological⁺
shrowd	shroud¹	sicopath	psychopath⁺
shrub /bery		sicosomatic	psychosomatic
shrug³		sicosis	psychosis⁺
shrunk /en		sicotherapey	psychotherapy
shudder¹		sicotherapist	psychotherapist⁺
shuffle² /r		sicotic	psychotic
shuful	shuffle²⁺	sicul	cycle²
shugar	sugar⁺	side² /board/line/ways	
shun³		sider	cider
shunt¹		sidle²	
shurbet	sherbet	sie	sigh¹
shurk	shirk¹⁺	siege	
shurt	shirt⁺	sienna	
shut /ter/ting		siense	science⁺
shuttle² /cock		sientific	scientific⁺
shutul	shuttle²⁺	sientist	scientist
shuv	shove²	siesta	
shuvel	shovel³⁺	sieve²	
shy⁴ /er/est/ly/ness		sieze	seize²
si	sigh¹	sifer	cipher¹
sianide	cyanide	sifilis	syphilis⁺

sifon	siphon [1]+	silidge	silage
sift [1]		silie	silly +
sigar	cigar +	silige	silage
sigaret	cigarette	silinder	cylinder
sigh [1]		silindrical	cylindrical +
sight [1]★ (see) /less		silk /ily/iness/y	
sight	cite [2]★+	sill	
sight	site [2]★	sillable	syllable +
sightsee r /ing		sillabub	
sign [1]★ /er/-writer		sill y /ier/iest/ily/iness	
sign	sine ★	silo	
signacher	signature	silogise	syllogise [2]+
signal [3] /ler		silogism	syllogism
signalise [2]		silooet	silhouette [2]
signator y /ies		siluet	silhouette [2]
signature		silvan	
signet ★ (ring)		silver [1] /y	
signet	cygnet ★	sily	silly +
signifi	signify [4]	simbiosis	symbiosis +
significan ce /t/tly		simbiotic	symbiotic
significans	significance +	simbol	cymbal ★+
signify [4]		simbol	symbol ★+
signpost [1]		simbolical	symbolical +
signul	signal [3]+	simbolise	symbolise [2]+
sikedelic	psychedelic	simbolism	symbolism
sikey	psyche	siment	cement [1]+
sikiatrist	psychiatrist +	simer	simmer [1]
sikiatry	psychiatry	simfoney	symphony +
sikick	psychic +	simian	
siks	six +	similar /ly	
sikstey	sixty +	similarit y /ies	
silable	syllable +	similer	similar +
silabus	syllabus +	similitude	
silage		simmer [1]	
silence [2] /r		simmetrey	symmetry +
silens	silence [2]+	simpathetic	sympathetic +
silent /ly		simpathise	sympathise [2]+
silestial	celestial +	simpathy	sympathy +
silf	sylph +	simper [1]	
silhouette [2]		simple /r/st/ton	
siliam	cilium	simplifi	simplify [4]+
silic a /osis		simplif y [4] /ication	
silicon ★ (hard mineral)		simplisitey	simplicity
silicone ★ (compound in polish)		simpl y /icity	
		simposium	symposium +

simptom	symptom [+]	sinopsis	synopsis [+]
simptomatic	symptomatic	sinoptic	synoptic
simpul	simple [+]	sinoshoor	cynosure
simpulton	simpleton	sinovial	synovial
simulashun	simulation	sinse	since
simulat *e* [2] /ion/or		sinsere	sincere [+]
simultaneous /ly		sinseritey	sincerity
simultanius	simultaneous [+]	sintactic	syntactic
sin [1] /ner		sintaks	syntax [+]
sinagog	synagogue	sintax	syntax [+]
sinamon	cinnamon	sinthesis	synthesis [+]
since		sinthesise	synthesise [2+]
sincer *e* /ity		sinthetic	synthetic
sinch	cinch [+]	sinue	sinew [+]
sincopate	syncopate [2+]	sinuous	
sindicalism	syndicalism [+]	sinus /es/itis	
sindicate	syndicate [2+]	sinuus	sinuous
sindrome	syndrome	sion	scion
sine ★ (maths)		sip [3]	
sine	sign [1★+]	sipher	cipher [1]
sinecamera	cine camera	siphon [1] /age	
sinecure		sipress	cypress
sinepost	signpost [1]	sir	
sinew /y		sirca	circa
sinful /ly/ness		sircharge	surcharge [2]
sing /er/ing		siren	
singe [2]		siringe	syringe [2]
single [2] /-minded		sirloin	
singul	single [2+]	siro stratus	cirro-stratus
singular /ity		sirocco	
singuler	singular [+]	sirocumulus	cirro-cumulus
sinic	cynic [+]	sirosis	cirrhosis
sinical	cynical [+]	sirup	syrup [+]
sinima	cinema [+]	sise	size [+]
sinimatograf	cinematograph [+]	sishun	scission
sinimatograph	cinematograph [+]	sismic	seismic [+]
sinisism	cynicism	sismograf	seismograph [+]
sinister		sismologey	seismology [+]
sink /er/ing		sissers	scissors
sinkromesh	syncromesh	sist	cyst [+]
sinkronise	synchronise [2+]	sistem	system [+]
sinod	synod [+]	sistematic	systematic
sinonim	synonym [+]	sistematise	systematise [2+]
sinonimus	synonymous	sister(s)/-in-law	
sinonym	synonym [+]	sistern	cistern

sistitis	cystitis
sistole	systole
sit /-in/ter/ting	
sitadel	citadel
sitashun	citation
site ²★ (place)	
site	cite ²★⁺
site	sight ¹★⁺
siteseeing	sightseeing
siteseer	sightseer ⁺
sitey	city ⁺
sithe	scythe ²
sitie	city ⁺
sitizen	citizen ⁺
sitologey	cytology
sitric acid	citric acid
sitron	citron ⁺
sitrus	citrus
situashun	situation
situat e ³ /ion	
siv	sieve ²
sivere	severe ⁺
sivic	civic ⁺
sivil	civil ⁺
sivilian	civilian
sivilisashun	civilisation
sivilise	civilise ²⁺
sivilitey	civility ⁺
sivit	civet
six /th/thly	
sixteen /th	
sixt y /ies/ieth	
siythe	scythe ²
size /able/ably	
sizemic	seismic ⁺
sizers	scissors
sizul	sizzle ²
sizzle ²	
skate ² /r	
skedule	schedule ²
skee	ski ¹★⁺
skein	
skelet on /al	
skematic	schematic ⁺
skeme	scheme ²⁺

skeptic	sceptic ⁺
skepticul	sceptical
skeptisism	scepticism
skermish	skirmish ¹⁺
skert	skirt ¹⁺
skerting bord	skirting-board
skertso	scherzo ⁺
sketch ¹ /ier/ily/iness/y	
skew ¹ /-whiff	
skewer ¹	
ski ¹★ (sport) /er	
ski	sky ⁴★⁺
skid ³	
skiff	
skil	skill ⁺
skilful /ly/ness	
skilite	skylight
skill /ed	
skim ³ /-milk	
skimp ¹ /ily/iness/y	
skin ³ /ner/ny	
skin-deep	
skin-div er /ing	
skiney	skinny
skinflint	
skintilate	scintillate ²⁺
skip ³	
skipper	
skirl ¹	
skirmish ¹ /es	
skirt ¹ /ing-board	
skiscraper	skyscraper
skism	schism ⁺
skist	schist
skit /tish	
skitsofrenia	schizophrenia ⁺
skittle ²	
skitul	skittle ²
skitzoid	schizoid
sku	skew ¹⁺
skulk ¹	
skull ★ (head) /-cap	
skull	scull ¹★⁺
skunk	
skurl	skirl ¹

If you cannot find your word under **skw** *look under* **squ**	

skwable	squabble [2]
skwod	squad
skwodron	squadron
skwolid	squalid [+]
sky [4][*][†] /-blue/-high †(atmosphere)	
sky	ski [1][*][+]
skyatic	sciatic [+]
skylark	
skylight	
skylite	skylight
skyscraper	
slack [1] /er/est/ly/ness	
slacken [1]	
slain	
slake [2]	
slaken	slacken [1]
slam [3]	
slander [1] /er/ous	
slane	slain
slang /y	
slant [1]	
slap [3] /dash/stick	
slash [1] /er	
slat *e*[2] /y	
slattern /ly	
slaughter [1] /-house	
Slav /onic	
slave [2] /ry	
slavish /ness	
slawter	slaughter [1][+]
slay [*] (kill) /ing	
slay	sleigh [*]
sleazy	
sled	
sledge /-hammer	
sleek /ness	
sleep /ing/y	
sleepi *er* /est/ly/ness	
sleepless /ness	
sleet [1] /y	

sleeve /d/less	
slege	sledge [+]
sleigh [*] (for snow)	
slender /ness	
sleuth	
slew	
sli	sly [+]
slice [2]	
slick [1]	
slid *e* /ing	
slight [1] /er/est/ly/ness	
slim [3] /mer/mest/ness	
slim *e* /ier/iest/y	
sling /er	
slip [3] /way	
slipper /iness/y	
slipshod	
slise	slice [2]
slit /ting	
slite	slight [1][+]
slither [1]	
sliver	
slo	sloe [*]
slo	slow [1][*][+]
slobber [1] /er	
sloe [*] (plum)	
sloe	slow [1][*][+]
slog [3] /ger	
slogan	
sloop	
sloose	sluice [2]
slooth	sleuth
slop [3] /py	
slope [2]	
sloppi *er* /est/ly/ness	
slosh [1]	
slot [3] /machine	
sloth /ful	
slouch [1]	
slough [1][*] (dead skin)	
sloven /liness/ly	
slow [1][*][†] /er/ly/-worm †(not quick)	
slow	slough [1][*]
slowch	slouch [1]

slowerm	slow-worm	smug /ger/gest/ly/ness	
sludg e /y		smuge	smudge ²⁺
slue	slew	smuggle ² /r	
sluff	slough ¹★	smugul	smuggle ²⁺
slug /gard/gish		smurch	smirch ¹⁺
sluge	sludge ⁺	smurk	smirk ¹
sluice ²		smut /tiness/ty	
slum ³ /mer/my		snack	
slumber ¹ /ous		snag ³	
slump ¹		snail ¹	
slung		snake ² /-bite	
slunk		snale	snail ¹
slur ³		snap ³ /dragon/shot	
slush /y		snapp er /ily/ish/y	
slut /tish		snare ²	
sly /er/est/ly/ness		snarl ¹ /er	
smack ¹		snatch ¹ /es	
small /er/est/pox		sneak ¹ /ingly/ily	
smarmy		sneek	sneak ¹⁺
smart ¹ /er/est/ly/ness		sneer ¹	
smarten ¹		sneeze ²	
smash ¹ /er		snicker ¹	
smatter /ing		snide	
smear ¹ /y		sniff ¹ /er/y	
smeer	smear ¹⁺	sniffle ²	
smell ¹ /ier/iest/ing/y		sniful	sniffle ²
smelling-salts		snigger ¹	
smelt ¹ /er		snip ³ /pet	
smirch ¹ /es		snipe ² /r	
smirk ¹		snivel ³ /ler	
smit e /ing		sno	snow ¹⁺
smith /y/ies		snobb ery /ish/ishness	
smithereens		snoberie	snobbery ⁺
smithey	smithy	snobish	snobbish
smitten		snooker ¹	
smock ¹		snoop ¹ /er	
smog		snooze ²	
smoke ² /r/-stack		snore ² /r	
smok ier /iest/y		snorkel	
smolder	smoulder ¹	snorkle	snorkel
smooth ¹ /er/est/ly/ness		snort ¹ /er	
smote		snot /ty	
smother ¹		snout	
smoulder ¹		snow ¹ /drift/drop/fall	
smudg e ² /y		snowball ¹	

snow-plough		soften [1]	
snowt	snout	software	
snub [3]		softwear	software
snuff [1]		sogg y /iness	
snuffle [2]		sogie	soggy [+]
snuful	snuffle [2]	Soho	
snuggle [2]		soia	soya
snugul	snuggle [2]	soil [1]	
so * (in this way)		soiray	soirée
so	sew *[+]	soirée	
so	sow [1]*	soiya	soya
soak [1]		sojern	sojourn [1+]
soap [1] /y		sojourn [1] /er	
soar [1]* (to fly)		soke	soak [1]
soar	sore *[+]	solace [2]	
sob [3]		solar /ium	
sober [1]		solar plexus	
sobriety		solar system	
sobrikay	sobriquet [+]	solas	solace [2]
sobriquet /s		solder [1]	
soccer		soldering iron	
sociab le /ility/ly		soldier [1] /ly/y	
sociabul	sociable [+]	sole * (shoe) /ly	
social /ite/ly		sole	soul *[+]
socialis e [2] /ation		solecism	
socialis m /t/tic		soleful	soulful [+]
societ y /ies		solem	solemn [+]
sociolog y /ical/ist		solemn /ity/ly	
sock [1]		solemnis e [2] /ation	
socker	soccer	solemnitey	solemnity
socket		solenoid	
soda /-water		solesism	solecism
sodden		sol-fa	
soden	sodden	solger	soldier [1+]
sodium		solicit [1] /ation/ude	
sodom y /ite		solicit or /ous	
sofen	soften [1]	solid /er/est/ity/ly	
sofism	sophism [+]	solidarity	
sofist	sophist	solidifi	solidify [4+]
sofisticashun	sophistication	solidif y [4] /ication	
sofisticate	sophisticate [2+]	solilokwise	soliloquise [2]
sofistication	sophistication	solilokwy	soliloquy [+]
sofistrey	sophistry	soliloquise [2]	
sofmore	sophomore	soliloqu y /ies	
soft /er/est/ly/ness		solisit	solicit [1+]

solisiter	solicitor +	soop	soup
solisitous	solicitous	soot * (black powder) /y	
solisitus	solicitous	soot	suit [1]*+
solitar y /ily/iness		sooth /sayer	
solitrey	solitary +	soothe [2]	
solitude		soovenir	souvenir
soljer	soldier [1]+	sop [3] /py	
solo /ist		sope	soap [1]+
solstice		sophis m /t/try	
solstis	solstice	sophisticat e [2] /ion	
solub le /ility		sophomore	
solubul	soluble +	soporific	
solushun	solution	soprano /s	
solution		sorcer er /ess (fem.)/y	
solv e [2] /able		sord	sword
solven cy /t		sordid /ly/ness	
solvensey	solvency +	sordust	sawdust
somber	sombre +	sore * (hurt) /ly/r/st	
sombraro	sombrero +	sore	saw *+
sombre /ly/ness		sore	soar [1]*
sombrero /s		sorey	sorry +
some *† /body/how		sorie	sorry +
†(a few)		sorna	sauna
some	sum [3]*	sornter	saunter [1]
some one /what/where		sorow	sorrow [1]+
somersalt	somersault [1]	sorrel	
somersault [1]		sorrow [1] /ful/fully	
somnolen ce /t		sorr y /ier/iest	
somnolens	somnolence +	sors	sauce *+
son * (male child)		sors	source *
sonar		sort [1]* (kind) /er	
sonata		sort	sought *
sonde		sortee	sortie
soner	sonar	sortie	
song /-bird/ster		sorul	sorrel
sonic		soshable	sociable +
son(s)-in-law		soshabul	sociable +
sonnet		soshal	social +
sonor ous /ity		soshalise	socialise [2]+
sonorus	sonorous +	soshalism	socialism +
soo	sue [2]	soshalist	socialist
soocher	suture	soshalistic	socialistic
sooflay	soufflé	soshiologey	sociology +
sooit	suet	soshiologist	sociologist
soon /er		sosidge	sausage

sosietey	society [+]	spanner	
sosige	sausage	Spanyard	Spaniard
sot /tish		spanyel	spaniel
sotto voce		spar [3]	
soufflé		spare [2]	
sought * (did seek)		spark [1] /ing-plug	
soul * (spirit) /less		sparkle [2] /r	
soul	sole *[+]	sparkul	sparkle [2+]
soulful /ly		sparo	sparrow [+]
sound [1] /er/est/less/ness		sparrow /-hawk	
soundproof [1]		spars	sparse [+]
soup		sparse /ly/ness	
sour [1] /er/est/ish/ness		sparsity	
source * (origin)		Spartan	
source	sauce *[+]	spase	space [2+]
souse [2]		spashal	spatial
south /erly/ern		spashus	spacious
souvenir		spasm	
sou'-wester		spasmodic /ally	
sovereign /ty		spastic /ism	
soverin	sovereign [+]	spate	
soviet		spatial	
sovrentey	sovereignty	spatter [1]	
sow [1]* (cast seed, pig)		spatula /te	
sow	sew *[+]	spawn [1]	
sown * (seed)		speak /er/ing	
sown	sewn *	spear [1] /head	
sownd	sound [1+]	special /ist/ly	
sowndproof	soundproof [1]	specialis e [2] /ation	
sowr	sour [1+]	specialt y /ies	
sowse	souse [2]	species	
sowth	south [+]	specifi	specify [4+]
sow-wester	sou'-wester	specific /ally	
soya		specif y [4] /ication	
spac e [2] /ious		specimen	
spade /-work		specious /ness	
spagetti	spaghetti	speck [1]	
spaghetti		speckle [2]	
span [3]		spectacle	
spaner	spanner	spectacular /ly	
spangle		spectator	
spangul	spangle	specter	spectre [+]
Spaniard		spectr e /al	
spaniel		spectrograf	spectrograph
spank [1]		spectrograph	

270

spectroscop *e* /ic	
spectr *um* /a (pl.)	
speculashun	speculation
speculat *e*² /ion/or	
speculative /ly	
speech /less	
speed¹ /y	
speedi *er* /est/ly/ness	
speedometer	
speek	speak⁺
speeker	speaker
speeking	speaking
speer	spear¹⁺
speerhed	spearhead
spekul	speckle²
spel	spell⁺
spelbownd	spellbound
spel *l* /ling/t	
spellbound	
spend /er/thrift	
sperm /-whale	
spermatoz *oon* /oa (pl.)	
spern	spurn¹
spert	spurt¹
speshal	special⁺
speshalise	specialise²⁺
speshalist	specialist
speshaltey	specialty⁺
speshes	species
speshialtey	specialty⁺
speshus	specious⁺
spesifi	specify⁴⁺
spesific	specific⁺
spesificashun	specification
spesify	specify⁴⁺
spesimen	specimen
spew¹	
spher *e*² /ical/ically	
spheroid	
sphincter	
sphinx /es	
spi	spy⁴⁺
spic *e*² /y	
spici *er* /est/ly/ness	
spick and span	

spider /y	
spik *e*² /y	
spil *l* /ling/t	
spin³ /ner/neret	
spinach	
spinaker	spinnaker
spindl *e* /y	
spindul	spindle⁺
spin *e* /al/eless	
spiney	spinney⁺
spinidge	spinach
spinige	spinach
spinnaker	
spinney /s	
spinster /hood	
spiracle	
spiral³ /ly	
spire	
spirichooal	spiritual⁺
spirichooalise	spiritualise²⁺
spirichooalist	spiritualist⁺
spirit¹ /less	
spiritual /ly	
spiritualis *e*² /ation	
spiritualist /ic	
spise	spice²⁺
spisey	spicy
spisier	spicier⁺
spit /ting/toon	
spite /ful/fulness	
spitfire	
spittle	
spitul	spittle
splash¹ /-down	
splay¹	
spleen	
splender	splendour
splendid	
splendour	
splice²	
splint¹	
splinter¹	
splise	splice²
split /ting	
splutter¹	

spoil¹ /sport/t	
spoke /n	
spokes *man* /woman	
spoliashun	spoliation⁺
spoliat *ion* /or	
spong *e*² /er/y	
sponser	sponsor¹
sponsor¹	
spontaneity	
spontaneous /ly/ness	
spontanius	spontaneous⁺
spontenaitey	spontaneity
spoof¹ /er	
spool	
spoon¹ /-fed/ful	
spoonerism	
spoor¹★ (track)	
spoor	spore★
sporadic /ally	
sporan	sporran
spore★ (seed, germ)	
spore	spoor¹★
sporn	spawn¹
sporran	
sport¹ /ive/ively	
sportsman	
spot³ /-check/ty	
spotlight¹	
spotlite	spotlight¹
spouse	
spout¹	
spowse	spouse
spowt	spout¹
sprain¹	
sprane	sprain¹
sprang	
sprawl¹	
spray¹ /er	
spread /ing	
spread-eagle²	
spred	spread⁺
spree	
spri	spry⁺
sprightl *y* /ier/iest	
spring /-board/bok	

springtime	
spring *y* /iness/ing	
sprinkle² /r	
sprinkul	sprinkle²⁺
sprint¹	
sprite /ly	
sprocket	
sproose	spruce⁺
sprout¹	
sprowt	sprout¹
spruce /ly	
sprung	
spry /er/est	
spu	spew¹
spume²	
spunge	sponge²⁺
spunk	
spur³	
spurious /ly/ness	
spurius	spurious⁺
spurm	sperm⁺
spurn¹	
spurt¹	
sputter¹	
sputum	
sp *y*⁴ /ies	
squabble²	
squabul	squabble²
squad	
squadron	
squalid /ly	
squall¹	
squalor	
squander¹	
square² /ly	
squash¹	
squat³ /ter	
squaw	
squawk¹ /er	
squeak¹ /er/y	
squeal¹ /er	
squeamish /ly/ness	
squeeze²	
squelch¹	
squerm	squirm¹

squert	squirt [1]	stale /ness	
squib		stalemate [2]	
squid		stalk [1] /er	
squiggle [2]		stall [1]	
squigul	squiggle [2] .	stallion	
squint [1]		stalwart	
squir e [2] /archy		stalwert	stalwart
squirm [1]		stalyun	stallion
squirrel		stamen	
squirt [1]		stamer	stammer [1+]
squod	squad	stamina	
squodron	squadron	stammer [1] /er	
squoler	squalor	stamp [1] /er	
squolid	squalid [+]	stampede [2]	
squonder	squander [1]	stance	
squosh	squash [1]	stanch [1]★ (stop flow)	
squot	squat [3+]	stanch	staunch ★
stab [3]		stand /-by/point/still	
stabilis e [2] /ation/er		standard	
stability		standardis e [2] /ation	
stable [2]		standerd	standard
stabul	stable [2]	standerdise	standardise [2+]
staccato		stane	stain [1+]
stacher	stature	stank	
stachooery	statuary	stans	stance
stack [1]		stanza	
stadi um /a/ums (pls.)		stapes	
staf	staff [1+]	staple [2] /r	
staff [1] /s		stapul	staple [2+]
stag		star [3] /less/light/ry	
stage [2] /-coach		starboard	
stager	stagger [1]	starbord	starboard
stagger [1]		starch [1]	
stagnant		stare [2]★ (gaze)	
stagnashun	stagnation	stare	stair ★+
stagnat e [2] /ion		starecase	staircase
staid ★ (steady)		starie	starry
staid	stayed ★	stark	
stain [1] /less		starling	
stair ★ (step) /case		starry	
stair	stare [2]★	start [1] /er	
stake [2]★ (post)		startle [2]	
stake	steak ★	startul	startle [2]
stalactite ★ (down)		starvashun	starvation
stalagmite ★ (up)		starv e [2] /ation/eling	

stashun	station [1]+
stashunrey	stationary *
stashunrey	stationery *
state [2] /less/ment	
stately /ier/iest/iness	
static /ally/s	
station [1] /ary * (at rest)	
stationer /y * (paper)	
statistic /ian/s	
statistical /ly	
statistishun	statistician
statuary	
statue /sque/tte	
statuesk	statuesque
statuet	statuette
stature	
status	
statute /ory	
staunch * (true)	
staunch	stanch [1]*
stave [2]	
stawk	stalk [1]+
stay /ed *† /ing	
†(remained)	
stayed	staid *
steadfast /ly/ness	
steadie	steady [4]+
steady [4] /ier/iest/ily	
steak * (beef)	
steak	stake [2]*
steal * (to take) /ing	
steal	steel [1]*+
stealth /ily/iness/y	
steam [1] /er	
stedfast	steadfast +
stedy	steady [4]+
steed	
steel [1]* (metal) /y	
steel	steal *+
steem	steam [1]+
steep [1] /er/est/ly/ness	
steeple /chase/jack	
steepul	steeple +
steer [1] /able/age	
stelar	stellar

stellar	
stelth	stealth +
stem [3]	
stench /es	
stencil [3] /ler	
stenografey	stenography +
stenography /er/ic	
stenotipe	stenotype [2]
stenotype [2]	
stensil	stencil [3]+
step [3]* (pace) /-ladder	
step	steppe *
step brother /sister	
step daughter /son	
step father /mother	
steppe * (plain)	
ster	stir [3]
sterdey	sturdy +
stereo /phonic	
stereoscope /ic	
stereotype [2]	
sterile /ity	
sterilise [2] /ation	
sterilitey	sterility
sterio	stereo +
steriofonic	stereophonic
sterioscope	stereoscope +
steriotipe	stereotype [2]
sterjun	sturgeon
sterling	
stern /er/est/ly/ness	
sternum	
stethoscope	
stevedore	
stew [1]	
steward /ess (fem.)	
sti	sty [4]+
stich	stitch [1]+
stick /er/ing/s * (wood)	
sticking-plaster	
stickleback	
stickler	
Sticks	Styx *
sticky /ily/iness	
stif	stiff +

stifen	stiffen [1+]
stiff /er/est/ly	
stiffen [1] /er	
stifle [2]	
stiful	stifle [2]
stigma /s/ta (pls.)	
stigmatise [2]	
stil	still [1+]
stilberth	still-birth [+]
stile * (steps)	
stile	style [2*+]
stiletto /s	
stilise	stylise [2+]
stilish	stylish
stilist	stylist
still [1] /ness	
still -*birth* /-born	
stilt [1]	
stilus	stylus [+]
stimie	stymie [+]
stimulashun	stimulation [+]
stimulat *e* [2] /ion/ive/or	
stimul *us* /i (pl.) /ant	
sting /er/ing	
sting *y* /ier/iest/ily/iness	
stink /er/ing	
stint [1]	
stipel	stipple [2]
stipend	
stipendiar *y* /ies	
stipple [2]	
stiptic	styptic
stipul	stipple [2]
stipulashun	stipulation
stipulat *e* [2] /ion/or	
stir [3]	
stirrup	
stirup	stirrup
stitch [1] /es	
stoat	
stock [1] /broker/taking	
stockade	
stockie	stocky [+]
stocking	
stockman	

stockpile [2]	
stock-still	
stock *y* /ier/iest/iness	
stodg *e* [2] /y	
stoge	stodge [2+]
stoic /al/ally	
stoicism	
stoisism	stoicism
stoke [2] /r	
stole /n	
stolid /ity	
stoma /ta (pl.)	
stomach [1] /-ache	
stone [2] /mason	
stonewall [1] /er	
ston *y* /ier/iest/ily	
stood	
stooge [2]	
stook [1]	
stool [1]	
stoop [1]	
stop [3] /cock/page/per	
stoper	stopper
storage	
store [2] /house	
storekeeper	
storey * (floor level) /s	
storey	story [*+]
storidge	storage
storie	storey [*+]
storie	story [*+]
storige	storage
stork	
storm [1] /ier/iest/y	
stormi *ly* /ness	
stor *y* * (narrative) /ies	
story	storey [*+]
stote	stoat
stout /er/est/ly/ness	
stove [2]	
stow [1] /age/away	
stowige	stowage
stowt	stout [+]
straddle [2]	
stradul	straddle [2]

275

straf	strafe [2]	streemline	streamline [2]
strafe [2]		street	
straggle [2] /r		strength	
stragul	straggle [2+]	strengthen [1]	
straight * (line)		strenth	strength
straight	strait *	strenthen	strengthen [1]
straightaway		strenuous /ly/ness	
straighten [1]		strenuus	strenuous +
straightforward		streptococc *us* /i (pl.)/al	
strain [1] /er		stress [1]	
strait * (sea passage)		stretch [1] /er	
strait	straight *	strew /ing	
straitaway	straightaway	strewn	
straiten	straighten [1]	striccher	stricture
straitforwerd	straightforward	stricken	
strait-jacket		stricneen	strychnine
strait-laced		strict /er/est/ly/ness	
strand [1]		stricture	
strane	strain [1+]	strid *e* /ing	
strange /ly/ness/r/st		striden *cy* /t	
strangle [2]		stridensey	stridency +
strangul	strangle [2]	strife	
strangulat *e* [2] /ion		strik *e* /er/ing	
strap [3] /hanger		strike-break *er* /ing	
stratagem		string /ing/y	
strate	straight *	stringen *cy* /t	
strate	strait *	stringensey	stringency +
strategey	strategy +	strip [3] /per	
strategic /ally		stripe /d	
strateg *y* /ies/ist		stripling	
stratifi	stratify [4+]	striv *e* /en/ing	
stratif *y* [4] /ication		stroboscop *e* /ic	
stratoscope		strode	
stratosfere	stratosphere +	stroke [2]	
stratospher *e* /ic		stroll [1] /er	
strat *um* /a (pl.)		strong /er/est/ly/ness	
straw		strontium	
strawberie	strawberry +	stroo	strew +
strawberr *y* /ies		strooen	strewn
stray [1]		strove	
streak [1] /y		struck	
stream [1]		struckcher	structure +
streamline [2]		structur *e* /al/ally	
streek	streak [1+]	struggle [2]	
streem	stream [1]	strugul	struggle [2]

strum [3] /mer
strung
strut [3]
strychnine
stu   stew [1]
stuard   steward +
stub [3]
stubbl e /y
stubborn /ly/ness
stubern   stubborn +
stubul   stubble +
stucco [1]
stuck
stud [3]
student
studey   study [4]+
studio /s
studious /ly/ness
studius   studious +
stud y [4] /ies
stuf   stuff [1]+
stuff [1] /y
stuffi er /est/ly/ness
stuko   stucco [1]
stultifi   stultify [4]+
stultif y [4] /ication
stumac   stomach [1]+
stumble [2]
stumbul   stumble [2]
stump [1]
stun [3]
stung
stunk
stunt [1]
stupefi   stupefy [4]+
stupef y [4] /action
stupendous /ly/ness
stupendus   stupendous +
stuper   stupor
stupid /er/est/ity/ly
stupify   stupefy [4]+
stupor
sturdie   sturdy +
sturd y /ier/iest/ily/iness
sturgeon

sturgon   sturgeon
sturgun   sturgeon
sturling   sterling
sturn   stern +
sturnum   sternum
stuter   stutter [1]+
stutter [1] /er
stuward   steward +
st y [4] /ies
styl e [2]*† /ish/ist
   †(manner)
style   stile *
stylis e [2] /ation
stylus /es
stymie /d
styptic
Styx * (river)
suage   sewage
suav e /ely/ity
subaltern
subcomitee   subcommittee
subcommittee
subconscious /ly
subconshus   subconscious +
subcontinent
subcontract [1] /or
subdivide [2]
subdivishun   subdivision +
subdivisi on /ble
subdue [2]
subedit [1] /or
suberb   suburb +
suberban   suburban
sub-human
subjecshun   subjection
subject [1] /ion/ive/ivity
subjoogate   subjugate [2]+
subjugat e [2] /ion
subjunctive
sublet /ting
sublimat e [2] /ion
sublim e /inal
submachine-gun
submarine
submerg e [2] /ence/ible

277

submershun	submersion +	subtenant	
submersi *on* /ble		subtend [1]	
submishun	submission +	subterfugé	
submisiv	submissive	subterranean	
submiss *ion* /ive		sub-title [2]	
submit [3]		subtitul	sub-title [2]
submurge	submerge [2]+	subtle /ness/r/st	
subnormal		subtlet *y* /ies	
subordinat *e* [2] /ion		subtly	
suborn [1] /ation/er		subtracshun	subtraction
subpena	subpoena [1]	subtract [1] /ion	
sub-plot		subtropical	
subpoena [1]		suburb /an/ia	
subscribe [2] /r		subvershun	subversion +
subscription		subvers *ion* /ive	
subsekwent	subsequent +	subversiv	subversive
subsequent /ly		subvert [1] /er	
subservien *ce* /t		subvurt	subvert [1]+
subserviens	subservience +	subway	
subsidarey	subsidiary +	succeed [1]	
subside [2] /nce		success /ful/fully	
subsidens	subsidence	success *ion* /ive/or	
subsidey	subsidy +	succinct	
subsidiar *y* /ies		succour [1]★ (help)	
subsidis *e* [2] /ation		succulen *ce* /t	
subsid *y* /ies		succumb [1]	
subsist [1] /ence		such	
subsistens	subsistence	sucher	suture
subsoil		suck [1]	
subsonic		sucker ★ (victim,	
subsoyl	subsoil	one who sucks)	
substance		sucker	succour [1]★
substandard		suckle [2]	
substans	substance	sucksun	suction
substanshal	substantial +	suckulens	succulence +
substanshiate	substantiate [2]+	suckulent	succulent
substantial /ly/ity		suckumb	succumb [1]
substantiat *e* [2] /ion		sucrose	
substantive		sucseed	succeed [1]
substashun	substation	sucseshun	succession +
substation		sucsess	success +
substitushun	substitution	sucsesser	successor
substitut *e* [2] /ion		sucsessful	successful
substrat *um* /a (pl.)		sucsessiv	successive
subtefuge	subterfuge	sucsint	succinct

suction	
sudden /ly/ness	
sudo	pseudo +
sudonim	pseudonym
suds	
sue ²	
suède	
suer	sewer ¹★+
suet	
sufer	suffer ¹+
suffer ¹ /ance/er	
suffice ²	
sufficien cy /t	
suffiks	suffix ¹+
suffise	suffice ²
suffishency	sufficiency +
suffishent	sufficient
suffix ¹ /es	
suffocat e ² /ion	
suffrage /tte	
suffus e ² /ion	
sufocashun	suffocation
sufocate	suffocate ²+
sufocation	suffocation
sufrajet	suffragette
sufrance	sufferance
sufrige	suffrage +
sufuse	suffuse ²+
sugar ¹ /y	
sugeschun	suggestion
sugest	suggest ¹+
sugestion	suggestion
sugestiv	suggestive
suggest ¹ /ion/ive	
suicid e /al	
suige	sewage
suiside	suicide +
suit ¹★† /ability	
†(clothes)	
suit	suet
suitab le /ility/ly	
suite ★ (rooms)	
suitor	
sulfate	sulphate
sulfer	sulphur +

sulferus	sulphurous
sulfide	sulphide
sulfuric asid	sulphuric acid
sulie	sully ⁴
sulk ¹ /ily/iness/y	
sullen	
sully ⁴	
sulphate	
sulphide	
sulphur /ous	
sulphuric acid	
sultan /a (fem.) /ate	
sultrey	sultry +
sultr y /ily/iness	
suly	sully ⁴
sum ³★ (total)	
sum	some ★+
sumbody	somebody
sumhow	somehow
summari ly /ness	
summarise ²	
summar y /ies	
summer /time/y	
summerise	summarise ²
summit	
summon ¹★ (call forth)	
summons ¹★ (before court)	
sump	
sumpshus	sumptuous +
sumptuous /ly/ness	
sumshus	sumptuous +
sumun	summon ¹★
sumuns	summons ¹★
sumwere	somewhere
sumwun	someone +
sun ³★† /beam/dial/ny	
†(planet)	
sun	son ★
sun inlaw	son(s)-in-law
sunbathe ²	
sunbern	sunburn +
sunburn /t	
sundae ★ (ice cream)	
Sunday ★ (day of week)	
sundrey	sundry +

279

sundr *y* /ies		supervis *e* [2] /ion/or/ory	
sung		supervishun	supervision
sunk /en		supine	
sunlight		suplant	supplant [1+]
sunlite	sunlight	suple	supple [+]
sunni *er* /est/ly/ness		suplement	supplement [1+]
sun *rise* /stroke		suplicate	supplicate [2+]
sun-tan [3]		suport	support [1+]
sup [3] /per * (meal)		suposishun	supposition
super * (fantastic)		suposition	supposition
super	supper *	supositrey	suppository [+]
superabundan *ce* /t		supplant [1] /er	
superannuat *e* [2] /ion		supple /ness	
superb /ly		supplement [1] /ation	
supercargo /es		supplementary	
supercharge [2]		suppli	supply [4+]
supercilious /ly/ness		suppliant	
superconductor		supplicat *e* [2] /ion/ory	
superficial /ity/ly		suppl *y* [4] /ier/ies	
superfine		support [1] /er	
superfishal	superficial [+]	suppos *e* [2] /ition	
superflooous	superfluous [+]	suppositor *y* /ies	
superflu *ous* /ity		suppress [1] /ible/ion/or	
superhuman		suppurat *e* [2] /ion	
superier	superior [+]	supremasey	supremacy
superimpos *e* [2] /ition		suprem *e* /acy/ely	
superintend [1] /ent		supreshun	suppression
superior /ity		supress	suppress [1+]
superlative		supression	suppression
super *man* /men (pl.)		suprintend	superintend [1+]
supermarket		supul	supple [+]
supernacheral	supernatural [+]	sur	sir
supernatural /ly		surayalism	surrealism [+]
supernova		surayalist	surrealist
supernumerar *y* /ies		surca	circa
superpos *e* [2] /ition		surcharge [2]	
supersede [2]		surcit	circuit [1*]
supersilious	supercilious [+]	surcitrey	circuitry
supersilius	supercilious [+]	surcitus	circuitous
supersonic		surcul	circle [2]
superstishun	superstition [+]	surcularise	circularise [2+]
superstishus	superstitious	surculashun	circulation
superstitio *n* /us		surculate	circulate [2+]
superstructure		surculer	circular
superven *e* [2] /tion		surcumfleks	circumflex

surcumflex	circumflex	surogat	surrogate
surcumfrance	circumference	suround	surround [1]
surcumfrans	circumference	surownd	surround [1]
surcumnavigate	circumnavigate [2+]	surpass [1]	
surcumscribe	circumscribe [2]	surplice ★ (robe)	
surcumscripshun	circumscription	surplis	surplice ★
surcumscription	circumscription	surplus ★ (excess)	
surcumsise	circumcise [2+]	surprise [2]	
surcumsision	circumcision	surrealis *m* /t	
surcumspecshun	circumspection	surrender [1]	
surcumspect	circumspect +	surreptitious /ly/ness	
surcumstans	circumstance	surrogate	
surcumstanshul	circumstantial +	surround [1]	
surcumstantial	circumstantial +	surt	cert
surcumvent	circumvent [1+]	surtaks	surtax +
surcus	circus +	surtax /es	
sure ★† /ly ★†/r/st		surtin	certain +
†(certain[ly])		surtn	certain +
sure	shore [2★]	survant	servant
sureptishus	surreptitious +	survay	survey [1+]
sureptitious	surreptitious +	survaylans	surveillance
suret *y* /ies		surve	serve [2+]
surf [1★] (sea) /er		surveillance	
surf	serf ★+	survey [1] /or	
surface [2]		survice	service [2+]
surfdom	serfdom	surviet	serviette
surfeet	surfeit [1]	survile	servile +
surfeit [1]		survilitey	servility
surfis	surface [2]	survis	service [2+]
surfit	surfeit [1]	surviv *e* [2] /al/or	
surge [2]		susceptib *le* /ility	
surgeon		suseptible	susceptible +
surger *y* /ies		suseptibul	susceptible +
surgun	surgeon	suspect [1]	
surley	surely ★	suspend [1] /er	
surli *er* /est/ly/ness		suspense	
surloin	sirloin	suspenshun	suspension +
surly ★ (uncivil)		suspens *ion* /ory	
surly	surely ★	suspicion	
surmise [2]		suspicious /ly/ness	
surmon	sermon	suspishun	suspicion
surmonise	sermonise [2]	suspishus	suspicious +
surmount [1]		sustain [1]	
surmownt	surmount [1]	sustayn	sustain [1]
surname		sustenance	

281

sustenans	sustenance
sut	soot *+
sutable	suitable +
sutabul	suitable +
suter	suitor
suthen	southern
sutherley	southerly
sutle	subtle +
sutletey	subtlety +
sutul	subtle +
suture	
swab [3]	
swaddle [2]	
swade	suède
swadul	swaddle [2]
swagger [1] /er	
swain	
swallow [1] /er	
swam	
swamp [1] /y	
swan [3] /sdown	
swane	swain
swank [1] /y	
sware	swear +
swarm [1]	
swarthy	
swash [1]	
swastika	
swat [3] /ter	
swath * (line of cut grass)	
swathe [2]* (bandage)	
sway [1]	
swear /-word	
sweat [1] /er/y	
Swed e /ish	
sweep /er/ing/stake	
sweet * (sugary)	
sweet	suite *
sweetchestnut	
sweeten [1]	
sweet heart /ly/meat	
sweetpea	
swell /ing	
swelter [1]	
swept	

swerve [2]	
swet	sweat [1]+
sweter	sweater
swich	switch [1]+
swift /er/est/ly/ness	
swig [3]	
swill [1] /er	
swim /mer/-suit	
swimming /-pool	
swindle [2] /r	
swindul	swindle [2]+
swin e /ish	
swing * (move) /ing	
swinge * (beat) /ing	
swipe [2]	
swirl [1]	
swish [1]	
Swiss /roll	
switch [1] /back	
swivel [3]	
swizul	swizzle [2]
swizzle [2]	
swob	swab [3]
swollen	
swollow	swallow [1]+
swomp	swamp [1]+
swon	swan [3]+
swoon [1]	
swoop [1]	
swop [3]	
sword	
swor e /n	
swostika	swastika
swot [3] /ter	
swum	
swung	
swurl	swirl [1]
swurv	swerve [2]
sybarit e /ic	
sycamore	
sycedelic	psychedelic
syciatrey	psychiatry
syciatrist	psychiatrist +
sycick	psychic +
sycoanalise	psychoanalyse [2]+

sycoanalisis	psychoanalysis	synops *is* /es (pl.)	
sycofant	sycophant +	synoptic	
sycologey	psychology +	synovial	
sycological	psychological +	syntaks	syntax +
sycologist	psychologist	synta *x* /ctic	
sycopath	psychopath +	synthes *is* /es (pl.)	
sycophant /ic		synthe *sise* ² /tic/tically	
sycosis	psychosis +	sypher	cipher ¹
sycosomatic	psychosomatic	syphili *s* /tic	
sycotherapey	psychotherapy	syphon	siphon ¹⁺
sycotherapist	psychotherapist +	syringe ²	
sycotic	psychotic	syrup /y	
syfilis	syphilis +	system /atic/atically	
sygnet	cygnet ★	systematis *e* ² /ation	
sylf	sylph +	systole	
syllab *le* /ic			
syllabus /es			
syllogis *e* ² /m		**T**	
sylph /like			
symbio *sis* /tic		tab ³	
symbol ★ (sign) /ic		tabard	
symbol	cymbal ★⁺	tabb *y* /ies	
symbolical /ly		tabernacle	
symbolis *e* ² /m		tabernacul	tabernacle
symmetr *y* /ical/ically		tabie	tabby +
sympathetic /ally		table ²	
sympathey	sympathy +	tableau /x (pl.)	
sympathise ² /r		tablespoon /ful	
sympath *y* /ies		tabl *et* /oid	
symphon *y* /ies/ic		tablit	tablet +
symplify	simplify ⁴⁺	tablo	tableau +
symposi *um* /a (pl.)		tabloyd	tabloid
symptom /atic		taboo ¹ /s	
synagog	synagogue	tabor	
synagogue		tabul	table ²
synchronis *e* ² /ation/m		tabular	
syncopat *e* ² /ion		tabulashun	tabulation
syncope		tabulat *e* ² /ion/or	
syncromesh		tabuler	tabular
syndicalis *m* /t		tabulspoon	tablespoon +
syndicat *e* ² /ion		taby	tabby +
syndrome		tacit /ly	
synic	cynic +	taciturn /ity	
synod /al/ical		tack ¹	
synonym /ous/ously		tackey	tacky +

283

tackle² /r	
tackul	tackle²⁺
tack y /iness	
tact /less/lessly	
tactful /ly/ness	
tactic /al/ian/s	
tactile	
tactishun	tactician
tacul	tackle²⁺
tadpole	
taffeta	
tafita	taffeta
tag³	
tail¹*† /less	
†(follow, of animals)	
tail	tale*
tailor¹ /-made	
taint¹	
tak e /en/ing	
takey	tacky⁺
taks	tax¹⁺
taksashun	taxation
taksi	taxi⁺
taksidermey	taxidermy⁺
talc /um	
tale * (story)	
tale	tail¹*⁺
talent /ed	
talie	tally⁴⁺
talie ho	tally-ho
talisman /s	
talk¹ /ative/er	
talk	talc⁺
talkum	talcum
tall /est/ness	
tallow	
tall y⁴ /ies	
tally-ho	
talon	
talor	tailor¹⁺
talow	tallow
tamarisk	
tamber	tambour⁺
tamboreen	tambourine
tambour /ine	

tam e² /able	
tam-o'-shanter	
tamper¹	
tampon	
tan³ /ner/nery/neries	
tandem	
taner	tanner
tang	
tangent /ial	
tangerine	
tangib le /ility/ly	
tangibul	tangible⁺
tangle²	
tango¹ /s	
tangul	tangle²
tanic	tannic⁺
tanjent	tangent⁺
tanjerene	tangerine
tank /age/ard/er/ful	
tanni c /n	
tant	taint¹
tantalis e² /ingly	
tantalum	
tantamount	
tantamownt	tantamount
tantrum	
tap³ /-dancing/-root	
tape² /worm	
tape measure	
tape recorder	
taper¹* (candle, narrow)	
taper	tapir*
tapestr y /ies	
tapioca	
tapir * (animal)	
tapistrey	tapestry⁺
tar³	
taragon	tarragon
tarantella * (dance)	
tarantula * (spider)	
tardie	tardy⁺
tard y /ily/iness	
tare * (weed)	
tare	tear*⁺
target	

targit	target	tawny	
tarie	tarry [4]	tax [1] /able/ation	
tarif	tariff	taxashun	taxation
tariff		taxi /cab/meter/s	
tarmac		taxiderm y /ist	
tarmigan	ptarmigan	Te Deum	
tarn		tea ★ (drink) /cup/pot	
tarnish [1]		tea	tee ★+
tarpaulin		teach /able/er/ing	
tarporlin	tarpaulin	teajuncshun	T-junction
tarragon		teak	
tarr y [4]		teal	
tarsals		team [1] ★ (group) /ster	
tarsus		team	teem [1]★
tart /let		team-work	
tartan		tear ★ (crying) /ful	
tartar		tear ★ (rip) /ing	
tarter	tartar	tear	tier ★
tartrate		tease [2] /r	
tasit	tacit +	teaspoon /ful	
tasiturn	taciturn +	teat	
task /master		teath	teeth ★
tassel [3]		teathe	teethe [2]★
tassul	tassel [3]	teatime	
taste [2] /less/r		teatotler	teetotaller
tasteful /ly/ness		teatotul	teetotal +
tast ier /iest/y		tech	teach +
tatle	tattle [2]	techer	teacher
tatoo	tattoo [1]+	technical /ly	
tatter /ed		technicalit y /ies	
tattle [2]		techni cian /que	
tattoo [1] /er		technocrac y /ies	
tatul	tattle [2]	technocrat /ic	
taught ★ (did teach)		technolog y /ical/ically	
taught	tort ★	tecneek	technique
taunt [1] /er		tecnical	technical +
Taurus		tecnicalitey	technicality +
taut ★ (tight) /ly/ness		tecnician	technician +
taut	taught ★	tecnishun	technician +
taut	tort ★	tecnocracy	technocracy +
tauten [1]		tecnologey	technology +
tautolog y /ical		teddy-bear	
taven	tavern	tedibare	teddy-bear
tavern		tedi um /ous/ously	
tawdr y /ily/iness		tedius	tedious

285

tee * (golf) /d/ing	
tee	tea *+
teech	teach +
teek	teak
teel	teal
teem 1* (swarm)	
teem	team 1*+
teenage /r	
teese	tease 2+
teet	teat
teeter 1	
teeth * (pl. of tooth)	
teethe 2* (develop teeth)	
teetotal /ism/ler	
tegument	
tekneek	technique
teknical	technical +
teknicalitey	technicality +
teknician	technician +
teknishun	technician +
teknocracy	technocracy +
teknocrasey	technocracy +
teknologey	technology +
teknological	technological
tekscher	texture
tekst	text +
tekstile	textile
telecommunications	
telefone	telephone 2+
telefonist	telephonist
telegraf	telegraph 1+
telegram	
telegraph 1 /ic/ist/y	
teleks	telex 1
telemeter	
telepath y /ic	
telephon e 2 /ic/ist	
telephoto /graph	
teleprinter	
telescop e 2 /ic/y	
teletipe	teletype
teletype	
televise 2	
televishun	television
television	

telex 1	
telicomunications	telecommunications
telie	telly
telifone	telephone 2+
telifoto	telephoto +
teligraf	telegraph 1+
teligram	telegram
telimeter	telemeter
teliprinter	teleprinter
teliscope	telescope 2+
teliscopic	telescopic
telitipe	teletype
telivise	televise 2
telivishun	television
telivision	television
tell /er/ing/-tale	
tellurium	
telly	
telurium	tellurium
temerity	
temper 1	
temperacher	temperature
temperament /al	
temperance	
temperans	temperance
temperat e /ure	
temperit	temperate +
tempest /uous	
tempestuus	tempestuous
temple	
tempo /s	
temporal /ly	
temporar y /ily	
temporis e 2 /r	
temprament	temperament +
temprecher	temperature
tempremental	temperamental
tempt 1 /ation/er	
temptashun	temptation
tempul	temple
temtashun	temptation
ten /fold/th/thly	
tenab le /ility	
tenabul	tenable +
tenacious /ly	

tenacity		terbine	turbine	
tenanc*y* /ies		terbium		
tenansey	tenancy +	terbo	turbo +	
tenant /ry		terbot	turbot	
tenashus	tenacious +	terbulence	turbulence +	
tenasitey	tenacity	terbulens	turbulence +	
tend [1]		terbulent	turbulent	
tendenc*y* /ies		tergid	turgid +	
tendensey	tendency +	terible	terrible +	
tendenshus	tendentious	teribul	terrible +	
tendentious		terific	terrific +	
tender [1] /er/est/ly/ness		terify	terrify [4]	
tenderhooks	tenterhooks	teritorey	territory +	
tendon		teritorial	territorial +	
tendril		terjid	turgid +	
tenement /-house		terkey	turkey +	
tener	tenor ★	terkish	Turkish	
tenet		terkwoise	turquoise	
teniment	tenement +	term [1]		
tenis	tennis	termagant		
tennis		terminable		
tenon /-saw		terminabul	terminable	
tenor ★ (voice)		terminal /ly		
tenor	tenure ★	terminat *e* [2] /ion		
tense /ly/ness/r/st		terminological /ly		
tenshun	tension	terminolog*y* /ies		
tensile		termin *us* /i (pl.)		
tension		termite		
tent		termoil	turmoil	
tentacle		tern ★ (bird)		
tentacul	tentacle	tern	turn [1]★+	
tentative /ly		ternip	turnip	
tenterhooks		terodactil	pterodactyl	
tenuous /ly/ness		teror	terror +	
tenure ★ (possession)		terorism	terrorism	
tenuus	tenuous +	terorist	terrorist	
tenyer	tenure ★	terpentine	turpentine	
tepid /ity/ly		terpitude	turpitude	
teracota	terracotta	terra firma		
terafurma	terra firma	terrace [2]		
terain	terrain	terracotta		
terapin	terrapin	terrain		
terass	terrace [2]	terrapin		
terban	turban +	terrestrial		
terbid	turbid +	terribl *e* /y		

287

terribul	terrible +
terrier	
terrifi	terrify [4]
terrific /ally	
terrify [4]	
territorial /ly	
territor y /ies	
terror /ism/ist	
terroris e [2] /ation	
terse /ly/ness	
tershan	tertian +
tertia n /ry	
tertle	turtle
teselashun	tessellation
teselate	tessellate [2+]
teselation	tessellation
tespoon	teaspoon +
tessellat e [2] /ion	
test [1] /-tube	
testament	
testat e /or/rix (fem.)	
testes	testis +
testicle	
testicul	testicle
testie	testy +
testifi	testify [4+]
testif y [4] /ier	
testimon y /ial	
testimonyal	testimonial
test is /es (pl.)	
test y /ily/iness	
tetanic	titanic
tetanus	
tetatet	tête-à-tête
tête-à-tête	
tether [1]	
tetragon /al	
tetrahedr on /al	
tetrarch /y	
tetrark	tetrarch +
Teutonic	
texcher	texture
text /ual/ually	
textile	
texture	

thach	thatch [1+]
thalidomide	
thallium	
than	
thank [1] /less	
thankful /ly	
thanksgiving	
that /'s (that is)	
thatch [1] /er	
thaw [1]	
thay	they +
the	
theater	theatre
theatre	
theatrical /ly	
theft	
theif	thief +
their * (possession) /s *	
their	there *
theirs	there's *
theis m /t/tical	
theives	thieves
theivish	thievish
them /selves	
them e /atic	
thence /forth/forward	
thens	thence +
theocra cy /tic	
theocrasey	theocracy +
theodolite	
theolog y /ian/ical/ist	
theolojun	theologian
theorem	
theoretic /al/ally	
theorey	theory +
theorise [2]	
theor y /ies/ist	
theosofey	theosophy +
theosoph y /ical/ist	
therapeuti c /st	
therapey	therapy +
theraputic	therapeutic +
therap y /ist	
therd	third +
there * (that place)	

288

there	their *+	thiroyd	thyroid
there	they're *	thirst [1] /ily/y	
therefore		thirteen /th	
therem	theorem	thirtie	thirty +
there's * (there is)		thirt y /ies/ieth	
theres	theirs *	thisis	phthisis
theretic	theoretic +	thisle	thistle +
theretical	theoretical	thisorus	thesaurus +
therey	theory +	thistl e /y	
therise	theorise [2]	thisul	thistle +
therist	theorist	thither	
therm /al/ally		tho	though
thermion /ic		thole	
thermite		thong	
thermocouple		thor	thaw [1]
thermocuple	thermocouple	thoraks	thorax +
thermodynamic /s		thora x /cic	
thermo-electric /ity		thorium	
thermomet er /ric/ry		thorn /y	
thermonuclear		thorough /ly	
thermos		thorough bred /fare	
thermostat /ic/ically		thort	thought
thersday	Thursday	thortful	thoughtful +
therst	thirst [1]+	thortless	thoughtless +
therstey	thirsty	those	
therteen	thirteen +	though	
therty	thirty +	thought	
thesaur us /i (pl.)		thoughtful /ly/ness	
these		thoughtless /ly/ness	
thes is /es (pl.)		thousand /th	
they /'re * (they are)		thowsand	thousand +
thi	thigh	thrall	
thick /er/est/ly/ness/set		thrash [1]	
thicken [1] /er		thread [1] /bare	
thie f /ves (pl.)/vish		threat	
thigh		threaten [1]	
thimble /ful		thred	thread [1]+
thimbul	thimble +	thredbare	threadbare
thime	thyme	three /fold/pence	
thin [3] /ly/ner/nest		three-dimensional	
thine		three-quarters	
thing		thresh [1] /er	
think /er/ing		threshold	
third /ly		thret	threat
thirm	therm +	threten	threaten [1]

threw * (did throw)		thurm	therm +
threw	through *	thurmal	thermal
threwout	throughout	thurmion	thermion +
thrice		thurmite	thermite
thrift /less/y		thurmocuple	thermocouple
thrifti er /est/ly/ness		thurmodinamic	thermodynamic +
thrill ¹ /er		thurmoelectric	thermo-electric +
thrise	thrice	thurmometer	thermometer +
thriv e /en/ing		thurmonucliar	thermonuclear
throat /y		thurmos	thermos
throb ³		thurmostat	thermostat +
throe * (pain) /s *		thurmyon	thermion +
throe	throw *+	Thursday	
thrombosis		thurst	thirst ¹+
throne * (chair of state)		thurteen	thirteen +
throne	thrown *	thurty	thirty +
throng ¹		thus	
throo	threw *	thwack ¹	
throo	through *	thwart ¹	
thrŏt	throat +	thwort	thwart ¹
throttle ²		thyme	
throtul	throttle ²	thyroid	
through * (penetrated)		tialin	ptyalin
through	threw *	tiara /s	
throughout		tibia	
throve		tic * (twitch)	
throw *† /ing/n *†/s *†		tick ¹* (sound) /er	
†(hurl[ed, s])		ticket	
throw	throe *+	tickl e ² /er/ish	
thrum ³		tickul	tickle ²+
thrush /es		ticoon	tycoon
thrust /er/ing		tidal	
thud ³		tiddler	
thug /gery		tiddlywinks	
thulium		tide /less	
thum	thumb ¹	tidie	tidy ⁴+
thumb ¹		tidi ly /ness	
thump ¹		tidings	
thunder ¹ /bolt/ous		tidliwinks	tiddlywinks
thunderstorm		tidul	tidal
thunderstruck		tid y ⁴ /ier/iest/ily/iness	
thunderus	thunderous	tie /d	
thurer	thorough +	tier * (layer)	
thurerbred	thoroughbred +	tier	tire ²*+
thurerfare	thoroughfare	tier	tyre *

tiff [1]		tipist	typist	
tiffin		tipit	tippet	
tifin	tiffin	tiple	tipple [2+]	
tifoid	typhoid	tipografey	typography +	
tifoon	typhoon +	tippet		
tifus	typhus +	tipple [2] /r		
tig er /ress (fem.)		tipsey	tipsy +	
tight /-laced/rope		tips y /ily/iness		
tighten [1]		tiptoe [2]		
tight er /est/ly/ness		tipul	tipple [2+]	
tights		tirade		
tike	tyke	tiraney	tyranny +	
tile [2]		tiranical	tyrannical +	
tilige	tillage	tiranise	tyrannise [2+]	
till [1] /able/age/er		tirant	tyrant	
tilt [1]		tirannical	tyrannical	
timber [1]		tiranus	tyrannous	
time [2] /keeper/less		tire [2*†] /less/lessly		
timepeace	timepiece	†(grow weary)		
timepiece		tire	tyre ★	
timid /er/est/ity		tiresome /ly/ness		
timorous /ly/ness		tiresum	tiresome +	
timorus	timorous +	tiro		
timpan o /i (pl.)/ist		tishoo	tissue +	
timpanum	tympanum +	tishue	tissue +	
tin [3] /foil/ny		tissue /-paper		
tincture		Titan		
tinder /y		titanic		
tinge [2]		titanium		
tingle [2]		titbit		
tingul	tingle [2]	tite	tight +	
tinie	tiny +	titen	tighten [1]	
tinkcher	tincture	titer	tighter +	
tinker [1]		titerope	tightrope	
tinkle [2]		tites	tights	
tinkul	tinkle [2]	tithe /-barn		
tinsel [3] /ly		titillat e [2] /ion		
tinsul	tinsel [3+]	titivat e [2] /ion		
tint [1]		title /d		
tin y /ier/iest/ily/iness		titm ouse /ice (pl.)		
tip [3] /ster		titmowse	titmouse +	
tipe	type [2+]	titrat e [2] /ion		
tiperiter	typewriter +	titter [1]		
tipical	typical +	tittle-tattle		
tipify	typify [4]	titul	title +	

titul tatul	tittle-tattle	toll¹ /-bar/-gate	
titular		tolrable	tolerable +
tituler ⟨	titular	tolrabul	tolerable +
T-junction		tomahawk	
to * (towards) /day		tomahork	tomahawk
to	too *	tomane	ptomaine
to	two *+	tomato /es	
to and fro		tomb /stone	
toad /stool/y		tomboi	tomboy
toast¹ /er		tomboy	
tobacco /nist		tome	
tobaco	tobacco +	tomfoolery	
toboggan¹ /er		tomorrow	
tocsic	toxic +	tomtit	
tocsicologey	toxicology +	ton * (weight) /nage	
tocsin * (bell)		ton	tun *
tocsin	toxin *	tonal /ity	
toddle² /r		tone /less	
toddy		tongs	
tode	toad +	tongue² /-tied/-twister	
todle	toddle ²+	tonic	
todstool	toadstool	tonight	
todul	toddle ²+	tonite	tonight
tody	toddy	tonsher	tonsure +
toe * (on foot)		tonsil /litis	
toe	tow ¹*+	tons ure /orial	
tofee	toffee	too * (also)	
toffee		too	to *+
together		too	two *+
toggle		took	
togul	toggle	tool¹	
toi	toy ¹+	toom	tomb +
toil¹ /er		toomstone	tombstone
toilet /ry		toor	tour ¹+
token		toot¹	
toksic	toxic +	tooth /ache/less	
toksicologey	toxicology +	toothake	toothache
tole	toll ¹+	tootle²	
tolemaic sistem	Ptolemaic system	tootul	tootle ²
tolerabl e /y		top³ /-heavy/sail	
tolerabul	tolerable +	topas	topaz
toleran ce /t		topath	towpath
tolerans	tolerance +	topaz	
tolerashun	toleration	topic /al/ally	
tolerat e² /ion		tople	topple ²

topografer	topographer	tortuus	tortuous +
topografey	topography +	torus	Taurus
topografic	topographic	Tor y /ies	
topograph y /er/ic/ical		toss ¹ /-up	
topple ²		tost	toast ¹+
topsy-turvy		total ³ /ity/ly	
topul	topple ²	totalis e ² /ator	
torch /light		totalitey	totality
torcher	torture ²+	totem pole	
torchlite	torchlight	totter ¹	
tordrey	tawdry +	totul	total ³+
toreador		touch ¹ /ier/iness/y	
torenshal	torrential	touchstone	
torent	torrent +	touchwood	
torential	torrential	tough /er/est/ly/ness	
torero		toughen ¹	
torey	Tory +	tour ¹ /ism/ist	
torid	torrid	tournament	
torie	Tory +	tourniket	tourniquet
torism	tourism	tourniquet	
torist	tourist	tousle ²	
torment ¹ /or		tout ¹	
tornado /es		tow ¹★ (pull) /age	
tornament	tournament	tow	toe ★
torney	tawny	toward /s	
tornt	taunt ¹+	towel ³	
torpedo ¹ /-boat/es		tower ¹	
torper	torpor	town /hall	
torpid /ity		towpath	
torpor		towsl	tousle ²
torrenshal	torrential	towt	tout ¹
torrent /ial		toxic /ity	
torrid		toxicolog y /ist	
torshun	torsion +	toxin ★ (poison)	
torsion /al		toxin	tocsin ★
torso /s		toy ¹ /s/shop	
tort ★ (law)		toylet	toilet +
tort	taught ★	toyul	toil ¹+
tort	taut ★+	trace ² /able/r/ry	
torten	tauten ¹	trache a /otomy	
tortoise /-shell		tracing-paper	
tortologey	tautology +	track ¹ /er	
tortuous /ly/ness		tracshun	traction
torture ² /r		tract	
tortus	tortoise +	tract able /ion/or	

293

tracter	tractor	transendental	transcendental
trade² /r/sman		transept	
tradishun	tradition⁺	transfer³ /able/ence	
tradishunal	traditional	transferens	transference
tradition /al/ally		transfiger	transfigure²⁺
traduce²		transfigur e² /ation	
traduse	traduce²	transfiks	transfix¹
traffic /ked/king		transfix¹	
trafic	traffic⁺	transform¹ /ation/er	
traged y /ies		transformashun	transformation
tragic /al/ally		transfus e² /ion	
trail¹ /er		transfushun	transfusion
train¹ /ee/er		transgreshun	transgression
traipse²		transgress¹ /ion/or	
trait		tranship³ /ment	
traitor /ous		transien ce /t/tly	
trajector y /ies		transiens	transience⁺
trajectrey	trajectory⁺	transishun	transition⁺
trajedey	tragedy⁺	transister	transistor
trakia	trachea⁺	transistor	
trakiotomey	tracheotomy	transistoris e²	
trakshun	traction	transit /ive/ory	
tram /car/-line		transition /al	
trammel³		translashun	translation
tramp¹		translat e² /able/ion/or	
trample²		translater	translator
trampoline		translucen ce /t	
trampul	trample²	translusens	translucence⁺
tramul	trammel³	translusent	translucent
trance		transmigrat e² /ion	
trane	train¹⁺	transmishun	transmission
trankwil	tranquil⁺	transmission	
trankwilise	tranquillise²⁺	transmit³ /ter	
trankwilitey	tranquillity	transmut e /ation	
tranquil /lity/ly		transparen ce /cy/t	
tranquillis e² /er		transparens	transparence⁺
trans	trance	transparensey	transparency
transact¹ /ion		transpir e² /ation	
transatlantic		transplant¹ /ation	
transceiver		transport¹ /ation/er	
transcend¹ /ence/ental		transportashun	transportation
transcribe²		transpos e² /ition	
transcript /ion		transsever	transceiver
transend	transcend¹⁺	transverse /ly	
transendence	transcendence	transvershun	transversion

transversion	
transvesti *sm* /te	
trap ³ /per	
trapez *e* /ium/oid	
trapse	traipse ²
trase	trace ²⁺
trash /y	
trasing paper	tracing-paper
trate	trait
trater	traitor ⁺
traterous	traitorous
traterus	traitorous
trauma /tic	
travail ¹	
travale	travail ¹
travel ³ /ler/ogue	
travelog	travelogue
traverse ²	
travest *y* /ies	
trawl ¹ /er	
trawma	trauma ⁺
tray /s	
treacherey	treachery ⁺
treacher *y* /ous	
treacl *e* /y	
treacul	treacle ⁺
tread /ing/le	
treason /able/ous	
treasonus	treasonous
treasure ² /r	
treasur *y* /ies	
treat ¹ /able/ment	
treatise	
treatiss	treatise
treat *y* /ies	
trebl *e* ² /y	
trebul	treble ⁺
trecherey	treachery ⁺
trecherus	treacherous
tred	tread ⁺
tree	
treecul	treacle ⁺
treet	treat ¹⁺
treetie	treaty ⁺
treetis	treatise

treetment	treatment
trefoil	
trefoyul	trefoil
trek ³ /ker	
trellis-work	
tremble ²	
trembul	tremble ²
tremendous /ly	
tremendus	tremendous ⁺
tremer	tremor
tremor	
tremulous	
tremulus	tremulous
trench ¹ /es	
trenchan *cy* /t	
trenchansey	trenchancy ⁺
trend ¹ /y	
treo	trio ⁺
trepidashun	trepidation
trepidation	
treshur	treasure ²⁺
treshurey	treasury ⁺
treson	treason ⁺
trespass ¹ /er/es	
tressul	trestle
trestle	
tri	try ⁴⁺
trial	
triang *le* /ular	
triangul	triangle ⁺
triangulat *e* ² /ion	
trianguler	triangular
trib *e* /al/alism	
tribul	tribal
tribulashun	tribulation
tribulation	
tribun *e* /al	
tributar *y* /ies	
tribute	
tributrey	tributary ⁺
trice	
triceps	
tricicul	tricycle
trick ¹ /ery/ster/y	
tricki *er* /est/ly/ness	

295

trickle[2]	
tricuspid	
tricycle	
trident	
trifle[2] /r	
triful	trifle[2]+
trigger[1]	
trigonometr*y* /ic	
trill[1]	
trilogy	
trim[3] /mer	
trimaran	
trinity	
trinket	
trio /s	
triode	
trip[3]* (fall)	
tripartite	
tripe * (food)	
triple[2] /t	
triplicat*e*[2] /ion	
tripod	
tripos	
triptick	triptych
triptych	
tripul	triple[2]+
trise	trice
trisicul	tricycle
trite /ly	
triumf	triumph[1]+
triumph[1] /al/ant	
trivia /l/ly	
trivialise[2]	
trivialit*y* /ies	
trod /den	
trofey	trophy+
troley	trolley+
trolie	trolley+
troll[1]	
trolley /s	
trollop	
trolop	trollop
trombon*e* /ist	
troo	true+
trooancy	truancy+

trooant	truant
troobadoor	troubadour
trooism	truism
trooley	truly
troop[1]* (military)	
troop	troupe *
troos	truce
trooth	truth
troothful	truthful+
troph*y* /ies	
tropic /al/ally	
tropism	
troposfere	troposphere
troposphere	
trorma	trauma+
trormatic	traumatic
trot[3] /ter	
troubadour	
trouble[2] /-maker	
troubleshooter	
troublesome	
trough	
trounce[2]	
trouns	trounce[2]
troup	troop[1]*
troupe * (actors)	
trousers	
trousseau /x (pl.)	
trout	
trowel	
trownce	trounce[2]
trowns	trounce[2]
trowsers	trousers
trowt	trout
truan*cy* /t	
truansey	truancy+
truble	trouble[2]+
trubul	trouble[2]+
truce	
truck	
truculen*ce* /t	
trudge[2]	
tru*e* /er/est/ism/ly/th	
truf	trough
truffle	

truful	truffle	tumultuus	tumultuous
truge	trudge [2]	tumulus	
trulie	truly	tun * (large cask)	
trump [1]		tun	ton *+
trumpet [1] /er		tuna	
truncat e [2] /ion		tundra	
truncheon		tun e [2] /able/er	
trunchon	truncheon	tuneful /ly/ness	
trundle [2]		tuney	tunny +
trundul	trundle [2]	tung	tongue [2]+
trunk /-line		tungsten	
trusow	trousseau +	tungtied	tongue-tied
truss [1] /es		tunic	
trust [1] /ee/ful/fully		tunie	tunny +
trustwerthey	trustworthy +	tunige	tonnage
trustworth y /iness		tunnel [3] /ler	
truthful /ly/ness		tunn y /ies	
tr y [4] /ier/ies		tunul	tunnel [3]+
trycicle	tricycle	turban /ed	
tsar		turbid /ity	
tub [3] /biness/by		turbine	
tuba /s		turbo /-alternator	
tub e [2] /ular		turbo-generator	
tuber /cle/cular		turbo-jet	
tubercul osis /ous		turbo-prop	
tuch	touch [1]+	turbot	
tuchstone	touchstone	turbulen ce /t	
tuchwood	touchwood	turbulens	turbulence +
tuchy	touchy	tureen	
tuck [1] /er		turet	turret +
Tuesday		turf [1] /s/ves (pls.)	
tuf	tough +	turgid /ity	
tuffen	toughen [1]	turjid	turgid +
tuft [1]		turkey /s	
tug [3] /-of-war		Turkish	
tuishun	tuition	turkwoise	turquoise
tuition		turm	term [1]
tuk	tuck [1]+	turminable	terminable
tuksedo	tuxedo	turminabul	terminable
tulip		turminal	terminal +
tumble [2] /r		turminate	terminate [2]+
tumbul	tumble [2]+	turmination	termination
tumer	tumour	turminologey	terminology +
tumour		turminological	terminological +
tumult /uous		turminus	terminus +

turmite	termite	twilight	
turmoil		twilite	twilight
turn [1]* (rotate) /er		twill [1]	
turn	tern *	twin [3]	
turn *coat* /key/pike		twine [2]	
turnikay	tourniquet	twinge [2]	
turniket	tourniquet	twinkle [2]	
turnip		twinkul	twinkle [2]
turn *stile* /table		twirl [1]	
turpentine		twise	twice
turpitude		twist [1] /er	
turquoise		twit [3]	
turret /ed		twitch [1] /es	
turse	terse [+]	twitter [1]	
turshan	tertian [+]	two * (number) /-way	
tursharey	tertiary	two	to *[+]
turtian	tertian [+]	two	too *
turtle		twodle	twaddle [2]
turtul	turtle	two *fold* /pence	
tusday	Tuesday	twurl	twirl [1]
tusk [1] /er		tyalin	ptyalin
tussle [2]		tycoon	
tusul	tussle [2]	tyfoid	typhoid
tutel *age* /ary		tyfoon	typhoon [+]
tutelige	tutelage [+]	tyfus	typhus [+]
tuter	tutor [1+]	tyke	
tutonic	Teutonic	tympano	timpano [+]
tutor [1] /ial		tympan *um* /a (pl.)	
tuxedo		type [2] /script	
twaddle [2]		typeriter	typewriter [+]
twain		typewrit *er* /ing/ten	
twang [1]		typho *on* /nic	
twayn	twain	typh *us* /oid	
tweak [1]		typical /ly	
tweed		typifi	typify [4]
tweek	tweak [1]	typify [4]	
tweezers		typist	
twel *fth* /ve		typografey	typography [+]
twelth	twelfth [+]	typograph *y* /er/ic	
twent *y* /ies/ieth		tyranical	tyrannical [+]
twice		tyrannical /ly	
twich	twitch [1+]	tyrann *ise* [2] /ous	
twiddle [2]		tyran *ny* /t	
twidul	twiddle [2]	tyre * (of a car)	
twig [1]		tyre	tire [2]*[+]

U

u	ewe *
U-boat	
ubikwitey	ubiquity +
ubikwitus	ubiquitous
ubiquit *y* /ous	
ucalyptus	eucalyptus +
Ucarist	Eucharist
uclid	Euclid
udder	
ufemism	euphemism
ufemistic	euphemistic +
ufoney	euphony +
uforia	euphoria +
uforic	euphoric
ug	ugh
ugenic	eugenic +
ugh	
uglie	ugly +
ugl *y* /ier/iest/iness	
ukaliptus	eucalyptus +
ukarist	Eucharist
ukelalee	ukulele
uksorius	uxorious
ukulele	
ulcer /ous	
ulcerat *e* ² /ion	
ulna	
ulogey	eulogy
ulogise	eulogise ²+
ulogism	eulogism
ulser	ulcer +
ulserate	ulcerate ²+
ulserous	ulcerous
ulserus	ulcerous
ulterier	ulterior
ulterior	
ultimate /ly	
ultimatum /s (pl.)	
ultramarine	
ultramicroscopic	
ultrasonic	
ultra-violet	
umbilical	

umbrage	
umbrella	
umbridge	umbrage
umpire ²* (referee)	
umpire	empire *
umpteen	
unable	
unabridged	
unabriged	unabridged
unabul	unable
unacceptable	
unaccompanied	
unaccompnid	unaccompanied
unaccountable	
unaccustomed	
unacowntable	unaccountable
unacquainted	
unacseptable	unacceptable
unacseptabul	unacceptable
unacumpanid	unaccompanied
unacustomd	unaccustomed
unaded	unaided
unadulterated	
unaffected	
unafrade	unafraid
unafraid	
unaided	
unalloyed	
unaloid	unalloyed
unanimity	
unanimous /ly	
unanimus	unanimous +
unanserable	unanswerable +
unanswer *able* /ed	
unapproachable	
unaprochable	unapproachable
unaprochabul	unapproachable
unarmed	
unashamed	
unasked	
unaskt	unasked
unassisted	
unassuming	
unatacht	unattached
unatainable	unattainable

unattached		uncann *y* /ily/iness	
unattainable		uncared-for	
unattended		unceremonious /ly	
unauthorised		unceremonius	unceremonious [+]
unavail *able* /ing		uncertain /ty/ties	
unavalabul	unavailable [+]	unchangable	unchangeable
unavaling	unavailing	unchangeable	
unavoidabl *e* /y		uncharitable	
unavoydable	unavoidable [+]	uncharitabul	uncharitable
unaware /s		uncharted	
unawthorised	unauthorised	unchristian	
unbalanced		uncivil /ised	
unbalanst	unbalanced	unclaimed	
unbarable	unbearable [+]	unclamed	unclaimed
unbarabul	unbearable [+]	uncle	
unbearabl *e* /y		unclean	
unbeat *able* /en		uncomfortabl *e* /y	
unbecoming		uncomfortabul	uncomfortable [+]
unbeknown		uncomftable	uncomfortable [+]
unbeleif	unbelief	uncomited	uncommitted
unbelevable	unbelievable [+]	uncommitted	
unbelevabul	unbelievable [+]	uncommon	
unbelief		uncommunicative	
unbeliev *able* /ing		uncompromising	
unbelievabul	unbelievable [+]	unconcern /ed	
unbend /ing		uncondishnal	unconditional [+]
unbenown	unbeknown	unconditional /ly	
unberden	unburden [1]	unconected	unconnected
unbeten	unbeaten	unconfirmed	
unbiased		unconfurmd	unconfirmed
unbiast	unbiased	uncongenial	
unbidden		unconnected	
unblemished		unconquerable	
unblemisht	unblemished	unconscionable	
unborn		unconscious /ly/ness	
unbounded		unconshonable	unconscionable
unbowed		unconshonabul	unconscionable
unbownded	unbounded	unconshus	unconscious [+]
unbridled		unconstitutional	
unbriduld	unbridled	uncontrolabul	uncontrollable
unbroken		uncontrollable	
unburden [1]		unconvenshunal	unconventional
unbutton [1]		unconventional	
uncalled-for		unco-operative	
uncanie	uncanny [+]	unco-ordinated	

uncooth	uncouth	underling	
uncorroborated		undermand	undermanned
uncouple ²		undermanned	
uncoupul	uncouple ²	undermine ²	
uncouth		underneath	
uncover ¹		undernourish ¹ /ment	
uncristian	unchristian	undernurish	undernourish ¹⁺
uncritical		underpass	
uncshun	unction ⁺	underprivileged	
unct *ion* /uous		underrate ²	
uncul	uncle	underrite	underwrite ⁺
uncultivated		underrote	underwrote
uncumftable	uncomfortable ⁺	undersell /ing	
uncuple	uncouple ²	undersigned	
uncuver	uncover ¹	undersined	undersigned
undated		undersised	undersized
undaunted		undersized	
undawnted	undaunted	understand /able	
undeceive ²		understatement	
undecided		understood	
undecieve	undeceive ²	understud *y* ⁴ /ies	
undefended		undertak *e* /er/ing	
undeniable		underto	undertow
undeniabul	undeniable	undertone	
under /arm/bid		undertook	
undercarige	undercarriage	undertow	
undercarriage		underwait	underweight
undercloth *es* /ing		underware	underwear
undercover		underwater	
undercurrent		underwear	
undercut /ting		underweight	
undercuver	undercover	underwerld	underworld
underdog		underworld	
underdone		underwrit *e* /ing/ten	
underdun	underdone	underwrote	
underfed		undeservd	undeserved
undergo /ing/ne		undeserved	
undergraduate		undeseve	undeceive ²
undergroth	undergrowth	undesirable	
underground		undesirabul	undesirable
undergrownd	underground	undeterd	undeterred
undergrowth		undetermind	undetermined
underhand		undetermined	
underl *ie* /ying		undeterred	
underline ²		undieing	undying

undifended	undefended	unfaned	unfeigned
undignifide	undignified	unfare	unfair +
undignified		unfasen	unfasten [1]
undisciplined		unfashionable	
undisided	undecided	unfashnable	unfashionable
undisiplind	undisciplined	unfasten [1]	
undo /ing/ne		unfathful	unfaithful +
undornted	undaunted	unfavourabl e /y	
undoubted /ly		unfavrable	unfavourable +
undowted	undoubted +	unfeigned	
undress [1]		unfit [3] /ness	
undu e /ly		unfold [1]	
undulat e [2] /ion/ory		unforeseen	
undying		unforgetabul	unforgettable
unearned		unforgettable	
unearth [1] /ly		unfortunate /ly	
uneas y /ily		unfounded	
uneatable		unfownded	unfounded
uneatabul	uneatable	unfriendl y /iness	
unecessary	unnecessary +	unfurl [1]	
uneconomic /al/ally		unfurnished	
uneducated		unfurnisht	unfurnished
uneek	unique +	ungainly	
unekspected	unexpected	unganley	ungainly
unekwal	unequal +	ungarded	unguarded
unemploiabul	unemployable +	ungodly	
unemploy able /ed/ment		ungovernable	
unenterprising		ungracious /ly	
unequal /led/ly		ungrammatical /ly	
unequivocal		ungrashus	ungracious +
unering	unerring	ungrateful	
unerned	unearned	ungreatful	ungrateful
unerring		unguarded	
unerth	unearth [1+]	unguent	
unesessary	unnecessary +	unguvernabul	ungovernable
unesey	uneasy +	unguvnable	ungovernable
unetable	uneatable	unguvnabul	ungovernable
uneven /ness		unhallowed	
uneventful		unhalowd	unhallowed
unexpected		unhapie	unhappy +
unfailing /ly		unhappi ly /ness	
unfaind	unfeigned	unhapp y /ier/iest	
unfair /ly/ness		unhealthy	
unfaithful /ly/ness		unheard-of	
unfaling	unfailing +	unhelthy	unhealthy

unherdov	unheard-of	unkshus	unctuous
unhinge [2]		unkwalified	unqualified
unholesum	unwholesome	unkweschunable	unquestionable [+]
unholy		unlawful /ly	
unhurdov	unheard-of	unleash [1]	
unicellular		unleavened	
unicicle	unicycle	unlesh	unleash [1]
unicorn		unless	
unicycle		unlevend	unleavened
unidentified		unlicensed	
unifi	unify [4+]	unlike /ly	
uniform /ity		unlimited	
unif y [4] /ication		unlisensd	unlicensed
unikwivocal	unequivocal	unload [1]	
unilateral /ly		unlock [1]	
unimpeachable		unlode	unload [1]
uninhabit able /ed		unluck y /ier/iest/ily	
uninteligibul	unintelligible [+]	unlukey	unlucky [+]
unintelligib le /ility		unmanageable	
union /ism/ist		unmanigable	unmanageable
unique /ly/ness		unmannerly	
uniquivocal	unequivocal	unmarid	unmarried
uniselular	unicellular	unmarried	
unisicul	unicycle	unmask [1]	
unison		unmenshunable	unmentionable
unit /ary		unmentionable	
unitarian /ism		unmistakabl e /y	
unite [2]		unmistakabul	unmistakable [+]
unit y /ies		unmitigated	
uniun	onion	unmoovd	unmoved
universal /ity/ly		unmoved	
universe		unnacheral	unnatural [+]
universit y /ies		unnamd	unnamed
univursal	universal [+]	unnamed	
univurse	universe	unnatural /ly	
univursitey	university [+]	unnecessar y /ily	
unjust		unnerv ed /ing	
unjustifi able /ed		unnesessarey	unnecessary [+]
unjustifiabul	unjustifiable [+]	unnowing	unknowing [+]
unkempt		unnown	unknown
unkemt	unkempt	unnumberd	unnumbered
unkind /ness		unnumbered	
unknow ing /n		unnurvd	unnerved [+]
unkristian	unchristian	unobserv ant /ed	
unkshun	unction [+]	unobtrusive	

unoccupied	
unocupied	unoccupied
unoffending	
unofficial /ly	
unoficial	unofficial [+]
unofishul	unofficial [+]
unopend	unopened
unopened	
unorthorised	unauthorised
unpack [1]	
unpaid	
unparaleld	unparalleled
unparalleled	
unparlamentrey	unparliamentary
unparliamentary	
unpayd	unpaid
unpick [1]	
unpleasant /ness	
unplesant	unpleasant [+]
unpopular /ity	
unpopuler	unpopular [+]
unpractical	
unprecedented	
unprejudiced	
unprejudist	unprejudiced
unpremeditated	
unprepard	unprepared
unprepared	
unprepossessing	
unpresedented	unprecedented
unpretenshus	unpretentious
unpretentious	
unprincipled	
unprinsipld	unprincipled
unprintable	
unprintabul	unprintable
unprofeshnal	unprofessional [+]
unprofessional /ly	
unqualified	
unquestionabl e /y	
unquestionabul	unquestionable [+]
unrap	unwrap [3]
unravel [3]	
unreadable	
unreadabul	unreadable

unread y /iness	
unreal /istic	
unreasnable	unreasonable [+]
unreasonabl e /y	
unrecognis able /ed	
unrecognisabul	unrecognisable [+]
unredabul	unreadable
unredey	unready [+]
unreel	unreal [+]
unrekwited	unrequited
unreleved	unrelieved
unreliab le /ility	
unreliabul	unreliable [+]
unrelieved	
unremitting	
unrequited	
unreservedly	
unresnable	unreasonable [+]
unresponsive	
unrest	
unrestraind	unrestrained
unrestrained	
unrighteous	
unrimitting	unremitting
unripe	
unritchus	unrighteous
unritten	unwritten
unrivald	unrivalled
unrivalled	
unroll [1]	
unruffled	
unrufld	unruffled
unrufuld	unruffled
unruly	
unsafe	
unsaid	
unsatisfactor y /ily	
unsatisfactrey	unsatisfactory [+]
unsatisfied	
unsavorey	unsavoury [+]
unsavour y /iness	
unscathed	
unscientific	
unscrupulous /ly	
unscrupulus	unscrupulous [+]

unseasnabul	unseasonable	unsucsesful	unsuccessful [+]
unseasonable		unsuitable	
unseat [1]		unsuitabul	unsuitable
unsed	unsaid	unsupported	
unseeing		unsurmountable	
unseeml *y* /iness		unsurmowntable	unsurmountable
unseen		unsurtan	uncertain [+]
unseet	unseat [1]	unsuspected	
unselfish /ly/ness		unsutable	unsuitable
unseremonius	unceremonious [+]	unsutabul	unsuitable
unsermowntable	unsurmountable	untactful /ly	
unsertan	uncertain [+]	untenable	
unsettle [2]		untenabul	untenable
unsetul	unsettle [2]	unthinkable	
unsientific	unscientific	unthinkabul	unthinkable
unsightl *y* /iness		unti	untie [+]
unsitely	unsightly [+]	untide	untied
unsivil	uncivil [+]	untid *y* /ier/iest/ily/iness	
unsivilised	uncivilised	unt *ie* /ied/ying	
unskathd	unscathed	untieing	untying
unskild	unskilled	until	
unskilful		untimely	
unskilled		untimley	untimely
unsociabl *e* /y		unto	
unsofisticated	unsophisticated	untold	
unsolicited		untouchable	
unsolisited	unsolicited	untouchabul	untouchable
unsootable	unsuitable	untoward	
unsootabul	unsuitable	untraceable	
unsophisticated		untrasable	untraceable
unsoshable	unsociable [+]	untrasabul	untraceable
unsoshabul	unsociable [+]	untroo	untrue
unsound		untrooth	untruth
unsownd	unsound	untroothful	untruthful [+]
unspeakabl *e* /y		untrue	
unspekabul	unspeakable [+]	untruth	
unspoiled		untruthful /ly/ness	
unspoyld	unspoiled	untuchable	untouchable
unstable		untuchabul	untouchable
unstabul	unstable	untuterd	untutored
unstead *y* /ily/iness		untutored	
unstedey	unsteady [+]	unuch	eunuch
unsubstanshiated	unsubstantiated	unuk	eunuch
unsubstantiated		unushual	unusual [+]
unsuccessful /ly		unusual /ly	

unvail	unveil [1]	upon	
unvareying	unvarying	upper /most	
unvarnished		uppish /ness	
unvarnisht	unvarnished	upright	
unvarying		upris e /ing	
unveil [1]		uprite	upright
unwanted		uproar /ious/iously	
unwarey	unwary +	uprore	uproar +
unwarrant able /ed		uprorius	uproarious
unwarrantabul	unwarrantable +	upset /ting	
unwar y /ily		upshot	
unweldey	unwieldy	upside-down	
unwell		upstairs	
unwerkable	unworkable	upstares	upstairs
unwerkabul	unworkable	upstart	
unwerthey	unworthy +	upstream	
unwholesome		upstreem	upstream
unwieldy		upward	
unwilling		upwerd	upward
unwind /ing		ur	err [1]
unwise /ly		uranium	
unwitting /ly		Uranus	
unworantable	unwarrantable +	Urazian	Eurasian
unworantabul	unwarrantable +	urban	
unworkable		urban e /ely/ity	
unworkabul	unworkable	urbanis e [2] /ation	
unworldl y /iness		urbun	urban
unworth y /iness		urchin	
unwound		urea	
unwownd	unwound	ureter	
unwrap [3]		urethra	
unwritten		urge [2] /ncy/nt	
unyun	onion	urinate [2]	
upbrade	upbraid [1]	urin e /al/ary	
upbraid [1]		urithmics	eurhythmics
upbringing		urjensey	urgency
update [2]		urjent	urgent
upheaval		url	earl +
upheld		urley	early +
upheval	upheaval	urlier	earlier +
uphill		urmin	ermine
uphold /ing		urn * (vase)	
upholster [1] /er/y		urn	earn [1]*+
uphoney	euphony +	urnest	earnest +
upkeep		urolog y /ist	

Uropian	European	vacseen	vaccine
urstwile	erstwhile	vacsinashun	vaccination
urth	earth [1+]	vacsination	vaccination
urthen	earthen [+]	vacsine	vaccine
urthkwake	earthquake	vacu *ous* /ity	
urthquake	earthquake	vacuum	
us *e* [2] /able/age/er		vacuus	vacuous [+]
useful /ly/ness		vagabond /age	
useless		vagar *y* /ies	
userp	usurp [1+]	vage	vague [+]
usher [1] /ette (fem.)		vagina	
usheret	usherette	vagran *cy* /t	
usless	useless	vagransey	vagrancy [+]
usorius	usurious	vague /ly/r/st	
usual /ly		vail	vale ★
usurp [1] /ation/er		vail	veil [1]★
usur *y* /ious		vain ★(proud)/er/est/ly	
utensil		vain	vane ★
uter	utter [1+]	vain	vein [1]★
uter *us* /ine		vainglor *ious* /y	
uthanasia	euthanasia	vainglorius	vainglorious [+]
uther	other [+]	vajina	vagina
utherwise	otherwise	valance	
utilis *e* [2] /able/ation		valans	valance
utilitarian /ism		valay	valet [3]
utilit *y* /ies		vale ★ (valley)	
utmost		vale	veil [1]★
Utopia /n		valedicshun	valediction [+]
utríc *le* /ular/ulus		valedict *ion* /ory	
utter [1] /ance/ly		valentine	
uvula /r		valer	valour [+]
uxorious		valerus	valorous
uxorius	uxorious	valese	valise
		valet [3]	
		valiant	
V		valid /ity	
		validashun	validation
		validat *e* [2] /ion	
vacanc *y* /ies		valise	
vacansey	vacancy [+]	valley /s	
vacant /ly		valor	valour [+]
vacashun	vacation	valo *ur* /rous	
vacat *e* [2] /ion		valt	vault [1]
vaccinat *e* [2] /ion/or		valuashun	valuation
vaccine		valu *e* [2] /able/ation/er	
vacillat *e* [2] /ion			

valueless	
valv *e* /ular	
valy	valley +
valyu	value ²⁺
valyuble	valuable
valyubul	valuable
valyuer	valuer
valyuless	valueless
vamp ¹	
vampire	
Van de Graaff generator	
vanadium	
vandal /ism	
vane ★ (weather)	
vane	vain ★⁺
vane	vein ¹★
vangard	vanguard
vanglorey	vainglory
vanglorious	vainglorious +
vanglorius	vainglorious +
vanguard	
vanilla	
vanish ¹	
vanity /-bag	
vankwish	vanquish ¹
vanquish ¹	
vantage	
vantidge	vantage
vantige	vantage
vaper	vapour +
vapid	
vaporis *e* ² /ation/er	
vaporus	vaporous
vapo *ur* /rous	
varia *ble* /bility/tion	
variabul	variable +
varian *ce* /t	
varians	variance +
variashun	variation
varicose	
varie	vary ⁴⁺
variegated	
variet *y* /ies	
varikose	varicose
varius	various

varnish ¹ /er	
var *y* ⁴ /iation/ious	
vascular	
vase	
Vaseline	
vasillate	vacillate ²⁺
vasleen	Vaseline
vast /er/est/ly/ness	
Vatican	
vault ¹	
vaunt ¹	
veal	
vech	vetch +
vector	
veel	veal
veemence	vehemence +
veemens	vehemence +
veement	vehement
veer ¹	
vegetable	
vegetarian /ism	
vegetashun	vegetation
vegetat *e* ² /ion/ive	
vegtable	vegetable
vegtabul	vegetable
vehemen *ce* /t	
vehic *le* /ular	
veiculer	vehicular
veil ¹★ (disguise)	
veil	vale★
vein ¹★ (blood)	
vein	vain ★⁺
vein	vane ★
veks	vex ¹⁺
veksashun	vexation
veksashus	vexatious
veksation	vexation
veksatious	vexatious
vekter	vector
veld	
vellum	
velocit *y* /ies	
veloors	velours
velositey	velocity +
velours	

velt	veld	verbiage	
velum	vellum	verbos *e* /ity	
velvet /een		verdant	
vena cava		verdict	
venal /ity/ly		verdur *e* /ous	
vencher	venture ²⁺	verge ²	
vend ¹ /or		verger	
vendetta		verie	very
veneer ¹		verifi	verify ⁴⁺
venerab *le* /ility		verif *y* ⁴ /iable/ication	
venerabul	venerable ⁺	verily	
venerashun	veneration	verisimilitude	
venerat *e* ² /ion		verit *y* /ies/able/ably	
venereal		vermicelli	
venerial	venereal	vermilion	
veneshun	Venetian	vermin /ous	
Venetian		vermouth	
venge *ance* /ful		vernacular	
vengence	vengeance ⁺	vernal	
vengens	vengeance ⁺	versatil *e* /ity	
venial		verse /s ★ (poetry)	
venison		verses	versus ★
venom /ous		versif *y* ⁴ /ication	
venomus	venomous	version	
venous ★ (of veins)		versus ★ (against)	
venous	Venus ★	vertebra /e (pl.)/l/te	
vent ¹		verteks	vertex ⁺
ventilashun	ventilation	vert *ex* /ices (pl.)	
ventilat *e* ² /ion/or		vertical /ly	
ventral /ly		vertig *o* /inous	
ventrical	ventricle	verve	
ventricle		very	
ventrilokwism	ventriloquism ⁺	vesa	visa
ventriloquis *m* /t		vescher	vesture ²
venture ² /some		vespers	
venturous		vessel	
venturus	venturous	vest ¹ /ment	
Venus ★ (planet)		vestal	
venus	venous ★	vestibule	
venyet	vignette	vestig *e* /ial	
veraci *ous* /ty		vestrie	vestry ⁺
veranda		vestr *y* /ies	
verashus	veracious ⁺	vestul	vestal
verasitey	veracity	vesture ²	
verb /al/ally/atim		vesul	vessel

vet [3]	
vetch /es	
vetenarey	veterinary +
vetenrey	veterinary +
veteran	
veterinar y /ies	
veto [1] /es	
vex [1] /ation/atious	
vexashun	vexation
vexashus	vexatious
veza	visa
vezave	vis-à-vis
vi	vie +
via	
viab le /ility	
viabul	viable +
viaduct	
vial ★ (glass)	
vial	vile ★+
vial	viol ★+
viands (pl.)	
vibrant	
vibrashun	vibration
vibrat e [2] /ion/or	
vicar /age	
vicarious /ly	
vicarius	vicarious +
vice	
vice versa	
vice-chancellor	
vice-president	
vicer	vicar +
viceregal	
viceroi	viceroy +
viceroy /alty/alties	
vicinity	
vicious /ly/ness	
vicissitude	
vicount	viscount +
vicownt	viscount +
victim	
victimis e [2] /ation	
victor /ious/iously	
victorey	victory +
victorius	victorious

victor y /ies	
victual [3] /ler	
video /-frequency	
vidio	video +
vie /d	
vieing	vying
view [1] /er	
view-point	
viger	vigour +
vigil /ance/ant/ante	
vigilans	vigilance
vignette	
vigorus	vigorous
vigo ur /rous/rously	
vijun	vision +
Viking	
viksen	vixen
vilan	villain +
vile ★† /ly/ness/r/st †(loathsome)	
vile	vial ★
vile	viol ★+
vilidge	village +
vilifi	vilify [4]+
vilif y [4] /ication/ier	
vilige	village +
villa	
village /r	
villain /ous/y	
villaney	villainy
villanus	villainous
vill us /i (pl.)	
vindicashun	vindication
vindicat e [2] /ion/or	
vindictive	
vine /ry	
vinegar /y	
viniger	vinegar +
vintage	
vintidge	vintage
vintige	vintage
vinul	vinyl
vinyet	vignette
vinyl	
viol ★ (music) /a/in/inist	

viol	vial ★
viol	vile ★+
violashun	violation
violat e ² /ion/or	
violen ce /t	
violens	violence +
violet	
violoncello /s	
violonchelo	violoncello +
viper /ish/ous	
virgin /al/ity	
Virgo	
viril e /ity	
virilitey	virility
virolog y /ist	
virtual /ly	
virtu e /osity/ous	
virtuoso	
virulen ce /t	
virulens	virulence +
virus	
visa	
visage	
vis-à-vis	
viscera /l	
viscid /ity	
viscos e /ity	
viscositey	viscosity
viscount /ess (fem.)	
viscous	
viscuus	viscous
vise	vice
vise chanseler	vice-chancellor
vise president	vice-president
visera	viscera +
viseregal	viceregal
viseroi	viceroy +
visevursa	vice versa
vishiate	vitiate 2+
vishun	vision +
vishunrey	visionary
vishus	vicious +
visib le /ility/ly	
visibul	visible +
visid	viscid +
visiditey	viscidity
visinitey	vicinity
vision /ary	
visionrey	visionary
visissitude	vicissitude
visit ¹ /ant/ation/or	
visitashun	visitation
visiter	visitor
viskositey	viscosity
vista	
visual /ly	
visualis e ² /ation	
visul	visual +
visulise	visualise 2+
vital /ity/ly/s	
vital	victual 3+
vitalis e ² /ation	
vitalitey	vitality
vitamin	
vitaminis e ² /ation	
vitiat e ² /ion	
vitreous	
vitrifi	vitrify 4+
vitrif y ⁴ /ication	
vitriol /ic	
vitrius	vitreous
vitul	vital +
vituperat e ² /ion/ive/or	
viul	vial ★
viul	vile ★+
viva voce	
vivac ious /ity	
vivashus	vivacious +
vivasitee	vivacity
vivavosi	viva voce
vivid /ly/ness	
vivifi	vivify 4+
vivif y ⁴ /ication	
viviparous	
viviparus	viviparous
vivisecshun	vivisection
vivisect ¹ /ion/or	
vixen	
vocabular y /ies	
vocal /ist/ly	

vocalis *e* ² /ation		vote ² /r	
vocashun	vocation +	votive	
vocation /al		vouch ¹ /er	
vocative		vouchsafe ²	
vocifer *ate* ² /ous		vow ¹	
vociferus	vociferous	vowch	vouch ¹⁺
vodka		vowchsafe	vouchsafe ²
voge	vogue	vowel	
vogue		vowul	vowel
voice ²		voyage ² /r	
void ¹		voyd	void ¹
voiige	voyage ²⁺	voys	voice ²
voiiger	voyager	vue	view ¹⁺
voile		vulcanis *e* ² /ation	
vois	voice ²	vulcher	vulture
volatil *e* /ity		vulgar /ity	
volatilis *e* ² /ation		vulgaris *e* ² /ation/m	
volcanic		vulnerab *le* /ility	
volcano /es		vulnerabul	vulnerable +
voley	volley ¹⁺	vulnrable	vulnerable +
volishun	volition +	vulture	
volition /al		vulva	
volkano	volcano +	vurb	verb +
volley ¹ /s		vurchoo	virtue +
volt /age/meter		vurchual	virtual +
volub *le* /ility/ly		vurchuous	virtuous
volubul	voluble +	vurchuus	virtuous
volum *e* /etric/inous		vurgin	virgin +
voluminus	voluminous	vurginitey	virginity
voluntar *y* /ily		vurgo	Virgo
volunteer ¹		vurtue	virtue +
voluntrey	voluntary +	vurtuoso	virtuoso
voluptu *ous* /ary		vurtuous	virtuous
voluptuus	voluptuous +	vwal	voile
vomit ¹		vye	vie +
voraci *ous* /ty		vying	
vorashus	voracious +		
vorasitey	voracity		
vornt	vaunt ¹	**W**	
vorteks	vortex +		
vort *ex* /exes/ices (pls.)		wack	whack ¹
vorticella		wad /ding	
vosiferate	vociferate ²⁺	waddle ²	
vosiferus	vociferous	wade ² /r	
votar *y* /ies		wadle	waddle ²

wadul	waddle ²	walow	wallow ¹
wafe	waif	walrus /es	
wafer		walts	waltz ¹+
waffle ² /-iron		waltz ¹ /er	
wafle	waffle ²+	wan ★ (pale) /ness	
waft ¹		wan	won ★
waful	waffle ²+	wander ¹★ (roam) /er/lust	
wag ³ /gish/tail		wander	wonder ¹★+
wage ²		wane ²	
wager ¹		wangle ² /r	
waggle ²		wangul	wangle ²+
wagon /er/ette		wanskot	wainscot ¹+
wagul	waggle ²	want ¹	
waif		wanton /ness	
wail ¹★ (cry)		war ³ /-paint/-path	
wail	whale ★+	warant	warrant ¹+
wainscot ¹ /ing		warantee	warranty +
waist ★ (body) /coat		warble ² /r	
waist	waste ²★+	warbul	warble ²+
wait ¹★† /er/ress (fem.)		ward ¹ /er/room	
†(stay for)		warden	
wait	weight ★+	wardrobe	
waitey	weighty	ware ★ (avoid) /s ★†	
waive ²★ (give up)		†(goods for sale)	
waive	wave ²★+	ware	wear ★+
waiver ¹★ (law)		ware	where ★
waiver	waver ¹★+	warehouse	
wake ² /ful/fulness		warehowse	warehouse
waken ¹		waren	warren
waks	wax ¹+	wares	wears ★
wakswork	waxwork	warey	wary +
walabey	wallaby +	warf	wharf +
wale	wail ¹★	war fare /like	
wale	whale ★+	warior	warrior
walk ¹ /-over		warm ¹ /er/est/ly/ness/th	
walkie-talkie		warmonger ¹	
walking-stick		warn ¹	
wall ¹ /flower/paper		warp ¹	
wallab y /ies		warrant ¹ /able	
wallah		warrant y /ies	
wallet		warren	
wallop ¹		warrior	
wallow ¹		wart /y	
walnut		warves	wharves
walop	wallop ¹	war y /ily/iness	

was	
wash ¹ /able/er	
washed-up	
wasl	wassail ¹
wasn't (was not)	
wasnt	wasn't
wasp /ish	
wassail ¹	
wast e ²★† /age/er/rel	
†(squander)	
waste	waist ★+
wasteful /ly/ness	
wat	watt ★+
wat	what ★+
watch ¹ /ful/fulness	
wate	wait ¹★+
wate	weight ★+
water ¹ /cress/fall	
waterlogged	
water mark /tight	
waterproof ¹	
watt ★ (power) /age	
wave ²★† /form/length	
†(water, gesture)	
wave	waive ²★
waver ¹★ (falter) /er	
waver	waiver ¹★
wawlts	waltz ¹+
wax ¹ /en/work	
way ★ (direction) /side	
way	weigh ¹★+
way	whey ★
waybridge	weighbridge
wayfare ² /r	
way lay /laid/laying	
wayward	
waywerd	wayward
we ★ (us)	
we	wee ★
weak ★† /ling/ness	
†(feeble)	
weak	week ★+
weaken ¹	
weak er /est/ly ★† /ness	
†(sickly)	

weakly	weekly ★+
weal ★ (state)	
weal	wheel ¹★+
weald ★ (district)	
weald	wield ¹★
wealth /ier/iest/iness	
wean ¹	
weapon	
wear ★† /able/er/ing/s ★†	
†(have on the body)	
wear	ware ★+
wear	where ★
wearey	weary ⁴+
wearisome	
wears	wares ★
wear y ⁴ /ier/iest/ily/iness	
weasel	
weat	wheat +
weather ¹★† /cock	
†(atmosphere)	
weather	whether ★
weathervane	
weatmeal	wheatmeal
weave ²★ (make fabric) /r	
weave	we've ★
web ³ /-footed/-toed	
wed ³ /ding/lock	
wedge ²	
Wedensday	Wednesday
Wednesday	
wee ★ (small)	
weed ¹ /s/y	
weedul	wheedle ²
week ★† /day/end	
†(seven days)	
week	weak ★+
weeken	weaken ¹
weekling	weakling
weekl y ★ (every week) /ies	
weel	weal ★
weel	wheel ¹★+
weelbarrow	wheelbarrow
weeld	weald ★
weeld	wield ¹★
weelrite	wheelwright

314

ween	wean [1]
weep /er/ing/y	
weevil	
weeze	wheeze [2]+
wege	wedge [2]
weigh [1]*† /bridge	
†(how heavy)	
weight *† /less/lessness/y	
†(heaviness)	
weild	weald *
weild	wield [1]*
weir * (dam)	
weird /er/est	
weja	ouija
welch [1]* (cheat)	
welch	Welsh *
welcome [2]	
weld [1] /er	
welfare	
welk	whelk
welkin	
we'll * (we will)	
well [1]* (spring) /-advised	
well-appointed	
well-balanced	
well-behaved	
well-*being* /-bred	
wellingtons	
well-meaning	
well-*nigh* /-to-do	
welp	whelp [1]
Welsh * (from Wales)	
welter [1]	
welth	wealth +
wen	when +
wence	whence
wench [1] /es	
wend [1]	
wenever	whenever
went	
wepon	weapon
wept	
wer	weir *
werd	weird +
werd	word +

were * (to be)	
were	where *
were	whirr [1]*
we're * (we are)	
wereabouts	whereabouts
wereas	whereas +
wereby	whereby
werefor	wherefore
weren't (were not)	
werever	wherever
werewol*f* /ves (pl.)	
werey	weary [4]+
werisum	wearisome
werk	work [1]+
werkbox	workbox +
werker	worker
werkshop	workshop
werl	whirl [1]*+
werl	whorl [1]*
werld	world +
werldwide	worldwide
werligig	whirligig
werm	worm [1]+
werse	worse +
wersen	worsen [1]
wership	worship [3]+
werst	worst
wersted	worsted
werth	worth +
werthey	worthy +
werthwiul	worthwhile
werwoolf	werewolf +
wesel	weasel
Wesleyan	
weslian	Wesleyan
west /erly/ern/ward	
westernis *e* [2] /ation	
westwerd	westward
wet [3]*† /ness/ter/test	
†(soaked)	
wet	whet [3]*
wether	weather [1]*+
wether	whether *
wethercock	weathercock
wethervane	weathervane

315

we've ★ (we have)

weve   weave ²★+

wevil   weevil

whack ¹

whal *e* ★† /er/ing
   †(mammal)

whar *f* /ves (pl.)

what ★† /ever/soever
   †(question)

what   watt ★+

wheat /en/meal

whedul   wheedle ²

wheedle ²

wheel ¹★ /barrow

wheelwright

wheez *e* ² /ily/y

whelk

whelp ¹

when /ever/soever

whence

whens   whence

where ★ (which place)

where   ware ★+

where   wear ★+

where   were ★

whereabouts

where *as* /by/ever

wherefore

where *upon* /withal

wherl   whirl ¹★+

wherl   whorl ¹★

whet ³★ (sharpen)

whether ★ (if)

whether   weather ¹★+

whey ★ (milk)

which ★ (which one)

which   witch ★+

whiff ¹

Whig ★ (political)

whil *e* ★ (during) /st

while   wile ²★+

whim /sical

whimper ¹

whimsie   whimsy +

whims *y* /ies

whine ²★ (complain)

whinn *y* ⁴ /ies

whip ³ /cord

whipper-snapper

whippet

whirl ¹★† /igig
   †(swing round)

whirl   whorl ¹★

whirr ¹★ (whirl)

whisk ¹

whisker /ed

whiskey ★†
   †(alcohol—Irish)

whisky ★†
   †(alcohol—Scotch)

whisper ¹ /er

whist

whistle ² /r

whisul   whistle ²+

whit ★ (particle, jot)

white /bait/r/st

whiten ¹

whitewash ¹

whither ★ (where)

whiting

Whitsun

whittle ²

whitul   whittle ²

whiz ³

who /ever

whoa ★ (stop)

whole ★ (complete)

whole   hole ²★+

whole-hearted

wholesale /r

wholesome /ly

wholly ★ (fully)

wholly   holey ★

wholly   holy ★

whom

whoop ¹★ (shout)

whoop   hoop ¹★

whooping cough

whop ³

whore ² /monger

whorl [1]*†	
†(ring of leaves)	
whorl	whirl [1]*+
who's * (who is or has)	
whose * (possessive)	
whur	whirr [1]*
whurl	whirl [1]*+
whurl	whorl [1]*
why	
wick /er/et	
wicked /er/est	
wide /ly/r/st	
wide *awake* /spread	
widen [1]	
widow [1] /er	
width	
wield [1]* (hold and use)	
wield	weald *
wi*fe* /ves (pl.)	
wiff	whiff [1]
wig [3]* (hair)	
wig	Whig *
wiggl*e* [2] /y	
wigul	wiggle [2]+
wigwam	
wild /er/est/ly/ness	
wilderness	
wil*e* [2]* (trick) /iness/y	
wile	while *+
wilful /ly/ness	
will [1] /power	
will-o'-the-wisp	
willow /y	
willy-nilly	
wilst	whilst
wilt [1]	
wim	whim +
wimin	women +
wimper	whimper [1]
wimsey	whimsy +
wimsical	whimsical
win /ner/ning	
wince [2]	
winch [1] /es	
wind /bag/ed/ward	
wind /er/ing	
window /-pane/-sill	
wind*y* /ier/iest/iness	
wine * (drink) /-cellar	
wine	whine [2]*
wineglass /es	
wing [1]	
wink [1]	
winkle [2]	
winkul	winkle [2]
winnow [1]	
winsome /ness	
winter [1]	
wintrie	wintry
wintry	
wip	whip [3]+
wipcord	whipcord
wipe [2] /r	
wipper snapper	whipper-snapper
wippet	whippet
wire [2] /less	
wir *iness* /y	
wirl	whirl [1]*+
wirl	whorl [1]*
wirr	whirr [1]*
wisdom	
wise /acre/ly/r/st	
wish [1] /ful	
wishy-washy	
wisk	whisk [1]
wisker	whisker +
wiskey	whiskey *
wiskey	whisky *
wisp	
wisper	whisper [1]+
wist	whist
wistful /ly/ness	
wistle	whistle [2]+
wisul	whistle [2]+
wit * (flair, humour)	
wit	whit *
witch * (hag) /es	
witch	which *
witcher*y* /ies	
wite	white +

witen	whiten [1]
witer	whiter
witewash	whitewash [1]
with /al	
withdraw /al/ing/n	
withdrew	
withdroo	withdrew
wither [1]★ (decay)	
wither	whither ★
withers	
withheld	
withhold /ing	
within	
without	
withstand /ing	
witing	whiting
witness [1] /es	
witsun	Whitsun
witti *cism* /ness	
wittle	whittle [2]
witt *y* /ier/iest/ily	
witul	whittle [2]
wiz	whiz [3]
wizard	
wizened	
wo	whoa ★
wo	woe ★+
wobbl *e* [2] /y	
woble	wobble [2]+
wobul	wobble [2]+
woch	watch [1]+
wod	wad +
wodle	waddle [2]
wodul	waddle [2]
woe ★ (grief) /begone	
woe	whoa ★
woeful /ly	
wofle	waffle [2]+
woft	waft [1]
woful	waffle [2]+
woful	woeful +
wolabey	wallaby +
wolet	wallet
wol *f* [1] /ves (pl.)	
wolla	wallah

wolop	wallop [1]
wolow	wallow [1]
woman /kind/ly	
womb	
women (pl.) /folk	
won ★ (did win)	
won	wan ★+
wonder [1]★† /ful/fully †(remarkable thing)	
wonder	wander [1]★+
wondrous	
wondrus	wondrous
wont ★ (accustomed)	
wont	want [1]
wont	won't ★
won't ★ (will not)	
wonton	wanton +
woo [1] /er	
wood ★ (lumber) /cut	
wood	would ★
wooden /ly/ness	
woof	
wool /len/liness	
woolf	wolf [1]+
wooll *y* /ies	
wooman	woman +
woomb	womb
woond	wound [1]
wop	whop [3]
wor	war [3]+
worant	warrant [1]+
worantie	warranty +
worble	warble [2]+
worbul	warble [2]+
word /ily/ing/y	
word	ward [1]+
worden	warden
wordrobe	wardrobe
wore	
woren	warren
worf	wharf +
worfare	warfare +
work [1] /able/aday/er	
work *box* /shop	
worl	whirl [1]★+

worl	whorl [1]★
world /liness/ly/wide	
worm [1] /wood	
worm	warm [1+]
wormunger	warmonger [1]
worn /-out	
worn	warn [1]
worp	warp [1]
worrey	worry [4+]
worrier	warrior
worr y [4] /ies/ier	
wors e /t	
worsen [1]	
worship [3] /per	
worsted	
wort	wart [+]
worth /less/while	
worth y /ier/iest/ily	
wos	was
wosh	wash [1+]
wosht up	washed-up
wosl	wassail [1]
wosnt	wasn't
wosp	wasp [+]
wot	watt ★[+]
wot	what ★[+]
wotch	watch [1+]
wotchful	watchful
wotever	whatever
wotsoever	whatsoever
would ★ (conditional)	
would	wood ★[+]
wound [1]	
wove /n	
wrack ★ (seaweed)	
wraith	
wrangle [2] /r	
wrangul	wrangle [2+]
wrap ★ (pack) /per ★ /ping	
wrapped ★ (packed)	
wrath /ful	
wreak [1]★ (inflict)	
wreath ★ (flowers)	
wreathe [2]★ (twist)	
wreck [1] /age	

wren	
wrench [1]	
wrest [1]★ (pull away)	
wrestle [2] /r	
wresul	wrestle [2+]
wretch ★†	
†(unhappy person)	
wri	wry ★[+]
wriggle [2]	
wrigul	wriggle [2]
wring [1]★ (squeeze)	
wringer ★ (machine)	
wrinkle [2]	
wrinkul	wrinkle [2]
wrist /band/let/-watch	
writ	
writ e ★† /er/ing/ten	
†(put words on paper)	
writhe [2]	
wrong [1] /doer	
wrongful /ly	
wrort	wrought [+]
wrote ★ (did write)	
wrought /-up	
wrung ★ (squeezed)	
wry ★ (distorted) /ly	
wun	one ★[+]
wunce	once
wunder	wonder [1]★[+]
wundrous	wondrous
wundrus	wondrous
wuns	once
wunself	oneself
wur	whirr [1]★
wurey	worry [4+]
wurl	whirl [1]★[+]
wurl	whorl [1]★
wurligig	whirligig

X

xenofobia	xenophobia [+]
xenophob ia /e/ic	
xeroks	Xerox [1]

Xerox [1]	
X-ray [1]	
xylofone	xylophone
xylophone	

Y

y	why
yacht [1] /sman	
yak	
yam	
yank [1]	
Yankee	
yap [3]	
yard /age	
yarn [1]	
yashmak	
yaw [1]★ (of ship)	
yaw	yore ★
yaw	your ★+
yawl [1]	
yawn [1]	
yay	yea
yea	
yeald	yield [1]
year /ling	
yearn [1]	
yeast	
yeer	year +
yeest	yeast
yeld	yield [1]
yell [1]	
yellow /ish	
yelow	yellow +
yelp [1]	
yeoman /ry	
yerling	yearling
yern	yearn [1]
yes	
yest	yeast
yesterday	
yet	
yeti	
yety	yeti

yew ★ (tree)	
yew	ewe ★
yew	you ★+
yewse	use [2]+
yewsery	usury +
yewshual	usual +
yewsual	usual +
yiddish	
yield [1]	
yodel [3] /ler	
yodle	yodel [3]+
yoga	
yogert	yogurt
yogurt	
yoke ★ (round neck)	
yoke	yolk ★
yokel	
yokle	yokel
yolk ★ (of egg)	
yolk	yoke ★
yoman	yeoman +
yonder	
yore ★ (years ago)	
yore	yaw [1]★
yore	your ★+
yorself	yourself +
yorselves	yourselves
yot	yacht [1]+
yotsman	yachtsman
you ★ (person)	
you	ewe ★
you	yew ★
youboat	U-boat
you'll ★ (you will)	
young /er/est/ster	
your ★† /s	
†(belonging to you)	
your	yaw [1]★
your	yore ★
your	you're ★
you're ★ (you are)	
yourself /ves (pl.)	
youth /ful	
ytterbium	
yttrium	

yule *† /tide	
†(Christmas)	
yule	you'll *
yung	young [+]
yungster	youngster
yurn	yearn [1]
yuse	use [2+]
yuseful	useful [+]
yuserey	usury [+]
yusual	usual [+]
yutensil	utensil
yuterine	uterine
yuterus	uterus [+]
yuth	youth [+]
yutilise	utilise [2+]
yutilitarian	utilitarian [+]
yutilitee	utility [+]
yutopia	Utopia [+]

Z

zan y /ies	
zar	tsar
zeal /ous	
zealot	
zebra	
zeel	zeal [+]
zefer	zephyr
zelot	zealot
zelus	zealous
zenith	

zenofobia	xenophobia [+]
zenophobia	xenophobia [+]
zepher	zephyr
zephyr	
zeplin	Zeppelin
Zeppelin	
zerconium	zirconium
zero /s	
zeroks	Xerox [1]
zerox	Xerox [1]
zest /ful	
Zeus	
zigospore	zygospore
zigote	zygote
zigzag [3]	
zilofone	xylophone
zilophone	xylophone
zinc	
zink	zinc
Zion /ism/ist	
zip [3] /per/-fastener	
zirconium	
zither	
zodiac	
zon e [2] /al	
zoo /logical/logy	
zoologey	zoology
zoom [1]	
Zulu	
zus	Zeus
zygospore	
zygote	

APPENDIX I
Some Spelling Rules

A. y always stays when adding -ing but changes to i before adding -ed, e.g.:

    carry, carrying, carried   terrify, terrifying, terrified

B. i before e except after c, e.g.:

    field, mischievous, relief   deceive, perceive, receipt

Note that there are exceptions to the above rules.

C. q is always followed by u, e.g.:

    conquer, frequent, queen

D. all at the beginning of a word loses one l, e.g.:

    already, altogether, always

The double l is retained in hyphenated words such as all-fours and all-round, but the words all right should always be written as two separate words and in that form only.

THE FORMATION OF PLURALS

The following is a summary of the main rules involved in the formation of plurals:

1. Most words, including those ending in silent -e, add -s, e.g.:
   airport, airports
   sausage, sausages

2. Words ending in -ay, -ey, -oy, or -uy add -s, e.g.:
   day, days   toy, toys
   abbey, abbeys   guy, guys

3. Words ending in -fe change f to v and add -s, e.g.:
   knife, knives

4. Some words ending in -f change f to v and add -es, e.g.:
   half, halves   loaf, loaves

5. Some words ending in -f add -s, e.g.:
   chief, chiefs
   handkerchief, handkerchiefs
   But note that some words ending in -f can either add -s or change f to v and add -es, e.g.:
   hoof, hoofs *or* hooves
   scarf, scarfs *or* scarves

6. Words ending in -ff usually add -s, e.g.:
   cliff, cliffs
   sheriff, sheriffs

7. Words ending in -o add -s or -es, e.g.:
   concerto, concertos
   dynamo, dynamos
   buffalo, buffaloes
   domino, dominoes

8. Words ending in -ch, -s, -sh, -x, or -z add -es, e.g.:
   church, churches   thrush, thrushes
   gas, gases   box, boxes
   dress, dresses   buzz, buzzes

9. Words ending in -y (but not -ay, -ey, -oy, or -uy: see Note 2) change the y to an i and add -es, e.g.:
   baby, babies
   family, families

10. Some words form their plurals mainly by changing their vowels (or some of their vowels), e.g.:
    foot, feet   mouse, mice
    goose, geese   tooth, teeth
    man, men   woman, women

11. One word adds -**en**:
    ox, oxen
    One word adds -**ren**:
    child, children

12. Words ending in -us change us to i, e.g.:
    bacillus, bacilli
    fungus, fungi
    radius, radii
    rhombus, rhombi
    terminus, termini

13. Words ending in -is change is to -es, e.g.:
    analysis, analyses
    basis, bases
    metamorphosis, metamorphoses

14. Words ending in -ex add -es or change -ex to -ices, e.g.:
    apex, apexes or apices
    index, indexes or indices
    vortex, vortexes or vortices

15. Words ending in -ix add -es or change -ix to -ices, e.g.:
    appendix, appendixes or appendices
    helix, helices
    matrix, matrixes or matrices

16. Some words ending in -a simply add -s, e.g.:
    aroma, aromas
    drama, dramas
    idea, ideas
    but note:
    alga, algae
    antenna, antennae
    formula, formulas or formulae
    stoma, stomas or stomata

17. Some words ending in -um simply add -s, e.g.:
    museum, museums
    pendulum, pendulums
    premium, premiums
    but note:
    aquarium, aquariums or aquaria
    bacterium, bacteria
    curriculum, curricula
    memorandum, memorandums
                    or memoranda
    spectrum, spectra
    stadium, stadiums or stadia

18. Words ending in -on usually add -s, e.g.:
    electron, electrons
    neutron, neutrons
    but note:
    phenomenon, phenomena

19. Words ending in -eau add -x, e.g.:
    bureau, bureaux
    chateau, chateaux
    plateau, plateaux
    Note that some dictionaries allow a plural in -s for some of these words.

20. Some words have the same spelling for both the singular and the plural forms, e.g.:

bison	grouse	sheep
deer	salmon	trout

21. Compound words.
    Logically, the most important word should be changed into the plural, as, for example:
    brother-in-law, brothers-in-law
    man-of-war, men-of-war
    but note:
    court-martial, court-martials
    lord justice, lords justices

22. Some words are used only in the singular form, e.g.:

arithmetic	goodness	magic
courage	logic	music

23. Some words are used only in the plural form, e.g.:
    mathematics
    Among words frequently used in their plural form are:

acoustics	physics	tactics
athletics	politics	

24. Pairs.
    The following nouns do not have a singular form:

entrails	pliers	trousers
pincers	scissors	tweezers

APPENDIX II
Abbreviations in General Use

A. Advanced (level of G.C.E.)
A.A. Automobile Association
A.B.M. anti-ballistic missile
acc., a/c account
A.D. in the year of our Lord
A.D.C. aide-de-camp
A.F.C. Air Force Cross
A.F.M. Air Force Medal
a.m. before noon
Ave. avenue
A.W.O.L. absent without leave

B.A. Bachelor of Arts
Bart. Baronet
B.B.C. British Broadcasting Corporation
B.C. before Christ
B.D. Bachelor of Divinity
B.Ed. Bachelor of Education
B.E.M. British Empire Medal
Benelux Belgium–Netherlands–Luxembourg Union
B.M. Bachelor of Medicine
B.M.A. British Medical Association
B.Mus. Bachelor of Music
B.R. British Rail
B.R.C.S. British Red Cross Society
B.Sc. Bachelor of Science
B.S.T. British standard time, British summer time

C. Centigrade
c., ca. about
C.A.B. Citizens' Advice Bureau
C.A.C.M. Central American Common Market
CARICOM. Caribbean Community
C.B.E. Commander of the British Empire
C.B.I. Confederation of British Industry
C.C. County Council
C.E.N.T.O. Central Treaty Organisation
C.G.M. Conspicuous Gallantry Medal
C.G.S. Chief of General Staff
C.H. Companion of Honour
Ch.B. Bachelor of Surgery

C.I.D. Criminal Investigation Department
C.-in-C. Commander-in-Chief
C.M.E.A. (COMECON) Council for Mutual Economic Assistance
C.N.D. Campaign for Nuclear Disarmament
C.O. Commanding Officer
c/o care of
C.O.D. cash on delivery
Con. Conservative
C.S.E. Certificate of Secondary Education

D.B.E. Dame Commander of the British Empire
D.C.L. Doctor of Civil Law
D.C.M. Distinguished Conduct Medal
D.D. Doctor of Divinity
D.D.T. dichlor-diphenyl-trichlorethane (insecticide)
D.F.C. Distinguished Flying Cross
D.F.M. Distinguished Flying Medal
D.M. Doctor of Medicine
D.Mus. Doctor of Music
DNA deoxyribonucleic acid
D.O.E. Department of the Environment
D.Phil. Doctor of Philosophy
Dr. Doctor
D.Sc. Doctor of Science
D.S.C. Distinguished Service Cross
D.S.M. Distinguished Service Medal
D.S.O. Distinguished Service Order

E.E.C. European Economic Community
E.F.T.A. European Free Trade Association
e.g. for example
E.S.N. educationally subnormal
E.S.P. extrasensory perception
Esq. Esquire

F. Fahrenheit
F.A. Football Association

F.A.O. Food and Agriculture Organisation

F.B.A. Fellow of the British Academy

f.o.c. free of charge

F.R.S. Fellow of the Royal Society

G.A.T.T. General Agreement on Tariffs and Trade

G.B. Great Britain

G.B.E. Dame or Knight Grand Cross of the British Empire

G.C. George Cross

G.C.E. General Certificate of Education

G.D.P. gross domestic product

G.D.R. German Democratic Republic

G.H.Q. General Headquarters

G.L.C. Greater London Council

G.M. George Medal

G.M.T. Greenwich mean time

G.N.P. gross national product

G.P. general practitioner

G.P.O. General Post Office

H.E. His Excellency; His Eminence

H.M. Her Majesty

H.M.I. Her Majesty's Inspector

H.M.S. Her Majesty's Ship

H.M.S.O. Her Majesty's Stationery Office

H.N.C. Higher National Certificate

H.N.D. Higher National Diploma

Hon. honorary; Honourable

h.p. hire purchase; horsepower

H.Q. Headquarters

H.R.H. Her (His) Royal Highness

I.B.R.D. International Bank for Reconstruction and Development (World Bank)

I.C.C. International Chamber of Commerce

I.C.F.T.U. International Confederation of Free Trade Unions

I.C.I. Imperial Chemical Industries

i.e. that is

I.L.O. International Labour Organisation

I.M.F. International Monetary Fund

I.O.U. I owe you

I.Q. intelligence quotient

I.R.A. Irish Republican Army

I.T.V. Independent Television

J.P. Justice of the Peace

Jr. Junior

K.B.E. Knight Commander of the British Empire

K.C.B. Knight Commander of the Bath

Kt. Knight

Lab. Labour

L.A.F.T.A. Latin American Free Trade Association

lat. latitude

lbw leg before wicket

L.E.A. Local Education Authority

Lib. Liberal

LL.B., LL.D. Bachelor, Doctor of Laws

long. longitude

L.P. long-playing (of gramophone records, etc.)

L.S.D. lysergic acid diethylamide (hallucinogenic drug)

L.T.A. Lawn Tennis Association

Ltd. Limited

L.V. luncheon voucher

M.A. Master of Arts

M.B. Bachelor of Medicine

M.B.E. Member of the British Empire

M.C. Military Cross; Master of Ceremonies

M.C.C. Marylebone Cricket Club

M.D. Doctor of Medicine

M.F.H. Master of Foxhounds

M.O.H. Medical Officer of Health

M.P. Member of Parliament

m.p.g. miles per gallon

m.p.h. miles per hour

MS., MSS. manuscript(s)

M.Sc. Master of Science

N.A.S.A. National Aeronautics and Space Administration

N.A.T.O. North Atlantic Treaty Organisation

N.B. note well

N.C.O. non-commissioned officer

N.H.S. National Health Service

N.I. National Insurance

No. number

nr. near

N.S.P.C.C. National Society for the Prevention of Cruelty to Children

O. Ordinary (level of G.C.E.)
O.A.P. old aged pensioner
O.A.S. Organisation of American States
O.A.U. Organisation of African Unity
O.B.E. Officer of the British Empire
O.D.E.C.A. Organisation of Central American States
O.E.C.D. Organisation for Economic Co-operation and Development
O.H.M.S. On Her Majesty's Service
O.M. Order of Merit
O.N.C. Ordinary National Certificate
O.N.D. Ordinary National Diploma
op. cit. in the work named
O.P.E.C. Organisation of the Petroleum Exporting Countries

P.A.Y.E. pay as you earn
P.E. physical education
Ph.D. Doctor of Philosophy
P.M. Prime Minister
P.O. post office; postal order
P.O.W. prisoner of war
P.S. postscript
P.T.O. please turn over

Q.C. Queen's Counsel

R. Regina; Rex
R.A. Royal Academy; Royal Artillery
R.A.C. Royal Automobile Club
R.A.D.A. Royal Academy of Dramatic Art
R.A.F. Royal Air Force
R.A.M. Royal Academy of Music
R.C. Roman Catholic
R.C.A. Royal College of Arts
R.C.M. Royal College of Music
Rev., Revd. Reverend
R.G.S. Royal Geographical Society
R.H.S. Royal Horticultural Society
R.I.P. may he (she, they) rest in peace
R.M. Royal Marines; Royal Mail
R.N. Royal Navy
r.p.m. revolutions per minute
R.S.P.C.A. Royal Society for the Prevention of Cruelty to Animals
R.S.V.P. please reply
Rt. Hon. Right Honourable

s.a.e. self-addressed envelope
S.A.L.T. Strategic Arms Limitation Talks

S.A.Y.E. save as you earn
S.C.M. State Certified Midwife
S.E.A.T.O. South-East Asia Treaty Organisation
S.O.S. distress signal
S.R.N. State Registered Nurse
St. Saint; street
S.T.D. subscriber trunk dialling

T.A.S.S. Soviet Telegraph Agency
T.B. tuberculosis
T.N.T. trinitrotoluene (high explosive)
T.U.C. Trades Union Congress

U.A.R. United Arab Republic
U.D.C. Urban District Council
U.D.I. Unilateral Declaration of Independence
U.F.O. unidentified flying object
U.N. United Nations
U.N.D.P. United Nations Development Programme
U.N.E.S.C.O. United Nations Educational, Scientific and Cultural Organisation
U.N.I.C.E.F. United Nations International Children's Emergency Fund
U.S. United States
U.S.A. United States of America
U.S.S.R. Union of Soviet Socialist Republics

V.A.T. value added tax
V.C. Victoria Cross
V.D. venereal disease
V.H.F. very high frequency
V.I.P. very important person

W.C.C. World Council of Churches
W.H.O. World Health Organisation
W.I. West Indies; Women's Institute
W.R.A.C. Women's Royal Army Corps
W.R.A.F. Women's Royal Air Force
W.R.N.S. Women's Royal Naval Service
W.R.V.S. Women's Royal Volunteer Service

Y.H.A. Youth Hostels Association
Y.M.C.A. Young Men's Christian Association
Y.W.C.A. Young Women's Christian Association

APPENDIX III
Common Forenames

MEN
Adrian
Alan, Allan
Andrew
Anthony, Antony
Barry
Brian, Bryan
Bruce
Charles
Christopher
Claude
Clive
Cyril
Derek
Desmond
Douglas
Edmund
Edward, Ted
Eugene
Ewen, Ewin
Francis
Frederick, Fred
Gareth
Gary
Geoffrey
George
Gerald, Gerry
Giles
Gordon
Graham
Guy
Harold, Harry
Howard, Howerd
Hugh
Humphrey
Ian
Jack
James, Jim
Jeremy, Jerry
John
Jonathan
Julian
Keith
Kenneth
Leonard

Lewis
Malcolm
Mathew, Matt
Michael, Mike
Neil
Nicholas, Nick
Nigel
Oliver
Patrick, Paddy
Peter
Philip
Richard, Dick
Robert, Bob
Roger
Ronald
Roy
Sean
Sidney
Simon
Stephen, Steven
Terence, Terry
Thomas
Timothy
Tony
Trevor
Wayne
William

WOMEN
Alice
Alison
Angela, Angie
Ann, Anne
Anthea
Barbara
Belinda
Bridget
Carol, Carole
Caroline
Carolyn
Catherine, Cathy
Charlotte
Christine
Clare
Daphne

Dawn
Deborah, Debby
Denise
Diana
Doreen
Eileen
Elaine
Elizabeth, Betty
Ellen
Emily
Emma
Evelyn
Felicity
Fiona
Frances
Gillian, Jill
Hazel
Heather
Helen
Hilary
Irene
Isabel, Isobel
Jacqueline
Jane
Janet
Janice
Jean
Jennifer, Jenny
Jill
Joan
Joanna
Joy
Joyce
Judith, Judy
Julia
Julie
Karen
Laura
Lesley
Lilian
Linda, Lynda
Lisa, Liza
Lorna
Louise
Lynn

Margaret, Maggie
Marian
Marie
Marilyn
Marion
Marjorie
Mary
Miranda
Miriam
Monica
Natalie
Olivia
Pamela
Patricia
Paula
Pauline
Penelope, Penny
Phillipa
Phillis, Phyllis
Rachel
Rebecca
Rosemary
Ruth
Sally
Sandra, Sandy
Sarah
Sharon
Sheila
Shirley
Sonia
Stephanie
Susan, Sue
Suzanne
Sylvia
Theresa, Tessa
Tina
Tracy
Vera
Veronica
Victoria, Vicky
Virginia
Vivian
Wendy
Yvonne
Zoe

The British Isles

APPENDIX V

The World Today

APPENDIX VI

Metric Measures — Imperial Measures

Length

Metric Measures			Imperial Measures		
1 millimetre (mm)		= 0.039 in	1 inch (in)		= 2.540 cm
1 centimetre (cm)	= 10 mm	= 0.394 in	1 foot (ft)	= 12 in	= 30.48 cm
1 metre (m)	= 100 cm	= 1.094 yd	1 yard (yd)	= 3 ft	= 0.914 m
1 kilometre (km)	= 1000 m	= 0.621 mile	1 mile	= 1760 yd	= 1.609 km
			1 nautical mile	= 6080 ft	= 1.852 km

Surface or Area

Metric Measures			Imperial Measures		
1 sq cm (cm^2)	= 100 mm^2	= 0.155 in^2	1 sq in (in^2)		= 6.452 cm^2
1 sq m (m^2)	= 10000 cm^2	= 1.196 yd^2	1 sq ft (ft^2)	= 144 in^2	= 9.290 dm^2
1 sq km (km^2)	= 100 ha	= 0.386 mile^2	1 sq yd (yd^2)	= 9 ft^2	= 0.836 m^2
1 hectare (ha)	= 10000 m^2	= 11 960 yd^2	1 rood	= 1210 yd^2	= 1012 m^2
			1 acre	= 4840 yd^2	= 0.405 ha
			1 sq mile	= 640 acres	= 259.0 ha

Volume and Capacity

Metric Measures			Imperial Measures		
1 cu cm (cm^3)		= 0.061 in^3	1 cu in (in^3)		= 16.39 cm^3
1 cu dm (dm^3)	= 1000 cm^3	= 61.02 in^3	1 cu ft (ft^3)	= 1728 in^3	= 0.028 m^3
1 cu m (m^3)	= 1000 dm^3	= 1.308 yd^3	1 cu yd (yd^3)	= 27 ft^3	= 0.765 m^3
1 litre (l)	= 1 dm^3	= 1.760 pints	1 pint	= 4 gills	= 0.568 l
1 hectolitre (hl)	= 100 l	= 2.750 bushels	1 gallon (gal)	= 8 pints	= 4.546 l
			1 bushel	= 8 gal	= 36.37 l
			1 fluid ounce	= 8 fl drachms	= 28.41 cm^3
			1 pint	= 20 fl oz	= 568.2 cm^3

Weight

Metric Measures			Imperial Measures		
1 milligram (mg)		= 0.015 grain	1 ounce (oz)	= 437.4 grains	= 28.35 g
1 gram (gm)	= 1000 mg	= 0.035 oz	1 pound (lb)	= 16 oz	= 0.454 kg
1 kilogram (kg)	= 1000 g	= 2.205 lb	1 stone	= 14 lb	= 6.350 kg
1 tonne (t)	= 1000 kg	= 0.984 ton	1 cwt	= 8 st	= 50.80 kg
			1 ton	= 20 cwt	= 1.016 tonnes

Temperature Conversion

$$C = \tfrac{5}{9}(F - 32) \qquad F = (\tfrac{9}{5}C) + 32$$

98.4° Fahrenheit	= 36.9° Centigrade
32° Fahrenheit	= 0° Centigrade
50° Fahrenheit	= 10° Centigrade
68° Fahrenheit	= 20° Centigrade
212° Fahrenheit	= 100° Centigrade

Time

1 min	= 60 sec	
1 hr	= 60 min	= 3600 sec
1 day	= 24 hr	
1 year	= 365 days (366 in leap year)	

APPENDIX VII

Common Chemical Compounds

Common name	Chemical name	Formula
Alcohol, grain	Ethanol	CH_3CH_2OH
Alcohol, wood	Methanol	CH_3OH
Baking soda	Sodium hydrogen carbonate	$NaHCO_3$
Borax	Disodium tetraborate	$Na_2B_4O_7$
Brimstone	Sulphur	S
Calomel	Mercury(I) chloride	Hg_2Cl_2
Carbolic acid	Phenol	C_6H_5OH
Carbon tetrachloride	Tetrachloromethane	CCl_4
Carborundum	Silicon carbide	SiC
Chalk	Calcium carbonate	$CaCO_3$
Chloroform	Trichloromethane	$CHCl_3$
Cooking salt	Sodium chloride	$NaCl$
Corn syrup	Glucose, dextrose	$C_6H_{12}O_6$
Diamond	Carbon	C
Dry ice	Carbon dioxide (solid)	CO_2
Ethyl	Lead tetraethyl	$Pb(C_2H_5)_4$
Fire damp	Methane	CH_4
Glycerine	Glycerol	$C_3H_5(OH)_3$
Graphite	Carbon	C
Iron pyrites	Iron disulphide	FeS_2
Laughing gas	Dinitrogen oxide	N_2O
Lime water	Calcium hydroxide solution	$Ca(OH)_2$
Lye (or caustic soda)	Sodium hydroxide	$NaOH$
Magnesia	Magnesium oxide	MgO
Marble	Calcium carbonate	$CaCO_3$
Marsh gas	Methane	CH_4
Milk of magnesia	Magnesium hydroxide (with water)	$Mg(OH)_2$
Moth balls	Naphthalene	$C_{10}H_8$
Muriatic acid	Hydrochloric acid	HCl
Oil of vitriol	Sulphuric acid	H_2SO_4
Peroxide	Hydrogen peroxide	H_2O_2
Potash	Potassium carbonate	K_3CO_3
Quartz	Silicon dioxide	SiO_2
Quicklime	Calcium oxide	CaO
Quicksilver	Mercury	Hg
Sal ammoniac	Ammonium chloride	NH_4Cl
Saltpetre	Potassium nitrate	KNO_3
Sand	Silicon dioxide (impure)	SiO_2
Soap	Sodium stearate	$C_{17}H_{35}COONa$
Sugar (cane or beet)	Sucrose	$C_{12}H_{22}O_{11}$
Vinegar	Ethanoic acid (with water)	CH_3COOH
Water glass	Sodium silicate	Na_2SiO_3
Zinc white	Zinc oxide	ZnO

APPENDIX VIII

Physical Constants, Conversion Factors and Units

	Quantity	Name of unit	Symbol
There are nine basic units in the SI system (Système international d'unités)	length	metre	m
	mass	kilogram	kg
	time	second	s
	electric current	ampere ★	A
	thermodynamic temperature	kelvin ★	K
	amount of substance	mole	mol
	luminous intensity	candela	cd
	plane angle	radian	rad
	solid angle	steradian	sr
In addition there are a number of derived units, including the following	force	newton ★	N
	energy	joule ★	J
	power	watt ★	W
	electric charge	coulomb ★	C
	potential difference	volt ★	V
	electric resistance	ohm ★	Ω
	frequency	hertz ★	Hz
	customary temperature	degree Celsius	°C

The asterisk (★) indicates that the names of the relevant units begin with a small letter when they are written out in full, but are symbolised by a capital letter.

	Multiple	Prefix	Symbol
Special prefixes and symbols are used to indicate multiples and sub-multiples of the basic units in powers of ten	10^{12}	tera	T
	10^{9}	giga	G
	10^{6}	mega	M
	10^{3}	kilo	k
	10^{-1}	deci	d
	10^{-2}	centi	c
	10^{-3}	milli	m
	10^{-6}	micro	μ
	10^{-9}	nano	n
	10^{-12}	pico	p
	10^{-15}	femto	f
	10^{-18}	atto	a

APPENDIX IX

PERIODIC TABLE OF THE ELEMENTS

H 1 Hydrogen																	He 2 Helium
Li 3 Lithium	Be 4 Beryllium											B 5 Boron	C 6 Carbon	N 7 Nitrogen	O 8 Oxygen	F 9 Fluorine	Ne 10 Neon
Na 11 Sodium	Mg 12 Magnesium											Al 13 Aluminium	Si 14 Silicon	P 15 Phosphorus	S 16 Sulphur	Cl 17 Chlorine	Ar 18 Argon
K 19 Potassium	Ca 20 Calcium	Sc 21 Scandium	Ti 22 Titanium	V 23 Vanadium	Cr 24 Chromium	Mn 25 Manganese	Fe 26 Iron	Co 27 Cobalt	Ni 28 Nickel	Cu 29 Copper	Zn 30 Zinc	Ga 31 Gallium	Ge 32 Germanium	As 33 Arsenic	Se 34 Selenium	Br 35 Bromine	Kr 36 Krypton
Rb 37 Rubidium	Sr 38 Strontium	Y 39 Yttrium	Zr 40 Zirconium	Nb 41 Niobium	Mo 42 Molybde-num	Tc 43 Technetium	Ru 44 Ruthenium	Rh 45 Rhodium	Pd 46 Palladium	Ag 47 Silver	Cd 48 Cadmium	In 49 Indium	Sn 50 Tin	Sb 51 Antimony	Te 52 Tellurium	I 53 Iodine	Xe 54 Xenon
Cs 55 Caesium	Ba 56 Barium	La 57 Lanthanum●	Hf 72 Hafnium	Ta 73 Tantalum	W 74 Tungsten	Re 75 Rhenium	Os 76 Osmium	Ir 77 Iridium	Pt 78 Platinum	Au 79 Gold	Hg 80 Mercury	Tl 81 Thallium	Pb 82 Lead	Bi 83 Bismuth	Po 84 Polonium	At 85 Astatine	Rn 86 Radon
Fr 87 Francium	Ra 88 Radium	Ac 89 Actinium●	104	105													

Ce 58 Cerium	Pr 59 Praseody-mium	Nd 60 Neodymium	Pm 61 Promethium	Sm 62 Samarium	Eu 63 Europium	Gd 64 Gadolinium	Tb 65 Terbium	Dy 66 Dysprosium	Ho 67 Holmium	Er 68 Erbium	Tm 69 Thulium	Yb 70 Ytterbium	Lu 71 Lutetium
Th 90 Thorium	Pa 91 Protactin-ium	U 92 Uranium	Np 93 Neptunium	Pu 94 Plutonium	Am 95 Americium	Cm 96 Curium	Bk 97 Berkelium	Cf 98 Californium	Es 99 Einsteinium	Fm 100 Fermium	Md 101 Mendelev-ium	No 102 Nobelium	Lr 103 Lawrencium

Acknowledgements

In preparing this dictionary the following books have been particularly useful to me as resource material:

Cassell's New Spelling Dictionary
L. B. & D. Firnberg, Cassell, 1976

Collins Authors and Printers Dictionary
Stanley Beale, Oxford University Press, 11th rev. ed., 1973

The Concise Oxford Dictionary 3rd rev. ed.
Ed. C. T. Onions, Oxford University Press, 1976

Maxwell's Illustrated Colour Dictionary
Eds. J. P. Brasier-Creach, M.A. and
B. A. Workman, M.A. ILSC, London, 1969

The Oxford School Dictionary
Joan Pusey, Oxford University Press, 3rd rev. ed., 1974

The Perfect Speller
Harriet Wittels and Joan Griesman, Grosset & Dunlap, New York, 1973

I have benefited greatly from the help and advice of many people and schools. I would specially like to acknowledge the help of: Miss Judy Black, Miss Georgina Cox, Mr. Gordon Files, Mrs. Edna Goldman, Mr. Oliver Gregory, Mrs. Gretchen Ingram, Mr. C. R. Jacobs, Mrs. Jean Price, Mrs. Olive Robinson, Miss Avital Talmor and the teachers of Shepherds' Hill Middle School, Oxford. However, any mistakes contained in the dictionary are entirely my responsibility.

The final acknowledgement goes to my family who helped me out in so many ways and particularly to my father, without whose invaluable advice, constant encouragement and support, this project would never have got off the ground.